THE 100 GREATEST DAYS IN NEW YORK SPORTS

THE 100 GREATEST DAYS IN NEW YORK SPORTS

UPDATED EDITION

Stuart Miller

ROWMAN & LITTLEFIELD
Lanham • Boulder • New York • London

Published by Rowman & Littlefield
An imprint of The Rowman & Littlefield Publishing Group, Inc.
4501 Forbes Boulevard, Suite 200, Lanham, Maryland 20706
www.rowman.com

6 Tinworth Street, London, SE11 5AL, United Kingdom

Distributed by NATIONAL BOOK NETWORK

British Library Cataloguing in Publication Information Available

Library of Congress Cataloging-in-Publication Data

Names: Miller, Stuart, 1966– author.
Title: The 100 greatest days in New York sports / Stuart Miller.
Other titles: One hundred greatest days in New York sports
Description: Updated edition. | Lanham, Maryland : Rowman & Littlefield
  Publishing Group, 2020. | Includes bibliographical references and index. |
  Summary: "This book illuminates how important sports are to the life
  of New York but also of the city's preeminent place in American sports.
  It covers the most dramatic sporting events ever to take place in New
  York and features both the greatest stars-including Babe Ruth and
  Muhammad Ali-and the unlikeliest of heroes-such as Jeremy Lin and
  Roberta Vinci"—Provided by publisher.
Identifiers: LCCN 2019038936 (print) | LCCN 2019038937 (ebook) | ISBN
  9781538126851 (cloth) | ISBN 9781538126868 (epub)
Subjects: LCSH: Sports—New York (State)—New York—History.
Classification: LCC GV584.5.N4 M54 2020 (print) | LCC GV584.5.N4 (ebook) |
  DDC 796.09747/1—dc23
LC record available at https://lccn.loc.gov/2019038936
LC ebook record available at https://lccn.loc.gov/2019038937

For Caleb and Lucas,
and for their teammates on the Superbas and Atlantics,
whose championships were definitely my favorite moments in New York sports.

Contents

CONTENTS

CONTENTS

CONTENTS

Introduction

New York City sports history, like the city itself, is noisy, self-important, and endlessly fascinating.

Go on, admit it: If you live or have lived in New York for any length of time, deep inside of you there is at least a touch of that New York arrogance, a sense that for an event to truly matter it has to happen in New York. Well, when it comes to sports, that self-imposed myopia has historically been somewhat justified.

Pick a sport—baseball, professional or college football or basketball, horse racing, boxing, or tennis—and New York has consistently had front-row seats for every major development and many of the most memorable events in sports history.

The most prominent example is baseball: New York was home to the first well-formulated baseball rules; the first ballpark; the first paying customers; the first fastball, curve, and bunt; the creation of "Take Me Out to the Ball Game"; Babe Ruth; the first televised games; the first racially integrated game; the first free-agent signing; and on and on. But the same holds true for the other sports as well.

Sure, other cities have teams with rich and storied pasts (Boston Celtics, Green Bay Packers, St. Louis Cardinals, Montreal Canadiens); the Yankees alone, however, are more dominating, important, and influential than any team in any sport, and New York City's overall depth, breadth, and success blows everyone else away. And it's not just about "firsts" and historical developments: Beginning in 1921, local teams captured 41 championships in a 58-year span, with four major-league teams, two pro football teams, one pro basketball team, and one hockey team, along with several college basketball teams, winning their respective big ones. It's not just the titles themselves but the fact that no other city can match this one for sheer dramatic events and memorable personalities—from Bobby Thomson's homer to Mookie Wilson's grounder, from Louis–Schmeling to Ali–Frazier, from Knute Rockne to Joe Namath, from CCNY to Pat Riley, from Bill Tilden to Jimmy Connors.

And because New York is the nation's media capital, almost any great sports moment there has gotten extra amplification that guaranteed it was heard 'round the world. Would the 1958 New York Giants–Baltimore Colts NFL championship have been seen as the watershed game in the league's history if it had pitted Baltimore against Green Bay? Would "Broadway Joe" Namath have become as large an icon playing in St. Louis?

So, while all the world may be a stage, New York has the audience and the media to make it the grandest, most important arena of all.

I wrote that for the first edition of this book, which was published in 2006. I still mean all of it, but I'm taking a slightly different approach this time around. At the time, I wanted the book to be as much a tribute to the city itself as to sports; the result was a top 100 that segregated out any events that happened out of town (the Jets' Super Bowl III win, Bucky Dent's home run) into a "Top 25 on the Road," which excluded anything that happened in the suburbs: the Belmont Stakes, the New York Nets, and the New York Islanders. And, most significantly, the New Jersey versions of the Giants and Jets were all unceremoniously left out. I now feel that was a mistake—the hometown excitement for the Giants' Super Bowl win in, say, 2012, was no less than that for the Yankees' World Series title in 2009. Before you ask, only the New Jersey Devils remain on the outside; it seems that their fans take pride in being rooted in a different place than the Islanders and Rangers. (One note: There have been four Madison Square Gardens to date. The first, in Madison Square, lasted from 1879 to 1890; another in the same location lasted until 1925; the third held court at Eighth Avenue between 49th and 50th Streets through 1967, when the current version, above Penn Station, was built. For simplicity's sake, throughout the book I refer to all of these structures simply as Madison Square Garden.)

So this list of the 100 greatest folds in the best of the 2006 list, plus the 2006 "On the Road" list, plus the best moments in the suburbs . . . plus the great memories formed in the New York sports landscape since 2006. That makes this list much more selective than the original, of course, but I'll be recounting those that warrant honorable mention online and on social media throughout the year. (The greatest performances against New York teams, as well as the worst moments, from blunders to painful injuries to bad behavior to brawls, are also retold there.)

To some extent, this list drew on my years of writing about both sports and the life and history of the city, as well as my own deep local roots—my family has lived in Brooklyn for more than 100 years; I even married a native Brooklynite, and we raised our two boys there. I grew up on my dad's stories of Dixie Walker and Dolph Camilli (and knew the '41 Dodgers' starting lineup by heart at age eight) and my grandfather's tales of watching everyone from Babe Ruth to fellow New York University student Ken Strong, and the day Jackie Robinson came to the house for a business meeting. My kids have listened patiently to my memories of such events as "Gets by Buckner" and Jimmy Connors's run to the U.S. Open semifinals in 1991. And, of course, they lived through the highs (we were at Johan Santana's no-hitter, plus David Tyree's Helmet Catch and "Linsanity") and lows (everything else about the Knicks, plus too many Mets messes to recount here), and moments that offered both (Endy Chavez's catch, followed by the Mets' heartbreaking Game 7 loss in the National League Championship Series).

Beyond my own experience, I picked the brains of numerous sportswriters, historians, and other experts—plus my friends, especially diehard New York sports fans (David, Tom, and Charlie) and one tennis expert (Todd). But, ultimately, it was the days, weeks, and months of endless research—watching videotapes, studying stats online, and reading through hundreds of books and literally thousands of newspaper and magazine articles and even blogs—that provided the basis for not only what I wrote, but also what I included and how I ranked each event.

That was the tricky part, of course. This book is being published in reverse chronological order so it makes it easier for you to find your favorite sports moments. But after just a few more minutes of me justifying my decisions, you'll come to my new 100 greatest days ranked in order.

How do you weigh the relative merits of such wildly diverse sports and time periods, great comebacks versus dominant performances, and championship moments versus classic wins in a season that ended in defeat?

There is, of course, no objective way to do it—I changed my list daily, sometimes every hour (and would be tinkering still if not for my deadline), and every argument you could make I've probably already had in my head—at least twice, since I took each side as I shifted and slid every entry around. Still, as the book evolved, I tried to follow some basic criteria.

I had to start by thinking about what to leave out. I rejected mythical tales (many propagated online), like the story floating around about Giants outfielder Red Murray getting struck by lightning while catching a fly ball to end a 21-inning game in Pittsburgh in 1914. It never happened, although apparently Murray had made a great catch in the same ballpark on a stormy day five years earlier.

Another catch is that many of baseball's greatest moments—Bobby Thomson's homer, Sandy Amoros's catch, Don Larsen's perfect game—came at the expense of another hometown team and could be seen as absolutely awful from that perspective. But they brought glory to at least part of New York, and that's the way I measured them.

To pick the ultimate survivors I pitted noteworthy moments against one another. Each Yankees game was held to a higher standard because it competed against so many other great Yankees moments: Constant winning becomes a bit numbing. The Bronx Bombers' World Series wins in 1937, 1938, and 1939 didn't make the list because there was little suspense, as the Yankees won 12 of 13 games. Their 1949, 1950, and 1951 wins fell short because they were overshadowed by the Game 7s in 1952 and 1953. Of those, even the seventh game of the 1952 World Series, a true nail-biter, didn't crack the top 40, since it was less historically significant than the 1953 World Series, when the Yankees won their unprecedented fifth straight crown. (The same was largely true for the greats in other sports: Muhammad Ali's fight against Ken Norton doesn't compare to Ali–Frazier. American Pharoah makes the list because of the long gap between Triple Crown winners but Justify does not for repeating the feat three years later.)

By contrast, singular seasons create multiple memorable moments. Titles for such teams as the Mets, Knicks, and Rangers are so few and far between that each one stands out. And because these teams lack the Yankees' imperial air, their championship runs seem infused with more close calls and narrow escapes. So the top 100 includes two wins from the Mets' 1969 World Series and three from the 1986 postseason, plus two from the Rangers' 1994 Stanley Cup surge. The exception is the Brooklyn Dodgers' 1955 World Series—they'd been so close so many times in one generation that winning the final game was all that mattered.

The top 14 moments were easy to place—you might quibble with whether one belongs a spot or two higher or lower but will probably agree that these are the greatest of the greatest. (The only tough call was the number-10 slot: I chose Don Larsen's perfect game over Game 6 of the 1986 World Series because Larsen achieved perfection, while the Mets won because Boston blew it.)

Many of these would be near the top of lists covering sports, or even popular culture, across the entire nation's history. Most of the other top 25 entries are equally obvious—the Rangers winning after 54 years, Willie Mays making "the Catch"—but a few need explaining. Obviously, Babe Ruth's 60th homer in 1927, Roger Maris's 61st in 1961, and Joe DiMaggio's hitting streak in 1941 rank among baseball's greatest achievements. And so they made the top 25. But if they are there, why not Santana pitching the first Mets no-hitter or Derek Jeter becoming the first Yankee to reach 3,000 hits? Well, those moments were great but had no impact on the team's fortunes in that particular season. By contrast, Ruth, Maris, and DiMaggio had singular seasons that carried their teams to World Series titles, giving extra heft to these individual achievements. Why aren't they higher? Because they still ultimately had less impact than a Super Bowl win or a Game 7 of the Stanley Cup, the World Series, or the NBA Finals. (The Yankees would have won the Series in 1927 if only Ruth had hit 55 homers; DiMaggio's streak also ranks lower in this book because it is measuring singular days, while his streak was impressive because it was a seemingly endless string of games.)

After that, I weighed a number of other factors. If a season was already represented near the top of the 100, then the second or third entries from that team's season or era would get bumped further down; no matter how exciting those secondary games were, they were not defining. (This is true of the 1986 Mets but also various Yankee dynasties, the 1970s Knicks squads, and the 1930s Giants.)

And if the game in question was a classic but occurred in a season that failed to produce a championship, in the end it ranked lower than a similarly great event that helped lead to a crown. The Yankees' Game 7 win in the 2003 American League Championship Series may have been as dramatic as the finale of the 1953 World Series, but the 2003 season ended with a World Series loss, while the latter ended in the Yankees' record fifth-straight title. Taking that reasoning one step further, great games in which the home team didn't win the series— think Robin Ventura's grand-slam single or John Starks's dunk over Michael Jordan—don't even make the list this time around.

Still, this book gave me more of an appreciation for the near-misses—the years the home team came up short. Finishing second seems so frustrating at the time; in retrospect, however, not only can it be hailed as impressive, but we ultimately cherish the great moments from those seasons more than we stew over the disappointment of the aftermath. In 1951, the Giants lost the World Series, but we remember only that they won the pennant.

Additionally, the flawlessly played game or dominant win is admirable but often less memorable: Which stands out more, the breath-stopping end of the Giants' 1991 Super Bowl win or their dominant performance in the 1987 Super Bowl?

There are always, of course, exceptions to just about everything I've laid out here: The quirks of the list are what make it interesting, and I hope that will make you want to argue one way or another. So enjoy the read and start the debate.

THE TOP 100

1. Jackie Robinson shatters the color barrier, April 15, 1947, Ebbets Field
2. Joe Louis annihilates Max Schmeling, June 22, 1938, Yankee Stadium
3. The Fight: Ali–Frazier I, March 8, 1971, Madison Square Garden
4. Broadway Joe makes good on his guarantee, January 12, 1969, Orange Bowl, Miami
5. The Giants win the pennant, October 3, 1951, Polo Grounds
6. Eli Manning scrambles, David Tyree uses his head, and the Giants end the Patriots' dream season, February 3, 2008, University of Phoenix Stadium, Phoenix
7. "Next Year" finally arrives for Brooklyn, October 4, 1955, Yankee Stadium
8. Willis Reed hobbles to the rescue, May 8, 1970, Madison Square Garden
9. The Amazin' Mets win the World Series, October 16, 1969, Shea Stadium
10. Don Larsen pitches a perfect game in the World Series, October 8, 1956, Yankee Stadium.
11. Mookie Wilson hits a ground ball to first in Game 6 of the World Series, October 25, 1986, Shea Stadium
12. Bucky Dent tops the Green Monster, October 2, 1978, Fenway Park, Boston
13. Fifty-four years later, the Rangers finally win the Stanley Cup, June 14, 1994, Madison Square Garden
14. Secretariat ends horse racing's Triple Crown drought by dominating at the Belmont States, June 9, 1973, Belmont Park
15. Roger Maris beats the Babe, October 1, 1961, Yankee Stadium
16. The Babe hits 60, September 30, 1927, Yankee Stadium
17. Joe DiMaggio hits in his 45th straight game, a new record, July 2, 1941, Yankee Stadium
18. Willie Mays makes "The Catch," September 29, 1954, Polo Grounds

19. The Yankees win a fifth straight World Series on Billy Martin's Series-record 12th hit, October 5, 1953, Yankee Stadium
20. Jack Dempsey outslugs Luis Firpo, September 14, 1923, Polo Grounds
21. Buffalo misses wide right and the Giants escape with their second Super Bowl, January 27, 1991, Tampa Stadium, Tampa
22. Jimmy Connors defies Father Time, September 2, 1991, National Tennis Center
23. Babe Ruth christens the "House That Ruth Built" with a home run, April 18, 1923, Yankee Stadium
24. Lou Gehrig proclaims himself the "luckiest man," July 4, 1939, Yankee Stadium
25. Arthur Ashe wins the first U.S. Open, September 9, 1968, West Side Tennis Club
26. The Marathon expands to all five boroughs and Bill Rodgers wins it, October 24, 1976, Central Park
27. Matty shuts out the A's, again, October 14, 1905, Polo Grounds
28. Man o' War comes back to beat John P. Grier at the Dwyer Stakes, July 10, 1920, Aqueduct Race Course
29. Reggie, Reggie, Reggie, October 18, 1977, Yankee Stadium
30. CCNY wins its second national championship . . . of the month, March 28, 1950, Madison Square Garden
31. The Mets finally vanquish Houston in the 16th, October 15, 1986, Astrodome, Houston
32. The Knicks finally beat Boston in Game 7, April 29, 1973, Boston Garden, Boston
33. Phil Simms is almost perfect as the Giants win their first Super Bowl, January 25, 1987, Rose Bowl, Pasadena
34. This time Ralph Terry finds success in the ninth inning of a Game 7, October 16, 1962, Candlestick Park, San Francisco
35. Every match goes the distance on Super Saturday, September 8, 1984, National Tennis Center
36. The Giants crush the Bears in the NFL championship, December 30, 1956, Yankee Stadium
37. Babe Ruth "calls" his World Series home run, October 1, 1932, Wrigley Field, Chicago
38. The Subway Series rides again, October 21, 2000, Yankee Stadium
39. The Giants win, 1–0, to capture the first modern "Subway" series, October 13, 1921, Polo Grounds

1

Roberta Vinci Stuns Serena Williams to Stop Her Grand Slam Dreams, September 11, 2015, National Tennis Center

Serena Williams, arguably the greatest women's tennis player ever, was yet again closing in on history.

Williams had finished 2014 by winning the U.S. Open and the WTA Finals. She started 2015 by winning the Australian Open. En route to winning the Miami Open, she won her 700th singles match, putting her in elite company with only Roger Federer and Rafael Nadal. Soon Williams accomplished something neither man had, capturing four straight majors with triumphs at Roland Garros and then Wimbledon. During the French Open, she also became the first Open-era woman to win 50 matches at each of the four Slams; by winning Wimbledon, she became the oldest Open-era woman to win a major and the first player to win four consecutive Slams twice—she also achieved the feat in 2002–2003.

Only one task remained: win the Grand Slam, capturing all four majors in a calendar year. Only Martina Navratilova and Steffi Graf, Williams's two challengers for the greatest tennis player of all time, had won an Open-era Grand Slam. Winning in Queens would also tie Williams with Graf for most majors in the Open era.

The powerful, intimidating Williams seemed impervious to outside pressures. But she was also acutely aware of her place in tennis history, and while she was loathe to admit it publicly, the Grand Slam was on her mind. In 2014, without the same stakes, she won seven matches at the U.S. Open without losing more than four games in any set. This year was tenser. In the second round, she required a tiebreaker in the first set against qualifier Kiki Bertens; next she dropped the first set against wild-card Bethanie Mattek-Sands, then eked out a 7–5 second set before taking control in the third set. She also dropped a set against her sister Venus in their quarterfinal match.

Still, it was difficult, if not impossible, to see how Williams could be stopped. Her semifinal match was against Roberta Vinci—the slight Italian doubles specialist was ranked 43rd in singles. She reached her first Slam semis in part through the good fortune of not having to play any seeded players. She had lost all four of her previous matches to Williams. Bookmakers placed the odds at 300–1. Afterward, Vinci confessed that she didn't believe she could win either.

The indomitable Serena Williams was on the verge of completing a Grand Slam when she was stunned by Roberta Vinci at the U.S. Open. *Author photo*

Williams was expected to win, then finish her quest against second-seed Simona Halep, who Williams had beaten in six of their seven matches. On the off-chance that another unlikely Italian semifinalist, 26th-seed Flavia Pennetta, would surprise Halep, well, Williams had won all seven of those showdowns. (Pennetta did indeed shock Halep, 6–1, 6–3, just before the main event.)

Maybe after 33 straight wins at Grand Slam matches, the presumption of victory got to Williams. Maybe it was plain old-fashioned nerves, getting so close to a long-desired goal. Certainly, Vinci deserves plenty of credit for what was to follow: Smiling all the way, she stuck to her game plan of pestering Williams with defensive slices and offensive attacks of the net, where the longtime top-ranked doubles player won 18 of 25 points. She remained steady even as pressure on her mounted.

The first set seemed predictable. Despite body language that suggested lethargy, Williams did what she does best: She overpowered Vinci, 6–2, in a little more than a half-hour. She pounded 16 winners and made only eight unforced errors. That ratio changed dramatically the closer Williams got to the finish line: In the last two sets, Williams hit 34 winners but had 32 unforced errors. Vinci, by contrast, had only 20 errors the entire match.

Williams's footwork stagnated. Vinci's low slices required Williams to move well to generate her own pace; Williams kept hitting hard, but she was often off-balance, leading to bad misses. Williams also played tight on both her serve and Vinci's. In their previous match, Williams had pounded weak second serves, winning 60 percent of those points, while capturing 54 percent on her second serves. In the semis, Williams won just 49 percent on Vinci's second serves and 45 percent of her own second serves.

Vinci could see Williams battling her nerves and kept pressuring her to make one more shot, one more shot again. When Williams missed a backhand to give Vinci the second set, 6–4, she smashed her racket in frustration, earning a code violation that she barely seemed to notice. Still, Williams was 18–1 in 2015, in three-set matches, and was the superior talent. When she broke Vinci to go up 2–0 in the final set, it seemed normalcy had returned. It had not.

Instead of consolidating the break, Williams choked, double faulting to lose the game. With the score tied at 3–3, Vinci played the quintessential point: She battled for 18 shots, sliced a backhand, charged the net, and turned Serena's running power backhand into a forehand drop volley to bring the game to deuce. Afterward, she put her hand to her ear and asked the crowd for some love. "What about me?" she said.

Williams stood silently catching her breath. Williams had two double faults that game as Vinci broke for a 4–3 lead.

Vinci kept telling herself to keep the ball in play and run down everything. Soon enough, she was serving for the match at 5–4. On the first point, Williams missed a second serve. On the next, Vinci volleyed a winner. Down 30–0, Williams played the aggressor but dumped a backhand volley into the net. At triple match point, it was again Vinci surviving a second serve and coming in to the net; Williams hit a good shot at Vinci's feet, but the challenger was, once more, up to the task. She flicked a forehand half volley winner that Williams couldn't touch. After exactly two hours, the match was over. Vinci had won, and Williams had lost.

Williams would later deny that she felt pressure, but her coach, Patrick Mouratoglou, said she had "lost her way mentally," and Navratilova, who twice won three majors in a year, said, "She lost to the Grand Slam more than anything else. But still, Vinci had to finish it off."

On the court, the moment belonged to the victor, who joyously told the crowd, "I'm sorry for the American people, for Serena, for the Grand Slam. But today's my day. Sorry guys."

The next day, Vinci would lose the first all-Italian final to Pennetta, but this was the match everyone would remember. Vinci's win earned a spot on a shortlist of major upsets, just behind the Jets' Super Bowl win, the Mets' 1969 World Series, the Giants toppling the undefeated Patriots, and, on a national scale, Buster Douglas flooring Mike Tyson, Leon Spinks dethroning Muhammad Ali, Villanova winning the NCAA Men's Basketball Tournament against Georgetown, and, of course, the U.S. Olympic hockey victory over the Soviet Union in 1980.

In tennis, the only two matches that come close are Robin Soderling beating Nadal at the French Open and Juan Martin del Potro beating Federer in the U.S. Open Finals. In women's tennis, however, Vinci's 2–6, 6–4, 6–4 semifinal win against Serena Williams goes down as the greatest tennis upset of all time.

2

Wilmer Flores Becomes a New York Folk Hero, July 31, 2015, Citi Field

Sometimes even Met fans get lucky. On July 31, 2015, a 12th-inning home run against their divisional rivals by the most unlikely of heroes made the Mets into a team of destiny, giving them momentum they would ride all the way to the World Series.

Just days earlier, it had been difficult for most fans to believe their future held any such glory. It wasn't that a 13–3 start vanished into a struggle for .500 as the season approached the 100-game mark. It wasn't just that the face of the franchise, captain David Wright, had been diagnosed with spinal stenosis. Or that they lost closer Jenrry Mejia to a PED suspension. Or that their starting lineup, which often featured such players as Eric Campbell, John Mayberry Jr., Johnny Monell, and Darrell Ceciliani, was enough to make you yearn for the days of Bruce Boisclair and Joel Youngblood. The problem, by that point, was just how long things had been that bad.

It wasn't only that it had been almost three decades since the last World Series crown, it was that almost nothing had gone right since Endy Chavez's miracle catch in the sixth inning of Game 7 of the 2006 NLCS against St. Louis. Moments later, the Mets loaded the bases with one out but failed to score. Cue Yadier Molina's ninth-inning, two-run homer and Adam Wainwright's two-strike curveball to Carlos Beltran and the strongest Mets squad in a generation was done. Then came the late-season collapse of 2007, in which the Mets blew a seven-game lead with 17 to play, with Tom Glavine's miserable finale a fitting turd on top, followed by another implosion in 2008, with the team dropping six of the final nine, blowing the last game on the final day at Shea Stadium.

Sadly, those became the good old days, as the Wilpon family became embroiled in the Bernie Madoff scandal—Fred Wilpon and partner Saul Katz had for years profited handsomely from Madoff's Ponzi manipulations and turned a blind eye to what was going on, before losing hundreds of millions when the fraud was exposed. The owners were almost forced to sell the team—which most fans would have preferred—but while MLB had pushed out Los Angeles Dodgers owner Frank McCourt for less egregious problems, the commissioner of MLB, Bud Selig, protected his good friend Fred Wilpon. So the Mets moved into Citi Field and began losing and losing—six straight seasons below .500.

Not everything was driven by financial mismanagement, debt problems, and unwillingness or inability to invest in the team; Jeff Wilpon's constant meddling earned blame, as did the team's propensity to mishandle players—the disparaging comments about Carlos Beltran and anonymous slams of Justin Turner before he was allowed to leave for stardom in Los Angeles. Free agent signings (Jason Bay, Michael Cuddyer) went south, while every injury seemed to be mishandled (most notably Ryan Church and Bay's concussions). The Mets lost more wins above replacement and had a higher percentage of their payroll on the disabled list between 2010 and 2016, than any other team, except for the Texas Rangers. Even the highlights had dark undertones: Johan Santana destroyed his arm pitching the first no-hitter in Mets history; Jose Reyes won a batting title and failed to receive a serious offer in free agency.

This was the essence of modern Metsness—don't get your hopes up because things would go wrong, often spectacularly and frequently in unimaginable ways. So forgive Met fans who knew that 2015—despite a talented young staff headed by Matt Harvey, Jacob DeGrom, Noah Syndergaard, and Steven Matz—was heading down the same old drain. It was safe to presume that any move the Mets made would be insignificant or make things worse.

As the Mets spiraled downward—last in the major leagues in runs scored and batting average—general manager Sandy Alderson disparaged the local media as "citizens of Panic City." It was clever but inaccurate—there was no longer enough hope to warrant panic. As if to prove the point, Alderson nibbled around the edges, adding Kelly Johnson, Juan Uribe, and Addison Reed as the trade deadline approached—useful complementary pieces for a contender, which the Mets would not be without the addition of a major bat.

Then came July 29, one of the stranger days in Mets history, which makes it pretty unusual indeed. Alderson made a deal to trade Wilmer Flores and Zach Wheeler to Milwaukee for Carlos Gomez. Fortunately for New York, it soon became the trade that wasn't.

Gomez had been shipped by the Mets to Minnesota after the 2007 season as part of the package that brought Santana to New York. In 2013 and 2014, Gomez had finally fulfilled his potential, hitting for power, stealing bases, and finally raising his batting average and on-base percentage to decent levels (despite striking out more than 140 times each year). Gomez would provide offensive help while Wheeler was out for Tommy John surgery, and Flores was a poor fielder lacking the overall firepower Gomez potentially offered. But Gomez was reverting to form, with his on-base percentage dropping sharply. And Mets fans liked Flores: He had been in the Mets organization since age 16 and was an RBI machine in the minors (145 RBI in 644 at-bats in the previous two years). Even if Flores and Wheeler were not the next Amos Otis and Nolan Ryan, there was a sense that Gomez was not the next Keith Hernandez and more likely the next Jim Fregosi (or George Foster, Carlos Baerga, Roberto Alomar, Mo Vaughn, or Jason Bay, to name just a few big bats that whiffed in Queens).

The Brewers thought they had a deal and told Gomez. Teammate Martin Maldonado tweeted a farewell, and reporters broke the "news" on social media. Fans at Citi Field began buzzing, but Flores remained in the game, despite baseball's tradition of pulling a traded player to ensure he didn't get hurt. When Flores batted in the bottom of the seventh, the fans gave him a huge ovation. He soon learned why, and when he took the field for the eighth inning, he was emotional, crying quietly. Exposing a vulnerable young player in a difficult situation—classic Metsness. But this one was not the Mets' fault. Flores had not been traded, and everyone had jumped the gun; Gomez's MRI exams reportedly had the team worried, and the deal never went through. The Mets, meanwhile, got three homers from Lucas Duda but lost the game.

The next day brought its unique twist on Metsness: As the front office continued seeking deals (Jay Bruce from the Reds? Justin Upton from the Padres?), Flores sat out on a rainy night. New York built a 7–1 lead over San Diego after six. Hansel Robles yielded a grand slam to Derek Norris, making it 7–5. In the ninth with two outs and closer Jeurys Familia ahead, 0–1, on Norris, the umpires suddenly decided the downpour was too much and halted play. After a delay, Norris blooped a single, Matt Kemp singled, and Upton, of course, homered, propelling the Padres to an 8–7 lead. The Mets had found a new way to lose.

Friday, July 29, was the trade deadline and the beginning of a three-game series with first-place Washington. It was do or die for the Mets—they were three games out of first and a bad weekend could bury them yet again. But this was the day that would, instead, transform the team, bringing the Mets back to the World Series for just the fourth time in history and the first time in 15 years.

Three hours before the first pitch against Washington, Alderson pulled off the best deal in terms of immediate impact since the Mike Piazza trade. Moments before the deadline, he tossed two prospects to Detroit for Cuban-born slugger Yoenis Cespedes. It was initially questionable whether Cespedes was a better fit than Gomez since he too provided power but with a low on-base percentage. But Cespedes would quickly quiet critics by carrying the Mets, often single-handedly, to the playoffs. In a 39-game stretch soon after he arrived, he hit .315, with 17 homers and 42 RBI, and New York posted a 28–11 record. (Gomez was sent to Houston, where he hit .244, with four homers through year's end, while Upton batted .250, with eight homers.)

News of the trade gave the Mets an emotional lift, but Cespedes wasn't there for the first game of the weekend so the team would need to find another source of offense. That source would be non-Brewer Wilmer Flores.

In the first inning, Flores made a diving stop on Yunel Escobar's ground ball to earn a huge ovation from the home crowd. The fans gave him a standing ovation for each at-bat, but in the fourth, Flores earned a second rousing round of cheers with an RBI single for a 1–0 lead. It was the only run they'd score in nine innings.

It almost stood the entire game: Matt Harvey looked like his preinjury Dark Knight, striking out nine in 7 2/3 innings. But with two outs in the eighth, he hit Clint Robinson in the foot with a pitch, then yielded two singles to tie the game. Newly acquired Tyler Clippard relieved and engaged in a 13-pitch battle with Yoenis Cespedes before fanning him to escape the inning.

The Mets offense remained punchless as the game rolled on into the 10th— and the 11th. The highlight of the 11th came when Bryce Harper lost his cool, shrieking at the home plate umpire after being called out on strikes; the umpire tossed Harper, to the delight of New York fans.

Flores led off the bottom of the 12th. Again, the fans cheered his mere presence. On a 1–1 pitch, Felipe Rivero tried to bust Flores inside with a fastball, his supposed weakness. But Flores turned on the pitch and smacked it over the fence in left-center field. The Mets had won the game with one swing of the bat, by a player who wasn't even supposed to be there. The Mets ran out to greet Flores at home plate. Just before he arrived, the gleeful Flores tossed his helmet aside, pounded his chest twice in celebration, and plunged into the embrace of his teammates.

The Mets were reborn. They won the next night, then finished the sweep on Sunday, ascending to a first-place tie. They had won seven straight, going from 52–50 and three games out to 59–50 and 2½ games in front. It wasn't all Flores, of course. It was Cespedes and rookie Michael Conforto and the pitching, and

Daniel Murphy, who would briefly become Babe Ruth in the playoffs: In nine games against Los Angeles and Chicago, Murphy batted .421 and swatted seven homers.

The Mets lost the World Series to Kansas City, but still this was the only time throughout the decade that either New York team reached the Fall Classic. And after six losing seasons on the heels of two horrific collapses, 2015 was a season to savor. The magic was back (albeit briefly), and it all turned on the trade that didn't happen, the trade that did, and the extra-inning home run that kick-started the offense.

3

American Pharoah Ends the Triple Crown Wait, June 6, 2015, Belmont Park

In 1978, Affirmed won the Triple Crown, making it the first time this feat had been achieved in consecutive years. The next year, it almost happened again: Spectacular Bid won the Kentucky Derby and the Preakness Stakes, before falling to third at the Belmont Stakes. Still, the racing world didn't think it meant anything, especially when Pleasant Colony, Alysheba, and Sunday Silence won the first two legs in the next decade. But the drought stretched on . . . and on . . . and on. Real Quiet lost at Belmont Park by a nose in 1998, and in the next six years, four more horses fell short at the Belmont.

Racing's popularity had declined for a variety of reasons since the 1970s, and trainers, owners, and others grumbled that the Triple Crown was broken—too many owners skipped one or both of the first two races, pushing a fresh horse out to win the Belmont. This made the Triple Crown all but impossible and the Belmont an anticlimax. By 2014, six of the previous eight winners hadn't bothered competing in the Kentucky Derby or the Preakness.

But in 2015, American Pharoah finally changed the narrative. His race wasn't a thriller like the Affirmed–Alydar showdown, nor was it historic like Secretariat's record-setting coronation. But after 37 years without a Triple Crown, no one minded the lack of suspense.

The Kentucky Derby had been packed with 18 horses, but American Pharoah, the top two-year-old in 2014, headed off as the favorite. He won by a length, but he had been less than his best, pushed hard by some tough horses running an aggressive race. As the favorite again at the Preakness, he started in the number-one post position, a spot that hadn't produced a winner in more than two decades. Then the skies opened and a strong rain soaked the course for the first time in more than 30 years. But American Pharoah was the only horse to have run on such a sloppy track before, and he cruised to a seven-length victory. Trainer Bob Baffert brought the horse back to Kentucky to work out at Churchill Downs, instead of practicing at Belmont Park. Some were skeptical of his staying away, but it had worked for Affirmed, with the idea being that a relaxed horse is a winning horse.

The Belmont field featured eight horses, including five who passed on the Preakness and one who sat out both the Derby and the Preakness. In other words, while American Pharoah was both the betting and the fan favorite, he was facing fresher legs in the Triple Crown's longest race.

American Pharoah seized an early lead, and nothing else mattered. No one could mount a serious threat, and jockey Victor Espinoza built American Pharoah's lead larger and larger. He ran the final quarter-mile in 24.32 seconds, bettering Secretariat's 25 seconds. This race wasn't much of a race, but for race fans it was a hell of a celebration.

When American Pharoah finally bolted across the line in 2:26.65, 5½ lengths ahead, he was faster than every Triple Crown winner but Secretariat.

While the crowd was ecstatic, the win meant even more to Baffert and Espinoza. Baffert had won the first two legs in 1997, 1998, and 2002, but he fell short at Belmont; Espinoza had ridden for Baffert in 2002, and then in 2014, on California Chrome, who finished fourth in his Triple Crown chance. Now the Mexican-born jockey had become the first Latino racer to win the Triple Crown. At age 43, he was also the oldest, although, ironically, that label would be claimed just three years later when Justify captured the crown with 52-year-old Mike Smith aboard. Justify's trainer was Baffert, who became just the second trainer in history to win two Triple Crowns.

American Pharoah would make further history in 2015, becoming the first horse to capture the Breeders' Cup Classic after having won the Triple Crown, giving him racing's sole Grand Slam. But that historic win remains a footnote to most fans, who most cherish his performance in winning the first Triple Crown at Belmont Park in almost four decades.

4

The Rangers Finally Topple the Penguins in Seven, en Route to the Finals, May 13, 2014, Consol Energy Center, Pittsburgh

New York Rangers fans waited 54 years for a championship after 1940. Immediately after that glorious 1994 triumph, the team reached the conference semifinals twice and the conference finals. Then darkness returned, as the Rangers failed for seven straight years to reach the postseason. The team was not a threat again until 2011–2012, when they won 51 games and reached the Conference Finals. By the spring of 2014, it had been two full decades since the team had reached the Stanley Cup Finals, almost matching the worst drought in team history, a 22-year spell that ended in 1972.

The team entered the 2014 playoffs having finished fifth in their conference and second in their division, behind the Pittsburgh Penguins and superstar Sidney Crosby. New York's offense was mediocre, but the defense, led by Henrik Lundqvist in goal, was supremely stingy, allowing the second fewest goals in the conference.

The Rangers needed seven games to beat Philadelphia in the opening round, meaning that in the next round against favored Pittsburgh, they would become the first team in a quarter-century forced to play five playoff games in a seven-day span.

Riding high, the Rangers opened with a 3–2 overtime win in Game 1. Then the schedule and New York's offensive shortcomings caught up with them: You can't win if you don't score, and the sluggish squad did not score for the next seven periods, getting shut out in two straight losses before falling, 4–2, in Game 4 at Madison Square Garden.

Down 3–1 in games, the reeling Rangers seemed doomed; never before had they recovered from such a deficit. Less than 24 hours before Game 5, Martin

St. Louis's mother died. St. Louis had arrived via trade with Tampa Bay just months earlier, and the 38-year-old had contributed two goals and six assists in the first 11 playoff games for this scoring-starved team. St. Louis went home to Montreal, but after talking it over with his father, the veteran returned for Game 5. His devotion seemed to stir the team, which finally broke loose, capitalizing on power play opportunities to skate off with a 5–1 win.

Less than four minutes into Game 6, St. Louis scored the game's first goal, sparking the team to a 3–1 win that evened the series. The Penguins, despite their scoring prowess, had faltered repeatedly in the playoffs, and going home for Game 7 ramped up the pressure. The Rangers, meanwhile, had won four straight Game 7s, thanks in large part to Lundqvist, whose save percentage in those games was .963. He would outdo himself against Pittsburgh.

The Penguins outshot the Rangers in the first period, 10–7, but Lundqvist ensured the Penguins came up empty. The Rangers scored on a goal by Brian Boyle, who had been struggling during the series. The Penguins did slip in one of their 13 shots in the second period, but the Rangers countered that on another power play, again with St. Louis central to the action. He lured Penguins goalie Marc-Andre Fleury toward him, then backhanded a no-luck pass to his left for Brad Richards, who had a suddenly open net. That was all the offense the Rangers would get—they'd muster just seven shots in the final period—but it was all Lundqvist would need. He stopped 35 of 36 shots in total. At one point in the third period, the goalie turned away three shots in a row, with the third coming on a goal-mouth shot by Paul Martin that deflected off a lost stick lying in front of him after Lundqvist had lost his own stick on the first two saves during a desperate scramble. He headed the fluttering shot away with his mask.

Inspired by their stunning comeback, the Rangers carried their momentum into the next round, routing Montreal, 7–2, in Game 1—St. Louis scored the first goal—en route to a series win that culminated with Lundqvist shutting out the Canadiens. The Rangers came up short against Los Angeles in the Stanley Cup Finals, but being one of the final two teams standing for the first time in 20 years made it a season worth celebrating.

5

The Patriots Are Again the Favorites, but the Giants Are Again the Champions, February 5, 2012, Lucas Oil Stadium, Indianapolis

One week before Super Bowl XLVI, Rodney Harrison said on television that he trusted Eli Manning more than Tom Brady in the fourth quarter. It may have sounded crazy, but Harrison had been on the wrong end of Manning's magic four years earlier when he could not pry the ball loose from David Tyree's helmet as the Giants stunned the undefeated Patriots in Super Bowl XLII.

Manning played with that same confidence in the biggest moments of this Super Bowl rematch. With 3:46 left in the fourth quarter, the Giants again trailed the Patriots, 17–15, and they were pinned back at their own 12-yard line. His favorite targets, Victor Cruz and Hakeem Nicks, were on the right—Patriots coach Bill Belichick had urged his defense to focus on those two men. On the left was Mario Manningham. While Cruz and Nicks had combined for 35 catches in the first three playoff games, Manningham had only grabbed eight. But Manning knew he could trust Manningham in pressure situations—he was the only one of the three to catch a fourth-quarter touchdown pass in each of those games.

Manning saw the Patriots in a Cover Two defense and knew their safeties stayed further from the sideline in those situations. The Giants had just three receivers going downfield to maximize protection. With both Cruz and Nicks covered, the quarterback took his chances with Manningham running a deep go route up the sideline. He had misfired twice on deep passes to Manningham in the game, but with the championship on the line Manning played his best. When Manningham got past cornerback Sterling Moore, safety Patrick Chung was just a tiny bit too far away to shut him down—if Manning could get the ball in the right spot.

The quarterback let fly with a perfect pass, right into his receiver's hands; Manningham was then hit by both defenders but kept his feet in bounds before going down. Manning had done it again, and the Giants were on their way.

Afterward, in *Sports Illustrated*, Peter King marveled, "How did Manning make that throw? Why make that throw? . . . I ask you: What quarterback alive do you want with the ball in his hands in the last two minutes of a big game?"

Fans, radio hosts, and writers had sneered before the 2011 season, when Eli Manning responded to a question that he was an "elite" NFL quarterback. Sure, he'd won a Super Bowl, but his stats could not match Tom Brady, Aaron Rodgers, Drew Brees, Ben Roethlisberger, or his brother Peyton.

Manning lost two favorite pass catchers—Steve Smith and Kevin Boss—to free agency and was stuck with the worst running offense in the league. Yet, one year after leading the league with 25 interceptions, he backed up his claim by throwing for 4,933 yards and set an NFL record with 15 fourth-quarter touchdown passes, which paced the Giants to six late comeback wins. (He threw only 16 interceptions.) The Giants stumbled midseason but won their final two games to reach the wild card at 9–7. The team scored 394 points but yielded 400—and no team had ever reached the Super Bowl with a negative point differential.

The erratic play vanished in the playoffs. The Giants were an experienced team that knew how to win on the road, and they blew out Atlanta and Green Bay, and then outlasted and upset San Francisco in overtime to reach the Super Bowl.

The game started as if a fourth-quarter comeback would be an unneeded luxury. In this matchup of potent offenses, the game began with a defensive blow. On New England's first play from scrimmage, Brady looked fearful, throwing the ball away downfield just before getting nailed by Justin Tuck. With no receivers in the vicinity of the ball it was intentional grounding, but because Brady's panic move came in his own end zone it was a safety. The Giants led, 2–0, and got the ball.

Manning set a Super Bowl record by starting the game with nine straight connections. He led a 78-yard drive, finishing with a nifty touchdown pass to Cruz, sliding between a cornerback and a linebacker with just barely enough room for the football to find him.

But the Patriots got their act together in the second quarter. Brady outdid Manning by completing 10 straight passes to send New England into halftime up 10–9. The Giants had trailed at halftime of their previous four Super Bowls and won three, so there was no panic, even after Brady fired six more completions in a row to start the second half on a drive that gave New England a 17–9 lead.

The Giants responded with a field goal to pull within five, and then the Giants defense, which had been on its heels while Brady dumped passes in front of them, regained its footing. On the final three drives of the game, Brady was just 7-for-17 for 75 yards. First came a three-and-out, in which Tuck sacked him on 3rd and 8. Another field goal brought the Giants within two.

Brady started the fourth quarter by trying out his Eli Manning impression. He started out with the ideal Eli, ducking and escaping from two would-be sackers and then coming up to fire deep downfield, a la Manning in the 2008 Super Bowl, but he finished up looking like 2010 regular-season Eli, throwing deep on a first down into traffic, where Chase Blackburn outjumped Rob Gronkowski and intercepted the pass.

The Giants drive fell short, and again Brady was looking to finish them off. He had Wes Welker open deep downfield, but he pushed, or aimed the pass, sending it behind his receiver. The open Welker had to turn back and try for a spinning off-balance catch. He'd often made that play but failed this time. The Giants got the ball back deep in their own territory with time running out.

The Giants had run their two-minute drills before the Super Bowl by pitting the offense against the starting defense, instead of the second unit, which is what most teams did. Obviously, the defense was not allowed to hit Manning, but Peter King later reported that they were otherwise going hard and Manning had coolly taken his squad 75 yards in just six plays.

In the Super Bowl, Manning made his big play, but Patriots coach Bill Belichick gave the Giants an extra gift by challenging the call that Manningham had stayed in bounds. When he lost, the Patriots forfeited a time-out. They would soon regret that.

Manning tried Manningham deep again but failed. Yet, he connected on his next three passes, two to Manningham and one to Nicks, moving the ball 32 yards to New England's 18. The Giants were in field goal range with a chance to run down the clock and win it. Two runs by Ahmad Bradshaw sandwiched between another completion to Nicks, and the Giants had 1st and goal on the seven with 1:09 left. New England burned its second time-out, but they used this more wisely, discussing a strategy to maximize the remaining time.

When Manning handed to Bradshaw on the next play, the Patriots stepped aside to give the running back all the room he could possibly want. Bradshaw was running so hard, so fast that even when he heard Manning call for him to stop, his momentum was unbreakable—he tried to sit down on the one but fell backward into the end zone for an accidental touchdown.

The Patriots, having realized that they'd rather have a minute to try for a touchdown than no time for a field goal attempt, had lured the Giants into scoring quickly. New York led, 21–17, but now Brady had 57 seconds to go 80 yards.

Brady's first two passes to open receivers were dropped, and on third down, Tuck again broke through, nailing Brady for a loss of six. The Patriots used their final time-out with 36 seconds left. Brady made a brilliant play to find Deion Branch for 19 on fourth down, but New York had the clock on its side. By the time New England reached its 49, there was time for just two more plays. The first fell incomplete, leaving Brady to try a Hail Mary to see if the Patriots had a miracle on the level of Tyree's Helmet Catch. He scrambled and then heaved the ball well into the end zone, but there were more Giants in the air than Patriots and the ball was batted away; Gronkowski desperately dove for it, but the ball fell harmlessly to the turf.

Eli Manning, the first person to throw for more than 4,900 yards in a season and win the title, was elite on the game's biggest stage . . . again. And as a result, the Giants were Super Bowl champions . . . again.

6

Linsanity Takes over New York and the NBA, February 4, 2012, Madison Square Garden

By any standard, the New York Knicks have had a terrible twenty-first century. Constantly undermined by a spoiled and self-aggrandizing owner, James Dolan, the team has cycled through a dozen coaches and reached the playoffs just four times in 18 seasons since 2001–2002—that's the same number of seasons they've lost at least 59 games, matching or exceeding the worst totals in team history. The most memorable events since Dolan assumed more power have largely been miscalculations (a long list featuring the acquisition of players like Stephon Marbury and Steve Francis, and the trade for Carmelo Anthony when he was months from free agency) and controversies (an equally lengthy list, from everything in Isaiah Thomas's tenure—but especially the culture of sexual harassment—to the eviction of Charles Oakley from Madison Square Garden).

But for one brief moment in 2012, the Knicks were relevant for all the right reasons, electrifying New York and the NBA as everyone came down with a feverish case of Linsanity.

On February 3, 2012, Jeremy Lin, 23, would have barely qualified as a footnote in Knicks history. He was the first American-born player of Chinese or Taiwanese descent to play in the NBA and the first Harvard graduate to reach the league in almost 50 years, but he had achieved that (with a flurry of media attention) in his brief tenure with his hometown Golden State Warriors.

When the Warriors, who had another point guard named Steph Curry, released Lin in December 2011, he signed with Houston, only to find himself unemployed again on Christmas Eve. The Knicks were so awful and shorthanded they were looking for warm bodies to back up at point guard. Baron Davis was hurt. Toney Douglas was bad. Mike Bibby wasn't making an impact. Rookie Iman Shumpert got injured. The Knicks picked up Lin off waivers. Still, after bouncing between the Knicks and their developmental league team, Lin knew he was on the verge of being released before his contract became guaranteed.

On February 3, Lin, who'd been sleeping on his brother Josh's couch on the Lower East Side, was told he'd need to stay somewhere else that weekend. Lin found a new home: in the spotlight at Madison Square Garden.

On February 4, the Knicks had lost 11 of their last 13 games and were playing for the third consecutive night. Coach Mike D'Antoni pulled Lin off the end of the bench and stuck him into the game to face down the Nets' All-Star point guard, Deron Williams.

Lin had played just 38 games in his two-year career and only 55 minutes the entire season, but he was unfazed. He slowed Williams and ran the pick-and-roll as if he was a veteran leading a polished team, which the Knicks definitely were not. Carmelo Anthony, plagued by a groin injury that would soon sideline him, shot just 3-for-15; Amar'e Stoudemire committed so many fouls he was limited to just 13 minutes. But with the crowd chanting Lin's name, he shot 10-for-19, taking over the game in the fourth quarter with 12 points to finish with 25 (his previous high was 13), more than Williams, who had 21. Lin added seven assists and five rebounds. The Garden played Pearl Jam's "Jeremy" when the game ended with a 99–92 win for the Knicks.

Lin was surrounded by two dozen reporters afterward, prompting Stoudemire, whose locker was next door, to joke, "What's going on, Jeremy? Can I have my locker back?"

Had Lin starred just this one time, no one would have remembered, but this game launched Lin on a comet to worldwide fame. Against Utah, playing without Anthony and Stoudemire, he provided 28 points and eight assists in a Knicks win. In a win against Washington, he scorched rising star John Wall, while tallying 23 points and 10 assists. Then he stunned Kobe Bryant and the Los Angeles Lakers with 38 points and seven assists. The next night, he had 20 points and overcame a poor shooting night to clinch a win against Minnesota with a free throw. He topped that against Toronto by hitting a game-winning three-pointer with less than a second left on the clock. He was the first NBA player to score at least 20 points and have seven assists in each of his first five starts; his 136 points in his first five career starts were the most since the merger with the ABA in 1976. He also had 45 turnovers in his first seven starts but the Knicks were 8–0 with Lin. They were even back on track for the playoffs.

By this time, Lin had morphed from player into cultural phenomenon, a hero to Asian Americans and underdogs everywhere. Linsanity trended on Twitter, and YouTube commenters thanked him for being an inspiration, overcoming prejudice and racial taunts, and defying stereotypes about Asian Americans. His agent's e-mail server collapsed, and he had to hire people just to handle the interview requests from throughout the country and China and Taiwan. Lin was praised by everyone from Bryant to New York Giants star Justin Tuck. The Knicks' nine top-selling souvenirs were Lin-related, but none existed and they were sold as preorders; the Knicks were ironing his uniform number, 17, onto jerseys before games just to have merchandise. Lin was belatedly added to the Rising Stars Challenge during NBA All-Star Weekend, and the league had to schedule a separate press conference just for him, which 100 reporters attended.

It was Linsanity every day, all day throughout the league and the world; closer to home, New Yorkers were suddenly excited and hopeful about the Knicks for the first time in a long time.

Of course, nothing good lasts in Knicksville. In March, D'Antoni, who was feuding with Anthony, was forced out. New coach Mike Woodson shifted emphasis from Lin's pick-and-rolls to Anthony's isos. And in April, before he could enjoy even more national exposure in the playoffs, Lin's season ended with knee surgery for a torn left meniscus. Afterward, the Knicks declined to match Houston's contract offer, and suddenly Lin was gone. Linsanity was over. The Knicks improved the following year (before becoming exponentially worse), while Lin went on to a solid but unspectacular—and injury-prone—career bouncing around from team to team (including a brief stay with the Brooklyn Nets).

But Linsanity, at least briefly, brought unsurpassed joy to so many people it is impossible to remember it without a smile. And while people may remember other games more, it was the game against the Nets, when Lin began the game on the bench and uncertain of his future, that was the flame that ignited it all.

7

Novak Djokovic Dominates the Tennis World and Stuns Roger Federer, September 10, 2011, National Tennis Center

With one reckless, brilliant forehand service return late in the semifinals at the 2011 U.S. Open, Novak Djokovic changed tennis history.

From 2004 to early 2010, Roger Federer proved himself the greatest player of his era and, indeed, all time. He won 15 of 25 Grand Slams, reaching six other finals and three more semifinals. Three times he won three Slams in one year, something no other player had done more than once in the Open era.

The only threat was Nadal, who won six Slams in that span, including four straight in France and an epic battle against Federer at Wimbledon in 2008. In 2010, Nadal became just the fifth man to win three majors in a year. These friendly rivals were permanent fixtures at the top and seemed destined to be remembered as the greatest players of all time.

Then 2011—and Djokovic—happened. Djokovic had won the 2008 Australian Open and reached two U.S. Open finals, losing once to Federer and once to Nadal. He was known for his return game and ability to grind out points, but equally for his humorous impressions of other players, excessive ball bouncing before serves, and losing discipline and fading at the end of grueling matches, as much as his skills.

Then Djokovic started 2011 with a 41-match winning streak. He captured the Australian Open and tournaments in Dubai, Indian Wells, Miami, Madrid, and Rome. He beat Federer or Nadal in the finals of the latter five, notably Nadal on clay twice. After losing to Federer in the semis of the French, he bested Nadal in the Wimbledon finals. His only other loss before the U.S. Open came when he retired with a shoulder injury in Cincinnati.

In New York, Djokovic wanted to put an exclamation point on his historic season. Winning a third Slam would emphatically declare that tennis now had a Big Three. Federer had easily dispatched him in either the semis or the finals in their first three U.S. Open meetings, losing just one set. But in 2010, Djokovic had broken through, winning the fourth and fifth sets to quiet his critics and surprise Federer. He saved two match points while serving in the fifth set, first with a swinging forehand volley and then with a crosscourt forehand winner that nicked the line. While Djokovic lost the finals to Nadal, that five-set win was a springboard for Djokovic's success in 2011.

Federer began the 2011 semifinal by serving wide to Djokovic's forehand. That forehand was the game's most dangerous weapon that year, but the serve was a favorite of Federer's on the deuce side in big moments. The game's greatest returner lunged for the ball and hit it meekly into the net.

After a remarkably crisp and even first set—neither man reached deuce on his opponent's serve—Federer used that serve again at 5–3 in the tiebreaker. Once again, Djokovic couldn't get it over the net. Federer won the tiebreaker, 9–7.

Play continued at an impossibly high level, with both players hitting deep and with great angles. Still, Federer finally earned a break in the third game. When he found himself with a 5–4, 40–15 lead, Federer knew what to do. Djokovic had only come back once before from being down two sets, and Federer had only blown such a lead once at a Grand Slam (that summer, at Wimbledon, against Jo-Wilfried Tsonga). One more point could seemingly assure Federer of victory. Naturally, he served wide to Djokovic's forehand, and, again, the Serb dumped it into the net.

Then Djokovic rediscovered the mojo that had elevated him to the number-one spot. He won the next two sets easily, 6–3, 6–2, as Federer could not match his consistency. By match's end, Federer would have 59 errors to the Serb's 35 (they were almost even on winners), and Djokovic lost just three points on serve in the fourth set. Overall, Federer would win just 17 percent of the points on Djokovic's first serve while Djokovic would win one of every three of Federer's first serves.

But Federer was still Federer, and he still maintained that aura of sweat-free invincibility. He started the fifth set steadily, holding serve with authority, as the partisan crowd urged him on. On the first point of the eighth game, Federer, up 4–3, got a middling second serve from Djokovic. He hit a careful return, then meticulously set up the point until he had room for a forehand winner down the line. Djokovic pointed to his racket frame, essentially complaining to Federer's adoring fans that their hero just got lucky—the second-to-last shot was a mishit off Federer's frame. On the next point, Federer's brilliant running forehand brought even louder roars. Disheartened, Djokovic double-faulted and then missed an easy forehand.

Up 5–3, serving for the match, Federer jumped out to a 40–15 lead. He had won 11 of the previous 12 points. The ball was in his hands, the momentum was on his side, the fate of the match belonged to him. In this moment, he once again went wide with the serve to Djokovic's forehand.

This time, Djokovic, who had looked almost resigned before the point, didn't miss. But that's not the point. It was not that he made the return, it was the how, the why, the where. Djokovic must have guessed that Federer would go wide one more time. He was ready, and he went for broke. Federer's serve was not quite wide enough or fast enough, and Djokovic hammered it across court at a short, sharp angle for a winner that Federer could only watch without moving.

Djokovic hit the ball so hard he knocked the class out of the usually elegant Federer—after the match Federer would seem downright churlish.

Federer said Djokovic was simply slapping the shot and not playing like someone "who believes much anymore in winning." That made the end particularly galling. He added, "To lose against someone like that, it's very disappointing, because you feel like he was mentally out of it already. Just gets the lucky shot at the end and off you go. It's awkward having to explain this loss because I feel like I should be doing the other press conference."

Djokovic, who had faced a hostile crowd and seen Federer get his share of lucky breaks, obviously saw the shot differently. "Yeah, I tend to do that on match points," he said. "It kinda works." He pointed out that he had done the same thing to Federer the previous year, hitting big winners on match point, and that it was necessary to take chances at any small opportunity against a player as great as Federer. The shot was such a stunner that a year later, ESPN wrote that top players on the tour, from Bob Bryan to Nadal, were still referencing it in interviews as either an example of luck or bravery, or both.

In the moment, Djokovic wiped his brow and calmly walked to the other side before realizing the crowd was cheering his shot. He seized the moment, raising both arms and urging them on with a grin.

"I had to get some of the crowd energy behind me," he said afterward. "And it worked." Federer still had another match point, but Djokovic was still smiling when he readied himself to return the serve as the umpire tried quieting the crowd. Federer got a short ball to his forehand that he'd normally smash for an inside-out winner, but he seemed to rush the shot. The ball smacked the net cord, going over but landing wide. Federer's next forehand was even worse, and while he saved one break point with an ace, he could not recover. He ultimately double-faulted to give Djokovic the game.

Djokovic held, broke, held in a blur to finish the match. He was aggressive, while Federer looked a little lost. Down 15–30 at 5–5, he got trapped in a rally of more than two dozen shots, unwilling to go for broke until Djokovic finally hit a forehand winner. The pattern repeated itself on the next point. When Djokovic served up 40–15 with two match points, he went up the middle, and Federer's backhand return sailed long. After three hours and 51 minutes, Djokovic had, somehow, prevailed.

The next day, Djokovic swatted away Nadal, winning the final set, 6–1, to give him three Grand Slam titles in one year and serve notice to the tennis world. He was not only equal to Federer and Nadal, but also a genuine threat to surpass them in the long run. Pete Sampras called this the greatest tennis season in history, although some would place Federer's 2006 season above it. But it certainly was one of the greatest in sports, if only because for much of 2011, Djokovic could be compared to the 1927 Yankees or Lew Alcindor's UCLA team, but in that crucial moment against Federer he became Buster Douglas against Mike Tyson. Djokovic may have surpassed himself with his dominant 2015 season, with a stretch during which he won five of six Slams. It's too soon to tell whether he'll actually catch Federer in total Grand Slams or the more debatable title of GOAT, but it was in this match, with his one bold shot and almost four hours of gutsy shot-making, that he proved he was ready to take that challenge.

The Jets "Can't Wait" to Beat the Patriots in the Playoffs, January 18, 2011, Gillette Stadium, Foxborough

The New England Patriots didn't win every game against the Jets, it just seemed that way. The Patriots simply loomed over the psyche of Jets fans, the way the Yankees long did to Red Sox fans. While the Jets weren't worthy of the word *rival*, the enmity that reared up in a torrent of trash talk before the 2011 AFC playoffs was real and ran deep.

The bad blood dated to the 1990s, when former Giants mastermind Bill Parcells coached the Patriots to the Super Bowl then tried to leave for the Jets; Parcells and his top assistant, named Bill Belichick, moved to the Jets. After signing away running back Curtis Martin from New England, the duo soon brought the Jets to the conference championships while the Patriots regressed. But when Parcells bequeathed the head coaching job to Belichick, he promptly resigned and returned to New England. When Jets linebacker Mo Lewis flattened New England quarterback Drew Bledsoe in 2001, Belichick turned to his backup, Tom Brady, and promptly won three Super Bowls in four years. Equally disheartening, New England won 13 of the next 15 games against the Jets, from 2001 to 2008, featuring a 37–16 rout in the 2007 playoffs.

Controversies continued flaring. When the Jets hired Eric Mangini as coach in 2006, he called Belichick a friend. Belichick wouldn't even mention Mangini by name. The Patriots accused the Jets of tampering with receiver Deion Branch. Then came Spygate, when Belichick and the Patriots were punished for secretly filming the Jets' defensive signals, a controversy that tarnished the Patriots' reputation. On the field, the Patriots just kept winning at the Jets' expense. (It didn't help Jet fans that it was the Giants who derailed the Patriots' perfect season with their miracle Super Bowl win.)

In 2009, the Jets hired a new coach, Rex Ryan. A defensive mastermind with Baltimore, he took on Belichick in psychological warfare, although he preferred bluster and bravado to lurking under a hoodie.

Although the Jets had won four playoff games in the previous quarter-century, Ryan told Jets fans that unlike Mangini, he'd never "kiss Bill Belichick's Super Bowl rings." He also ramped up the Jets' defense, signing two top defenders from his Ravens squad, Bart Scott and Jim Leonhard. In the first matchup of the Ryan era, the Jets beat the Pats at home for the first time in nine years. The new Jets reached the AFC conference championship, and while they lost to the Indianapolis Colts, the future looked bright.

For 2010, the Jets bolstered their roster with Antonio Cromartie in the secondary and Santonio Holmes at receiver. In September, they again beat New England at home. By December, both teams had 9–2 records. The Jets went to New England for a *Monday Night Football* showdown. Maybe this would become a rivalry after all. Instead, the Patriots smacked the Jets on national television, humiliating them, 45–3. The Patriots won the division while the Jets settled for the wild card.

After avenging their playoff loss against the Colts with a last-second come-from-behind win, it was on to New England. But before a down was played, Ryan led his team, especially Cromartie and Scott, in a robust round of trash-talking against the Pats.

Securing the chip firmly on his team's shoulder, Ryan then devised a game plan with defensive coordinator Mike Pettine that made Belichick and Brady look unprepared and outclassed.

Brady would finish 29-for-45 for 299 yards, but those numbers belied a game in which he looked lost or harried much of the time. Brady had thrown 340 passes without an interception, but that record streak ended on the first series when he seemed unnerved by linebacker Calvin Pace and rushed a pass that David Harris picked off and returned for 58 yards. Brady was also sacked five times and looked confused as the Jets disguised coverages. He was surprised that they opened playing zones when he expected man-to-man defense, but then the Jets would switch back to man-to-man when Brady wasn't expecting it. Blitzes kept him on the run and wary of pressure, worried about getting hit and hurt.

Still, the Jets failed to convert that interception into points, and New England drove to the Jets five. But Alge Crumpler dropped a pass in the end zone, and then Shaun Ellis sacked Brady. The Pats had to settle for a field goal. When Drew Coleman's sack of Brady later set up the Jets with good field position, quarterback Mark Sanchez hurled a 37-yard pass to Braylon Edwards and a seven-yard touchdown pass to LaDainian Tomlinson. The Jets suddenly had the lead. Trailing, the Patriots tried a fake punt on fourth down late in the second. The play bombed when safety Patrick Chung fumbled the snap, and, with 33 seconds left, Sanchez found Edwards for 15 yards and a 14–3 halftime lead.

That shift in score and momentum gave the Jets confidence in the second half, so when New England mounted an 80-yard touchdown drive to close to 14–11, the Jets calmly countered with their own score. Jerricho Cotchery broke loose through a porous Patriots defense after a short pass for 58 yards. Then Holmes made a seven-yard touchdown catch, diving while keeping his knee and foot in bounds.

The Patriots did not score again until they hit a field goal to make it 21–11, with just two minutes left in their season. Their onside kick failed, and Cromartie ran the ball to the Patriots 20-yard line. Shonn Greene's 16-yard touchdown run had the Jets dancing gleefully on the sidelines. Brady's 13-yard touchdown pass to Branch with 24 seconds left to pull within 28–21 proved meaningless. The Jets recovered the onside kick and began celebrating—with passion and anger.

While the Jets were heading to their second straight AFC Championship Game, they still weren't through proving their point in New England. When ESPN's Sal Paolantonio put a mic on Scott, he got more than the typical sports clichés.

"To all the nonbelievers! Especially *you* Tom Jackson," Scott shouted, referring to Jackson's pregame prediction of a 30–10 Jets loss on ESPN.

Poetic Justice. . . . We were . . . we're pissed off. People gave us no chance. . . . Disrespect us. Talk crap about the defense. We're the third-best defense in the league. All we hear is about their defense. . . . They can't stop a nosebleed. Twenty-fifth in the league . . . and *we're* the ones who get disrespected.

When Paolantonio, perhaps worried that Scott would explode through people's TV screens and into their living rooms, signed off by saying, "Congratulations. See you in Pittsburgh," Scott roared, "Can't wait!"

This spontaneous mixture of rage and joy went viral. In the locker room, Scott served up another half-hour of emotional, often-fuming speeches, attacking everyone on the Patriots and in the media who treated Ryan like a "buffoon" and made fun of his weight and personal life.

Unfortunately, it was all downhill, rather rapidly, from there. The Jets lost in Pittsburgh the following week, then rapidly reverted to being the same old Jets: eight straight seasons (and counting) without reaching the playoffs, often losing badly and committing gaffes both on and off the field. The Patriots, meanwhile, reached five more Super Bowls. Thus, this victory was the one time in a dismal two-decade stretch when it was the Jets, not the Patriots, who were clearly the better, tougher, smarter, better-coached team.

9

Hideki Matsui Drives in Six as the Yankees Win Their Only Championship Post-2000, November 4, 2009, Yankee Stadium

Hideki Matsui had a flair for the dramatic. Nicknamed "Godzilla" in Japan, where he was a three-time MVP, he stomped on pitchers in the major leagues from the moment he arrived in 2003. He drove in a run in his first major-league at-bat, then became the first Yankee to hit a grand slam in his first game at Yankee Stadium. In Game 7 of the 2003 ALCS, he doubled off Pedro Martinez and scored the tying run against Boston, setting up Aaron Boone's eventual series-winning homer.

Matsui had more than 100 RBI in each of his first four full seasons, but even in his baseball dotage, he maintained his knack for timely knocks—on his 35th birthday, June 12, 2009, his three-run home run gave the Yankees a 7–6 lead over the Mets. Two months later, against Boston, he became the first Yankee to drive in seven runs in Fenway Park since Lou Gehrig in 1930. This would prove his final year with the Yankees, and Matsui saved his biggest performance for his last game in pinstripes.

Most teams consider reaching the playoffs or the championship a mark of success, even if they fall short of the crown. The Yankees are not most teams. From 1923 to 1962, the Yankees won 20 World Series while the rest of baseball also won 20. The Yankees never went more than three seasons without a title. That dynasty remains unparalleled. After George Steinbrenner revived the Yankees franchise in the 1970s, he declared that anything short of a World Series win was a disappointment. His teams often fell short of the mark but won twice in the 1970s and, after a disastrous drought, four times between 1996 and 2000.

Since 2000, however, the Yankees have, by their own standards, been a bust. They lost the World Series in 2001 and 2003, then watched as the Boston Red

Sox became baseball's best twenty-first-century team, winning four titles. From 2005 to 2007, the Yankees didn't even reach the ALCS, and, in 2008, they were locked out of the playoffs completely, finishing in third place, with 89 wins. Yankees fans were feeling like the Alex Rodriguez era was going to be a very long, very expensive bust—especially when he confessed in the spring of 2009, to having used steroids years earlier.

Instead, in 2009, the first year after George Steinbrenner ceded control to his sons, the Yankees moved into a new Yankee Stadium and returned to their former glory, giving a new generation of fans a taste of what it had traditionally meant to be a Yankees fan.

The front office spent big on pitching, and newcomers C. C. Sabathia and A. J. Burnett became the two best starters on this 103-win team. The new Yankee Stadium's homer-friendly jet stream toward right field helped another free agent addition, Nick Swisher, hit 29 homers. Rodriguez added 30 and Mark Teixeira hit 39, as part of an onslaught of 244 homers—a new team record. Derek Jeter passed Gehrig to become the team's all-time hit leader, en route to becoming first Yankee with 3,000 hits.

After sweeping Minnesota and beating the Los Angeles Angels, the Yankees faced the defending champion Philadelphia Phillies in the World Series. The Yankees lost Game 1 at home, but in Game 2, Matsui drove in what proved to be the winning run with a sixth-inning homer off Pedro Martinez. In Philadelphia, Matsui, the designated hitter, would be forced to the bench, but his pinch-hit home run helped put away Game 3.

The Yankees returned home for Game 6, looking to finish the Series. Back in the lineup, Matsui single-handedly made sure it happened. The game marked Andy Pettitte's 18th and final World Series win (a record) and Mariano Rivera's 11th and final World Series save (a record), but that was only possible because Matsui tied a record too, driving in six runs in a single World Series game. (Bobby Richardson, another Yankee, did it in 1960.)

In the second, Martinez walked Alex Rodriguez on four pitches, then tried to fool Matsui with a 3-2 changeup. Matsui fought it off to stay alive. Martinez's fastball was nothing but an 89-mile-per-hour fat meatball, and Matsui cranked it into the second deck in right field.

When Philly scored in the third, Matsui responded with a two-run single off Martinez to make it 4-1. In the fifth, Philadelphia's Chad Durbin yielded an RBI single to Teixeira and was replaced by J. A. Happ, who had the misfortune of facing Matsui with two on and one out. Matsui's two-run double put the game out of reach, and the Yankees cruised to a 7-3 win. Matsui barely smiled and didn't publicly celebrate, even when the fans chanted "MVP" or when he received a standing ovation while on second base and the scoreboard announced he had tied the single-game RBI record

Matsui became both the first Japanese-born player and the first full-time designated hitter (and 11th Yankee) to win the World Series MVP. Starting only three games, he had 3 homers, 8 RBI, and a .615 average.

Matsui's World Series heroics meant that when George Steinbrenner died on the day of the 2010 All-Star Game, he died with the Yankees restored as defending World Series champions.

There would be no new dynasty, as the Yankees crumbled afterward. Rodriguez was finally caught and suspended for his cheating and lying, and the team grew old and stale. The core four—Jorge Posada (2011), Andy Pettitte (2013), Mariano Rivera (2013), and Derek Jeter (2014)—retired, and the Yankees failed to even reach the divisional series for four straight years, even as the hapless Mets revived and went to the World Series. The Yankees closed in on two decades with just one championship—a dry spell the team has not experienced since acquiring Babe Ruth—making Game 6 of the 2009 World Series and Matsui's clutch performance something to cherish.

10

Unheralded Juan Martin del Potro Upsets Invincible Roger Federer, September 14, 2009, National Tennis Center

Roger Federer's dominance of the U.S. Open was unprecedented: Beginning in 2004, he captured five straight titles, unparalleled in the modern era. He was so brilliant, so unstoppable, his wins were largely devoid of drama. He lost only 15 sets in 41 straight wins through the 2009 semifinals. The best way to acknowledge the magnificence of his achievement is to celebrate what it took to defeat him. What it took was four-plus hours and five sets worth of blistering forehands from 6-foot-6 Argentinian howitzer Juan Martin del Potro.

The 21-year-old Del Potro had decimated Rafael Nadal in the semis, while Federer had beaten Novak Djokovic in (what else) straight sets. Those two were considered the biggest threats: In the previous 18 majors, Djokovic won one and Nadal six. (Federer won the other 11.)

This match initially seemed like another coronation. Federer had already won the French Open and Wimbledon, and was hoping to become the first man since Rod Laver to win three Slams on three surfaces in one year.

Federer kept the ball to del Potro's backhand, only going to the forehand when he could find a sharp angle. Federer had four break points in del Potro's first service game, completing the job by racing off the court to retrieve a short angle volley to his backhand and then gliding back to hit a seemingly impossible crosscourt forehand winner. Using his serve, attacking net game, and drop shots, Federer cruised through the first set, 6–3.

In the second set, Federer led, 5–4, 30–0, and was on the verge of an insurmountable two-set lead. But del Potro scrambled to even the score at 30–30, then unleashed one of those laser forehands down the line. The ball was called out, but del Potro challenged the call; this was a pet peeve of Federer, who never liked and only grudgingly accepted the relatively new Hawk-Eye replay technology. The replay showed that the ball nicked the line, so instead of set point for Federer, it was break point for del Potro. Federer was so frustrated that he purposely walked over to point out where he believed the ball really hit. (The ball looked in on traditional replays, but it's impossible to be certain.) By his standards, it was a McEnroe-esque tantrum. Del Potro capitalized, breaking serve with a forehand passing shot down the line. Del Potro's forehand then carried him through his service game and was the difference maker in the tie-break—he hit winners to start and finish it.

In the third set, Federer's first-serve percentage slipped, and del Potro broke for what seemed to be a crucial 4–3 lead. But the champion immediately broke back, then saved a break point. But on the point that seemingly gave him a 5–4 advantage, del Potro challenged a call long after he should have been allowed to. When the umpire, Jake Garner, inexplicably permitted it, Federer barked, "How can you allow that, do you have any rules in there?" When Garner was dismissive, Federer responded, "Don't tell me to be quiet, okay? When I want to talk, I'll talk. I don't give a shit."

(Garner had previously taken an ace away from Federer when del Potro claimed he wasn't ready even though he did not ask for time and appeared in position.)

Still, Federer held and then finished the set when his rival double-faulted twice. Again, the sixth title seemed close, especially when Federer earned two break points in the second game of the fourth set. But again, del Potro's forehand changed history. He hit a crosscourt winner off a short ball. And then he hit another, inside out to the other corner. Federer couldn't even move for either one. Back to deuce. Del Potro ended the game with another crosscourt forehand winner, this time launching it from behind the baseline. Del Potro faced another break point in his next service game. And yes, he got back to deuce with another crosscourt forehand winner. When he hit a winner down the line on the first point of Federer's serve, the legend seemed to wilt a little, and del Potro broke him at love. He ran his streak to 10 straight points before the champ rallied off the ropes to hold serve and even break del Potro back. The fourth set came down to a tiebreaker. If Federer could pull it out the title was his. But del Potro's forehand proved too much on the first three points, and he held on for a 7–4 finish.

In the fifth set, the young challenger proved physically and mentally tougher. Federer had played just two five-setters in his record run at Flushing Meadows and was broken early and then again, falling, 6–2, to the new champion. It was just one of eight five-setter finals in 50 years of the Open and the first of the twenty-first century.

Federer never again won the U.S. Open (through 2018), but he, Nadal, and Djokovic maintained their stranglehold on the sport, winning 14 of the next 16 Slams and 30 of the next 37. That fact, along with the multiple wrist surgeries that would derail del Potro for years, makes this win that much more special.

11

Eli Manning Scrambles, David Tyree Uses His Head, and the Giants End the Patriots' Dream Season, February 3, 2008, University of Phoenix Stadium, Phoenix

The New England Patriots had perfection within their grasp. And then, suddenly, shockingly, it slipped away, like a desperate quarterback eluding a certain sack.

The 18–0 Patriots, the record-setting Patriots—36.8 points per game, 75 touchdowns, +315 point differential—had been bruised and battered by the New York Giants defense. Yet, with 1:20 remaining in Super Bowl XLII, New England led, 14–10, and was about to cement its stature as football's greatest team ever: When New York quarterback Eli Manning overthrew David Tyree, Asante Samuel was there to make an interception that would end the game. But the ball glanced off the defender's hand and flew away.

The Giants faced 3rd and 5 from their own 44-yard line with just 1:15 left, but they were still alive—until Manning took the snap and was instantly confronted by one Patriot after another, each grabbing at the beleaguered quarterback. This became one of the greatest plays ever as Manning evaded, escaped, and spun himself free and then, with some help from David Tyree and his helmet, changed NFL history.

The Patriots were led by the inscrutable Bill Belichick, whose Spygate cheating scandal had just tarnished his image, and glamor boy quarterback Tom Brady, who threw 50 touchdown passes en route to an MVP Award. Each infuriated fans of opposing teams in different ways—their one common bond was that they seemed unstoppable.

Marching inexorably toward a fourth Super Bowl title in seven seasons, the Patriots also did their share to make a mockery of the long-standing New York–Boston rivalry. The Red Sox had ended their "curse" and yanked baseball supremacy from the Bronx with World Series crowns in 2004 and 2007. The Celtics were on their way to an NBA title as the Knicks, well, you don't really wanna remember. The Jets were the Pats' patsies. Even the lone bright spot, the Giants, lost to New England in the regular-season finale, 38–35, as Brady threw for 356 yards.

No one expected the Giants to then be New England's final obstacle in the Super Bowl. The team collapsed in 2006, and lost their first two games in 2007. Manning took much of the blame—notably a public slam from retired running back Tiki Barber—with some justification. He loved looking deep, often on first and second down, and while he had a flair for big plays, he also frequently put the offense in a hole, completing just 54 percent of his passes. But Coach Tom Coughlin changed his rigid ways, and, after starting 0–2, the Giants finished 10–6, despite injuries to tight end Jeremy Shockey, defensive end Mathias Kiwanuka, and running back Derrick Ward. They relied on receivers Plaxico Burress and Amani Toomer, and 1,000-yard rusher Brandon Jacobs, plus an intimidating front line lead by Michael Strahan, Justin Tuck, and Osi Umenyiora. The Giants eked out three straight playoff victories on the road, against Tampa Bay, the top-ranked Dallas Cowboys, and the Green Bay Packers.

Still, no one put them on equal footing with the Patriots. The Patriots seemed invincible, same as the Baltimore Colts before their 1969 Super Bowl against the Jets. Being double-digit underdogs certainly built up resentment, along with all the love and attention showered on New England's pretty boy superstar.

"Everywhere you went, it was all about the Patriots and 19–0," said cornerback R. W. McQuarters later. "We go into the city, and there's Tom Brady on the buildings. We get to the stadium today, and there's a Super Bowl program in our locker, and it's like a Tom Brady magazine. We come out to warm up, and Tom Brady is on the big screen. It's like Tom Brady was everywhere."

In the Super Bowl, the Giants put Brady in a new place—on the ground, sacking him five times and knocking him down six more, leaving him harried and even gun shy. Tuck was constantly shifting positions so Brady didn't know where to look, while Umenyiora had All-Pro left tackle Matt Light so off-balance he committed two false starts in the second half. Manning's final drive made the headlines, but it was the swarming defense, which also shut down the Patriots' running game, that made the comeback possible.

New York started with a throwback to Super Bowl wins of yore—beat the other team's offense by keeping them off the field. With four third-down conversions, the first Giants drive lasted one second shy of 10 minutes, breaking the record for the longest drive in Super Bowl history (set by the Giants against the Buffalo Bills). After 16 plays, the Giants stalled, settling for a field goal. Then

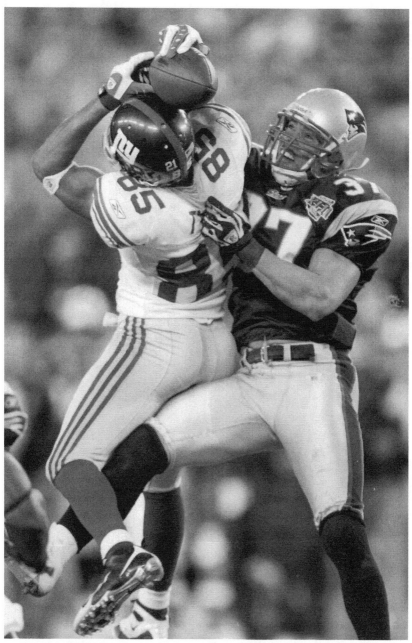

David Tyree's Helmet Catch helped the Giants stun the Patriots, short-circuiting their dreams of going undefeated. *ASSOCIATED PRESS*

the Patriots—as per usual—benefited from a penalty when Giants linebacker Antonio Pierce was called for pass interference on an incomplete pass on 3rd and 10. Given the ball on the one-yard-line, the Patriots easily took a 7-3 lead.

Then both defenses took over, and no one scored for 33 minutes and 52 seconds, a Super Bowl record.

The Patriots got a free first down at the start of the second half when Belichick noticed the Giants had a 12th man still on the field before a New England punt, but then Strahan nailed Brady for a six-yard loss on third down, killing the drive.

When the final quarter began, the scoring suddenly resumed. Manning found rookie tight end Kevin Boss for 45 yards. Later, Steve Smith added a third-down, 17-yard catch. From the five, Manning looked into the end zone, and, instead of his favorite targets, he found an open man in New Jersey native David Tyree.

Tyree was in his fifth year, but he was best known as a special teams guy. In 2007, he caught just four passes, plus one in the playoffs. He dropped more than that total in practice on the Friday before the Super Bowl, but afterward Manning told Tyree he still believed in him. Tyree rewarded that faith with his touchdown catch, putting the Giants up, 10-7. But Brady soon found his rhythm on a drive where he completed six of his first eight passes for a total of 55 yards. From the New York six, the Giants twice halted his quest for the end zone, but on third down Corey Webster slipped and Randy Moss was left wide open for an easy touchdown. With just 2:39 left, the Patriots had a 14-10 lead. New England was firmly in control. The season suddenly seemed over.

The Giants started at their own 17. After small steps forward, they soon faced a 4 and 1. But Jacobs climbed through the middle for two yards to keep the drive alive. Two plays later came the plays that transformed this into one of the greatest upsets in sports history.

After Manning was forced to scramble for five on first down, he threw the pass that Samuel could have—should have—intercepted. Manning's target was Tyree, but there was a miscommunication between quarterback and receiver about the route. The drive's momentum was gone. Manning had been off-balance or off the mark on four of his previous five attempted pass plays. The play call from the sidelines on 3rd and 5 was "62 Sail-Y Union," which gave Manning two receivers on each side. The "Union" translates as Burress, from the left wideout, and Toomer, from the slot on that side, cutting across, Toomer at 12 yards and Burress behind him—deep enough for a first down but short enough that Manning should have time to read the coverage and still look for other options. The "Y," Smith, ran a corner from the right slot, while Tyree ran a post to take defenders out of coverage. Burress had been Manning's favored target throughout the season but was hobbled by an injured knee and had only caught one pass in the game, meaning Toomer was the likely first choice.

Manning saw the Patriots in dime coverage with six defensive backs, but he also noticed that free safety James Sanders was so tight on Smith that Tyree might have a shot at beating Samuel deep. This was Manning at his best and worst—an expert at reading defenses at the line with a tendency to look for the deepest, flashiest, most dangerous option. So, Tyree was first in his mind. Then the ball was snapped.

Linebacker Adalius Thomas blew past left tackle David Diehl, creating instant pressure. Manning did a little dance to move forward, but his pocket had a defensive lineman-sized hole in it. Two actually. Jarvis Green and Richard Seymour both closed in as the Giants lineman tried in vain to protect their quarterback. Seymour grabbed number 10 but couldn't catch hold; Green got a stronger grasp on Manning's back and then his jersey. If Manning went down it would be 4th and very long. The Patriots pass rush was almost perfect, but while both big men got to Manning, almost simultaneously, neither could get him firmly in their clutches, thanks in part to the extra effort by Shaun O'Hara and Rich Seubert, the linemen who had been beaten but kept shoving back at the Patriots defenders.

Manning took a blow to the head but then ducked, turned, and retreated. That Manning didn't go down was astonishing, but it is the next second that is perhaps more remarkable. Manning stumbled away at his own 37, looking down, his body turned from the action. One second later he was five yards further back and upright, and—a second can be an eternity in sports—he had spotted Tyree. The receiver broke from his route and came back to provide a midfield target. A second later, Manning unleashed a beautiful bomb downfield just before getting leveled.

Tyree knew the pass was on target, but he also knew ferocious Pro Bowl safety Rodney Harrison was on top of him. They went up. Tyree grabbed the ball. Harrison smacked into Tyree. The ball could have—should have—come loose, but as Harrison slammed Tyree to the ground on his back and the receiver's left hand came away, he pressed the ball to his helmet with his right, ensuring that it would stay in his control.

The Helmet Catch turned the momentum, but the outcome was no more secure than a midair one-handed catch. The 32-yard gain put the Giants at New England's 24-yard line, and the clock was running low. The Giants no longer needed a miracle, but they soon faced 3rd and 11. Manning produced another big play, connecting with Smith for 12 yards. Smith stepped out at the 13 to stop the clock.

On the next play, Burress found space and the spotlight: The Giants lined up three receivers on the right and Burress in isolation on the left. With the Patriots blitzing, Hobbs was in single coverage. He guessed the receiver would slant across the middle; instead, Manning pump-faked and Burress faded into the corner of the end zone and found himself alone when Manning's pass fell into his hands. After 12 plays and 83 yards—more than a third of that accomplished on one seemingly impossible play and more than half on third downs—the Giants led, 17–14. Manning became the first quarterback to throw two go-ahead touchdowns in the fourth quarter of one Super Bowl.

There were 35 seconds left on the clock, and the Patriots still had Tom Brady, his generation's Joe Montana. But these Giants were unyielding. Jay Alford sacked Brady on second down, and Webster batted away a bomb to Moss on third down. After a Hail Mary was knocked to the turf, 19–0 was, impossibly, 18–1.

For New York sport fans, no other wins from the season mattered. The Giants were the best team in football. Full stop. Four years later, more than a dozen key players, led by Manning and Tuck, would still be on the Giants squad when they were again Super Bowl underdogs against New England and again trailed late in the game. But, in 2012, everyone who had witnessed the Helmet Catch knew better than to doubt Manning and the Giants when the Super Bowl was on the line.

Aaron Boone Sinks the Sox, October 16, 2003, Yankee Stadium

Aaron Boone's middle name is John.
Russell "Bucky" Dent's middle name is Earl.

Yet, if you pronounce both middle names with a Boston accent, they sound exactly the same: "Bleeping."

Boone's 11th-inning blast into the night at Yankee Stadium on October 16, 2003, drove the stake through the heart of the Boston Red Sox, slamming down the exclamation point on a titanic seven-game battle. By then a Yankee win seemed inevitable, after an explosive eighth inning when Boston manager Grady Little incited in Red Sox Nation a winter's worth of expletives as his inaction gave easy runs to the Yankees in what was then the annual Boston clearance sale on World Series dreams.

The Yankees had, of course, lorded their superiority over Boston for decades, from the acquisition of Babe Ruth through the pennant-clinching win over Boston in 1949's final game, through Dent's homer in the Yankees' 1978 tiebreaker playoff win, through New York's six straight first-place finishes over second-place Boston from 1998 to 2003.

In the offseason before 2003, agitated Boston president Larry Lucchino dubbed big-spending New York the "Evil Empire," which only heightened the bad feelings. The Yankees, however, remained imperturbable. Although they hadn't won the World Series since 2000, they had an unassailable core with Derek Jeter, Bernie Williams, Jorge Posada, and Mariano Rivera. The Yankees won 101 games and then flicked away Minnesota in the ALDS.

Boston, the wild-card winner, was waiting in the ALCS, believing they finally had the team to topple the big, bad bullies, with a bullpen trio (Alan Embree, Mike Timlin, and Scott Williamson) that had flourished down the stretch.

In Game 1, when Tim Wakefield walked two batters in the seventh, Little immediately called on Embree, Timlin, and then Williamson to preserve the lead. After New York evened the series, Game 3 added a touch of WWE melodrama to the tension. Ex-Boston ace Roger Clemens faced Boston's new ace, Pedro Martinez, who gave up four early runs, then grazed the head of Yankees right fielder Karim Garcia with a fastball. Both teams soon started jawing, and Martinez appeared to threaten Posada. The next inning Manny Ramirez overreacted to a high fastball from Clemens, heading toward the mound with his bat, which brought out both benches. Leading the Yankees charge was 72-year-old bench coach Don Zimmer, who foolishly attacked Martinez; forced to defend himself, the pitcher slammed the old-timer to the ground. Later Garcia and reliever Jeff Nelson got into a fight with a Boston groundskeeper. The Yankees eked out a 4–3 win, but the tone was set even, as the teams split the next two games.

The best sports dramas are built on stories and relationships, and the stage for Game 7 was set for an epic of Shakespearean dimensions. It was America's greatest rivalry at the cathedral of baseball, and it again pitted Clemens against Martinez, who had won all five American League Cy Young Awards from 1997 to 2001 (although Clemens was likely enhancing his performance illegally).

Clemens was gone in the fourth after yielding two homers. The Red Sox seemed ready to reverse the curse, with Martinez retiring 16 of 18 at one point and throwing faster than he had in weeks. In Boston that afternoon, the Fenway Park grounds crew had painted the 2003 World Series logo onto the field, a bit of hubris or optimism that was beginning to seem justified.

With the Sox up 4–1, it might have seemed logical for Little to call on the bullpen after six: Martinez's statistics grew markedly worse as his pitch count grew, while Timlin, Embree, and Williamson had allowed just one run in their previous 16-plus innings, fanning 24. Additionally, the Yankees' over-the-top stretching of the seventh-inning stretch (allegedly for patriotic reasons, with their absurdly long rendition of "God Bless America") left Martinez cooling for an extra seven minutes. But Little did nothing.

Jason Giambi ripped his second solo homer. Little didn't move. When the Yankees' number eight and nine hitters, the unthreatening Enrique Wilson and Garcia, both singled, Little failed to recognize the warning signs. When Martinez struck out Alfonso Soriano with a 94-mile-per-hour heater, Little misinterpreted it as a sign of strength, not a tired hurler finding one last big pitch.

Martinez thought he was through, pointing to the heavens and hugging his teammates in the dugout. When David Ortiz's homer built the lead back to 5–2, Red Sox fans finally let themselves relax. Then Little defied rational thinking.

Martinez had pitched into the eighth only four times throughout the year. The Yankees hadn't hit him well all day, but they'd remained poised and made him work for each out because they knew he'd fade. He had thrown exactly 100 pitches. In 2003, the batting average against him on pitches 85 to 100 was .230; after that it was .370.

Nick Johnson popped out after wringing seven pitches out of Martinez's arm. The Red Sox were five outs away from the World Series. Jeter, playing despite a ruptured ligament in his thumb, slammed a double to right. Little stayed put. The baseball gods had sent the Yankees another gift, and they capitalized.

On pitch 115, Williams roped a single to left, making it 5–3. Little trotted to the mound but left his authority in the dugout. "Take him out," the entire New England region yelled at their television sets. Martinez said he could get lefty Hideki Matsui, even though Matsui had already doubled off Martinez twice in the series, and even though the southpaw Embree was ready. Little bowed before his ace and left. Matsui pulled Martinez's failing fastball down the right-field line for a ground-rule double. The tying runs were in scoring position, and Martinez had thrown 118 pitches.

Still, Little failed to do the obvious thing. Posada worked the count to 2–2, pushing Martinez above 120 pitches. Then he blooped a ball over second; Williams and Matsui raced home.

Credit the Yankees for patient and clutch at-bats—in Martinez's final nine batters, New York produced three singles, three doubles, and a home run.

Posada's hit tied it at 5–5, but now it felt like just a matter of time. Little finally called on Embree, who got Giambi on a fly-out, then Timlin walked two men to load the bases before escaping. Mariano Rivera limited the Red Sox to one hit in the ninth and one in the 10th. He hadn't pitched three innings in a game in seven years, but in the 11th he retired the side in order, fanning two. Wakefield, who had carried the Red Sox to two wins as a starter, pitched a 1–2–3 10th.

Leading off the Yankees 11th was Aaron Boone, taking his first at-bat after entering as a pinch-runner in the eighth. Boone had been acquired midseason from Cincinnati but slumped in New York. Just 5-for-31 in the postseason, he'd been benched for Enrique Wilson. A dancing knuckleball is the last pitch a struggling hitter wants to see. But Wakefield's first pitch didn't knuckle, didn't flutter, didn't do much of anything—until Boone cracked it hard, launching it into the history books. "Derek Jeter told me that if we just waited the ghosts would show up," Boone said.

As perennial winners, the Yankees tended to be relatively low-key in their celebrations. Not this time. Rivera ran to the mound and lay down while everyone jubilantly greeted Boone at the plate. "To beat our rival like we did, it couldn't be more satisfying," manager Joe Torre said.

The Yankees lost the World Series that year. Usually that's all that mattered for George Steinbrenner and his fans, but they rocked comfortably by baseball's hot stove that winter, content at least with the shot heard breaking hearts 'round New England.

13

Justine Henin's Comeback Undoes and Outdoes Jennifer Capriati's, September 5, 2003, National Tennis Center

Before the 2003 U.S. Open, Serena Williams had won five of six Grand Slam crowns, defeating her sister Venus in the finals each time. The sisters had also won the previous four U.S. Opens. But with both sidelined by injuries, a new champion would be crowned. The favorites were top-ranked Kim Clijsters and second seed Justine Henin, who won her first Slam that spring by defeating Clijsters in the French Open final.

Henin, who had never made it past the fourth round in Queens, had been dogged by controversy. In her French Open semifinal against Serena Williams, it appeared Henin raised her hand to ask for time; when Williams's serve missed, Henin did not acknowledge the motion, forcing Williams into a second serve. Then in a final in San Diego, she asked for a medical time-out after dropping the first set to Clijsters. After Henin won the match, Clijsters accused her of faking an injury to wreck her rhythm.

At the Open, Clijsters cruised through her semifinal against Lindsay Davenport, leaving Henin to face off against crowd favorite and feel-good story Jennifer Capriati. Capriati, who wore an outfit of red, white, and blue, replete with stars to appeal to the locals, was a former teen phenom whose career—and life—had derailed soon after her 1991 U.S. Open semifinal loss as a fifteen-year-old to Monica Seles. Capriati made headlines for being arrested for shoplifting, entering drug rehab, and admitting that she had contemplated suicide, before essentially vanishing from the tour. But she gradually stitched herself back together and, in 2001, won both the Australian and French Opens, defending her Australian title successfully in 2002. In Flushing, the sixth seed stormed into the semifinals, losing just 24 games in her first five matches.

CHAPTER 13

But the fiercely competitive Henin had been equally dominant. She possessed superb footwork and timing, plus a flair for attacking early in points with a topspin forehand and a dynamic one-handed backhand, finishing at the net, where she was more comfortable than many women players. Early on against the bigger, stronger Capriati, Henin asserted herself as the superior overall player, running down everything, moving Capriati around, and racing out to a 4–1 lead. Henin was a point from 5–3 when the chair umpire overruled a game-winning shot. The ball was actually in, but instant replay challenges did not exist then and Capriati seized this small opening. Playing to the crowd enhanced her momentum, as she ultimately won five straight games to close out the set, 6–4.

Despite occasional concentration lapses, Capriati was flowing effortlessly— early in the second set she defended against an overhead, then raced in on the subsequent drop volley to hit a winner down the line. She relentlessly pounded the ball deep and on great angles, while Henin's forehand faltered again and again in lengthy rallies; the Belgian's 24th forehand error put Capriati in control, 5–3, in the second set.

But with Capriati two points from the finals, Henin created stunning shots on successive points. At the net she casually fielded a bullet at her feet, dispatching it with a perfect touch volley. On break point, Capriati raced in to retrieve Henin's volley and threw up a perfect lob, over Henin into the corner on her backhand side. Somehow, Henin not only ran it down, but also responded with a lob over Capriati to the baseline, winning the point and the game, to get back on serve. Moments later Henin dug out another tough shot from Capriati, who tore in from the baseline and arrived in time to hit a running forehand down the line, only to see Henin stab a backhand volley into the open court. That evened the set at 5–5; now it was Henin's turn to capitalize on her momentum, and she did, winning, 7–5.

Henin broke Capriati in the first game of the final set by retrieving a ball that looked past her in the forehand corner, then running down Capriati's lackluster volley to the backhand corner and hitting an astonishing short angle passing shot. After losing five straight games, Capriati could have collapsed mentally, but she kept attacking too, and broke right back. Capriati kept coming to the net and kept winning, pushing out to a 5–2 lead—she sprinted to her chair then, ramped up and ready to close out the match. Meanwhile, Henin was grimacing and clutching her thigh after many points. This time she did not seek medical help, even as the match inched toward the three-hour mark.

Instead, Henin kept herself in the fight with shorter points—she won the first one of her next service game at the net, the second on a backhand down the line with a more concise swing than usual, and a third on short ball hit for a winner off the baseline. Capriati had a chance to serve out the match, but Henin had her rhythm and broke back.

But Henin's cramping returned, and Capriati again got within two points of victory. Awaiting the serve, Capriati crept well inside the baseline to attack, then thought better of it and backed up; that uncertainty returned later in the point when she watched Henin's windblown lob land at her feet before awkwardly moving around it, giving up her control of the rally. Henin came through with the big blow, a forehand winner. Each woman then held serve after a multitude of long and dramatic rallies.

Fittingly, the match required a tiebreaker to determine the winner.

The crowd gave a standing ovation to both players. Fatigue produced more unforced errors, but Henin seemed the steadier presence, and Capriati, who had been within two points of a win 11 times, had less composure in reserve. She dropped the first three points on backhand errors, and while she'd battle back to win four of the next seven—including saving two match points—it was too late. At 6–4, Capriati made one last attack; she was in position to handle Henin's passing shot down the line, but after 183 minutes she was a half-step slow and her volley landed in the net.

Conquest complete, Henin then limped off the court, unable to even carry her rackets. The loser was too distraught to show grace, barely shaking Henin's hand and leaving without acknowledging the crowd. Capriati did, however, put on her brave face for the press conference and confessed she felt like her "heart was being ripped out." Henin didn't even make it there, needing an IV to recover and not leaving until 3:00 a.m. Initially uncertain whether she'd play the next day's final, she somehow recovered, beating Clijsters for the second of seven career Slam titles. But the semifinal remained the tournament's biggest thrill. "This match has just become part of the USA Network rain delay library," said commentator John McEnroe. "We will be watching this for years to come."

In a Match for the Ages, Pete Sampras Beats Andre Agassi One Last Time, September 8, 2002, National Tennis Center

Thirty-three straight winless tournaments in 26 months. That's quite the dreary oh-fer.

When people are calling you the greatest ever, you need to win some trophies. Pete Sampras had fallen from his peak by 1999, but because he won Wimbledon that year and the next, garnering accolades for his record 13th Grand Slam crown in 2000, no one wrote him off.

Then came the drop. In his next eight Slams, Sampras reached just two finals—the 2000 and 2001 Opens, where he was raked by confident young guns Marat Safin and Lleyton Hewitt. He wasn't reaching the quarters at other majors and lost four first-round matches in early 2002. Tasting fear and failure, Sampras whipped through three coaches. Mutterings and murmurings burbled in the press and on the tour: Sampras should retire before he embarrassed himself. Sampras kept on losing, falling in Wimbledon's second round to someone named George Bastl, on a side court no less.

Sampras knew history would treat him well: He'd ranked number one in the world six years running, won Wimbledon seven times in eight years, and took four U.S. Opens in seven. But Sampras wanted respect in his own time and to go out on his own terms. He wanted his peers, the press, and the fans to remember him as a winner who was at his best when it counted most. To do that, Sampras, 31, would have to prove himself one last time.

Sampras was seeded just 17th at the Open but looked like his younger self, tearing through lesser opponents like Greg Rusedski and Sjeng Schalken.

Back in the final, Sampras saw his destiny on the other side of the net, in sixth-seeded Andre Agassi. After an early career marred by frivolous distractions, Agassi, 32, had become a genuine champion in his own right, winning seven Slams, featuring four between 1999 and 2001; unlike Sampras, who'd never conquered the French Open, Agassi had won all four majors. Agassi also burnished his off-court reputation in ways Sampras the loner never could, helping younger players while committing more to Davis Cup play and philanthropic work.

Yet, Agassi remained keenly aware that in their inextricably linked careers, Sampras's legend burned brighter. Agassi won their first match, when he was 10 and Sampras nine, and their first pro match in Italy in 1989, in front of perhaps 100 people. But when the stakes were highest, Sampras would go from great to unfathomable, finding a way to win. He'd done it in their 1990 and 1995 Open finals, the 1999 Wimbledon final, and the fourth-set tiebreaker of their classic all-tiebreak 2001 Open quarterfinals.

Their on-court differences made this rivalry shimmer. Sampras had an overpowering serve, but Agassi was his generation's premier returner; Sampras's sharp volleys and leaping overheads countered Agassi's passing shots and lobs; Sampras swung aggressively with long, fluid strokes, while Agassi had a compressed game—superior reaction time, a compact swing, and great speed through the zone—that gave him the edge in baseline rallies. Agassi was emotionally vulnerable and played from a sense of insecurity but was remarkably fit (he ran sprints up the mountains in Nevada); Sampras played from confidence and a sense of belonging to history but was often lax in his conditioning, counting on superior ability to pull him through. Even practicing on adjacent side courts in their prime, they were a study in contrasts. Agassi played to the crowd, acknowledging their cheers and going between his legs to return a lob. Sampras just worked. Agassi approached Sampras and suggested they hit together, put on a show for some lucky fans. He coaxed, he charmed, he goaded—no luck. Sampras simply wanted to hone his game.

Sunday was a guaranteed winner, with tension and emotion rarely matched on the court. Back then, the Open era had never seen two players in their 30s reach the finals, nor two finals opponents who owned 20 Grand Slam titles; this would be Sampras and Agassi's 34th and final meeting, equaling the Jimmy Connors–John McEnroe rivalry. Sampras held a 19–14 edge.

For Sampras, this was his last chance to declare emphatically, "I am Pete Sampras. I am the greatest."

The crowd was wracked with emotion even before the first point— September 8, 2002, was the first men's final since 9/11, so a pregame ceremony honored the attack's victims and featured Queens native Art Garfunkel singing a heartbreaking version of "Bridge over Troubled Water."

CHAPTER 14

Agassi was usually the crowd favorite, but Sampras was the underdog for the first time ever, and fans backed him from the start. He didn't play like an underdog—he played like the winner of four Opens. With Agassi sluggish after his arduous semifinal against Hewitt, Sampras blasted 16 aces (reaching 132 miles per hour) and 36 winners in winning the first two sets, 6–3, 6–4. When Agassi earned a break point down 5–3 in the first, Sampras unleashed a 109-mile-per-hour second-serve ace. In the second set, he held at love four times, ending the set with another ace.

Then Agassi found his legs while Sampras's started to wobble. In the sixth game of the third set, Agassi's crosscourt passing shot on the run gave him three break points. But Sampras produced two aces and escaped. The crowd, wanting more tennis, switched sides, cheering even when Sampras missed a serve. Up 6–5, Agassi dragged Sampras through deuce after deuce, finally earning a break point and sizzling a backhand return that Sampras volleyed meekly into the net. The crowd gave Agassi a standing ovation.

Sampras shrewdly took a bathroom break to build some reserves. He'd need them desperately. The fourth set would be the deciding one—if Sampras couldn't finish Agassi, it was unlikely he'd stand a chance in the fifth.

It was a taut set, filled with potential turning points. With Agassi up, 2–1, the fourth game took everyone's breath away. Sampras, slow to the net and struggling with his serve, found himself looking into the abyss. Agassi punched backhands into the corners. Sampras twice saved break points. First, he picked a backhand half-volley off his shoestrings. On the second, a fatigued Sampras resorted to a drop shot to short-circuit the rally; from off the court Agassi tried flicking it around the side, but it ricocheted off the net post. On the 20th point of the game, Sampras put away a forehand volley, pulling back from the precipice, winning back the fans with his tenacity.

At 4–4, Agassi, the terrier who wouldn't let go, fought for another break point, then got it when Sampras double-faulted. But Agassi botched his backhand return, and Sampras revived the great champion within, the one who seized on the smallest of openings and cracked them wide. He finished that game with an ace, then used the momentum to break Agassi. Almost three hours after they began, Sampras finished Agassi off with his 84th winner of the day, a crisp backhand volley.

"I've needed Andre over the course of my career," Sampras would say afterward. "He's pushed me, forced me to add things to my game. He's the only guy that was able to do that."

Sampras had rewritten the record book, which confirmed his place at the top of the tennis pantheon (albeit briefly), but he'd also polished his legacy, touching everyone with his determination and resilience. Sampras hugged Agassi at the net, then climbed into the seats to embrace Bridgette Wilson, his pregnant wife and steadfast supporter. "This [title] might mean more than any of them," Sampras said. Having done what no one thought he could, he walked away from tennis, satisfied.

Mike Piazza Picks Up New York with His Post-9/11 Game-Winning Homer, September 21, 2001, Shea Stadium

It is all too easy to summon up—or perhaps all too impossible to completely bury—the visceral reactions people felt on the surface and in their souls on September 11, 2001: disbelief, nausea, sorrow, outrage, fear.

What has dissipated more with time are the emotions that have spun us this way and that in the aftermath: the perpetual shakiness, the despair over innocence lost, the sense that not only was our future forever altered, but also that there might not be a future. From that muddle of emotions there emerged a desperation for some semblance of normalcy, for a diversion, something to pump life into our hearts. If ever sports seemed frivolous and unnecessary it was in mid-September 2001, but it was precisely those traits that made games so vital.

There was no baseball for six days. Everything was just too raw, too confusing, too chaotic. The Mets and Yankees pitched in by carrying supplies to rescue workers, making morale-boosting visits, and doing anything else asked of them. Shea Stadium's parking lot became a staging area for supplies and a rest area for Ground Zero cleanup workers, so when play resumed, Mets home games were shifted to Pittsburgh.

The Mets replaced their regular caps with NYPD, FDNY, and other emergency services caps in tribute to the rescue workers and their fallen brethren. They won three straight, starting with a tiebreaking, three-run, ninth-inning rally. Throughout the nation it seemed that everyone was suddenly pulling for the Mets. New York City was wearing the persona of the downtrodden and the underdog, an image that fit the Mets far better than the first-place Yankees, winners of three straight World Series.

On September 21, the Mets returned to Shea Stadium. This was more than a ballgame. As the city's first large-scale event since 9/11, it was a national news story, and it provided a catharsis, a communal experience, a chance to pay tribute to those who had died and those still working heroically.

Long lines caused by new security measures delayed the start time, but New Yorkers, the world's most impatient people, did not complain. The Mets darkened the lights of the Twin Towers in their scoreboard skyline, wrapping those missing icons in red, white, and blue ribbon. The pregame program moved many to tears: a joint color guard from agencies that had lost personnel in the Towers (NYPD, FDNY, EMS, the Port Authority Police, and the State Court Officers Association), the NYPD bagpipe troupe, a Marine Corps 21-gun salute, Diana Ross singing "God Bless America," and Marc Anthony singing the national anthem. Before the game, the Mets and Atlanta Braves, bitter rivals for years, shook hands and hugged one another.

It was time to play, to acknowledge that for the living, life must go on. It was hardly a marquee matchup—Bruce Chen versus Jason Marquis—but it was a close contest. The Braves snagged a 1–0 lead in the fourth, but the Mets responded immediately, sparked by Mike Piazza's double. But the Mets left two on and did it again in the fifth. In the eighth, closer Armando Benitez yielded an RBI double, putting the Mets in a 2–1 hole. Recent events had redefined everyone's perspective. Yet, it still was hard not to feel glum about this special night ending with Benitez blowing another important game.

But in the Mets' eighth, Edgardo Alfonzo walked. A moment later, Piazza's bat whipped through the strike zone, finishing on his shoulder as the ball launched high and deep into the night. New Yorkers finally had cause, no matter how inconsequential, to be briefly, blissfully happy. "A small miracle," manager Bobby Valentine called the blast.

In the long run, it was nothing to get excited about, as the Mets' long-shot pennant hopes faded in the final week, but on that night the victory wasn't about the National League East standings. Many players lingered on the field afterward, and many fans stayed in the stands, knowing New York would never experience anything quite like this again—the anguish, joy, and relief commingling in the community of baseball.

16

The Williams Sisters Take Women's Tennis into Prime Time, September 8, 2001, National Tennis Center

Okay, so the match was kinda boring for a U.S. Open final: A 6–2, 6–4 yawner, it lasted just 69 minutes and was littered with 55 unforced errors. Yet, that doesn't diminish what the 2001 finals meant for women's tennis. Venus and Serena Williams, like Billie Jean King, transformed their sport, giving the women's game its own identity. The women's final had traditionally been sandwiched between two men's semifinals, but the Williams's star power insisted that women's tennis had players ready for prime time, live from New York on a Saturday night. This match—with the splendor and spectacle surrounding it—showed that, thanks to these riveting, willful, and immensely talented sisters, women's tennis was indeed able to stand on its own.

Back then, before the Williams's legends were secure, the most famous member of the family might have been their father, the brash rebel Richard Williams. He had proclaimed long and loud that his daughters would take over the game, irritating the (often racist) white establishment.

But Richard was right. His daughters were indeed the best in women's tennis, and the best thing for women's tennis, too. They might not have made lots of friends early on, but they were good—and compelling. Everyone wanted to see what they'd wear, what they'd do, and how they'd win.

Serena won the U.S. Open in 1999, at age 17. Venus won it at 20 in 2000. But to some extent they were still better known as celebrities, with no guarantee that they'd truly rule the game for an extended period the way Richard had promised. They'd also never faced one another in a Grand Slam final, and heading into the 2001 tournament, that was no sure thing.

Venus, the defending champion who had just won her second straight Wimbledon, came in seeded fourth. Serena, weeks shy of her 20th birthday, had just the one Grand Slam title and came in seeded 10th, after losing in the quarters of her last four Slams. That gave her a tougher draw. No matter, Serena and Venus wiped out all five of the other top six seeds. Serena beat sixth-seed Justine Henin, third-seed Lindsay Davenport, and top-seeded Martina Hingis, while Venus eliminated fifth-seed Kim Clijsters and second-seed Jennifer Capriati. This final wasn't about destiny, it was about dominance.

As kids in Compton, the two played a game called Do or Die—get your first serve in or lose the match. Their mother, Oracene, said of these showdowns between sisters, "It was do or die, and it was always for the U.S. Open championship."

Now it really was for the U.S. Open championship, and the two remained as inseparable as ever, practicing together that morning, taking prematch naps together, too. This would be the first time two black players met in any major finals and the first time two sisters had met in a major final since the Watson gals (Maud and Lillian) at Wimbledon in 1884. Before play began, the Harlem Gospel Choir performed, a Marine guard unfurled a court-sized flag, Grucci provided fireworks, and Diana Ross sang "God Bless America." There was enough celebrity glitter to recall Ali–Frazier: Joe Namath, Robert Redford, Carl Lewis, Robert Duvall, P. Diddy, and countless others—not to mention Billie Jean King—were there to witness the event.

Venus had beaten Serena in the early rounds of the Australian Open in 1998, and in the semis of Wimbledon in 2000, in addition to two of their three non-Slam matchups. None were great tennis—as much as each sister loved to win, their killer instinct was muted against the one person they hated to see lose. This match was a slight improvement, very slight. Two of the best servers in the game's history were broken seven times in 15 games, a total that indicates nerves. Venus was, if not more serene, less erratic, making 19 unforced errors to her younger sister's 36 in a humdrum 6–2, 6–4 win.

But the match also justified the hype in that it served notice to the rest of the sport: The sisters would face off again in five of the next seven Slam finals, leaving little room for anyone else at the top of the game. Serena won all of those matches, before losing her dominance for almost five years. Her recovery began at Wimbledon in 2008, when she lost to Venus in the final. (That was Venus's seventh and final Slam.) That fall at the U.S. Open, the two finally gave New Yorkers the match they'd hoped for: a two-and-a-half-hour slugfest in which Serena barely escaped in two tight tiebreakers with a 7–6 (6), 7–6 (7) victory.

CHAPTER 16

Inspired, Serena won 15 of the next 38 slams, one of which, remarkably, was a 2017 final against 36-year-old Venus at the Australian Open.

This 2001 final also gave the two women—especially Venus—the platform and the voice to fight on behalf of the tour. While the U.S. Open had long had pay parity thanks to King and the Australian Open had ponied up in 2001, it took until 2006 for the French and 2007 for Wimbledon to shed their sexist traditions and share the wealth equally. King cited Venus's commitment as crucial in that fight; both sisters, outspoken for a good cause, also lent their clout to the Billie Jean King Leadership Initiative, to push for equal pay across jobs outside of tennis.

So, even if the match on that night in 2001, was undermined by the fact that neither player wanted to see the other lose, the big winner turned out to be women's tennis. It had indeed come a long way.

17

The Subway Series Rides Again, October 21, 2000, Yankee Stadium

New York, New York. How sweet it sounds. After a 44-year wait, local fans rejoiced when the Subway Series roared back into action on October 21, 2000. They would not be disappointed. The opener was a dynamite game, the first Subway Series confrontation to extend to 12 innings and the turning point in the Series.

From 1921 to 1956, the Yankees faced the Giants six times and the Dodgers seven times in the Fall Classic. With seven clashes between 1947 and 1956, the Subway Series seemed like a ritual of autumn sandwiched in between the first day of school and Thanksgiving.

Then the Giants and Dodgers went west, and when the Mets were born the two New York teams were never competitive at the same time. In 1999, the Mets fell just short of the Series, both of which the Yankees won.

In 2000, everything finally came together with a newly stoked rivalry when Yankee Roger Clemens beaned Mets catcher Mike Piazza in the head during interleague play and was too lacking in class to apologize.

The Yankees lost 16 of 19 near season's end, then struggled to get past Oakland and Seattle in the playoffs. The Mets, led by Piazza's 38 homers and .324 average, appeared stronger—although only a wild card, their 94-68 record was seven games better than the Yankees, and they looked sharper in the playoffs. The Subway Series dominated hometown papers and local conversation, and even became national news, with Derek Jeter and Piazza gracing the cover of *Newsweek* and reporters exploring the rooting preferences of senatorial candidates Hillary Clinton and Rick Lazio.

The Yankees still had poise and steely confidence built on their vast experience, their superior grasp of baseball's fundamentals, and, of course, their unparalleled bullpen, headed by demigod Mariano Rivera. They played with a cool efficiency that reflected manager Joe Torre's persona, while the Mets' bubbly, almost hyper style flowed from manager Bobby Valentine. The Mets showed up at Yankee Stadium with camcorders to capture the carnival atmosphere; for the Yankees it was just another day at work.

Game 1 would be more extraordinary than ordinary. Don Larsen, hero of the last Subway Series, tossed out the first ball to former batterymate Yogi Berra. Billy Joel sang the national anthem, as a bald eagle was released in center field.

Both teams started tough lefties who thrived under pressure, Andy Pettitte for the Yanks and Al Leiter for the Mets. Both teams left runners on, but while Yankee Chuck Knoblauch was picked off in the third, the Mets displayed inexperience and nerves with multiple mistakes. In the fourth, Piazza was picked off first, then Todd Zeile hit a grounder that started foul but rolled fair—he didn't run and was thrown out. In the fifth, after Benny Agbayani doubled, Jay Payton hit a grounder and started arguing that it was foul, but the umpires called it fair and he was thrown out.

But these guys were kids compared to the big-horned goats of the sixth inning. With two outs and the Mets' late-season sparkplug, Timo Perez, on first, Todd Zeile smashed the ball to deep left. Both he and Perez trotted as if the ball was a certain home run. Zeile had his arm ready to pump in celebration when the ball hit the padded wall and bounced back into play.

Embarrassed, Perez tried to score anyway. David Justice fielded the carom perfectly and fired home. When his throw tailed, he was rescued by Jeter, who sprinted across the foul line, caught the ball, jumped, spun, and threw home to nail Perez at the plate. It was a crushing blow for the Mets and a reaffirmation for the Yankees that their old pros, who had won eight straight World Series games, would lift them up when the game was on the line.

After the Yankees scored twice off Leiter, the Mets demonstrated resilience by tying the score off Pettitte on a pinch-hit two-run single by Bubba Trammell. Edgardo Alfonzo's infield single off reliever Jeff Nelson gave the Mets a 3–2 lead.

The ninth inning was a battle of the closers. With his placid demeanor and darting cutter, Mariano Rivera was not only the best closer, but also the best clutch closer in the history of the game. Since 1996, he'd pitched 385 regular-season innings, allowing 401 baserunners and 91 runs—and since blowing a save in the 1997 divisional playoffs against Cleveland in his first year as a closer, Rivera had allowed 24 baserunners and one—that's right, just one—single, solitary run in 35-plus innings against baseball's best teams in the postseason.

Mets closer Armando Benitez was the opposite in temperament, a big man with a tough glare and an explosive fastball but who was easily rattled, with a disquieting tendency to melt in the tightest situations. In Baltimore, Benitez had a 7.71 ERA against the Yankees in the 1996 ALCS. He then triggered a brawl with an unnecessary bean ball in 1998. With the Mets, Benitez blew a save in the 1999 NLDS clincher, an extra-inning lead in the NLCS to kill their comeback against Atlanta, and a save in the 2000 NLDS.

When Paul O'Neill misplayed Kurt Abbott's line drive into a double, giving the Mets second and third with one out, Rivera remained calm, got Perez on a grounder to second, and fanned Alfonzo. The Mets lead remained a sole run. Benitez's lack of composure became evident when O'Neill came up seeking redemption. The 37-year-old's bat speed had slowed considerably, and he was overmatched by Benitez's heat, but he fouled off pitch after pitch with defensive swings until Benitez finally lost the strike zone, walking O'Neill on the 10th delivery. Against weaker hitters, Benitez let up: Pinch-hitter Luis Polonia and ex-Met Jose Vizcaino, who'd had only two at-bats in the first two playoff rounds, both singled, and Knoblauch tied the game on a sacrifice fly.

The last time the Yankees come back from a ninth-inning deficit in the World Series was way back in 1941, when the Dodgers' Mickey Owen famously failed to catch the third strike of the third out. Although "what if" is a foolish and ultimately futile exercise, it is one Mets fans (like Dodgers fans before them) find themselves playing all too often. What if they hadn't traded Nolan Ryan or Tom Seaver? What if Doc and Darryl hadn't succumbed to the temptation of drugs? What if Mike Scioscia hadn't hit that ninth-inning homer in the 1988 NLCS? What if Benitez hadn't blown Game 1? That question ranks up there in this painful memory game, for the Series probably would have played out quite differently.

But in the real world, where Yankees fans never needed to daydream, Rivera and Mike Stanton retired 11 straight Mets through the 12th inning. Meanwhile, the Yankees poked and prodded for vulnerable spots. In the 10th, they drew two walks off Dennis Cook; Glendon Rusch came on and wild-pitched them over a base, but the Mets drew the infield and outfield in and slipped the noose. In the 11th, after two walks and another Rusch wild pitch, Turk Wendell came on, and the Mets again escaped the gallows. But the Yankees were much closer to victory than the Mets, and both sides knew it.

This was just the second game since the 1977 Yankees–Dodgers to last a dozen innings. In the Yankee 12th, Tino Martinez singled, and Jorge Posada doubled. The Mets were at the end of their rope. Wendell walked O'Neill intentionally and Luis Sojo popped up, but on the game's 396th pitch,

Vizcaino—who Torre had almost pinch-hit for several times—picked up his fourth single to win the game.

The Yankees had an edge, and in typical Yankee fashion they would not surrender it. The Series contained plenty of other memorable moments: Clemens hurling a broken bat at Piazza and the Mets almost overcoming a six-run ninth-inning deficit in Game 2; Orlando Hernandez fanning 12 but the Mets keeping hope alive with a comeback 4–2 win in Game 3; Jeter demonstrating both his skill and leadership yet again by homering to lead off Game 4, suffocating those Mets hopes; and Leiter's brilliant, gutty effort in Game 5 before he lost the game and the Series by yielding singles on his 141st and 142nd pitches of the night. But the first game remained the most exciting and pivotal, the one that delineated the differences between the two teams.

When it was all over, even the Yankees acknowledged that this had been something special, that there was something to that viewpoint offered in the famous *New Yorker* cartoon showing the local perspective on the city versus the rest of the world.

Bernie Williams admitted that being king of the hill in the battle for New York mattered more than just being top of the heap in an ordinary season: "It really made us feel like we were playing for something other than the World Series."

Allan Houston Beats the Buzzer
and Miami, May 16, 1999, Miami Arena

With four and a half seconds to save the New York Knicks' season, Allan Houston caught the ball and took two dribbles. The Miami Heat's Dan Majerle was with him, Tim Hardaway was lurking, and Alonzo Mourning was looming. Perhaps two seconds elapsed. Houston went airborne from about 14 feet out. With his classic form and sweet touch, Houston was the Knicks' best pure shooter, but he lifted an ugly, running, leaning jumper, short-armed off the front rim. The Knicks watched the ball bounce, not away, toward doom, but up there it floated, as if deciding which team fate should smile upon, before it kissed the backboard and dropped through the net—78–77, New York.

Houston's astonishing game-winner in the opening round of the playoffs earned the save. The W—which made the Knicks the first eighth seed in the East to upset the top seed—belonged to Patrick Ewing, whose brave and bravura performance was the highlight of the Knicks' soapiest and most improbable year of the decade. The 1990s Knicks led the NBA in melodrama: the headline-grabbing rivalries with Chicago, Indiana, and Miami, and the brawls and stunning losses that accompanied them; the never-ending search for a point guard; the much-heralded arrival of Pat Riley and his subsequent resignation by fax; the disastrous but short-lived Don Nelson era.

Still, nothing could match 1998–1999, when each key person seemed to come with the phrase "oft-maligned" attached to his name. As union president, the aging Patrick Ewing, still in search of a championship, showed up out of shape after rancorous and controversial negotiations led to a shortened season. Latrell Sprewell, the infamous coach-choker who cost the team sentimental favorite John Starks, irked team officials and the media with shooting sprees and inconsistent defense, then worsened his reputation by yukking it up after a shameful loss in Chicago and letting his agent trash coach Jeff Van Gundy in the press. Van Gundy's status remained imperiled as the Knicks barely snuck into the playoffs. President Dave Checketts drew heat for firing general manager Ernie Grunfeld over dessert after a two-hour dinner and lying to Van Gundy about negotiating behind the coach's back with Phil Jackson.

Allan Houston buries the Miami Heat at the buzzer to win the first round of the Eastern Conference playoffs and help send the Knicks to the finals for just the second time in a quarter-century. *ASSOCIATED PRESS*

Still, no matter how deep their wounds, the Knicks remained dangerous, especially as Sprewell came around late in the season, igniting the Knicks and electrifying the crowd, going from NBA public enemy number 1 to number 8, the jersey worn by Spike Lee and countless other fans.

On the season's final day, Pat Riley, by then the head Heat honcho, even rested three players, hoping to lose and avoid New York in the first round.

But a New York–Miami matchup was destiny. There was a bitter rivalry built on two intense playoff series marred by headline-grabbing brawls—the 1997 bench-clearing fight that cost the Knicks that series and the 1998 scrum that ended up with Van Gundy wrapped around the ankle of Miami star Alonzo Mourning—and a simmering feud between two coaches who had once been mentor and protégé. For the third straight year, the Knicks–Heat series went the distance. The Knicks grabbed the advantage with a 32–2 run in Game 3, but Miami trounced New York in Game 4.

In Game 5, the Heat breezed to a 21–8 lead, and Mourning even mimicked Knick Larry Johnson's signature move of forming an "L" with his arms. Then the Knicks shoved back, metaphorically this time, behind Sprewell's 11 first-half points. The teams were deadlocked at 60 after three, but when Ewing, already hobbled by sore knees and a strained Achilles tendon, badly injured his rib cage in the third, his mobility was reduced to that of a wobbly statue. Still, he kept scoring, rebounding, and leading, remaining in the game the entire fourth quarter.

The Knicks fell behind, 69–62, but clawed back once more. Houston, long castigated by fans and the press as too soft with the game on the line, sat during the first-half comeback but rose up with two jumpers to help tie the contest.

Rugged defense, always central to these battles, then devoured whatever offensive opportunities remained. The Knicks grabbed their first lead at 72–71, with 4:05 remaining; it took Miami three minutes to inch ahead to 77–74.

One defensive stop was an all-time classic. With about 1:20 left, Ewing found himself guarding Mourning to the left of the basket. Seven years Ewing's junior, Mourning was a fellow Georgetown alum who had once treated Ewing as a mentor, but in this series, he had often mistreated him. With the game, the series, and the season on the line, Mourning expected to have his way with the invalid in front of him.

Mourning threw a fake. Ewing didn't bite. Mourning moved toward the hoop. Ewing managed to shift his feet laterally, cutting him off. The Knicks center would not give in. Finally, Mourning was forced to go baseline—what Ewing wanted, demanded, of the situation—falling out of bounds and trying to pass as the 24-second clock buzzed. Ewing wasn't done. When Sprewell missed off the rim, Ewing grabbed a crucial offensive rebound to keep hope alive. Mourning fouled him with 39.7 seconds left. Two shots. Despite Ewing's tremendous effort under extraordinary physical duress to keep the Knicks close throughout the game, in their souls most Knicks fans groaned. For everything Ewing had done throughout the years, Knicks fans saw only his failures—the occasions when he displayed stone hands, refused to share the ball, clogged up a running offense, or fell for the head fake—and they added up to one grand failure: the inability to win that elusive championship. Never mind that Michael Jordan couldn't win without Scottie Pippen and that neither John Starks nor Allan Houston was Scottie Pippen. The perception was that the Big Fella would come close but fall short. But for the third time in less than a minute, Ewing came through, calmly sinking both free throws—77-76, Miami.

After the Knicks recovered the ball with 19.9 seconds left, Van Gundy called a pick-and-roll for Sprewell. But these teams knew one another too well, and Sprewell got trapped, then had the ball knocked out of bounds by Terry Porter. From the bench, Van Gundy signaled for Triangle Down, a play in which Sprewell inbounded, ideally to Houston, who Ewing should free with a high screen. Sprewell and Johnson would crisscross underneath to provide another option, but with four and a half seconds left, Houston didn't look for second choices. Instead, he finally shed his image as a player who disappeared at crunch time. (Call it the "$100 Million Shot," since it later helped persuade Knicks management to foolishly pay him that sum.)

Houston sank the shot, and Miami was sunk. The momentum propelled New York through a General Sherman-esque sweep of Atlanta and a memorable upset over Indiana that catapulted them back to the Finals, where their enchanted playoff run ended.

Houston's game-winning shot made it all possible, but Game 5 was also Ewing's final great moment as a Knick—he outscored Mourning, 22-21, outrebounded him, 11-5, and made the biggest plays at the biggest moments, while in excruciating pain that would have felled a less-committed player. In other words, he pulled a Willis Reed but added results to the inspiration.

Jim Leyritz Powers a Yankees Comeback, October 23, 1996, Fulton County Stadium, Atlanta

The Yankees spent decades as the team many baseball fans loved to hate— rooting for them was likened to rooting for an omnipotent corporation. Yet, the 1996 New York Yankees were different, a team that even a Mets fan or old Brooklyn Dodgers fan could root for . . . almost.

Winning seemed fresh and surprising in the Bronx—the Yankees hadn't won the World Series in 18 seasons, and the Mets had an equal number of titles during the previous 30 years. For all the advantages their bloated budget and impetuous owner offered (a bench with Tim Raines and Cecil Fielder), they entered the World Series against the dynastic Atlanta Braves as underdogs. Their core was immensely appealing, a mix of homegrown young talent (Derek Jeter, Bernie Williams, Andy Pettitte, Mariano Rivera) and unsung old-school guys (Joe Girardi, Paul O'Neill).

Additionally, the script of this Yankees journey was an exceedingly sentimental one. New manager Joe Torre hailed from Brooklyn, played for and helmed the Mets, and endured an un-Yankee-like record of 32 seasons and 4,110 games as a player or manager without reaching the Series. His older brother Frank, who had played for the Braves against the Yankees in two World Series, was now gravely ill, awaiting a heart transplant.

Bench coach Don Zimmer played on the 1955 Dodgers, and pitching coach Mel Stottlemyre was an ex-Yankee but more recently the Mets pitching coach in 1986. The starters included popular ex-Met David Cone and Dwight Gooden, the erstwhile Mets icon who revived his career with a no-hitter and 11 wins. The lefty slugger picked up from the independent Northern League was Darryl Strawberry, another fallen ex-Met who George Steinbrenner signed as much to give another chance as to bolster the roster. These were not Babe Ruth's Murderers' Row or Joe DiMaggio's Bronx Bombers.

The Yankees came back three times against the Texas Rangers in the ALDS, then twice against the Baltimore Orioles in the ALCS. The defending champion Braves stomped New York, 12–1, in the opener and 4–0 in Game 2, the most lopsided two-game margin ever. In Game 2, Greg Maddux required just 82 pitches for eight innings, only 20 of which were called balls.

Counting the NLCS, the Braves had outscored their opponents 48–2, the greatest postseason streak of all time. They had not trailed in 45 innings. They were cocky, and they were going home to Fulton County Stadium. Cone's clutch Game 3 outing gave New York a slim ray of hope, but Game 4 starter Kenny Rogers was the antithesis of the gutsy Cone, nibbling at the strike zone, becoming unnerved by a botched defensive play, and recording just six outs while allowing five runs. By the fifth, the Yankees trailed, 6–0. Only twice had teams overcome such a deficit in World Series play, and New York had only two hits. Thus, overcoming the Braves seemed faintly ludicrous. A loss would give Atlanta a 3–1 edge with Cy Young winners John Smoltz, Maddux, and Tom Glavine ready.

But in the sixth, fate smiled on the Yankees just as it had in days of yore. As in olden days, the Yankees seized the opportunity. An umpire inadvertently blocked right fielder Jermaine Dye as he chased Jeter's pop foul. Jeter subsequently singled, sparking a three-run rally that knocked out starter Denny Neagle, getting the Yankees into Atlanta's shaky bullpen.

In the eighth, Braves manager Bobby Cox called on closer Mark Wohlers, just the second time he'd done so all year. A weak but well-placed roller and a blown double-play ball put two Yankees on. Jim Leyritz suddenly represented the tying run at the plate, although he had just 14 homers in 529 at-bats in the previous two years. Despite a 15th-inning game-winning homer against Seattle in the 1995 ALDS, he was just 4-for-22 in two postseasons.

Wohlers unleashed a 100-mile-per-hour fastball, but Leyritz took a good rip, fouling it straight back. A 98-mile-per-hour blazer followed, and Leyritz again fouled it straight back—for all that velocity, Leyritz was timing Wohlers.

Afraid to repeat himself, Wohlers went to his third-best pitch, his slider. He chose poorly. The selection fooled Leyritz, but there's a reason for avoiding plan C in that situation—the slider was awful, a big, fat meatball. Leyritz clocked it over the wall in left, silencing the obnoxious tomahawk chop routine of the Braves fans.

The game was tied. After the Yankees left the bases loaded in the ninth, their inexperienced set-up man, Mariano Rivera, almost let the game slip away. But he was yanked with two on, and Graeme Lloyd coaxed a double-play grounder from slugger Fred McGriff.

In the 10th, the Yankees got two on with two outs. Lefty Steve Avery intentionally walked Bernie Williams—New York's most dangerous hitter—rather than bring in righty Brad Clontz to switch Williams to his weaker side. Rookie Andy Fox, who had pinch-run for Fielder in the ninth, was due up next, but Torre had saved one man on his bench. It was another lefty but a special one: Wade Boggs, a Hall of Fame singles hitter with a keen plate discipline. Avery's 1–2 pitch was so close that catcher Eddie Perez reacted as if the inning was over. Boggs got the call. On 3–2, Avery missed with a slider, walking home the go-ahead run.

Cox then made a double switch that put Ryan Klesko at first, where he promptly muffed a soft liner—Clontz failed to cover and Jeter scored for an 8–6 lead. Atlanta got a man on against closer John Wetteland in their last licks, and Terry Pendleton smashed a long drive to left. Raines slipped but caught the ball just as he lost his balance, ending the game.

The Braves were crushed. The Yankees won Game 5, 1–0, then returned to New York to learn that Frank Torre, hospitalized since August, was finally getting a new heart—the donor had lived in the Bronx and the doctor's last name was Oz. The Yankees finished off the Braves in Game 6, becoming the first team to win four straight games after losing the first two at home. They were champions despite a .216 team batting average. This was a fairy-tale season after all.

Leyritz was a new hero, the man who launched a dynasty that captured four World Series in five years. "That was the hit," Torre said, "that made us believe we were going to win this thing."

20

Steffi Graf, Struggling with Her Father's Arrest, Faces Off against Monica Seles, Struggling to Overcome Her Stabbing Injury, September 9, 1995, National Tennis Center

Call it Soap Opera Saturday. September 9, 1995 was, after Super Saturday 1984, the most dramatic all-day affair in U.S. Open history. This episode of *As the Tennis World Turns* starred six current or former number ones with 43 Grand Slam titles to their combined credit. Yet, much of the drama was about more than shotmaking.

The men's semis matches were *All Nick Bollettieri's Children*. The top two seeds—friendly rivals since childhood, winners of the two previous Opens, and costars in an attention-getting Nike ad—fulfilled virtually everyone's hopes and expectations by winning hard-fought matches, setting the stage for a dynamic final; however, these tense showdowns were overshadowed by the *Young and Anguished* melodrama of the women's final, in which two haunted victims, ranked number one together, both emerged triumphant even though only one walked off the winner.

First, two-time champion Pete Sampras faced off against Jim Courier, with whom he'd done time at Bollettieri's famed Florida tennis academy. It was vintage Sampras—his numbers weren't great, but he capitalized on opportunities and slammed the door on Courier's chances. Sampras saved two break points at 4–4 in the first set. In the third set, he responded to triple break point with five straight points. Eventually, and seemingly inevitably, Sampras emerged on top, 7–5, 4–6, 6–4, 7–5.

The other men's semifinal between defending champion Andre Agassi and Boris Becker was closer and tenser. At Wimbledon, Becker had upset Agassi, then bad-mouthed Nike and Agassi, claiming the corporate sponsor got its star preferential treatment. Tensions were heightened because Becker was working with Bollettieri, Agassi's former coach, with whom Agassi was feuding.

Becker boomed in 25 aces, but Agassi forced Becker to engage from the base-line, especially in tiebreakers—both times Agassi won big points on Becker's serve to go up 7–6 (7–4), 7–6 (7–2). Becker, down 4–1 in the third, dashed off five straight games and had two break points at 2–2 in the fourth set, before Agassi rallied. Later Agassi finished his foe with three huge, untouchable fore-hand serve returns.

Agassi offered a lukewarm handshake, then criticized Becker's Wimbledon comments before refocusing by looking into the camera and declaring, "Pete, I'm coming." (Soon enough, he was going, as Sampras won the men's final.)

But on this day, even Sampras and Agassi seemed secondary. The women's final was more than eagerly awaited; it felt absolutely necessary, as closure on one of the sport's most horrifying chapters.

In the late 1980s, Steffi Graf took over women's tennis. In 1988, she won the Grand Slam. In 1989, she captured three more majors. Then Monica Seles emerged, wielding her racket with two hands from both sides and grunting with the ferocity of a feral animal. She won three majors in both 1991 and 1992, and after winning the 1993 Australian, she seemed to be playing for the record books with eight Slams by the age of 19. But that April, during a changeover at a Hamburg tournament, a deranged man stabbed Seles in the back. He proclaimed himself a diehard Graf fan committed to restoring his favorite to number one.

Seles was out of action for more than two years, recovering physically but battling the psychic wounds. For Graf, too, this period felt endless, her career stuck in purgatory. She won 65 of her next 67 matches, including the next four Grand Slam tournaments, but the whispers and articles repeated endlessly, "Would she have won if not for the stabbing?" At home, Seles cried when watching those tournaments.

Then Graf began disintegrating as she battled injuries and Seles's spectral absence: She failed to win any of the next four Slams. When Seles finally began preparing to return, Graf's play recovered—despite back problems she won the 1995 French Open and Wimbledon. Seles would play the U.S. Open (after just one warm-up tournament), but new trouble found Graf.

Just before the Open, her father, Peter Graf, was arrested at home in Germany on tax evasion charges; compounding the issue was Peter's role as manager of Steffi's multimillion-dollar business empire. Although she wasn't implicated, she was not allowed to speak to him because German authorities didn't want them coordinating stories. The German media hungrily devoured this tabloid tale, trailing Graf everywhere, even in a supermarket.

Graf, 26, and Seles, 21, had been ranked as co-number ones, to acknowledge the unfortunate incident that bound them together. Graf was actually cheered by

Seles's gleeful parade through the other half of the draw—the return of Seles's smile and smashes lifted one ghost. Seles not only reached the finals without losing a set, but also took the time to enjoy the sights and sounds like she never had done before. She bought hats at Barney's, caught Broadway shows, served as a presenter at the MTV Video Music Awards at Radio City, and hung out on the sidelines of a Dallas–New York *Monday Night Football* game.

Although she still had occasional flashbacks of the stabbing, every interview seemed peppered with happy words like "fun." Once shunned by Open crowds for her thrashing of local favorites and offhanded arrogance, she was now embraced, held up as testimony to human resilience and bravery, and credited with reviving women's tennis. It was, Stefan Edberg said, the "Seles Open."

Finally, they faced off at Louis Armstrong Stadium. In a taut first set, both remained on serve, forcing a tiebreaker. Seles finally had the tiniest opening, a mini-break for a 6–5 tiebreak lead. At set point, Seles blasted a set-ending ace and trotted happily toward her chair. But wait, it was called wide. (Replays supported the call.) Graf had new life. The original Seles incarnation was so tough, so willful, she'd have simply plowed ahead. Having lost the habits of a lifetime, she couldn't shake off this reversal and lost three straight points and the set.

After the changeover, Seles reasserted herself, while Graf began thinking about what this victory would mean. Seles drove her from one corner to the other, shocking Graf and the crowd by taking the second set at love.

That awoke Graf. The two women were even in the third until two-all, when Graf pulled off her first—and only—service break of the match for a 3–2 lead. If she could hold serve three times, she'd be champion. With each game she inched closer, until, at 5–4, she finally had double match point at 40–15. On a second serve, Seles mashed an untouchable crosscourt backhand. The crowd cheered and screamed and wondered. Could Seles cap her comeback with the ultimate comeback? But Graf wanted this badly, too, and on her second match point she nailed a stronger serve. When Seles misfired a forehand, it was over—not just the match but the waiting. The women hugged and kissed, grateful and relieved.

"I want to thank you," Seles told the fans afterward. "This is one of the reasons I wanted to come back, to feel the electricity."

Although the soap opera was far from over for Graf—she fled questions about her father during her postmatch press conference to cry in private—she had proved herself where it mattered most to her: on the court, against Seles.

"This is the biggest win I have ever achieved," Graf said. "There is nothing that even comes close to this one."

21

Fifty-Four Years Later, the Rangers Finally Win the Stanley Cup, June 14, 1994, Madison Square Garden

Parity was the word in the early days of the NHL. For 13 years, starting in 1927, no NHL team won the Stanley Cup more than twice. Then the New York Rangers broke through, winning their third title in 1940. Could the Rangers establish hockey's first true dynasty?

Fifty-four years later, the answer was clear. Rangers fans no longer thought about league dominance, they just wanted the weight of that year, 1940, lifted away. From 1941 to 1993, the Yankees won 14 World Series. The Dodgers, the Giants, and their replacement, the Mets, won four total. The Knicks won two NBA crowns. The football Giants won an NFL championship and two Super Bowls, and the Jets won one Super Bowl. Worst of all, the New York Islanders, born in 1972, captured Lord Stanley's trophy four straight times in the 1980s. Meanwhile, the New York Rangers failed every year. In fact, they reached the finals only three more times, in 1950, 1972, and 1979.

Rangers fans grew so desperate they created not one curse, like the Boston Red Sox, but two. After winning the 1940 trophy, the Rangers' owners, who'd just paid off their mortgage, celebrated by burning the paperwork in the Cup. Such desecration was naturally frowned upon by the hockey gods. Then Red Dutton issued a personal hex. Dutton had run the New York Americans, the first hockey team to play at Madison Square Garden. But Garden management created its own hockey team, the Rangers, and years of high rent and inadequate ice time damaged the Americans, who folded in the 1940s. Dutton decreed that the Rangers would not win the Cup either in his lifetime or until the Americans played the Garden again (depending on the story). The truth, of course, lay in terrible management, decade after decade.

CHAPTER 21

Still, in 1993, Rangers general manager Neil Smith tried exorcising one curse by creating an award honoring Dutton through the NHL. He had also made vital moves in 1991, by signing Adam Graves and trading for Mark Messier, both stars in the recent Edmonton Oilers dynasty. Messier was a great talent but also a leader who could impose his formidable will on his team. In 1993, Smith hired hard-edged Mike Keenan as coach. Before the season, Keenan showed his team a video of New York ticker tape parades, then put them through torturous training to make sure they'd be the league's most physically fit team. The Rangers finished with a team-record 52 wins, thanks to Smith's infusion of midseason talent, notably Stephane Matteau and Craig MacTavish.

In the playoffs, the Rangers blew out the New York Islanders and Washington Capitals before falling to a 3–2 deficit against the New Jersey Devils. Messier stepped forward, guaranteed a victory, then backed it up with a hat trick to force a Game 7. When Matteau blasted a game-winner in double overtime, the Rangers were finally back in the finals. Favored against the surprising Vancouver Canucks, the Rangers grabbed a 3–1 lead.

But New York got slapped, 6–3, at home, then 4–1 in Vancouver. The finals were tied at 3–3, but the Canucks had the momentum. Before Game 7, Keenan delivered a pregame speech that Messier called the best ever. "Go out and win it for each other," Keenan urged them. "If you do, you will walk together the rest of your lives."

The Rangers had fallen behind in each of the previous five games, but in the finale, they seized the lead and never relinquished it. In the first period, Messier burst past Canucks star Pasha Bure, then dumped the puck to Sergei Zubov. When the pursuing Canucks left Brian Leetch wide open, Zubov found him, and Leetch angled in a wrist shot for his 11th goal of the playoffs and his fifth of the finals. Three minutes later, Graves, who hadn't scored since Game 3 of the Devils series, smacked home another goal for a 2–0 lead.

The Canucks halved the lead in the second period, but before it ended the Rangers retaliated. After Brian Noonan's shot missed, the puck either hit a Vancouver defender or was hit by a diving Graves or a swiping Messier. The scorer gave the goal to Messier, and since the Rangers made it stand as the winning goal, that was, symbolically anyway, the perfect call. It wasn't pretty, but it counted.

Vancouver scored on a power play in the third, and with 15 minutes remaining, the Rangers lead was down to one. In the next two-plus minutes, Mike Richter kicked away a Nathan LaFayette shot, Leetch stopped a 2-on-1, and Trevor Linden almost snuck in a shot from the corner. Heart attacks all around. With seven minutes remaining, Vancouver's Martin Gelinas's shot hit the outside of the post and ricocheted off Richter. A half-minute later, Richter blocked a shot, but Vancouver recovered and LaFayette missed by a half-inch on Richter's glove side. One period was lasting an eternity.

In the final minute, Vancouver pulled its goalie for an extra scorer, but the Rangers smothered every desperate Canucks attempt. Finally, Zubov controlled the puck and found Steve Larmer, who backhanded the black disk away and down the ice, out of danger. The final seconds drained away—but wait. The ref called icing, halting any premature celebration with 1.1 seconds left—and the refs added a half-second back onto the clock. One last danger. The puck dropped. MacTavish slid the puck harmlessly into the corner.

At 10:59 p.m, the Rangers were NHL champions, and "1940" was just a year, not a taunt. Messier, who notched 12 goals and added 18 assists in 23 playoff games, leaped into the air, and the party began. Moments later, Commissioner Gary Bettman stated, "Captain Mark Messier, come get the Stanley Cup." To the tune of Tina Turner's "Simply the Best," Messier, in a Rangers sweater, took the Cup and lifted it over his head. The team passed it around, skating across the ice, while the fans chanted, "We got the Cup!" and "1994!" In the stands, one sign read, "Now I can die in peace."

There'd be no peace that night or in the days ahead. Only wild, giddy, prideful fun. The Rangers took the Cup to a party on the Upper East Side, and so many fans flocked there that the police had to block off the street. Late into the night (or early in the morning), Messier and others began the Cup's public tour by taking it to the strip club Scores. Then it was on to David Letterman's show, Gracie Mansion, Belmont Park, center court back at the Garden during the NBA Finals, and Yankee Stadium. Finally, they took it down Broadway for a ticker tape parade, Keenan's preseason video finally come to life.

Patrick Ewing Lifts the Knicks into the NBA Finals, June 5, 1994, Madison Square Garden

Patrick Ewing, triumphant at long last.

With 24 points, 22 rebounds, 7 assists, and 5 blocks to his credit, with the game-defining play fresh in everyone's memory—a thunderous dunk off a rebound to recover the lead with just 26.9 seconds left—Ewing celebrated the New York Knicks' long-awaited return to the NBA Finals by leaping onto the courtside press table, throwing out his arms, and bellowing a marvelous, unabashed roar of elation as the crowd's unrestrained gratitude washed over him.

For nine years, the reticent Jamaican had shouldered the expectations of New York Knicks fans. That's never an easy task in a tabloid town, but Ewing had arrived at a particularly cruel juncture—sports radio, in the form of WFAN, was taking root, and the city, accustomed to and even demanding of championships, was hitting a rare dry patch. After the Mets' 1986 World Series victory and the Giants' 1987 Super Bowl win, the 1980s ended with a whimper right as the city's real-life troubles exploded with crack, crime, and racial strife. In the early 1990s, the Giants won once more, but the rest of the city's teams kept falling short. Ewing, unable to overcome his on-court weaknesses, his off-court shyness, front-office mismanagement, and, of course, Chicago's Michael Jordan, often bore the brunt of the fans' frustrations. Yes, he was one of the game's top centers, but why couldn't this team win it all—or at least reach the Finals? The Knicks hadn't accomplished either goal since 1973.

When Jordan abandoned hoops for baseball in 1993–1994, Pat Riley's Knicks sensed their opportunity. To the beat of their customized song (and video), "Go New York Go," the team captured the division and paraded through the playoffs to the Eastern Conference Finals against Indiana. New

York won two at home in games that were pugnacious, low-scoring, and occasionally ugly. Then New York went to Market Square Arena and collapsed. Ewing went 0–10 from the field in Game 3, scoring one point in an 88–68 trouncing. Then Indiana's Reggie Miller shook free for 31 points in Game 4. Still, the Knicks had home court advantage and a comfortable 70–58 lead in Game 5—until Miller took over. After scoring 25 points in the fourth quarter and taunting New York's most famous heckler, Spike Lee, he became an instant villain. Irate fans and the back pages of New York's tabloids turned on the Knicks, with headlines blaring, "Chokers," and "Gag City."

Ewing remained defiantly confident. When the Knicks headed back to Indiana, he told the New York media just one thing: "See you Sunday." This gritty, resilient squad won, 98–91, forcing a return to New York for Game 7.

There the Knicks demonstrated one more time that the selection of Billy Joel's "All about Soul" as a theme song was more than just marketing. Five Knicks scored in double figures, and they beat Indiana off the boards, 59–38, hustling for 28 offensive rebounds, all of them seemingly crucial. They dug in for a thrilling third-quarter comeback, then Ewing provided the final moments Knick fans had long hoped for.

With 4:39 left in the third, Indiana led, 65–53. Ewing picked up his fourth foul, but Riley couldn't afford to remove his leading scorer, his leading rebounder, and his entire game plan, so he left him in. Ewing, Anthony Mason, and Derek Harper fueled a 14–4 run. With 8:26 left to play, Ewing launched a long touchdown pass to Harper, who put the Knicks ahead, 76–74. With 4:52 left, Ewing was whistled for his fifth foul; again, Riley risked it all, and, again, his decision paid dividends. Seconds later, Ewing zipped a crisp pass to Mason, who gave New York an 85–80 lead.

Then Miller silenced the crowd, burying a three-pointer that sparked a 10–4 run. After Ewing swished a 21-foot turnaround jumper, Miller hit his own jumper, and Dale Davis dunked with 34 seconds left—90–89, Indiana. Suddenly, the Knicks were back at the precipice.

During their time-out, Ewing urged Riley to forget the outside shots and pound the ball inside to him one last time. "If we lose, I'm going to take the blame anyway," he said afterward.

Riley called a pick-and-roll with John Starks handling the ball, ideally to find a passing lane down to the Big Fella. It didn't work. Starks went right but had no place to pass. He did see an opening, however, and burst in and flipped up a layup. No good. The ball clunked off the backboard, then clanged off the front rim. Indiana's Dale Davis, Antonio Davis, and Derrick McKey were underneath—if any of them grabbed the ball, the game was over. Instead, Ewing leapt over all three, capturing the rock and smashing home a resounding dunk with both hands—91–90, New York.

There was still time for one last Miller miracle, but when the Knick-killer shook off Starks, Charles Oakley hurled himself into the fray, throwing up a hand, which prompted an air ball. Miller's subsequent foul on Starks was called flagrant, giving the Knicks two shots and possession.

Seconds later, it was over, 94–90. New York was going to the Finals, and Patrick Ewing had put them there. Erase the asterisk of Jordan's absence (and Chicago's dominance upon his return). Forget what would happen in the Finals when Hakeem Olajuwon blocked Starks's championship-winning shot in Game 6, and when Riley allowed Starks to shoot the Knicks into oblivion in Game 7. Block out how extra sweet a title would have been in the same month the Rangers ended their 54-year championship drought. Instead, appreciate reaching the Finals as an accomplishment, something the Knicks have done just four times since 1953. And savor the memory of Ewing's dunk and his subsequent celebration. It was a roar for the ages.

23

Stephane Matteau Scores in Double Overtime in Game 7 of the Eastern Conference Finals, May 27, 1994, Madison Square Garden

Tick. Tock. Tick. Tock. The Eastern Conference Finals never should have lasted this long. In their winter of great expectations, the 1993–1994 New York Rangers had posted the league's best record and raced through blowouts of the New York Islanders and Washington Capitals in the playoffs. Their conference finals foe was the New Jersey Devils, a team that had not beaten the Rangers once that year.

Tick. Tock. Tick. Tock. The Devils gained their first win against New York in Game 1, in double overtime. Soon enough time was running out on the Rangers as the Devils took a 3–2 lead home to New Jersey. Mark Messier hauled New York back from the abyss: He guaranteed victory in Game 6, then delivered with a hat trick.

But in Game 7 at Madison Square Garden, the Rangers still seemed unable to vanquish the Devils. In the first period, Rangers veteran goalie Mike Richter was flawless, but the Devils' outstanding rookie, Martin Brodeur, matched him. Halfway through the second, the Rangers finally grabbed the lead when Messier won a face-off, Adam Graves pushed the puck toward the blue line, and Messier sprung Brian Leetch free with a pick. Leetch raced down the ice, spun around, and powered home a goal.

Tick. Tock. Tick. Tock. In the game's final minute, the Devils pulled Brodeur for an extra attacker, and loyal Rangers fans counted down the seconds until their first Finals since 1979. But the clock started and stopped in maddening fits.

With 48 seconds to go, the Rangers were called for icing.

With 24 seconds left, another icing call.

CHAPTER 23

With 16.4 seconds remaining, the whistle blew again. Yup, icing. This time the Devils argued that 2.2 seconds should be put back, and the officials agreed.

Tick. Tock. Tick. Tock. Back to 18.6 seconds.

New Jersey's Bernie Nicholls won the face-off, and the puck headed to the boards near the Rangers' goal. Claude Lemieux got a shot off, but Richter deflected it off his pads. Just 7.7 seconds left.

Richter looked like the hero—a remarkable turnaround for a goalie who'd taken the blame for the 1992 playoff loss to Pittsburgh, lost his confidence, and been shipped to the minors. Stellar throughout the regular season, Richter knew he had to prove himself in the playoffs, in the clutch, and he had, with four shutouts already to his credit. With 23 Devils shots stopped in Game 7, Richter was a tick and a tock away from his fifth.

But the puck rebounded to Valeri Zelepukin, who thrust it into the net. The shutout, the lead, the role of hero, the end of the series—all gone.

Overtime came with the Rangers reeling. Silence enveloped the locker room during the break, and the smell of defeat began creeping in until Messier, the man with five Stanley Cups to his credit, took control, urging his teammates to be aggressive and stay positive.

"We'll win this game," he told them. "We'll play all night if we have to."

Tick. Tock. Tick. Tock. Perhaps it would take all night. Another overtime period elapsed, and Richter and Brodeur were again unassailable, with Brodeur turning away 15 shots. (The Rangers ultimately took 48 shots to the Devils' 32.)

As the teams headed to the third double overtime of the series, officials moved the Prince of Wales Trophy into position between the two locker rooms for its postgame presentation. Left wing Stephane Matteau, a midseason acquisition who had scored the winning goal in Game 3's second OT, had stayed behind to repair his skate. Heading to the ice he noticed the trophy and touched it for luck.

Richter redeemed himself by stopping five difficult shots; almost four minutes into the period he dove across the length of the crease to flick away a loose puck. The Rangers made the most of it. Less than a half-minute later, Matteau zipped around the net and took his first shot of the game. He banked a wraparound off Brodeur's stick and into the goal. At 4:24 of the period, the Rangers were Eastern Conference champions.

Garden fans were ecstatic, but they also knew that this could not be the end of the 1994 season. "We want the Cup," they chanted. "We want the Cup."

One Cup coming right up.

24

Grete Waitz and Fred Lebow Run Side by Side, November 1, 1992, Central Park

Each morning of the New York Marathon, Fred Lebow was awakened by a 2:30 a.m. phone call to the Manhattan hotel where he stayed with his staff and the top runners. He'd start prepping everything before leading the race, his baby, in his pace car. But 1992 was different. Lebow was sleeping in Staten Island just yards from the starting line. And he approached the line not as leader of the pack but as a runner.

Lebow's run was two years in the making, a testimony to determination and resilience. In early 1990, doctors found a large brain tumor in this energetic marathon man and gave him six months to live. Lebow realized that while he'd run 68 marathons throughout the world, he had been too busy to run the race he'd founded with the exception of the first year, 1970, when the race was confined to circling Central Park. So, the Romanian immigrant who had endured World War II work camps and escaped communism decided he would defy expectations and survive—not just survive, but also run—in celebration of hope, through the streets of his adopted city.

"It is the most dramatic way I know to fight my illness," he said later.

Lebow's training began in hospital hallways, where he calculated how many laps equaled a mile. He dragged his body, while encouraging other patients to join him. That fall the doctors declared him in remission, crediting both his remarkable attitude and physical relentlessness. But he remained woefully frail. He tried some mid-length races but some days was too weak to run even two miles.

Lebow persisted, and a plan fell into place. Grete Waitz, who had won New York nine times before retiring, volunteered to run alongside him, although she privately fretted that her friend was pushing himself too hard. Lebow's deputy, Allan Steinfeld, formed an entourage that included a local fireman and a policeman, as well as television meteorologists Storm Field and Irv "Mr. G" Gurofsky, as a buffer from such distractions as spectators looking for a handshake or photo.

Lebow devoted most of his energy that final week to promoting and managing (make that micromanaging) the marathon. Although the staff moved him to Staten Island so he'd relax and sleep, he awoke on race day five hours before start time, checking over everything with his usual gusto.

At race time, Lebow, wearing number 60 for his age, supposedly became just one of 26,000 runners hoping to finish. When some second-tier runners pushed forward a minute early, triggering a false start that couldn't be undone, Lebow was unhappy about yielding control, yelling, "I don't want to run. I shouldn't have run this race." Waitz calmed him, however, and off they went.

A motorcycle policeman and television camera truck rode alongside while 2 million people lining the streets rooted for the marathon's biggest celebrity. But Lebow, although buoyed by the heartfelt outpouring, rarely waved or responded, and he spoke almost exclusively to Waitz. She asked him to rest at the three-mile mark, but he blew right through, instead slowing to a walk several times after mile 10.

On the Queensboro Bridge, Lebow appeared drained, stopping to stretch and buy time, but with loudspeakers announcing his progress he could hear crowds along First Avenue roaring in anticipation and he pushed on. At the 17-mile mark, he made an exception and stopped to wave and hug spectators— cancer patients and their doctors at Memorial Sloan-Kettering Cancer Center, where he'd been treated. (Lebow also added a charity component to the marathon, raising $1.2 million for the center.)

Soon Lebow wilted. He seemed uncertain, tilting toward the right, guided gently back by his entourage. At 92nd Street, the tired old man bent over, clutching his stomach. This was the end, everyone thought. Tenacity could take you only so far. But when Waitz comforted her friend, Lebow lifted his head and, in his heavy accent, chortled, "Fooled you, fooled you," and bolted ahead, rejuvenated.

The homestretch was a genuine struggle. At 135th Street, pain shot through Lebow's knee. A spectator produced a chair, and Lebow sat briefly, donning a knee brace he had carried just in case. After mile 20, Lebow's stride became wobbly, and he repeatedly slowed to a walk. At times he was unable to recognize people he knew.

The spectators passionately, desperately urging him on boosted his energy, Waitz said. When 80-year-old Joe Kleinerman, Lebow's close friend and mentor, stepped out and kissed Lebow, Waitz was so moved she began crying. Lebow asked if she was hurt, since she'd never run that slowly before, but when she explained, he welled up, too. For the last two miles, Lebow and Waitz cried and held hands—and kept going.

It wasn't just street crowds rooting for Lebow. ABC's regular coverage had long since ended, but the network cut into programming to update Lebow's progress. Finally, Waitz and Lebow neared the finish line, where "New York, New York" played on the sound system. Waitz briefly stepped ahead, windmilling her arm to wave Lebow home, as he had done for thousands of others. Then she held out her hand and together they crossed the tape—held by winner Willie Mtolo and Mayor David Dinkins—and embraced. After 5 hours, 32 minutes, and 34 seconds Lebow had made it.

He hugged friends, coworkers, and family, then bent down to kiss the finish line. He needed help getting up, but when he did, he was the same old Fred, ready to charm the media. "I never realized that a marathon can be this long," he said.

Lebow's illness returned, and he died on October 9, 1994. About 4,000 people, one of whom was Waitz, paid tribute to Lebow at a memorial service in Central Park, where a statue of him now stands. "I know Fred wanted me to win 10, and I got only nine," Waitz recalled. "But crossing that finish line with Fred in 1992 made up for it."

25

Monica Seles and Jennifer Capriati Introduce Power to Women's Tennis, While Martina Navratilova Does Her Best Jimbo, September 6, 1991, National Tennis Center

In the midst of a U.S. Open focused on Jimmy Connors's miraculous resurrection, women's tennis produced a pair of classic matches of their own: a semifinal between the two greatest women before Serena Williams and another between the game's newest queen and its next heralded princess.

This foursome offered a little bit of everything: aging veteran and teen prodigy, net-rusher and baseliner, poise and breathless emotion, classic forehands and an unorthodox two-handed version. Martina Navratilova and Steffi Graf, with 28 singles Grand Slams between them already, thrilled the crowd with their remarkable precision in a back-and-forth tussle that produced three times as many winners as unforced errors. Then youngsters Monica Seles and Jennifer Capriati wowed the crowd with their raw, unharnessed power.

Navratilova, the best women's player of the 1980s, was seeded just sixth but was doing her best Connors impression. At age 34, she'd survived several three-setters to reach the semifinals. The 22-year-old Graf, who replaced Navratilova as the dominant player, had battled a shoulder injury after winning Wimbledon but still coasted to the semis. Their rivalry was even at 7–7, but Navratilova hadn't won since the 1987 U.S. Open final.

The match pitted the game's best attacker (Navratilova) against the owner of the most powerful baseline forehand (Graf). The margin of victory would be impossibly thin. To impose her will at the net, Navratilova bullied Graf's second serve and even her backhand. At 5–5, Graf altered her game to approach the net twice but was burned both times and Navratilova broke serve. Navratilova briefly unraveled after a bad call and lost her own serve before recovering to win the tiebreaker, 7–2.

Graf proved her mettle down 5–3 in the second set, converting on her fourth break point to fight her way to another tiebreaker. Graf grabbed a 6–2 lead only to watch Navratilova run off four points before she steadied herself and won, 8–6, on her first winner at the net, a beautifully angled backhand volley.

In the final set, however, Navratilova, pumping her fist a la Connors, broke twice for a 3–0 lead. Graf again rallied, pulling within 4–3, love–30 on Navratilova's serve. But Navratilova produced two inspired volley winners and eventually held. When Navratilova served for the match at 5–4, Graf managed two break points, but Navratilova responded first with an ace and then with a service winner. She won, 7–6, 6–7, 6–4, and would play the final against someone half her age—or younger.

Seles, just 17, had risen to number one after winning the 1991 Australian and French Opens with overwhelming two-handed shots from both sides. Although she'd alienated purists and lost her top ranking to Graf by skipping Wimbledon, she'd crushed the opposition at the Open. A win would get her back to number one. Capriati, 15, had been reaping millions in endorsements even before playing her first pro match at 14. She beat defending champion Gabriela Sabatini and was bidding to become the youngest player ever in the Open final.

Navratilova had transformed women's tennis with her superb athleticism and attacking style, but her unique skill set yielded few imitators. These two girls were both baseliners, but you'd never mistake Seles or Capriati for Chris Evert or Tracy Austin—they brought Navratilova-style oomph to the back of the court. This match emphatically introduced a new power game, setting the stage for an era ruled more by Seles, Lindsay Davenport, and later the Williams sisters than smaller, cagier champs like Martina Hingis or Justine Henin.

This was tennis as hand-to-hand combat, with no stinting on either recklessness or bravery, depending on your viewpoint. Although Seles mixed in some lobs and drop shots, every point featured heavy artillery fired within inches of the lines. Both players were remarkably free-swinging, going for broke at the slightest opportunity. At first, it seemed there'd be no third set as Seles bombarded the crowd favorite to win nine of the first 11 games for a 6–3, 3–1 lead. But Capriati pounded back, reeling off five straight games for the second set.

The third set was topsy-turvy, roiling and turbulent, perfect for a couple of adolescents. More than half of the match's 84 unforced errors came in this set, and neither player held serve through the last seven games. Capriati broke then fought off a break point for a 3–1 lead. But at 5–4 and at 6–5, with Capriati serving for the match, Seles hit harder, deeper, and with more aggression. Capriati even missed entirely on some swings.

CHAPTER 25

Finally, they went to a tiebreaker. Seles had more firepower left, subduing her younger foe with a service winner, a backhand down the line, and a forehand into the corner to win, 7–3. Capriati left in tears and soon tumbled away from the cusp of greatness. By contrast, two days later, Seles beat Navratilova, winning her sixth crown of the year and establishing herself as the future of the game.

26

Jimmy Connors Defies Father Time, September 2, 1991, National Tennis Center

Jimmy Connors won five U.S. Opens on three different surfaces at two different sites. Yet, he's best remembered for a tournament in which he didn't even reach the finals. That 1991 performance was the third and final act for Connors, who had won as the brash bully of the 1970s and the curmudgeonly craftsman of the 1980s. This time Connors, seemingly washed up, transformed himself into a feel-good story for a society built on both a Peter Pan complex and the worship of true grit.

This aging inspiration captivated even casual sports fans, attaining a new level of celebrity and forging an unforgettable legacy with his blend of tenacity and showmanship. It was surprising Connors was even there. His iron man records—109 pro titles, 159 straight weeks at number one, 12 straight Open semifinals, and 16 straight years in the top 10—were in the past. He'd played and lost three matches in 1990, before submitting to wrist surgery. He plummeted to 936th in the world, defaulted at the French Open in 1991, owing to a cranky back—the defining symbol of old age—and lost in Wimbledon's third round. He was ranked just 174th by Open time and needed a wild-card berth just to gain entrance to his "home court."

In the first round he faced McEnroe. Sure, it was Patrick, not his more talented older brother, but he was ranked 35th, was an Australian Open semifinalist, and had beaten Boris Becker that summer. McEnroe grabbed the first two sets and took a 3–0 lead in the third. Connors was limping (an act, perhaps, lulling his prey or laying groundwork for an alibi) and the stadium was emptying, everyone writing Connors off. By the next game, perhaps 6,000 loyalists remained from the sellout crowd.

Then, at 0–40, one mistake from oblivion, Connors finally turned it on. McEnroe could not finish off tennis's Rasputin, who drew his lifeblood from the screaming, stomping, bowing fans who remained. With his vibrant new Estusa racket flashing in the night, proclaiming the return of the king, Connors held, saved two more break points at 2–3, won five of six games for the third set, and stampeded McEnroe in the final two sets. The four-hour and 18-minute epic ended at 1:35 a.m.

"The crowd won it for me," Connors said. "The crowd was an awful heavy burden for Patrick."

By the fourth-round Connors was the story of the tournament: Becker stopped practicing to come over and congratulate him; defending champion Pete Sampras's third-round press conference included 12 out of 16 questions about Connors before Sampras snapped that he wanted questions about his own tennis; Nuprin rushed its new Connors commercial onto the air; and Ted Koppel explored the Connors phenomenon on *Nightline.*

September 2 was Connors's 39th birthday, and as he entered the court for his match against Aaron Krickstein, the fans greeted him with a rousing rendition of "Happy Birthday." He gave them the ultimate present: a match for the ages. Connors always used the crowd better than any other player, in defiance as a strident young outcast being booed before earning respect and adoration in the late 1970s. And no crowd connected better with Connors than the New York crowd, which fed off his working-class humor, his drive, his urgency.

Against Krickstein, Connors perfectly played and played to his audience, exulting, exhorting, slapping his thigh, pumping his pelvis, and thrusting his fist for four hours and 42 minutes. He still resorted to base tactics—calling an umpire "an abortion"—but mostly he oozed charm, even as he used the ovations as a stalling tactic to catch his breath and psych out Krickstein. At one point he directly addressed the nation, turning to a courtside television camera and boasting, "This is what they come for. This is what they want."

Although he'd fallen further behind against McEnroe, this was no simple task. Krickstein, who had idolized Connors, then become a friend and occasional hitting partner, was fresh off a win over 1990 finalist Andre Agassi.

Connors lost the first set, then clawed back to win the second in a tiebreaker. Worn down, he tanked the third, 6–1, while waiting for his second wind. He recovered to win the fourth set, but it took a toll. In the fifth set, he seemed finished after dropping a 17-minute, 23-point game.

But trailing 5–2 in the fifth was apparently right where Connors wanted to be. He was as aggressive as ever. He won one game with a touch backhand volley and another with an overhead, while Krickstein remained pinned to the baseline, unable to slow the attack.

Tennis writer Peter Bodo was in the press box near Arthur Ashe, who had loathed Connors for his refusal to join the players' union, his unwillingness to play for America's Davis Cup team, and his on-court behavior. Witnessing Connors's voodoo magic, Bodo asked Ashe if he thought Connors was still an asshole. Ashe paused, then replied, "Yes. But he's my favorite asshole."

As the crowd screamed and shrieked, Connors pulled even. By the time they reached a tiebreaker, the outcome seemed preordained. Connors flattened Krickstein, 7–4, to end the night. Well, not quite. This time the stands remained full to the end, and the fans serenaded their Jimbo with an encore of "Happy Birthday."

Even nemesis John McEnroe was impressed enough to search out Connors in the locker room to congratulate him. "I've just got to go in there and touch him and see if he bleeds," McEnroe said.

Connors reached the semifinals, thanks to one more miraculous moment. He was down a set and a break at 5–4, in the second set of his quarterfinal match against Paul Haarhuis. There was no way Connors could endure another five-setter, so if he couldn't solve Haarhuis here, the run would end. Haarhuis grabbed a 30–15 lead. Two points for the set.

Connors snatched two quick points. Break point for the old man. Haarhuis approached the net behind a deep backhand. Connors flung a lob skyward. Haarhuis slammed an overhead. Connors, back literally against the wall, managed another backhand lob. Another overhead to the backhand corner. Connors threw up one more lob. The crowd was electrified by his perseverance. This time Haarhuis rifled his shot toward Connors's forehand. Scampering relentlessly, he hurled another lob, turning even tennis's most defensive shot into a statement of aggression and defiance, thrusting his jaw out, and saying, "Hit me again, I won't ever go down."

Haarhuis was exhausted, mentally, if not physically. His last overhead was his weakest, and Connors, the game's finest opportunist, whacked a crosscourt forehand. Haarhuis reached it, but his backhand volley was soft. Connors raced in, driving a vintage backhand winner up the line.

The crowd, on its feet, roared—for this point, for almost two decades of unsurpassed thrills. Connors won that set, 7–6, and cruised through the next two as well. Although Connors lost to Jim Courier in the semifinals, he was clearly the tournament's biggest winner—make that 1991's biggest sports story. "F. Scott Fitzgerald once commented that there are no second acts in American lives. Jimmy Connors would probably tell Fitzgerald exactly where he could shove that remark," writer Joel Drucker once commented in a magazine piece.

The McEnroe match featured the longest road back at a time when no one expected anything, and it served as a reminder that Connors was more than just a great talent and a mesmerizing entertainer: He had succeeded so often and for so long because of his intense dedication to the game and the idea of competing. But for the history books, choose the Krickstein match—although Connors always thrashed Krickstein, this confrontation marked the apex because it put Connors back in the spotlight he loved and he always preferred facing the pressure of high expectations and somehow exceeding them.

27

Buffalo Misses Wide Right and the Giants Escape with Their Second Super Bowl, January 27, 1991, Tampa Stadium, Tampa

With 2:16 remaining and the New York Giants clinging to a one-point lead, Super Bowl XXV would come down to one last drive by the Buffalo Bills and their top-ranked offense. It was up to the Giants' heralded defense to stop them—just enough. Big Blue could yield plenty of yardage if they kept Buffalo out of field goal range.

What was field goal range? Narrower than you might think. During the previous five years, kickers had missed more than half of all kicks from at least 47 yards on grass. Buffalo's Scott Norwood lacked great leg strength and played home games on turf. He was just 8-of-17 lifetime on grass and 1-of-5 on grass field kicks of more than 40 yards. He'd tried just once the previous two seasons and had missed a 42-yarder—without the pressure of an entire Super Bowl on his shoulders.

So when Buffalo quarterback Jim Kelly started at his own 10, the Giants, leading 20–19, knew if they gave ground grudgingly, slowly, the clock would stop Buffalo short. Keep Buffalo beyond New York's 23 and Norwood would almost definitely miss.

The Bills started the day as heavy favorites—their no-huddle offense, featuring Kelly, running back Thurman Thomas, and receivers James Lofton and Andre Reed had piled up 95 points in two playoff victories.

But the Giants, led by coach Bill Parcells and defensive coordinator Bill Belichick, had Super Bowl experience. (The Bills supposedly didn't impose a curfew early in the week, and the team, thrilled just to be in the Super Bowl, reportedly enjoyed themselves quite a bit. The Giants were more businesslike.) The Giants were also smarter on the field and more fundamentally sound in classic old-school football: power running behind an unrelenting offensive line, no turnovers, and devastating defense. In seven games against opponents that made the playoffs, the Giants yielded just 13.2 points per game. "Power wins football games," was Parcells's mantra.

Even after losing quarterback Phil Simms to a broken bone in his foot (in a loss to Buffalo), the Giants cruised through their final two wins behind backup Jeff Hostetler. In the playoffs, they stomped the Chicago Bears, 31–3, by controlling the ball for more than 38 minutes. In the NFC Championship Game, the defense stopped the two-time defending Super Bowl champion San Francisco 49ers, 15–13.

Thus, the Giants weren't worried about betting odds. Parcells's offense could keep Kelly's gunners off the field for huge swaths of time. To earn the Vince Lombardi Trophy, Parcells coached a Super Bowl Lombardi would have loved. The Giants ran 72 offensive plays: 19 used three tight ends, 23 used two tight ends, and 20 used one tight end but had two running backs. MVP Ottis Anderson and Dave Meggett punished Buffalo for 150 yards rushing on 30 carries. But Parcells also knew Buffalo was geared to stop the run, so on first down he had the Giants pass 19 times and rush only 12 times—nothing fancy, just enough to keep the Bills off balance and help the Giants move the chains. (This was also the first turnover-free Super Bowl, and the teams combined for only 66 yards worth of penalties.)

By game's end, New York had set a Super Bowl record with 40 minutes and 33 seconds worth of possession. Meanwhile, Belichick's game plan—which is now in the Hall of Fame—used only two down linemen (usually nose tackle Erik Howard and end Leonard Marshall) and sometimes one linebacker in position to handle the run. He was willing to give ground to Thurman Thomas to add linebackers and defensive backs against Kelly's passing game, relying largely on zone coverage to stop Kelly from throwing deep.

The Giants alternated cover plans on each drive, making it harder for Kelly to audible in his no-huddle offense. Belichick believed that if Thomas ran for more than 100 yards, the Giants would win, because it meant the quick strike offense had been neutralized: Thomas gained 135 yards, but Kelly threw for only 212 yards and didn't convert a third-down play until the game was almost done. Kelly managed just one completion thrown more than 12 yards beyond the line of scrimmage, and 16 of his 18 completions were screens, swing passes in the flat to his backs, or shallow crosses to Reed in the slot.

New York's defenders hit every receiver hard every play. Reed was hit so hard he began dropping passes and caught just one short pass in the second half.

"No other team ever hit me this hard," Reed later admitted. "They bruised up my whole body."

New York grabbed an early lead with a 10-play, 58-yard drive that ate 6:15 off the clock. Buffalo's lone big pass play required luck—cornerback Perry Williams had Lofton covered but tipped Kelly's 42-yard pass and Lofton grabbed it then ran for 19 more yards. The Bills then stalled out before Norwood kicked a 23-yard field goal. The next time Kelly threw deep to Lofton, he was shut down. The quarterback never threw his way again.

Kelly did fire six straight short completions on an 80-yard touchdown drive. But even after Buffalo defensive end Bruce Smith nailed Hostetler in the end zone for a safety, making it 12–3, the Giants remained calm—many had played for the previous Super Bowl squad, which had grown stronger as that game wore on against Denver.

"Two drives, that's all it takes, two of those long, time-consuming drives," Simms had said days before the game. "That's all it takes to screw up the other team's offense, to foul up the tempo of their game."

With 3:43 left in the half, the Giants started an 87-yard drive that culminated when Hostetler connected with Stephen Baker on a 14-yard touchdown pass with 25 seconds left. They went into the locker room down just 12–10, knowing that they'd get the ball back to start the new half.

The first drive of the second half defined the game, not because the Giants' touchdown produced a 17–12 lead, but because the 75-yard drive took 14 plays, keeping Kelly's squad sidelined as New York wiped nine minutes and 29 seconds off the clock. (It was a Super Bowl record since surpassed only by the Giants 17 years later against Belichick's Patriots.) Four times the Giants faced third down, and each time they converted. On 3rd and 8 at New York's 27, Hostetler dumped a short pass to Meggett, who squirmed away from a tackler and gained 11 yards. The biggest play came on 3rd and 13, when wide receiver Mark Ingram grabbed a short pass and deked his way through four Buffalo defenders to get a first down at Buffalo's 18. The Giants defense never would have missed so many tackles, but, of course, the Bills defense was exhausted by this point.

"Any time you see a great player like Bruce Smith just barely getting down in his stance, you know he's tired," said fullback Maurice Carthon.

Still, Buffalo was too good to go away. On the first play of the fourth quarter, Thomas scored on a 31-yard run, putting Buffalo back in front, 19–17. The Giants stuck to their game plan, eating 7:32 off the clock in 14 plays, as Hostetler repeatedly found tight end Mark Bavaro until the drive stalled out at Buffalo's 3. New York settled for a field goal. The Giants stopped Buffalo once more and chewed up more time before Kelly came back on the field with 2:16 left to play.

Kelly still could not find receivers downfield and was forced to scramble three times on the drive, losing valuable seconds he couldn't afford to squander. On first down, Kelly ran for eight yards. Productive, but not dangerous. Two plays later, Thomas broke free for 21 yards on a run. That, of course, only highlights how badly outsmarted Buffalo had been: Unwilling to adapt to the Giants defense, Kelly gave the ball to Thomas on barely more than a quarter of Buffalo's plays. The Giants probably would have adjusted their defense to a running game, but that may have freed Kelly to throw downfield.

With 48 seconds left, the Bills used their final time-out on the Giants 46. The next play yielded only another short pass for six yards.

Thomas ran 11 to the Giants 29, where cornerback Mark Collins became an unsung hero by stopping Thomas from getting out of bounds—the Bills would have had time for another play, a chance to truly get within Norwood's range. Instead, the Bills had to throw an incompletion to stop the clock with eight seconds left. Norwood was brought out to kick. If he could hit it, Buffalo would fulfill its destiny. But the Giants had really done their job: A 47-yard field goal was beyond his reach.

It was (and still is) the only potential Super Bowl–winning field goal attempt in which the team would lose on a miss.

Norwood was right-footed and the ball was on the right hashmark, while the wind was blowing slightly left to right. The holder, Frank Reich, did not get the laces directly facing the goalpost, which would have been ideal. From such a great distance, Norwood seemingly overcompensated, focusing on launching the ball as far as he could, depriving himself of a follow-through that might have brought the kick back.

Norwood kicked it far enough, but the ball tailed off. On ABC, Al Michaels summed it up succinctly and memorably: "No good . . . wide right."

Only one Super Bowl has ever been decided by one point. The Giants, with skill, savvy, and power, took home the trophy.

28

The Knicks Beat Boston in Boston, Finally, May 6, 1990, Boston Garden

This was a game—and a series—the New York Knicks were just not supposed to win. The Knicks lost the first two games of the first-round playoff series against the Larry Bird–led Boston Celtics, the second one in humiliating fashion: a 157–128 drubbing, a NBA playoff record for points allowed. Only one team in the previous three decades had won after losing the first two games of a best-of-five series. Sure, the Knicks bounced back to win two straight at home (with a club-playoff record 43 assists in a Game 4 rout, 135–108).

But to complete the comeback New York would have to win in Boston Garden. New York was weak on the road (they'd lost 10 of their previous 11) and Boston was invincible at home (they'd won 13 straight), but it was this particular combination that seemed so daunting: New York had dropped 26 straight regular-season games in Boston, dating to 1984, and they had lost nine consecutive playoff games there since 1974.

And yet, led by Charles Oakley, mid-season acquisition Maurice Cheeks, and, of course, center Patrick Ewing, the Knicks defied the odds and deposed the Celtics, leaving the Boston crowd stunned.

The Celtics grabbed a comfortable 32–24 lead early on, and even after New York's 11–0 run, Boston was unfazed. Down 46–44, Boston scored eight straight and, with less than a minute remaining in the half, held a 52–46 edge. But the Knicks scored, got a stop, and then cut the lead to four when Ewing buried a 10-foot jumper with just six-tenths of a second left.

The third quarter let Boston know New York was not going to fade. The lead changed hands five times. Boston's 73–66 lead vanished amid New York's 18–6 run: After a Gerald Wilkins dunk put New York ahead, 80–79, the lead changes

New York Knicks center Patrick Ewing, left, reaches in from behind to block a shot by Boston Celtics forward Larry Bird, right, in the first period of a NBA playoff game, Sunday, May 6, 1990, Boston, Massachusetts. *ASSOCIATED PRESS*

were done. Ewing had 14 points and Cheeks 11 in the quarter, which ended with New York ahead, 87–83.

Boston haunted the Knicks throughout much of the fourth, but the Knicks, who shot 59 percent for the game, stepped it up at crunch time, shooting 69 percent in the fourth. When Boston pulled within 101–99, Ewing hit a short hook. When Bird went up for a layup, he heard Ewing's footsteps and was scared he was about to have his shot blocked (Ewing had four blocks) so he tried to dunk it—and missed. New York capped its 12–2 run with 2:03 left when Ewing chased a bad pass into the corner, grabbed it, and, as the shot clock expired, heaved a three-pointer—just the second of his career. It was 113–101, Knicks, en route to a 121–114 final.

Ewing finished with 31 points and eight rebounds, and beat Boston's double teams by dishing out 10 assists. He played 47 minutes, while Cheeks played every second and added 21 points and seven assists. Wilkins, not known for his passing, had eight more (along with 12 points), and Trent Tucker and Johnny Newman both added double-digit scoring off the bench. Those four men drove to the basket but also spaced the court well, giving Ewing good looks while hitting their own shots. It was the fiery Oakley, however, who was the stabilizing presence throughout the game, contributing 26 points and 17 rebounds.

The Knicks were eliminated by the eventual champions, the Detroit Pistons, but this win was a sign of a decade of competitive, hard-fought basketball to come, featuring two trips to the NBA Finals. In the moment, it was plenty satisfying simply hearing Bird, the Knicks' longtime tormentor, say, "This is as low as it gets since I've been here, we're in shock."

29

Phil Simms Is Almost Perfect as the Giants Win Their First Super Bowl, January 25, 1987, Rose Bowl, Pasadena

In the New York Giants' first playoff game in 1987, quarterback Phil Simms threw nine passes that were caught but 10 that were not. He wasn't even needed on the field in the fourth quarter, as the 14–2 Giants demolished the San Francisco 49ers, 49–3. The Giants were led by running back Joe Morris and a dominating defense that yielded just 29 rushing yards and forced four turnovers. The game essentially ended in the second quarter, when Pro Bowl tackle Jim Burt knocked San Francisco superstar Joe Montana out of the game as league MVP and Lawrence Taylor snatched Montana's pass and ran it back 34 yards for a touchdown.

In the NFC Championship Game, Simms was just 7–14, for 90 yards, but the defense had four sacks and an interception, shutting out the Washington Redskins, 17–0.

Heading into the Super Bowl, Simms was, as much as any quarterback could be, an afterthought. He had thrown 104 touchdowns to 103 interceptions since joining the Giants in 1979. While the Giants had made three straight playoffs, Simms's penchant for throwing deep meant he'd finished in the top five in interceptions and yards lost on sacks in three seasons without ever reaching the top 10 in pass completion percentage or passer rating.

Thus, the focus was on whether the Giants' fearsome front line and terrifying linebackers could throttle Denver Broncos quarterback John Elway.

In other words, no one was ready for what was about to happen.

In the first half, Elway completed 13 of 20 passes for 187 yards, but brilliant plays in crucial situations by New York's defense, along with poor kicking and bad luck, meant Denver entered the half with just 10 points and a one-point lead.

In the second quarter, the Broncos had 1st and goal on New York's one-yard line and were at the cusp of a commanding 10-point lead. Taylor slammed through the line and, with rookie Erik Howard, nailed Elway for a one-yard loss. Then Pro Bowl inside linebacker Harry Carson stopped a run up the middle by Gerald Willhite. On third down, the Broncos tried a sweep away from Taylor and Carson, but outside linebacker Carl Banks met Sammy Winder and tossed him for a four-yard loss.

This play summed up much of the day. The Broncos gained only 14 yards rushing in the first half; forced to abandon the running game in the second half, they left Elway more vulnerable to pressure. And as the Broncos tried to minimize Taylor's impact, other players stepped up, especially Banks, who led the team with 10 unassisted tackles, while Leonard Marshall added two sacks and rookie Eric Dorsey contributed one. The play was also revealing because the Broncos had run a similar play, for a score, against the Giants in their regular-season 19–16 loss. Banks, who studied game film all week, was ready. "They didn't get away from their tendencies," he said later. By contrast, the Giants would make play calls in the second half that shocked everyone and completely changed the game.

On fourth down, Rich Karlis attempted a 23-yard field goal. No one had ever missed such a short shot in Super Bowl history. Karlis did. The Giants were still down by just three.

Late in the half, Elway found tight end Clarence Kay for 25 yards. The officials ruled the pass incomplete and, on the first instant replay review in Super Bowl history, could not find evidence to overturn the call. (Later, CBS found an angle showing Kay definitely made the catch.) On the next play, Howard and George Martin chased Elway back from the 13, and Martin captured him in the Denver end zone. The safety made it 10–9. With less than a minute to go before halftime, Elway again moved the ball, reaching the Giants 20. Again, the Giants, after bending, refused to break, forcing three straight incompletions. And again, Karlis missed the field goal.

Simms had a strong first half, throwing 12 completions in 15 attempts, but after starting with an impressive nine-play, 78-yard drive, the Giants had not scored again until the safety. No Super Bowl had been this close at intermission. The second half would be a totally different story.

Credit for the Giants' success in the season and the game gets divided among general manager George Young, coach Bill Parcells, and Parcells's young defensive coordinator, Bill Belichick. Young's five selections in the first two rounds of the 1986 draft were on defense, despite that being the team's strength. In the Super Bowl, all five players contributed. Beyond Dorsey's sack and Howard's play on the goal line stand, they, along with linebacker Pepper Johnson and Mark Collins and Greg Lasker in the secondary, also rotated through to keep the stars' legs fresh while Denver's top players wore down.

Parcells created a game plan that, unlike Denver's, was full of surprises, starting with a pass-first offense for a team that relied on its ground game. In the first half, the Giants threw on nine of 11 first-down plays, and Simms completed all nine. Parcells also took two huge risks on play calls in the second half that left the Broncos reeling. Belichick, having stopped Denver's run, fine-tuned the defense at halftime, which helped turn the game around.

But that was all secondary to Simms's dazzling performance. Ten passes in the second half. Ten completions. Three touchdown passes.

The first turning point of the second half came on the fourth play, with the Giants facing 4th and a foot from their own 46. Pro Bowl punter Sean Landeta trotted onto the field. But so did backup quarterback Jeff Rutledge, who was never part of the punting team. Parcells figured that if Denver didn't notice and adjust, he'd make a last-minute call. He knew that if it didn't work, his defense would have his back.

Denver failed to respond, so Parcells nodded his head and Rutledge slid under center at the last second and plunged for two yards. The Broncos were back on their heels. Simms zipped a 12-yarder to Morris and a 23-yarder to Steve Rousey, and then, two plays later, he delivered a 13-yard touchdown pass to his favorite target, Mark Bavaro.

The Giants had the lead. Primed for the pass, the Giants hurried Elway to two incompletions and a useless five-yard pass. After the Giants tacked on a field goal, Elway again missed on two passes and had one short completion. Now Denver's defense was feeling the pressure. Simms, however, was not. He threw a 17-yarder to Lionel Manuel. Then, after a run, Parcells delivered the knockout punch. On the Denver 45, the straightlaced, smashmouth Giants ran a trick play: the flea flicker, the kind of play that kids love running in pickup games but rarely works in the NFL.

Simms handed off to Morris, who ran a few steps, then, once he'd frozen the defensive backs, tossed the ball back to his quarterback. Simms had Bobby Johnson open in the end zone, but rather than make the riskier move, he fired a pass 25 yards to a wide open Phil McConkey at the 20. McConkey sprinted to the five, then, after taking a hit, dove to the one. Morris took it in on the next play.

"We've run the flea-flicker in practice for I don't know how long, and we've never hit on the damn thing," said Simms later. "When I hit McConkey down on the one, I thought, 'That's it. We've won it.'"

The score was 26–10. On the final play in the third quarter, Marshall sacked Elway for a loss of 11 yards. The Broncos finished the quarter with negative two yards total offense. Denver opened the fourth with a penalty, and then Elvis Patterson intercepted Elway. Simms lofted a 36-yarder to Stacey Robinson and later a six-yard touchdown pass to Bavaro—but he didn't catch it and as it bounced off his fingertips, it looked like Simms had his first incompletion of the half—until the ball landed in McConkey's hands. It was 33–10. The rest of the game was essentially garbage time: Simms didn't bother passing anymore, and Elway was lifted for the game's final series. His replacement, Gary Kubiak, was, fittingly, sacked (by Dorsey) on the game's final play.

The Giants set a record with 30 second-half points. Simms was 22 of 25 for 268 yards and three touchdowns. His 88 percent completion percentage broke both a Super Bowl and NFL postseason record.

The Giants had appeared more lackluster than giddy in their practice after the NFC Championship Game, and Parcells ripped into the team the next day. On the Monday before the big game, he put them through a brutal workout, ending it with six 80-yard sprints. Two days later, he stepped up the intensity. The Giants didn't complain. They trusted their coach.

"It paid off, didn't it," Burt said after the Super Bowl. "All the running got us in shape. We finished the game strong."

30

The Mets Come Back One More Time in Game 7, October 27, 1986, Shea Stadium

I t almost felt cruel to force the Boston Red Sox to play Game 7.

It wasn't because they'd faced three Game 7s since 1918, losing all three. This was about Game 6 of 1986. The New York Mets' Mookifizing comeback doused the Sox with defeat—they positively reeked of it. Boston legend Carl Yastrzemski confessed afterward, "After they lost the sixth game, you just knew somehow they wouldn't win the seventh game."

The Mets felt invincible, certain that having returned from the dead, they had a firm grip on their destiny.

Sure, a day of rain worked to Boston's advantage, allowing them to start the tough lefty Bruce Hurst instead of mediocre loudmouth Oil Can Boyd.

Yes, Ron Darling looked awful, yielding back-to-back homers to Dwight Evans and Rich Gedman as Boston jumped out to a 3–0 lead, while Hurst twirled a one-hitter through five.

Still, the Mets and their fans were not worried. (In Red Sox Nation, everyone recalled being up 3–0 in Game 7 in 1975, but losing 4–3.) A comeback was on the way. This game, this championship had been locked up with their resurrection, perhaps the moment Mookie Wilson jackknifed away from Bob Stanley's pitch, perhaps when he tumbled that roller toward Bill Buckner.

Just look at Sid Fernandez's relief job to keep the Mets in Game 7 after Darling faltered. The portly El Sid had grumbled about being bumped from the rotation in the Series but made the most of his moment, retiring seven straight with four strikeouts. "The necessary hero," Keith Hernandez called him afterward.

For inspiration, the video scoreboard replayed Bill Buckner's infamous error just before the home sixth. That was playing dirty, but it did the trick.

Lee Mazzilli's pinch-hit single, Wilson's single, and Tim Teufel's walk made it clear Hurst was wearing down. But Boston's bullpen could only charitably be described as unreliable, so Hurst stayed in, lefty against lefty, facing Keith Hernandez. The Mets' leader was only 5–24 in the Series, but he was one of his generation's fiercest clutch hitters. (The short-lived "game-winning RBI" stat seemed to have been invented to show off his prowess under pressure.) As Roger Angell wrote in the New Yorker, knowledgeable fans "understood that this was the arrangement—this particular batter and this precise set of circumstances—that the Mets wanted most and the Red Sox least at the end of their long adventures."

When Hurst left a fastball up over the plate, Hernandez smoked it into the gap in left-center, scoring both Mazzilli and Wilson. It was a one-run game. Gary Carter took a terrible cut and lifted a pathetic pop to right. On this day, for this team, that was enough. Dwight Evans dived and smothered the ball, recovering quickly to force Hernandez at second base. But Wally Backman, running for Teufel, was already home with the tying run.

Roger Clemens was in the bullpen, but for the seventh Boston manager John McNamara inexplicably turned to Game 6 loser Calvin Schiraldi, who'd said beforehand, "I don't deserve another chance."

Schiraldi quickly bid farewell to the ball, the game, and the season when the first hitter, Ray Knight, blasted a meaty 2–1 fastball over the wall and off the bleachers in left-center field.

Schiraldi only got worse. With taunts of "Caaaalll-viiiin" in his ears (revenge for Boston fans' "Daaar-yll" at Strawberry), he yielded a Lenny Dykstra single, then heaved the ball to the backstop on a pitchout, which sent Dykstra to second, allowing him to score on Rafael Santana's single. McNamara tried another former Met, Joe Sambito, who walked two hitters and then yielded another run on a sacrifice fly.

The Red Sox valiantly staged their own rally but fell short, not because of the "Curse of the Bambino," but because the Mets had the better manager, better bullpen, and better team. Ater Evans's two-run double made it 6–5. Davey Johnson replaced Roger McDowell with Jesse Orosco. He set down Gedman, Dave Henderson, and pinch-hitter Don Baylor. Crisis over.

Then the Mets added not one, but two finishing touches, showing off their multifaceted ballclub one last time. McNamara shoved Al Nipper, who had a 5.38 ERA and had pitched only once in three weeks, onto the hill in this tight spot instead of Clemens. Darryl Strawberry—who had done more sulking than hitting—greeted him with a moonshot. Then, with two men on base, Johnson had Orosco fake a bunt and swing away; the Mets reliever, who was 0–3 in 1986, punched a single through the drawn-in infield, scoring Knight.

CHAPTER 30

In 1969, Jerry Koosman was on the mound when the Mets won their first World Series. In 1978, the Mets traded Koosman to Minnesota for two young pitchers, one of whom was Jesse Orosco (the other, Greg Field, became the answer to a trivia question). In 1986, Orosco was on the mound as the Mets won their second World Series. At 11:26 p.m., Orosco struck out Marty Barrett on a high 2-2 fastball, leaped into the air, threw his glove even higher—an echo of the wild finish to the NLCS—and dropped to his knees, where he was buried beneath a pile of Mets crazed with triumph.

For all their historic success, New York teams have generally fared poorly in World Series Game 7s. Not counting the four in the Subway Series (which produced both winners and losers), the Yankees, Giants, and Mets have lost eight times in deciding games, winning only three times: 1958, 1962, and 1986. The win gave New York its first championship in any sport since the 1978 Yankees, an unusually long dry spell for a city built on winners. (From 1921 to 1986, the only longer stretch was 1963-1968.) Hence, this win, capping the unforgettable year of 108 wins, 4 brawls, 3 NLCS thrillers, and the miracle of Game 6, was particularly satisfying.

Even Mookie Wilson got swept up in the glory of it all. "Now," he said, "we can be as cocky as we want to be."

31

Mookie Wilson Hits a Ground Ball to First in Game 6 of the World Series, October 25, 1986, Shea Stadium

Disbelief gave way to despair. You knew in your heart you shouldn't feel so despondent—this was a baseball game, there were far graver problems, much larger injustices. Still, as the Boston Red Sox scored one run in the top of the 10th inning and then a second, your body slumped. As your New York Mets made one out, then a second, in the bottom of the 10th, your soul shrank. It was Game 6 of the World Series, and the Red Sox led, three games to two. No team had ever come back to win a Series from two down with two outs, while facing elimination.

The Mets' scoreboard congratulated Boston on breaking their curse. How could it have come to this? After enduring the Tom Seaver trade, the Mike Vail hype, the George Foster disappointment, after excusing 1984's close call and 1985's heartbreak as learning experiences, how could it have come to this for one of the best, most dominating baseball teams of all time?

A single. It meant nothing, merely delaying the inevitable.

A second hit started a stirring. Ah, if only there weren't already two outs—and then an 0–2 count. No team had ever come back to win a Series when down to its final strike.

Then something happened. Call it ghosts, call it history, call it the irresistible force of greatness. Whatever. It happened in slow motion and all at once—an avalanche that you rode atop, full-throated in your cheering. A weak looping single cut the lead to one. An eternal at-bat, forever fending off strike three, elicited a wild pitch. The game was tied, but its fate, indeed the fate of the entire Series, was tilting in New York's favor. Then the clincher: a slow roller, just a trickler, but the batter's blazing speed and the first baseman's fragility and the

Mookie Wilson evades Bob Stanley's wild pitch and the Mets tie Game 6. Moments later, Wilson hits a slow grounder to first. "Gets by Buckner." *National Baseball Hall of Fame*

most beautifully ugly play of all. And there you were in midair, hovering in the sky, flying, delirious. Someone bring back Red Smith: On October 25, 1986, fiction took another deadly beating.

The 1986 Mets—a ferocious combination of talent and ego, pitching and hitting, youth and experience, All-Stars and bench depth—were built for history. After an ugly, despairing stretch that began in 1977, the Mets started afresh in 1983, when general manager Frank Cashen promoted Darryl Strawberry from the minors and swiped Keith Hernandez from the St. Louis Cardinals for Neil Allen. They finished a strong second in 1984, and almost won the National League East in 1985. Each year brought more talent from within and without— Dwight Gooden, Bobby Ojeda, Lenny Dykstra, Gary Carter.

In 1986, they'd be great, and they knew it. In spring training, they left T-shirts declaring, "New York Mets 1986 NL East Champions," in the locker room of St. Louis, the defending National League champs. Manager Davey Johnson boasted, "We don't want to just win. We want to dominate." They did. After one-third of the season, Cardinals manager Whitey Herzog conceded.

The endless curtain calls, rally caps, and endorsements, and irked opponents, who provoked four bench-clearing brawls with New York. But no one could stop those damn Mets, whose 108 wins tied the 1975 Cincinnati Reds for the National League record. They clinched the East on September 17, the earliest date in divisional history, and won by 21.5 games, the largest margin since 1920.

The Mets weren't typical bullies, collapsing when someone stood up to them. They were tough as nails, as in the spark plug Dykstra, of the perpetually dirty uniform. They proved their resilience in a scintillating playoff against Houston, winning three games by the thinnest of margins.

All that remained was Boston. The Mets had traveled to Fenway Park on an offday in September for a charity exhibition game. No one knew what it foreshadowed when Rick Aguilera gave Boston a two-run lead (albeit in the third inning), when Bill Buckner booted a ball to set up a Mets rally (in the fourth), or when the Mets came back from two down with two outs to win thanks to a Boston error (by third baseman Ed Romero in the eighth).

The Red Sox had not won the Series since 1918, allegedly cursed after selling Babe Ruth to the Yankees. The Mets were better, but Boston was armed—Roger Clemens was that year's Gooden and Oil Can Boyd and Bruce Hurst combined for 29 wins—and they had their own dramatic comeback to beat California in the ALCS. Now Boston could end its spell in the city responsible for its most anguished memories, a city that gave many Bostonians an inferiority complex. And they'd do it against an arrogant team that symbolized New York's reputation (and success) to the nth degree.

The early going provided Met-bashers with a delightful schadenfreude. Boston won the opener, 1–0, when Jim Rice scored after Rich Gedman's grounder rolled through second baseman Tim Teufel's legs. Game 2 featured the best pitching matchup in a generation: Clemens versus Gooden. Clemens was shaky; Gooden was awful. The Mets tumbled to a 9–3 loss. The previous year, Kansas City had become the first team to win the Series after losing the first two at home. The Mets won, 7–1, as Ojeda, traded from Boston (for Calvin Schiraldi and others), became the first lefty postseason victor at Fenway Park since, yup, Babe Ruth in 1918, then riding Carter's two homers in Game 4. But Gooden faltered again in Game 5, and the Mets came home facing elimination.

Ojeda looked shaky early in Game 6, allowing one run in each of the first two innings. But in that first inning the Mets received a sign from above—literally. With Buckner coming up, unknown actor Mike Sergio earned instant fame and 21 days in jail by parachuting onto the field, displaying a banner cheering, "Go Mets." Buckner applauded, Dwight Evans grinned, and Ron Darling high-fived Sergio as he was led away through New York's dugout. In the fifth, the Mets tied it by scraping together two runs on a walk and a steal, two singles, an error, and a double play. Boston regained the lead in the seventh thanks to a throwing error by Ray Knight, although the Mets caught a break when Mookie Wilson nailed Rice at home. Going two runs down would have been disheartening so late in the game.

In the eighth, the season again almost slipped away, but Boston manager John McNamara outbungled Davey Johnson and delivered the Mets the raw material for victory. With a man on second and one out, McNamara pinch-hit for Clemens. He had thrown 135 pitches, popped a blister on his index finger, and torn a fingernail on his middle finger. Still, Clemens was baseball's best pitcher, and McNamara ditched him in search of an insurance run, despite his shaky and weary relief corp. Pinch-hitter Mike Greenwell whiffed. Then Roger McDowell loaded the bases with two walks, so Johnson called on southpaw Jesse Orosco to face lefty Bill Buckner.

The perpetually aching Buckner had endured nine cortisone shots in 1986, and strained his Achilles tendon in the playoffs. An inspiration but also a liability, he was seeking support from hideous high-top sneakers that served as a visual reminder of his decrepitude. In all seven postseason wins, McNamara had removed Buckner at game's end for defensive purposes. Dave Stapleton was ready to once again play the final six outs. Buckner wasn't contributing offensively anyway, with just a .216 OBP in the postseason. McNamara wanted to send up righty Don Baylor, who'd smashed 31 homers that year and had a .381 OBP in the postseason. (The designated hitter was not used at Shea Stadium.) Buckner, just 3-for-19 lifetime against Orosco, persuaded McNamara to let him bat. He flew out on the first pitch.

Johnson, meanwhile, had failed to make a double switch at the pitching change, so Orosco was due up first in the Mets' eighth and had to be pulled for a pinch-hitter. The Mets reached back to their ignoble past for Lee Mazzilli. The Brooklyn-born Maz had been hailed as a hunky savior in 1977, but was traded after failing to match the hype. He'd returned in 1986, to replace another old favorite, Rusty Staub, retired pinch-hitter extraordinaire.

Fortunately for the Mets, Boston also reached back to the Mets' ignoble past, for their closer, Calvin Schiraldi. The Mets once drafted Clemens out of high school, but Clemens chose instead to attend the University of Texas, where his teammate was Schiraldi. The next time around, Boston got Clemens and the Mets got Schiraldi, who had equally impressive stuff. But the Mets decided Schiraldi lacked mental toughness and dumped him to pry Ojeda loose.

Schiraldi buckled immediately, allowing a single to Mazzilli, then rushing a throw on a bunt. He loaded the bases with one out, then pumped three straight balls to Carter. Given the green light, Carter smacked a long fly, scoring Mazzilli with the tying run. The Mets threatened again in the ninth, but with two men on, Johnson inexplicably sent slugger Howard Johnson up as a pinch-hitter, then asked him to bunt. After one feeble attempt, he was allowed to swing away, but he whiffed. Mazzilli's subsequent out was the sacrifice fly that wasn't. Still, the Mets, outhit 10–5, were alive after nine innings.

On the second pitch of the 10th, Aguilera yielded a home run to ALCS hero Dave Henderson, who rubbed it in New York's collective face with an annoying hop and infuriating backward jog down the line as he watched his death blow sail on. It would get darker before it got any lighter. With two outs, Wade Boggs doubled, and Marty Barrett singled him home, making it 5–3. An extra run is often called a cushion, and this one seemed capable of suffocating the Mets, down to three last breaths.

"It is tough enough to lose, but when you make a decision that will stick in your craw, the long winter is interminable," Vin Scully intoned. He was talking about Johnson, not McNamara.

Despite Schiraldi's tentative performance and creeping fatigue, McNamara left him in. He also let Buckner return to the field so he could be there for the celebration.

Wally Backman flied out to left. Hernandez flied out to deep center. History dictated that the Mets could not revive themselves this time. The scoreboard, ready for the inevitable, inadvertently flashed, "CONGRATULATIONS BOSTON RED SOX." Clemens, showered and freshly shaved, sat in Boston's dugout, his teammates mostly on the top step or edging onto the field, ready to burst onto the scene. In Boston's clubhouse, bottles of bubbly waited, along with broadcaster Bob Costas. NBC announced Barrett as Player of the Game and Hurst as World Series MVP.

But Gary Carter had caught Schiraldi. He believed he could hit him: "I knew that he was gutless," said Carter. He lined a single.

Kevin Mitchell, who was undressed and on the clubhouse phone making plane reservations for the flight home, dashed out to pinch-hit for Aguilera. Schiraldi, his roomie in the minors, once claimed he'd get Mitchell out with a fastball in, then a slider away. Remembering that conversation, Mitchell fouled off the fastball, then hit the slider for a single. No one wanted to make that final out. In the clubhouse, the dejected and downcast souls—Hernandez, Orosco, Darling, Ojeda, McDowell—either froze, afraid to change what they were doing, or donned rally caps. They felt something now. Throughout the postseason the Mets had scored more than half their runs after the sixth inning.

Knight fell in the hole, 0–2. One more strike and Schiraldi could escape into the loving embrace of a grateful Red Sox Nation. He was so eager he forgot to waste a pitch; Knight looped a soft single, scoring Carter.

McNamara brought on veteran Bob Stanley, who had lost his closing job to Schiraldi that season but had not allowed a run in the Series. Stanley faced

Mookie Wilson. Neither scrub nor superstar, Wilson was a solid but flawed player and a fan favorite, beloved for his work ethic, team spirit (accepting Dykstra's arrival without much grumbling), and exhilarating speed. He was the longest-tenured Met and a low-key voice of sanity in this rowdy crew.

The first pitch was high and away, but Mookie's hitting philosophy was, "Thou shalt not pass at thy offering." He fouled it off. He took two pitches well out of the strike zone before fouling off another. Again, the Mets faced their final strike. Wilson hacked another foul ball. And another.

Stanley grew desperate to finish things. Knowing Stanley was working him away, Wilson crept closer to the plate. Perhaps Stanley saw that and changed his location at the last minute. The next potentially final pitch of 1986 burst inside, dusting Gedman's glove as Wilson jackknifed away. The ball rolled to the backstop, and Mitchell tore home with the tying run. Red Sox fans have debated ever since whether Stanley or Gedman deserved more blame. Mets fans don't care. They credit Wilson for keeping the at-bat going.

With the game tied at 5–5, the momentum was all New York. Wilson fouled off two more pitches. On the 10th pitch, he hit a grounder to first.

A healthy first baseman like Stapleton would have charged, but the mangled Buckner stayed back, letting the ball play him. Wilson knew he hadn't hit the ball well, but he tore down the line nonetheless. He had played every moment hard since 1981, when he hadn't hustled in the outfield on a single dumped in front of him—the Chicago Cub veteran who poked that hit was someone who never loafed, and he took advantage of Wilson's laxness to snatch the extra base, embarrassing the Mets youngster. That Cub—who inadvertently taught Wilson that speed was inextricably linked to effort—was Bill Buckner.

Wilson's grounder headed toward Buckner, who must have suspected Wilson would probably win a race to the bag unless he hurried. In a Boston television interview before the Series, Buckner said he hoped to be a hero. He didn't fret about striking out or hitting into a double play but said the nightmare would be to "let the winning run score on a ground ball through your legs."

"Gets by Buckner," longtime Mets announcer Bob Murphy shouted as Knight bounded home with the winning run. After steamrolling baseball for the entire season, the 1986 Mets had saved themselves by returning to their Mets roots, to the defining character of the 1969 and 1973 clubs, which won the games no one expected them to win, in ways no one imagined. There would be a Game 7, and a great one at that, but after this amazin' miracle, you had to believe the Mets would win it all.

The Mets Finally Vanquish Houston in the 16th, October 15, 1986, Astrodome, Houston

The famed Houston Astrodome roof blocked out the sunlight. Yet, shadows—cutting forward and backward in time—spread across one of the baseball's most thrilling baseball games, Game 6 of the 1986 NLCS.

Every pitch, every play was made with the shadow of Houston ace and Game 7 starter Mike Scott looming over it. And 10 days after the Mets won this 16-inning battle—then the longest postseason game ever—it was covered by the shadows of another extra-inning Game 6, in the World Series.

Throughout this game the Mets demonstrated the tenacity that made them great, prevailing not because of one factor, but because of many—pitching prowess, solid fundamentals, depth, resiliency, a knack for clutch hits, and a flair for capitalizing on an opponent's mistakes. Their triumph was a wild finish to a hold-your-breath, clutch-the-edge-of-your-seat-and-don't-even-leave-to-go-to-the-bathroom series, in which five games were decided by one run and three Mets wins came in their last at-bat.

Those '86 Mets were supremely talented and arrogant, crushing opponents and intimidating them in the process. With their easy ride and cocky manner, they seemed set to coast into history; on paper the weak-hitting Astros were no match. But occasionally one pitcher can dominate a series. Mike Scott was that pitcher. After May 9, the ex-Met was 15–8, with a 1.87 ERA, clinching the National League West with a no-hitter against San Francisco, fanning 55 in his last five starts.

There was already bad blood between the teams. Pitchers Bobby Ojeda, Rick Aguilera, Ron Darling, and infielder Tim Teufel had been arrested that July in Houston after a spat with off-duty cops moonlighting at a nightclub.

The Mets also publicly accused Scott of success through scuffing, not merely because of his new split-finger fastball. That controversy psyched the Mets out. In the first inning of Game 1, Carter asked umpire Doug Harvey to check a ball. Then he whiffed. Scott won, 1–0, tying a NLCS record with 14 strikeouts. On three days' rest in Game 4, he retired 20 of the first 22 batters. Scott yielded 8 hits, 1 walk, and 1 run in two complete games.

When Scott wasn't pitching, the Mets were better, but not by much: They needed Lenny Dykstra's ninth-inning two-run homer in Game 3 and Carter's 12th-inning single in Game 5 to go to Houston up 3–2. The Mets still felt their backs to the wall because of Scott. Game 6 was, for all practical purposes, a Game 7.

Houston manufactured three first-inning runs off Ojeda but lost a chance for more on a missed suicide squeeze. Lefty Bob Knepper, whose guile style contrasted starkly with that of the power-pitching Scott and Ryan, clamped down on the Mets in eight innings. The Astros bounced around their dugout chanting, "Scotty tomorrow! Scotty tomorrow!"

The ninth changed everything. Mets manager Davey Johnson sent the left-handed Dykstra to pinch-hit against Knepper. With two strikes, center fielder Billy Hatcher figured an uncomfortable Dykstra would try for contact and edged toward left field. Knepper threw an outside slider, but Dykstra turned on it, driving it into right-center for a triple. Mookie Wilson blooped a soft liner that second baseman Bill Doran misjudged. The ball skimmed his glove and landed for an RBI single. Wilson scored on Keith Hernandez's one-out double, and Knepper, who'd blown a lead in Game 3, was done.

Closer Dave Smith lacked composure. He walked Carter on a full count and complained about the call. He walked Darryl Strawberry on a full count. The bases were loaded. Smith complained about another call with Ray Knight batting, as did manager Hal Lanier and catcher Alan Ashby. When Knight—an ex-Astro—snapped at Ashby to "stop umpiring," Dickie Thon came in from shortstop to yell at Knight. Order was restored, but Smith pitched cautiously and left his next pitch over the plate. Knight drove it to right field, his sacrifice fly tying the game.

The Mets held the advantage, thanks to their stronger bullpen. Rick Aguilera had already posted three scoreless innings, and Roger McDowell stepped up with five of his own. In the 14th, Houston's depleted bullpen coughed up 38-year-old Aurelio Lopez. With two on and one out, Wally Backman singled to right. The Astros had already suffered Ashby's missed bunt, Hatcher's bad guess, Doran's mistimed leap, and Smith's lost temper; now right fielder Kevin

Bass couldn't get the ball out of his glove quickly enough and Strawberry scored from second.

When Mets co-closer Jesse Orosco struck out Doran, New York could smell victory. Then Hatcher, with only six homers for the season, swung for the fences and crushed a fastball high and deep into the left-field stands. It curved just left of the foul pole. With the count full, Orosco tried another fastball, and Hatcher hit it to virtually the same place, conjuring up enough Carlton Fisk to will the ball onto the fair side of the pole. The game was tied, 4–4. The Mets were shocked. Hatcher was shouting, "We're going to win it."

Lopez and Orosco both survived the 15th. No postseason game had ever gone 16 innings, but the Mets' knack for marathons included the longest regular-season game in time (six hours, 10 minutes, in 1985), the longest completed game in innings (25, in 1974), the longest 1–0 game (24 innings, in 1968, against Houston), and the longest doubleheader (32 innings, in 1964).

The 16th inning had enough dramatics for an entire game. Strawberry led off with a high, short fly to center. Hatcher was playing deep and couldn't reach it. Once more the Mets made the most of a small break as the hang time and Astroturf bounce allowed Strawberry to stretch it into a bloop double. Knight smacked an outside fastball down the right-field line. Bass made an ill-advised attempt to throw Strawberry out, allowing Knight to seize an extra base and an opportunity for insurance.

In came Jeff Calhoun, who pitched just 26 innings all season and none in the playoffs. Calhoun's first wild pitch advanced Knight to third. His second brought Knight home. Backman walked and scored on a Dykstra single for a seemingly insurmountable 7–4 lead.

But Orosco often unnerved fans by pitching himself into trouble. A one-out walk and singles to Doran and Hatcher made it 7–5. Unlike Houston, the Mets made the big play. Denny Walling hit a sharp bouncer in the hole, and Hernandez, the greatest defensive first baseman, robbed Walling of a hit and threw from one knee to second base for the force. Keeping the tying run out of scoring position proved crucial when Glenn Davis singled home Doran, making it 7–6.

Hernandez made another key contribution by storming the mound and threatening Orosco: "If you throw another fastball, I'll kill you," he declared. Orosco's first slider to Bass was down and in, out of the strike zone. Bass swung and missed. He took strike two. Then ball one, ball two, and—on an extremely close pitch—ball three.

The count was full. The runners were going. Mike Scott was lurking in the dugout.

Orosco threw one more slider. Down and in, way out of the zone. Bass chased it. Strike three.

Orosco threw his glove in the air as the Mets simultaneously celebrated and sighed in relief. Houston's fans applauded both teams, while back in New York the city went crazy—thousands of New Yorkers had gone to the nearest bar right after work; the result was a raucous celebration and a rush hour that arrived three hours late that day.

Soon Bill Buckner would be the Mets opponent everyone talked about, but that Game 6 might never have happened had it not been for this one. "Mike Scott haunted us," Carter said later of the playoff MVP. "We didn't want to face him the following day for all the marbles. . . . The man had a power over us even when he was spending the game on the bench."

33

Every Match Goes the Distance
on Super Saturday, September 8, 1984,
National Tennis Center

When you shell out big bucks for U.S. Open tickets, especially for the final weekend's glamour days, you hope to get your money's worth with a tense five-setter, elite rivals going at one another, or history being made. One of those is exciting, two a lifetime memory, but to go 3-for-3, well, you had to be at Louis Armstrong Stadium on September 8, 1984.

Super Saturday starred the game's greatest players, facing off in epochal rivalries: Chris Evert Lloyd versus Martina Navratilova and Jimmy Connors versus John McEnroe (the only two men who'd won the Open since it moved to Flushing Meadows in 1978); with two other matches also going the distance, the cumulative impact was indeed historic.

Evert and Connors had detonated a tennis boom in 1974, infusing an explosion of excitement about the sport; McEnroe's 1980 Wimbledon and U.S. Open matches with Connors and Bjorn Borg marked the era's apex. Super Saturday was the last, great high, 979 points across 165 games in the morning, afternoon, evening, and nighttime, a signature event representing tennis at its emotional, dramatic, and exhausting best—an only-in-New-York kind of day. "New Yorkers love it when you spill your guts out there. You spill your guts at Wimbledon, they make you stop and clean it up," Connors said beforehand.

The day started with the men's 35 semifinal between former Open champions Stan Smith and John Newcombe, a match added to maximize CBS's telecast. Smith lost the first set, 6-4, but won the second, 7-5, forcing a deciding set, which he won, 6-2. No one knew that a template had been established: Every match pushed to the limit.

Next was a riveting semifinal between Ivan Lendl and Pat Cash, in which Lendl started shedding his "choker" reputation. A taciturn 24-year-old Czech, Lendl had come from two sets down to beat McEnroe at the French Open, but New Yorkers remembered him falling apart in two previous Open finals against Connors. The second seed dropped his first service game, 10 straight points, and the first set 6–3, as the fans cheered Cash, a roguish Australian teen whose strong serve and frenetic net play had catapulted him into the Wimbledon semis. But Lendl captured the next two sets, 6–3, 6–4, by exploiting Cash's weak first volleys with his signature passing shots. Lendl held 19 straight times, but with Cash up 6–5 in the fourth, the crowd implored the brash youngster to force a fifth set.

Cash earned three break points, but the stoic Lendl refused to crumble, forcing a tiebreaker. Cash hung on to win, 7–5, to force a fifth set. Lendl opened the finale with a misstep—double-faulting on break point—but he recovered by scorching a backhand passing shot down the line to break back. Cash, down 4–5, saved one match point, but Lendl, down 6–5, did the same. With the howling fans hoping he'd unravel, Lendl steeled himself instead, lifting a magnificent running topspin lob. When he broke to force another tiebreaker, he actually emoted, pumping his fist, Connors-style. A frustrated Cash pointed at him and shouted. But Lendl was not intimidated—he pointed back, retorting, "Don't you yell at me."

In the tiebreaker, Lendl trailed, 3–2, but he played aggressively to win back the mini-break, whipped in two service winners for a 5–4 lead, and moved to match point on a running backhand passing shot. After three hours and 39 minutes, Cash misplayed his serve and volley, and Lendl finally won. *Washington Post* columnist Thomas Boswell speculated that future historians might see this match as a turning point, "when a tin man found his heart." While Lendl lost the 1984 final, he'd win the next three Opens.

With the preliminaries out of the way, two epics remained: Chrissie versus Martina and Jimbo against Junior.

Evert Lloyd and Navratilova had shared a bagel and watched the men's semi together. This was the 10th straight year at least one of the two had been in the finals in Flushing. But the results were starting to feel predetermined: Evert Lloyd, the Ice Maiden, the iron-willed baseliner who no one could crack, reigned supreme beginning in 1974, but Navratilova, once plagued by a reputation for blowing big matches, had captured nine of the previous 11 Grand Slams, including her first U.S. Open in 1983. She'd lost only once in 1983, and once in 1984. She was riding a 74-match winning streak, and her unsurpassed athleticism and quick thinking allowed her to attack the net with abandon and precision. Evert Lloyd had begun working out with weights. Yet, she'd still lost to Navratilova 12 straight times, evening their rivalry at 30 wins apiece.

With Navratilova cloaked in an aura of invincibility, this easily could have been a quickie. Another rout would have been devastating for Evert Lloyd, so she came out charging, keeping Navratilova on her heels. Swinging early, Evert Lloyd hit her crosscourt backhands with impunity, scoring numerous winners. Down a break, Evert Lloyd broke back at love with a backhand service return winner and a forehand into her opponent's body. With an ecstatic New York crowd urging her on—"I thought Chris was a blood relative of the Mets," Navratilova quipped afterward—she went up 5-4, then drove backhand and forehand winners to earn two set points. On the second, Evert Lloyd lobbed off Navratilova's approach, then crushed a crosscourt forehand and surprised everyone by racing to net, finishing the set with a forehand volley.

Her opponent's shift in tactics and a crowd openly against her might once have rattled Navratilova, but she remained calm. She adapted, gradually working her way to the net instead of simply rushing in. It was Evert Lloyd whose nerves melted. Trailing 5-4 in the second set she had two break points but turned indecisive, failing to attack Navratilova's serve. Navratilova escaped to win, 6-4.

In the third set, Navratilova broke at love, coming in four straight times off her service return. When she dug out a low forehand volley to finish the deciding set, 6-4, she ended one of the best-played matches in their long and storied history.

It was almost 7:30, and only now was it time for the main event. Despite the wait, Connors and McEnroe produced one of their finest Open battles, second to their 1980 semifinal. Connors, 32, had won two straight Opens but lost seven straight to McEnroe, six years his junior, including a thrashing at Wimbledon. It was widely (and accurately) presumed that this match would produce the tournament's champion.

Connors set the bar high on the first point with a backhand winner down the line. Both men met the challenge—McEnroe nailed 70 percent of his dangerous first serves and delivered 19 aces, yet Connors, the game's best returner, broke him seven times.

They traded 6-4 sets. In the third set, McEnroe, a net magician, switched up and rallied from the baseline. With Connors serving at deuce, 3-4 in games, the foes battled for 31 shots: Connors drove McEnroe from one corner to the other, but when he charged the net, McEnroe hoisted a deep lob, resetting the rally. Connors again took control but on his next attack netted a forehand down the line. Newcombe—now in the broadcast booth—said, "You could teach a whole lesson out of that rally." McEnroe broke for 5–3, Connors clawed back to 5–5, then McEnroe won the set 7–5, coming from behind in the last game and winning on a crosscourt backhand volley placed perfectly on the line.

In the fourth set, McEnroe tired, dumping volleys into the net, and Connors snagged a 5–2 lead. Then came the hidden turning point, according to Joel Drucker, author of the biography-memoir *Jimmy Connors Saved My Life*. McEnroe broke Connors and held, grinding down the elder statesman of tennis. Although Connors won the set, 6–4, his momentum and much of his energy evaporated.

A revitalized McEnroe leapt to a 3–0 fifth-set lead, winning 12 of 13 points. Yet, Connors never surrendered, charging to the net, where he and McEnroe batted the ball at one another with startling ferocity. Down 4–2, Connors—who would finish with 45 winners to McEnroe's 20—earned one last break point by whistling a crosscourt service return past McEnroe. But he couldn't even things up, and McEnroe clinched at love for a 6–3 final set.

After three hours, 45 minutes, this match was over; after more than 12 hours, with every food concessionaire long since sold out, Super Saturday was finally complete. "It was," said longtime *Tennis* magazine writer Peter Bodo, "the greatest single day in tennis."

34

Bernard King Buries Detroit,
April 27, 1984, Joe Louis Arena, Detroit

U p, up, and away. Bernard King lifted off and, while still on the rise, fired away, releasing the ball so quickly that no defender could stop him. Swish. And again. Swish. And again. Swish.

In his prime, King's turnaround jump shot was a thing of explosive beauty— unconventional yet unstoppable, as thrilling as Earl Monroe's hip-shattering jukes yet as reliable as Patrick Ewing inside the paint. In his glory, King's shot lifted a distinctly mediocre Knicks squad beyond its capabilities. At Detroit's Joe Louis Arena on April 27, 1984, the 6-foot-7 Brooklyn native shot New York to a win that outshines every other one between New York's 1973 championship and 1994's Eastern Conference Finals Game 7.

King's early promise with the Nets was derailed by alcoholism. After bouncing to Utah and Golden State, he straightened out his life and career. Acquired in 1982, that season King led the Knicks to their first playoff series win since 1974.

The next season, King, fueled by back-to-back 50-point games, became an All-Star, finishing fifth overall with his 26.3 scoring average. Carrying the team took its toll, however, and by the Detroit series he had dislocated both middle fingers. He could play, but with his fingers splinted, he had to catch passes with his palms and shoot with an altered motion to avoid banging and bending the damaged digits.

King managed 36 points in a Game 1 victory and then, despite a strained left knee, added 46 in a Game 2 loss, including a NBA-record 23 consecutive points for his team. He poured in 46 as New York won Game 3, and 41 in Game 4, when Detroit's young guard, Isiah Thomas, sparked the Pistons to a win. By then, King was also hampered by the flu, with a 102-degree temperature.

CHAPTER 34

A scheduling conflict bumped Game 5 from the Silverdome to downtown Detroit's old arena, a boiling building that gave the showdown between Thomas and King the feeling of a fever dream. Thomas later recalled that it felt a bit like a "summer league game where everyone is crammed into the gym," adding, "and it was a two-man shootout between me and Bernard."

King was too ill for the game-day shoot-around, and the stifling, smoky arena made it worse; by halftime he needed an IV feed to resuscitate him. Yet, nothing could stop him.

In the third quarter, King had 26 points, but his fourth foul forced him to the bench. The Knicks maintained their lead and were cruising, 106–98, with 1:57 left, when Thomas left Knick Rory Sparrow so befuddled he fouled the pumping Piston three times in 30 seconds. In a little more than 90 seconds, Thomas hit two jumpers, four foul shots, a layup with a free throw tacked on, and another jumper, and with 23 seconds left—after King's 39th and 40th points gave the Knicks a 114–111 cushion—he buried a three-point killer to tie the game.

With everything slipping away, New York headed off disaster on the last play of regulation when Darrell Walker stripped the ball from Thomas before he could score the winning basket.

Overtime, however, was King's coronation. With the game tied at 116, King slammed home a dunk off an offensive rebound, sparking a 7–0 run. When Thomas hit a three-pointer, King responded with his trademark jumper as the Knicks finally won, 127–123. King finished with 44, giving him a 42.6 average for the series on 60 percent shooting; his 213 points broke Elgin Baylor's five-game playoff record, which had stood since 1961.

King added to his legend with two 40-point games in the next round as the Knicks stretched Boston to the limit. The next year, he led the NBA with a 32.9 average before a devastating knee injury cost him almost two years. If that scoring title marked King at his apex, then this Detroit series was King still on the rise—the moment when he was most deadly.

35

St. John's Revs Up the Big East, March 12, 1983, Madison Square Garden

It had been three decades since Madison Square Garden was the center of the college basketball universe. College hoops had been huge once—Nat Holman's CCNY teams, Clair Bee's LIU squads, and Joe Lapchik's St. John's were fan favorites in the 1930s and 1940s. But after the infamous 1951 point-shaving scandal, the game largely died at the Garden, sending up only occasional flares as a sideshow between Knicks and Rangers games.

The mythology of the city game still held, but most talk was about kids who had left the city and made their name elsewhere: Lew Alcindor and Dean Meminger, Bernard King and Ernie Grunfeld, Billy Cunningham and Charlie Scott. Or they'd talk about those who didn't get out, the legends of the playgrounds, the Goat and the Destroyer and the Helicopter, wraiths whom only a privileged few in Harlem ever saw.

But in 1983, a tribal drumbeat rose out of the glorious past, a huge noise that boomed tradition yet set a cadence for a shout to the future: "We are . . . St. John's! We are . . . St. John's!"

The Big East Tournament, just four years old, was making its Madison Square Garden debut, with St. John's facing off in the final against Boston College. The old-timers were saying, "This is how college basketball used to be. This is how it oughta be." Indeed, this was how college basketball would be for the next decade—bigger than ever, thanks to a convergence of television, money, and opportunity.

Big East commissioner Dave Gavitt had successfully designed a made-for-TV league featuring popular schools in the major East Coast media markets of New York, Washington, Boston, and Philadelphia, which played in front of an estimated 30 percent of the nation's TV homes. Gavitt auditioned it Off-Broadway in Hartford, Providence, and Syracuse for three years. With such emerging stars as Patrick Ewing, Chris Mullin, and Ed Pinckney, plus coaches like John Thompson, Jim Boeheim, Lou Carnesecca, and Rollie Massimino, Gavitt's show was ready for the big town.

All year people hoped Looie Carnesecca's St. John's club could make a run. Nine of 11 kids were from the city or Long Island, making it a home team of sorts. Mullin, a Brooklynite, was the most estimable underestimated player ever. He could shoot and handle, had great body control, and, at 6-foot-6, was too long for guards and too quick for forwards. His story was a city version of Midwestern corn: gym rat begs for keys to the gym at his parish and hones his game there.

Mullin's lefty jumper buried Villanova in the semifinals, as he erupted for 25 second-half points. The final was against Boston College, which had beaten St. John's twice during the season, thanks to a tenacious press and 5-foot-9 dynamo Michael Adams. This time, St. John's backed off Adams, forcing him to shoot jumpers (he finished 1–13), and beat the press by hitting Mullin and Bronx boy Billy Goodwin with long passes for easy layups. Mullin, the tournament MVP, finished with 23 points, Goodwin with 20.

St. John's 85–77 victory gave them a school record of 27 victories. The triumph ended the tournament and marked a beginning, the return of New York hoops to the national stage and a run of Big East dominance—the tournament helped convince top talent like Alonzo Mourning, Pearl Washington, and Mark Jackson that the Big East was the place to be. Two years later, Georgetown, St. John's, and Villanova reached the Final Four together, and by decade's end Seton Hall would take a nucleus of New York natives to the NCAA final.

But there was a flip side to success. The big bucks that lifted the Big East to unimaginable heights would ultimately tear it apart as college sports became an even bigger business. But that was all in the future. On this one day, as the Big East announced itself loud and clear with this first salvo in the Garden, the Garden crowd grew louder and louder, the drumbeat ever steadier: "We are . . . St. John's! We are . . . St. John's!"

36

The Jets Win and Help the Giants, Too, December 20, 1981, Shea Stadium

There was no Super Bowl on the line on December 20, but this New York Jets win offered something equally rare in New York football in those days: excitement and hope for the future—times two.

New York football fans had just endured their darkest decade. From 1933 to 1963, the Giants reached 14 championship games, winning four. But after the Mara family refused to push out head coach Jim Lee Howell, his offensive and defensive coordinators left for head coaching opportunities elsewhere: Vince Lombardi and Tom Landry moved on to Green Bay and Dallas, respectively, coaching their teams to a combined 11 championship games and seven crowns in the next two decades. After the new Giants coach, Allie Sherman, led the team to the final three of those title games (all losses), his insecurities led to bad decisions, poorly handled, most notably the trade of linebacker Sam Huff. From 1964 to 1980, the Giants managed just two winning seasons and won 84 games, while losing 156. The team was so bad that in 1978, after "The Fumble" (when Joe Pisarcik didn't take a knee with the lead and 31 seconds left, instead botching a handoff, causing a fumble run back for a game-winning touchdown by Philadelphia), three fans rented an airplane to fly over Giants Stadium bearing a sign that read, "15 Years of Lousy Football. . . . We've Had Enough."

The Jets initially stepped into the void with their stirring 1969 Super Bowl win and a playoff appearance the next year but then collapsed like Joe Namath's deteriorating knees. The team's record from 1970 to 1980 was 57–103, and they didn't produce a single winning season.

In April 1981, both teams were coming off 4–12 seasons, landing the Giants the second draft pick and the Jets the third. The Giants snared a singular talent who transformed the game: linebacker Lawrence Taylor. The Jets fared well, too, grabbing running back Freeman McNeil. These two floundering franchises entered a rare era of mutual success. The Jets would reach the playoffs four times in the next six years, while the Giants would make it to the postseason six times in the next decade, capturing two Super Bowls.

It all started the final weekend of the 1981 regular season. The Giants were 8–7, and their playoff hopes seemed slim. First, they'd have to beat the 12–4 Cowboys, who had the second-best offense in the NFC. Even if they won, they'd only get the NFC wild-card berth if the 9–5–1 Jets beat the 8–7 Green Bay Packers—a game the Jets needed to win to clinch an AFC wild-card berth.

The Giants game on Saturday was far more dramatic, thanks to the erratic performance of the usually steady kicker Joe Danelo. The Giants defense was magnificent, holding Tony Dorsett, the league's top running back, to 39 yards on 21 carries and Dallas to just 10 points, thanks to three turnovers on its final three possessions. But on a windy day, Danelo missed field goals from 21 and 27 yards in the first quarter. After redeeming himself by tying the score with 25 seconds left on a 40-yarder, he hit the upright on a 33-yard try in overtime. (He hadn't missed all season from inside 36 yards.) Fortunately for Danelo, Taylor pressured quarterback Danny White into throwing an interception. The Giants gave Danelo one more shot, and he connected from 35 yards as the Giants escaped with a 13–10 win. Coach Ray Perkins helped carry the kicker off the field.

So, 1981 would be the first year both New York teams had a winning record. But would they both make the playoffs? The Giants came back to Giants Stadium Sunday, not to play, but to sit, helplessly, in the press lounge to watch the Jets battle the Packers at Shea Stadium. The Jets had won six of their previous seven. The Giants—and their numerous fans at Shea—roared in approval early on as the Jets blocked a punt on the first drive to set up an easy touchdown. Then Joe Klecko sacked Lynn Dickey, and Lance Mehl picked off a pass. But in an awkward bit of déjà vu, the Jets' kicker, Pat Leahy, missed a field goal from 33 yards out. He'd miss from 40 in the third quarter. Still, the Jets were dominant—they outgained the Packers 393 yards to 84 as the New York Sack Exchange threw Dickey to the grass nine times. The Jets began piling on in the second with a 20-play, 80-yard drive that lasted almost 10 minutes. And, with 42 seconds left, quarterback Richard Todd connected with Johnny "Lam" Jones for a 47-yard score to give the Jets a 21–3 halftime lead. In the only score of the second half, Todd would find Wesley Walker for a 38-yard touchdown, running the score to 28–3.

When the game ended, both teams—and all of New York's football fans—celebrated, sharing common cause for one glorious weekend.

37

John McEnroe Gets Revenge against Bjorn Borg, September 7, 1980, National Tennis Center

Revenge is a match best served hot—and sweaty and exhausted and filled with shouts and grunts, served after five sets in the unfriendly confines at the National Tennis Center, and served in the trademark style—the impossibly wide leg spread, the short backswing, and the deadly uncoiling at awkward angles—unique to the ultimate bad boy of tennis, New York's own John McEnroe.

On September 7, 1980, McEnroe attained glorious and grand (slam) revenge at Louis Armstrong Stadium in five exhilarating sets against his polar opposite and favorite dueling partner, the stoic Swede Bjorn Borg.

The two had staged the tennis equivalent of Ali–Frazier I at Wimbledon that summer, with Borg prevailing, 1-6, 7-5, 6-3, 6-7, 8-6. McEnroe had staved off seven match points in a 34-point fourth-set tiebreaker that was the zenith of this tennis heyday. Although the U.S. Open rematch is often overlooked, it was the rivals' Thrilla in Manila.

Borg, 24, was the sport's dominant force, winning three straight French Opens and Wimbledon three straight times. He had lost only once in 1980, and was reaping $3 million a year in endorsements. But he had yet to solve the U.S. Open—he lost two finals to Jimmy Connors and was upset by Roscoe Tanner under the lights in 1979. After his Wimbledon epic, Borg publicly declared himself ready to conquer New York, stating his aim of a complete Grand Slam. At Flushing Meadows, Borg overcame Tanner in five sets in the quarterfinals, then dropped two sets to Johan Kriek in the semifinals before whipping him, 6-1, 6-1, 6-1. McEnroe, the defending champion, was all that stood in his way.

McEnroe, 21, had beat up-and-comer Ivan Lendl in four sets in the quarterfinals on Thursday, gone five sets in the men's doubles final Friday, and on Saturday outlasted his other archrival, the hard-punching, menacing Jimmy Connors in the role of George Foreman. Mac had mouthed off and rope-a-doped through Connors's pounding in the middle sets to emerge the victor after four hours and 16 minutes, with a hard-fought fifth-set tiebreaker.

Lefties like McEnroe had won the previous six Opens, but Borg seemed unbeatable. The U.S. Open had hard courts, McEnroe's favorite surface and Borg's least favorite, but Borg had defeated McEnroe in four of their five previous meetings—on grass, carpet, and even hard courts twice. The New York environment—noisy fans, noisy planes, the glare of the lights—favored the hometown kid, but the crowd preferred the polite foreigner to the bratty native. (Oddly, McEnroe's fiery tenacity had won over the snooty British crowd at Wimbledon, but at the Open, where the equally voluble Jimmy Connors had become a New York hero, McEnroe remained the enemy.) This seemed both the top-ranked Borg's best shot at capturing the elusive crown and the second-ranked McEnroe's best hope at breaking Borg's hold on tennis.

The first set was suitably close, despite Borg's cautious play, atypical sloppiness (he'd finish with 95 unforced errors, almost two per game), and poor serving. Borg broke McEnroe for a 5–4 lead but then made just three of six first serves, and Mac broke back. Borg returned the favor, although he lost his focus standing around while McEnroe yelled at the linesman and umpire about a call, then lost his serve at love. In the tiebreaker, Borg got a bad break when McEnroe's apparent double fault was called in for a second-serve ace. McEnroe often used anger and frustration to rally himself (when he didn't become totally unhinged), but Borg, after a Swedish outburst (shooting a dirty look at the linesman), became dispirited, rolling over and losing the last two points as McEnroe finished him with winners at the net.

Borg's confidence was shaken. Zeroed in, McEnroe was among the most talented players ever, with quick feet and an uncanny ability to read shots. Employing a dazzling arsenal of weapons from the baseline and particularly the net, he had a magical sense of timing, touch, and restraint (although this self-discipline in shot-making often didn't extend to the emotional and mental side of the game). In the second set, McEnroe trampled a diffident Borg into submission, winning 13 straight points. Borg botched easy baseline shots and blew an overhead smash. He again seemed to be running the white flag up the pole of surrender.

In the third set, Borg recovered his equilibrium, pitting his inimitable passing shots against McEnroe's unsurpassed net game and his aggressive return against McEnroe's array of serves. McEnroe remained in fine fettle: When Borg served for the set up 5–4, McEnroe broke easily; when Borg served to stay in the match down 5–6, McEnroe dragged him through four deuces before Borg's passing shot down the line and sharply angled crosscourt backhand beat him. The tiebreaker began with Borg's backhand winner down the line. At 3–3,

John McEnroe avenges his historic Wimbledon loss to Bjorn Borg with a five-set victory of his own at the U.S. Open. *Courtesy of International Tennis Hall of Fame, Newport, Rhode Island*

McEnroe yelled at chair umpire Ken Slye, "You just made the worst call I've seen in the biggest match of all time." But it was Borg who was the real obstacle, firing five winners to pull it out, 7–5.

The fourth set was almost as close, with both players holding before Borg, switching his backhand from down the line back to crosscourt, broke McEnroe after four deuces to win, 7–5.

After three and a half hours, it was time for another fifth set. "Ice Borg" had been unsinkable, winning 13 straight five-setters since 1976. He won with talent, conditioning, and an unruffled mystique. McEnroe was more than fatigued—he was psyched out. "I started to think I was never going to beat the guy," he confessed after the match. Although there was no change of sides, McEnroe shrewdly took advantage of the crowd's lengthy ovation to walk off and sip some water. "I wanted to take a minute to get my head back together," he said.

As the heat of the day gave way to the cool of the evening, momentum shifted from the hotheaded New Yorker to the cold-blooded Swede. Even though the final set would be played under the lights, and even though McEnroe would nail 70 percent of his first serves in the final set to Borg's 49 percent, it was Borg who held easily in the first three tries, while McEnroe twice struggled past deuce. Eventually, it seemed McEnroe would give in.

But at 3–3, when McEnroe's return of Borg's serve appeared deep by an inch, Borg didn't play it, and the linesman never called it out. Love–15. The normally placid Borg angrily blurted out his disagreement and briefly lost his composure—at 15–15 he double-faulted, and at 30–30 he did it again. He passed McEnroe once on break point, but McEnroe chipped and approached again, and Borg missed. McEnroe converted this break with a crosscourt backhand Borg couldn't handle.

Down 5–3, Borg held at love, but McEnroe would not relinquish his hard-earned lead. Relentlessly attacking and slashing his way to the net, he finally finished Borg with a volley after four hours and 11 minutes, and an unimaginable 55 games. (No final since 1970 has required so many games.) "I thought my body was going to fall off," McEnroe said.

McEnroe lounged in the locker room afterward, but Borg fled as quickly as possible. He said all the right things before departing, but his flat tone betrayed his devastation. Like Frazier after Manila, Borg was never the same—in 1981, McEnroe became number one, beating Borg in four sets at both Wimbledon and the Open, chasing the Swede into early retirement. For McEnroe, this triumph did more than just avenge Wimbledon. He became the first man to win two straight U.S. Opens, marking his ascendancy to the top of the tennis world. It helped make the brat into the greatest.

38

Bob Nystrom's OT Goal Gives the Islanders Their First of Four Straight Stanley Cups, May 24, 1980, Nassau Coliseum

The New York Islanders could only stare in disbelief. Their lead, born of a lucky break here and a blown call there, was gone. When the Philadelphia Flyers tied Game 6 of the 1980 Stanley Cup Finals at 4–4 in the third period, the Islanders were suddenly in danger of frittering everything away, giving fresh ammunition to everyone who called them choke artists.

In 1978, the Islanders had the best record in their conference but dropped three of their final four games in a quarterfinal loss to the Toronto Maple Leafs. In 1979, the Islanders were the top-seeded team but were stunned in the semifinals by their local rivals, the Rangers.

This year the top-seeded Flyers faced higher expectations.

Philadelphia's 327 goals put them just one behind Montreal for league lead; the Islanders were just 12th in goals scored, although they were fourth in goals against, with goalies Chico Resch and Billy Smith among the league's best. While the Isles lacked the Flyers' offensive balance, they boasted the two biggest threats on the ice in the finals: Mike Bossy and Bryan Trottier.

The Islanders eked out a surprise overtime win in the opener in Philadelphia but were routed in Game 2. After the Islanders easily won twice at home, the Flyers beat them badly back at the Spectrum. Thus, the Islanders were desperate to win Game 6 back at the Coliseum.

Interest in the game was high enough that CBS ditched a bicycle demolition derby to put a NHL game on national TV for the first time in six years. The temperature was in the 90s outside, and the Coliseum ice was slushy. The players were hot, too, their nerves seemingly jangled from the tension—Gord Lane fought with Philadelphia's Paul Holmgren a minute into the game, and a dozen more penalties were handed out in the first period. There would be 94 minutes in penalties doled out overall.

Bob Nystrom was one of the few remaining players from the first Islander squad of 1972–1973 that had won just 12 games. He spent 10 minutes in the penalty box early on, which was frustrating, but given the heat—"the conditions were a little bit more towards beach than hockey," he'd recall later—also kept him fresh as the battle waged on.

The Islanders trailed, 1–0, when fortune smiled down—Dennis Potvin took a high swipe at an airborne puck and sent it into the goal, tying the game. The Flyers, to no avail, claimed his stick was illegally above shoulder level. They should have saved their howls for the next noncall, one of the worst in NHL history.

Clark Gillies was skating down the left boards when he crossed the Flyers' blue line and dumped a pass to Butch Goring, the center who was trailing him. Despite Goring's effort, the puck clearly passed back across the blue line and into the center-ice zone—a definitive offsides penalty. Linesman Leon Stickle swallowed his whistle, and Goring quickly sent the puck off to right wing Duane Sutter, who fired it home for a 2–1 Islander lead. The Flyers went nuts, justifiably, but the goal counted. (Stickle later admitted he blew it.) Still, it barely even shifted the momentum since Philadelphia tied the score less than five minutes later.

The Islanders seized control of the game in the second period, with Trottier's puck work setting up Bossy on a power play. Nystrom, on a perfect pass from John Tonelli, added a goal for a 4–2 lead just 14 seconds before the period ended.

In two periods, Smith had defended 12 shots. Yet, the Isles played the third as if their choker label was deserved. Their aggressiveness was gone, and the team stumbled around on defense as if they were new to skating. The Flyers tied it with two quick goals, and Smith later admitted he felt a panic rising in him. The Islanders escaped the third period with a tie.

Overtime almost ended quickly and badly when Smith failed to react to Bobby Clarke's shot heading to the top of the net—only to have it soar harmlessly just over the crossbar. Then Flyer Ken Linseman seemingly had a clean look at the goal, but defenseman Bob Lorimer used his body to stop the shot.

Finally, after almost seven unsettling minutes, Coach Al Arbour sent in his third line: Nystrom, Tonelli, and another original Islander, Lorne Henning, who was only on the playoff roster because of an injury to Anders Kallur. Nystrom had not only scored in the second period, but also landed the winning goal in three overtime playoff games before this series

Henning got the puck on the Isles' side, between the blue and red lines. He sent it Tonelli, cutting from the left toward the middle; Tonelli took it past the Philadelphia blue line and right at Moose Dupont before firing a pass to Nystrom, on his left, out ahead of defenseman Bob Dailey. Nystrom, who rarely backhanded shots because his blade was bent to enhance his slap shots, took the puck on the back of the blade and flipped it in the air, past Pete Peeters and into the history books, as the New York Islanders became NHL champions.

Queen's "We Are the Champions" blared in the Coliseum. With their destiny finally achieved, the Islanders could finally move on to becoming a dynasty.

39

The Rangers Beat the Islanders to Reach the Stanley Cup Finals, May 8, 1979, Madison Square Garden

The New York Rangers' triumph over the New York Islanders on May 8, 1979, did not yield a Stanley Cup, but it provided the next best thing, giving long-suffering Garden rooters an upset of epic proportions against the one team the Rangers most wanted to beat.

To truly appreciate the victory, steep yourself in the sorrows of Rangerdom, which stretched back decades. After winning the 1940 Stanley Cup, the Rangers failed to reach the postseason for five straight years in the 1940s and again in the 1950s. Starting in 1958–1959, the Rangers went eight straight years under .500. When they later reached the playoffs, they fared terribly. Finally, in 1972, they reached the finals for the first time in 22 years. The future finally seemed bright, despite the loss to the Boston Bruins. Then the Rangers began backsliding while an expansion team—a suburban club that encroached on their fan base amid 1970s "white flight" —surpassed them with surprising ease. In 1972–1973, the fledgling New York Islanders managed just 12 victories. A mere two years later, the Rangers were shocked by these upstarts in the playoffs. In the next three seasons, while the Islanders challenged the Philadelphia Flyers and eventually gained supremacy atop the division, the Rangers languished in the cellar.

The 1978–1979 Rangers improved to 40 wins. At age 37, the legendary Phil Esposito scored 42 goals and provided glamor and leadership. Newcomers Anders Hedberg and Ulf Nilsson added speed and skills, while John Davidson was the rock in goal. Still, even after rolling through two playoff rounds, they seemed no match for the 51-win Islanders, a team expected to win its first Cup.

Hockey rarely captures headlines in New York, in part because of the Rangers' perennial struggles and in part because it can't compete with baseball, football, and baseball. But in May 1979, the Rangers–Islanders showdown was *the* story in town. Scalpers reaped $250 for $22 tickets and, with limited TV coverage, thousands paid to watch on closed circuit at the Felt Forum and Roosevelt Raceway.

The teams' personas matched their geography—many Rangers were single and enjoyed Manhattan's nightlife, while more Islanders were married and settled down. The rivalry became venomous near season's end when a rough— Ranger fans still think dirty—check by Islander Dennis Potvin broke Nilsson's ankle. The play would echo throughout the years at the Garden with thousands of "Potvin sucks" jeers (sometimes even at Knicks games).

In the conference finals, the Rangers hounded Potvin, an All-Star defenseman, but more for tactical reasons than revenge, using hard forechecking to cramp his style. The Rangers showed surprising toughness as well against the front line of Brian Trottier, Mike Bossy, and Clark Gillies. The Rangers played disciplined but loose, while the Islanders seemed tight, fretting about falling to a lesser squad. The media's constant pronouncements on the subject exacerbated the difference, which Islander goalie Chico Resch dubbed "Newton's Law of Tightivity."

Up three games to two, the Rangers wanted to win at home in Game 6 instead of playing Game 7 in enemy territory. The Islanders snatched an early lead on a power play when righty Mike Bossy shot lefty and flipped in a rebound. It was the first score from the Islanders' famed triumvirate since the first goal of Game 1. Was this a signal that the dike was about to burst? The Islanders played their best hockey of the series in the opening period, but they could not score again as Walt Tkaczuk and company again throttled the Trio Grande. At 5:03 of the second period, Ranger Mario Marois bounced a shot off Resch's pads and into Don Murdoch's skates, almost tripping him. Murdoch recovered, spun, and wristed the puck into the net. The Rangers were back on an even rink. Less than four minutes later, the Rangers converted on a power play of their own—Esposito blocked Resch's view while Don Maloney fed Ron Greschner near the blue line, and he banged home a slap shot for the go-ahead goal. (The goal was originally credited to Esposito because the ref thought he tipped it in, but Esposito insisted to the official scorers that Greschner get the score.)

The momentum had turned, and the Rangers never let the Islanders recover, swarming the puck at every opportunity—they allowed only three shots in the final 20 minutes, and Davidson, who had been stellar throughout, turned away each. The clock wound down, and the raucous fans screamed and cheered, counted down and threw confetti, and celebrated like there was no tomorrow.

CHAPTER 39

There was a tomorrow, of course, and it wasn't as wonderful: Davidson struggled with an injured knee and Coach Fred Shero failed to rein in his bachelors partying in Montreal. The Rangers lost to the Canadiens in the Stanley Cup Finals. Subsequently, the Rangers mounted their longest sustained run of quality hockey, winning five playoff series, but the Islanders handily trumped them, beating the Rangers in the playoffs four straight years and winning four straight Stanley Cups. But on May 8, 1979, the Rangers finally had a win no one could ever take away.

40

Bucky Dent Tops the Green Monster, October 2, 1978, Fenway Park, Boston

Mike Torrez checked the runners. He rocked and delivered. Bucky Dent swung and shattered his bat as Rick Burleson gathered the infield pop for the third out, ending New York's threat. The Boston Red Sox held on to win this special tiebreaker and the 1978 American League East.

It didn't happen that way, but if not for the vigilance of Mickey Rivers, that alternative history might have become a reality.

On October 2, 1978, with two out and two on in the seventh inning, Rivers noticed his teammate swinging a cracked bat and gave him fresh lumber. On the next pitch, Dent broke his 0–13 streak, earned a new "bleeping" nickname, and made history with his game-changing three-run homer. Perhaps the most astonishing thing about this regular-season tiebreaker is the way Dent's homer has grown in baseball lore until it has obscured the remaining nine innings. Dent's shot over the Green Monster in Fenway Park's left field transformed a 2–0 deficit into a 3–2 lead, but in the 163rd game of the season, these archrivals would wrestle one another down to the final out in the bottom of the ninth.

In the spring, it had seemed the only tension in the American League East in 1978, would be the arguments spilling out of the fractured Yankees clubhouse. While Boston started 47–26, the Yankees battled injuries and one another. Only Ron Guidry's 13 straight wins kept Boston within sight. On July 17, the Yankees were in fourth, 14 games behind Boston, when another conflagration between Reggie Jackson, manager Billy Martin, and George Steinbrenner finally cost Martin his job. Replacement Bob Lemon dispelled Martin's contentious clubhouse atmosphere and showed the players he trusted them. As injured players like Rivers and Catfish Hunter returned, the Yankees started winning,

Bucky Dent becomes the most unlikely of heroes, puncturing Boston's hopes with a timely three-run homer in the 1978 tiebreaker. *ASSOCIATED PRESS*

while a local newspaper strike helped Lemon keep the focus on baseball. In Boston, manager Don Zimmer pushed his club too hard, and some, like Torrez, began playing tight under pressure.

The Yankees were within four upon arriving in Boston on September 7. They left tied for first, having pounded the scared and slumping Sox into submission, 15–3, 13–2, 7–0, and 7–4. A week later and two more wins against Boston gave the Yankees a three-and-a-half-game lead. The Red Sox recovered, winning 12 of their last 14, leading to just the second tiebreaker playoff in American League history. (In 1948, Cleveland, with 20-game winner Bob Lemon on its staff, had beaten Boston.)

Zimmer had used Dennis Eckersley and Luis Tiant to reach the playoff, so he turned to Torrez, who won two games for the Yankees in the 1977 World Series, then signed with Boston. He'd won 16 games but dropped six straight late, and his ERA was the worst among Red Sox starters. The Yankees countered with Guidry, 24–3. They were so confident they sent their bags on to Kansas City for the ALCS.

Guidry, who'd made two straight starts on three days' rest, did not have his Zeus-like lightning bolts, but he got by on his slider and his determination, allowing a homer by Carl Yastrzemski in the second but just one other hit through five innings. Torrez was even better, however, holding New York scoreless.

Before the sixth inning, Lou Piniella checked with catcher Thurman Munson, who confirmed that Guidry's pitches lacked zip, meaning good hitters would pull him. Rick Burleson proved this by doubling into the left-field corner. He scored one out later on Jim Rice's single. The southpaw Guidry walked Carlton Fisk to face lefty Fred Lynn, who worked the count full, then ripped a shot into the right-field corner. On any other day or against any other outfielder, he'd have had a two-run double for a 4–0 Boston lead. But Piniella had shifted 50 feet toward the line, easily corralled the ball, and snuffed the rally.

The squandering commenced immediately. Torrez gave up two one-out singles, and Lemon sent up pinch-hitter Jim Spencer for second baseman Brian Doyle, playing for the injured Willie Randolph. Had Randolph been healthy, Lemon would have saved Spencer to bat for the number-nine hitter, Bucky Dent.

After Spencer flied out, Dent fouled the second pitch hard off his foot. He hobbled away, and trainer Gene Monahan numbed the foot with ethyl chloride. During this interlude, Rivers brought in the new bat—during batting practice, he'd noticed that the Roy White model both he and Dent used was chipped, so he asked clubhouse man Nick Priori for a duplicate and taped up the handle. Now, noticing that Dent was still using the cracked bat, Rivers switched him to the healthy lumber; Torrez, meanwhile, failed to request any warm-up pitches after the lengthy delay, which disrupted his rhythm.

Torrez's 0–2 pitch, meant as a waste pitch inside, sat out over the plate. Dent lifted a fly to left. In any other ballpark, it would have been the third out—Fisk, Torrez, and Zimmer thought that was the case in Boston, too. But the 37-foot-high Green Monster sat just 315 feet away. Dent and Yastrzemski, the left fielder, thought the ball would carom off the wall, scoring a run. But the wind was blowing out, and to everyone's astonishment, the ball carried beyond the wall. Ernie Harwell's call expressed it perfectly: "It's a fly ball to left field. Oh, it's a home run."

It would only get worse for Boston. Torrez walked Rivers, prompting Zimmer to call on Bob Stanley to face Munson. After Rivers stole second, Munson doubled him home for a 4–2 lead. In the seventh, Jackson blasted a homer to center to make it 5–2.

Smacked down again, the Red Sox got up once more. Goose Gossage yielded four hits, and the Sox pulled within one. Ninth inning. Last chance. Burleson walked. Jerry Remy poked a ball to right. By this point, the sun was so blinding that even though Piniella knew where the ball was heading, he couldn't see it. Thinking fast, he decided to look like he was about to catch it. Burleson was watching Piniella instead of the third-base coach waving him on and froze between first and second.

By the time Burleson realized Piniella was fortunate just to catch the ball on the bounce, he had to stop at second so he could not score the tying run on Rice's out to deep right on the next play. Two out. The tying run was at third, with the winning run at first. Gossage, a power pitcher, was going up against Yastrzemski, a fastball hitter with two hits already. Gossage threw his fastest pitch of the season. Yaz swung late—way late—and lifted a harmless foul pop. The Yankees had finally prevailed, with the tying run just 90 feet away. Not much margin for error, but in the case of New York and Boston, it was, as always, just enough.

Affirmed Edges Alydar for the Third Straight Time to Win the Triple Crown, June 10, 1978, Belmont Park

"Alydar's got a lead! Alydar put a head in front right in the middle of the stretch," announcer Chic Anderson shouted as the great horse finally passed his archrival, Affirmed, in the last leg of the Triple Crown. Alydar stayed strong, running that final half-mile of the Belmont Stakes faster than any horse had ever run before. Unfortunately, that speed was matched step for step—and then some—by Affirmed. Alydar's push was enough to ensure he'd become a racing legend, but it wasn't enough to win. Alydar was a superb horse, but Affirmed was superior, not by much but by just enough to win the Triple Crown and affirm his status as one of the all-time greats.

The horses' history together actually began before they were born. Both chestnuts were conceived in Kentucky, in the same breeding shed. Alydar was sired by Raise a Native, a descendant of the great Native Dancer, while Affirmed was sired by Exclusive Native, a son of Raise a Native, so Affirmed was essentially Aldyar's half-nephew.

Affirmed's first race was a win at Belmont Park in May 1977; the next month, Alydar was the favorite in his debut, at Belmont's Youthful Stakes. But Affirmed won that day, too. Alydar evened their head-to-head record at Belmont Park in early July, but Affirmed soon pulled ahead, definitively, winning in Saratoga with teen jockey Steve Cauthen riding him for the first time and by a nose at Belmont in September. Jorge Velasquez rode Alydar for the first time at Belmont in October, besting Cauthen and Affirmed. In their final race that year, Affirmed held off Alydar by a neck to become the 2-year-old champion.

Yet, Alydar still was the favorite at the 1978 Kentucky Derby. Their pattern was predictable: Affirmed would start strong and then stave off a late run by the hard-charging Alydar out in the open. But Aldyar's miserable start at the Derby left him so far behind that his strong finish fell short. At the Preakness, Alydar hung closer and crept right up to the front-runner, but Cauthen calmly prodded Affirmed to victory by a neck.

All that remained was the Belmont Stakes. There had been seven Triple Crown winners from 1930 to 1948, then none until Secretariat in 1973. Seattle Slew did it in 1977, and, suddenly, there was a chance for the first ever back-to-back winners. But while it seemed everyone rooted for clear champs like Secretariat and Seattle Slew, Affirmed and Alydar, inseparable on the track, split the fans. Cauthen likened it to the Ali–Frazier battles of the 1970s, although he likened Affirmed to a street fighter. "He was like that guy in a bar looking for a fight," Cauthen once said. "He loved to fight horses off."

That mentality shows up in the statistics: Affirmed had nine races when less than a length separated him from another horse. He won every one. Alydar, by contrast, had seven such races and lost all seven, usually to Affirmed.

Still, Alydar was the only horse to have beaten Affirmed, and he had done it twice on Belmont's turf, with the long, sweeping turns that let him stretch out his stride. And this 1½-mile "Test of the Champion" would be the longest race either had run, which favored the stronger Alydar, allowing him more time to come from behind and wear down Affirmed.

With only three other, lesser horses at the gate, this shaped up as a match race. Some critics felt Velasquez was too patient, saying Alydar needed an attacking jockey instead. Trainer James Veitch was indeed desperate to change the game plan, but rather than switch riders, he raced Alydar without blinkers, hoping the horse would see his rival, feel the urgency, and "use his speed to get closer to Affirmed early."

Affirmed's trainer, Laz Barrera, had his horse take it easy so he'd feel relaxed on the big day. Cauthen was nervous himself but confident in his horse and their game plan—force Alydar inside where he wasn't comfortable and keep the pace slow early, since Alydar did not like leading the pack.

Affirmed grabbed his early lead, then slowed the pace, conserving energy. "I was daring Velasquez to go by," Cauthen later wrote. "He and Alydar wanted no part of that, so a cat-and-mouse game ensued as we crawled along."

The first half-mile took 50 long seconds; only three Belmont States had a slower start. Veitch had promised that if the pace was slow, his horse would jump to the front, but with Alydar stuck on the inside until the first turn, Velasquez was again perhaps too cautious. When Affirmed grabbed the rail, Alydar, in third behind Judge Advocate, lost time slipping to the outside.

Then Velasquez ramped up the speed. The crowd's roars told Cauthen the challenger was coming. This was the moment. They were side by side, the other horses all but forgotten. The trainers for Darby Creek Road and Judge Advocate both admitted afterward that they were watching the dynamic duo, not their own charges.

Affirmed was feeling fatigue when Alydar inched ahead, sending the delirious crowd into a frenzy. With no room to whip his horse, Cauthen tried something he'd never done to Affirmed before, switching his stick to his left hand and hitting Affirmed on his left side. Jolted, the horse caught Alydar, then eked back ahead. Alydar evened things up, but with perhaps 100 yards to go, Affirmed showed that even at the longer distance he was still unbeatable, getting his nose in front by the finish line.

The slow start was offset by the flying finish—the final time was 2:26 4/5, the third-fastest ever. Alydar had the fastest second-place finish, while becoming the first horse to finish second in all three Triple Crown races. Affirmed's combined margin of victory—a little less than two lengths—was by far the smallest ever for a Triple Crown winner.

Did people remember who finished second to Secretariat or Seattle Slew a year later or even a day later? Four decades later, it is impossible to hear Affirmed's name without instantly thinking of Alydar. After the Belmont Stakes, Affirmed's owner, Lou Wolfson, sent a letter to Calumet Farm thanking them for Alydar, acknowledging that the rivalry had elevated both horses to a level neither could have attained without the other.

42

Reggie, Reggie, Reggie,
October 18, 1977, Yankee Stadium

One swing. One homer.

In 1977 the New York Yankees had not won a World Series in 14 years, more than four times longer than any stretch since Babe Ruth arrived.

A second swing. A second homer.

The missing ingredient: a superstar slugger so dynamic he could be a household name, no surname necessary. A ballplayer, one might say, who was famous enough to have a candy bar named after him.

A third swing. A third homer.

The Yankees had won with the Babe, Joltin' Joe, and the Mick. Finally, in the 1977 World Series, a new king of the hill brought New York to the top of the heap.

Reggie! Reggie! Reggie!

Reginald Martinez Jackson became a superstar in 1969, by clouting 47 homers for Oakland. He was perhaps the most colorful and talented of that rambunctious A's crew, which won three straight World Series beginning in 1972. He won the 1973 MVP, landed on the cover of *Time* in 1974, and led the league in homers in 1975. Impending free agency prompted owner Charlie Finley to trade Jackson to Baltimore in 1976.

Then the man who once said, "If I played in New York, they'd name a candy bar after me," passed up more lucrative offers to bask in the spotlight of the nation's media capital, where George Steinbrenner had become the Yankees' unlikely savior, resurrecting the franchise and revolutionizing the game with his headfirst slide into free agency. The Yankees had reached the World Series in 1976, but they were swept by the powerful Cincinnati Reds, so Steinbrenner imported the big bat and defining presence he thought the Bombers needed, even though his manager, Billy Martin, a tactical genius but an alcoholic with no people skills, vehemently objected.

Jackson wasted no time in shining the light on himself. "I didn't come to New York to become a star," he said. "I brought my star with me."

Martin purposely antagonized Jackson, refusing to bat him cleanup, even though that hurt the club. Jackson's jealous teammates alienated him. Fans and the media poured on more pressure. Some of this was racism—baseball's old school (including Martin and much of the press) still couldn't handle a commanding, outspoken black man. Martin was a hero among the blue-collar New Yorkers in full "white flight" for the 'burbs in 1977. But Jackson, with his massive ego and a mouth to match, deserved his share of blame. In June, *Sport* magazine quoted Jackson calling himself "the straw that stirs the drink," while badmouthing catcher and captain Thurman Munson.

The Yankees' "Bronx Zoo" dysfunction matched a spiraling city in fiscal disarray and anxious about Son of Sam, a blackout, and looting. The South Bronx may have been consumed by fire, but the Yankees' most notorious conflagration took place in Fenway Park, when Martin yanked Jackson from the outfield in the middle of an inning for failing to hustle, inciting a heated, in-your-face shouting match that NBC's cameras showed to a nationwide audience. At a reconciliation meeting, Martin called Jackson "boy," igniting new flames.

Finally, in August, Steinbrenner told Martin he'd be fired if he didn't bat Jackson cleanup. Jackson began hitting, and the Yankees began winning. In the ALCS, Jackson went 1-for-14 in the first four games against Kansas City, and Martin benched him for the deciding Game 5. Jackson responded with a crucial eighth-inning pinch-hit single. In Game 1 of the World Series, Martin pulled him for defensive purposes, and his replacement, Paul Blair, singled home the winning run in the 12th inning. By the time the Yankees lost Game 2, Jackson was just 3-for-22 in the postseason.

Away from New York, Jackson found his stroke, with a hit in Game 3, a double and a homer in Game 4, and a homer in his final at-bat of a Game 5 loss. With the Yankees up 3–2, the Series returned to New York. Before Game 6, Joe DiMaggio—there to throw out the first ball—made a point of visiting Jackson at his locker and heaping compliments on him. Inspired, Jackson put on a Ruthian batting practice display that had players stopping to stare. Dodgers starter Burt Hooten, who had whiffed Jackson twice in Game 2, was among those witnesses and walked Jackson on four pitches in his first at-bat. But when first baseman Chris Chambliss homered, scoring Jackson, the Dodgers were forced to throw Jackson strikes the rest of the night.

CHAPTER 42

In the fourth, with the Dodgers hugging a 3–2 lead and Munson on base, Jackson suspected that Hooten would try tying him up inside, so he surreptitiously backed off the plate six inches. The first pitch did come in, and Jackson smacked it right out, a low hummer into the first row of the bleachers. The next inning, Jackson faced hard-throwing Elias Sosa with a man on base. Having phoned scout Gene Michael for a quick report, Jackson guessed fastball. Sosa threw it, and Jackson again clouted one into the bleachers. Afterward, Jackson looked into the television camera and gleefully held out two fingers and mouthed the word "two."

In the eighth, with New York winning, 7–3, Jackson got a rousing ovation from the Yankee Stadium crowd. No one had ever hit five homers in a six-game Series, and at that point only the immortal Babe Ruth had homered three times in one Series game. Jackson had one shot at history. It was all he'd need.

Charlie Hough tried his signature pitch, a knuckleball. Dancing to the plate, it was a stark contrast to the fastballs Jackson had walloped. Yet, he calmly waited before turning on the ball so hard and quick that even his jaded teammates were impressed. On his first two homers, the trajectory was so low that Jackson ran hard to first. This time, Jackson stood and watched his final masterpiece climb into the night sky before coming to rest some 475 feet away in dead center. As Jackson trotted around the bases blowing kisses, the chants of "Reg-gie" were deafening, and Los Angeles first baseman Steve Garvey silently applauded in his glove.

Jackson won the game and the Series for New York, and with his unprecedented display, he won over the city. In the ninth, fans chanted his name and showered him with confetti. (Afraid they might throw heavier artillery—this was the bleachers, after all—he ran in for a batting helmet.)

Jackson built his Mr. October persona off this, embracing his image so wholeheartedly it distorted the historical lens. Jackson had been inconsistent in Oakland's postseasons: He'd been a career .271 postseason hitter, with five homers and 15 RBI in 118 at-bats. After his dismal 3-for-22 start in 1977, it's easy to imagine Steinbrenner calling Jackson "Mr. May." In fact, "Mr. October" was first bestowed upon him by Munson during the ALCS with a heavy dose of sarcasm.

Jackson cemented his reputation by smashing a crucial home run in the famous one-game tiebreaker at Fenway Park, batting .462 in the 1978 ALCS and .391 in the rematch against Los Angeles, totaling four homers and 14 RBI in the postseason. Still, subsequent Octobers were lackluster, with Jackson hitting just .200 in 45 at-bats, with two homers and four RBI. Others equally deserve the title Mr. October, including, ironically, Billy Martin, who batted almost 80 points above his lifetime average in the postseason and banged 12 hits in the 1953 Series. But few wore the mantle of greatness more comfortably than Jackson. Of all his exploits, this historic slugging display remains the centerpiece, when he brought the championship back to the Bronx and slammed three exclamation points on his debut season in pinstripes.

43

The Marathon Expands to All Five Boroughs, and Bill Rodgers Wins It, October 24, 1976, Central Park

S tand on Fourth Avenue in Brooklyn or First Avenue in Manhattan on the first Sunday in November and you'll witness a miracle: Instead of rushing around, New Yorkers stop to cheer, support, and celebrate others as they stream by. Some runners are certainly New Yorkers, but many come from elsewhere in the United States and 100 other nations; some don serious running gear, others goofy wigs or costumes; most jog or run, but others keep on trucking even after they're reduced to a walk, while some zoom past in wheelchairs.

The New York City Marathon is most definitely a sporting event, but more than any other endeavor on this list, the emphasis is on "event." It attracts more than 2 million spectators, the most of any live sporting event anywhere, but most don't know, or care, who will win. With bands playing and spectators urging on those brave or foolhardy marathoners, it is, *New York* magazine once declared, a pageant that "exalts not only those who participate, but those who observe."

The Marathon is a glorious municipal holiday, a tribute to the city and its people, touching every borough and providing Gothamites with a unifying reminder of how special life can be in this often-challenging metropolis. And it's free. Fittingly for New York, this festival of a race was cooked up by a Jewish immigrant from Transylvania working in the garment industry and a black transplant from Texas working in politics.

Fishl Lebowitz was forced into labor camps in Romania during World War II, then fled when communism proved almost as threatening as fascism. On his way to becoming Fred Lebow, Lebowitz bounced around Europe and the United States, working as everything from a television salesman to a comedy club owner before settling in New York. Lebow eventually owned clothing companies that designed knockoffs. His only exercise was tennis, but he wasn't very good. To improve his fitness and thus his game, Lebow decided to race his tennis partner around the Central Park Reservoir. Lebow won easily. He dropped tennis and joined the New York City Road Runners Club. In 1970, he ran its annual Cherry Tree Marathon in the Bronx. Navigating through streets open to traffic, Lebow was struck by how uninviting and poorly organized the race was. He and fellow runner Vince Chiappetta launched the New York City Marathon later that year.

The race looped around and around Central Park. Lebow drummed up some press and spent $1,000 on soda and prizes, but the race drew just 127 runners, making little dent in the city's psyche—most people in the park didn't even realize a marathon was underway. Within three years, Lebow was club president and had attracted more than 400 entrants, plus a few sponsors. But growth stalled, and it remained a small-time race for diehards considered eccentrics by outsiders.

Then one marathoner, Ted Corbitt, decided that New York could celebrate America's bicentennial by having teams from each borough. A fellow runner, George Spitz, misunderstood this idea, thinking Corbitt was suggesting a marathon traversing all five boroughs. He took this to Lebow, who flatly rejected it. Lebow longed to create a "people's race," and he'd eventually morph into the P. T. Barnum of running, but he believed the concept logistically impossible.

Undeterred, Spitz asked Manhattan borough president Percy Sutton for help. Sutton, a former Tuskegee airman and lawyer for Malcolm X, had greatly enjoyed himself shooting the starter's gun at the 1975 race. Now he was contemplating a 1977 mayoral run, and in that era of fiscal calamities and white flight, he loved this bold way to embrace the city and its ethnic groups. When Lebow named the issues—street closings, police for crowd control, sanitation workers to clean up, and so on—Sutton simply asked how much it would cost. Lebow said $20,000, a number he thought would kill the notion.

Sutton didn't flinch. He persuaded Mayor Abe Beame to give him authority to coordinate the involvement of city agencies, thus eliminating most obstacles—the highway department even painted blue lines through the streets so runners wouldn't get lost. Sutton persuaded real estate developers Lewis and Jack Rudin to donate $25,000, and turned his own office space and staff over to Lebow to help.

Now Lebow embraced his task, learning quickly and on the fly. No reporters showed for his first press conference in 1976, so he persuaded 1972 Olympic gold medalist Frank Shorter to sign up and flew him in for another press conference, at which Beame fired a starter's gun and Shorter briefly ran "against" four borough presidents. That got photos in the paper. Lebow then paid $2,000 out of his own pocket and under the table to land another big name: Bill Rodgers, winner of the prestigious Boston Marathon. He ran premarathon parties and a Club 21 luncheon, while frantically arranging volunteers in the outer boroughs to provide water to the marathoners.

On October 24, 1976, at 10:30 a.m., it was readily apparent that this was not the same old race, but rather an event of, by, and for the people. There were 2,090 runners, ages 10 to 71, from 35 states and 12 other nations. Fifty-eight women ran (a record for any marathon). Dick Traum, who had lost a leg and wore a prosthetic, started early and finished in seven hours and 24 minutes; his inspiring story even inspired himself—he later started the Achilles Track Club for disabled runners.

Soon after Sutton fired the starter's gun, Finnish Olympian Pekka Paivarinta grabbed a lead, while Shorter and Rodgers hung back. They passed through Brooklyn and entered Queens, where Rodgers—wearing borrowed soccer shorts because he forgot to pack his own—took the lead. He never relinquished it.

Rodgers led virtually unchallenged the rest of the way, finishing in 2:10:10— the fastest time in the world that year—while Miki Gorman won the women's side in 2:39:11. They received Tiffany sterling silver trays, courtesy of the Rudins. Most noteworthy was the street turnout—about 500,000 spectators came to watch and party. Rodgers recalled that he "fed off their energy," but it wasn't just the front-runners who were saluted. (Lebow even made the one sour note sweet: Rodgers had unwittingly parked his car illegally, and it was towed during the race. Lebow paid the fine.)

One runner, Melvin Marks, noted in a letter to the *New York Times* that supposedly jaded New Yorkers bubbled with enthusiasm and appreciation. "Children everywhere called out just to touch my hand," he wrote. "Pretty girls smiled at me, and men as old or older than I urged me forward as if they were in this race too." After the supposed onetime success of 1976, there was no turning back—and not only for New York, but also for marathons that followed in London, Chicago, Paris, and Berlin. Organizers picked up on the populist attitude and stopped closing courses after four hours. (There are now online lists of runners who did not officially finish but reached the end as many as nine hours after starting.)

The New York City Marathon is now a week of parties followed by a race that's part folk festival, part street fair. It attracts more than 50,000 runners (also featuring competitive wheelchair and handcycle divisions), 12,000 volunteers, 2 million spectators, dozens of bands, prize money, title sponsors, television coverage, special newspaper sections, and millions of dollars flowing into the local economy. It was a long road from a concept pulled out of the rejection pile to serve as a singular bicentennial special, but the stunning success of 1976 prompted Lebow to push, prod, and promote the marathon into what Rodgers has called "maybe the most spectacular race in the world."

44

Chris Chambliss Homers the Yankees Back into the World Series, October 14, 1976, Yankee Stadium

Chris Chambliss was not alone. The bases were full as he made his triumphant circuit—not with fellow Yankees, since Chambliss had led off the
bottom of the ninth inning, but with Yankees fans. This was no metaphorical
"with him in spirit" kind of thing. This crowd was too spirited for that—if you
take "crowd" to mean mob and "spirited" to mean exuberantly rambunctious
in a frightening, 1970s, city-on-the-brink-of-chaos way.

For the first generation of Yankees fans in memory to grow up with a second-
rate club, this moment was too stimulating to be witnessed passively from their
seats. The fans wanted in on this celebration. So they joined Chambliss on the
basepaths—well, if you take "joined" to mean stampeded him and his teammates, making his journey as memorable as the game-winning, playoff-clinching
home run itself.

It made sense that the highlight of 1976 would be a home run and that it
would be tumultuous. The homer was fitting, since the Yankees had returned
that year to a renovated "House That Ruth Built" after a dismal two-year exile
to Shea Stadium. And turmoil—from feuds with the players' union and commissioner to on-field brawls—was a Bronx staple, since 1976 marked Billy Martin's
first full season as manager and George Steinbrenner's return after a suspension caused by felonious contributions to Richard Nixon's 1972 presidential
campaign. This stormy 97-win team was a perfect fit for a city barely holding it
together amid financial ruin, demographic shifts, and societal upheaval.

After 12 dismal years in the wilderness, most actually near the bottom of the
American League, a mere divisional title would not suffice. The Yankees need
to reach the World Series for the first time since 1964.

New York and Kansas City split the first four games in the best-of-five ALCS. The stakes were high enough for Game 5 that Baltimore-Oriole-turned-free-agent Reggie Jackson, moonlighting as a television color commentator, declared, "Everything is magnified tonight. You hit a home run, it'll be, for sure, heard 'round the country."

The Royals' John Mayberry struck a two-run shot in the opening inning off Ed Figueroa, but the Yankees struck back immediately, with hits by Mickey Rivers, Roy White, and Thurman Munson, and a sacrifice fly by Chambliss. Those top four hitters would produce all 11 of the team's hits, plus two walks and two steals. The Royals snuck ahead, 3–2, in the second, but in the fourth the fab four produced another two-run rally for a 4–3 lead as Chambliss added his second RBI on a groundout. In the sixth, the fearsome foursome sacked the Royals staff again. Rivers bunted for a hit, advanced on White's sacrifice, and scored on Munson's single. Munson was thrown out trying to stretch his hit, but Chambliss singled and even swiped second (just his second steal of the year), allowing him to score on an error.

Up 6–3 in the eighth, Martin went to the bullpen after a leadoff single but bypassed closer (and American League save leader) Sparky Lyle for veteran lefty Grant Jackson, who'd allowed an eighth-inning run the previous day. Jackson was touched for a single by pinch-hitter Jim Wohlford.

That brought up George Brett, whose .333 average had led the American League. Jackson allowed just one homer in 58 2/3 innings since the Yankees acquired him, while Brett hit just seven homers in more than 600 at-bats. But Brett poked a ball into the short porch in right. Whoosh. All the air was sucked out of Yankee Stadium. It was 6–6.

With two outs in the ninth, the Royals threatened again when Buck Martinez singled and Cowens walked, bringing up Wohlford. Brett and his eight ALCS hits were on deck. With the runners in motion, Dick Tidrow induced a chopper to Graig Nettles, who nipped Cowens at second base.

The Yankees were excited and jittery, but the fans were rabid. Bottles and beer cans, toilet paper and firecrackers appeared out of the night, littering the field and disrupting play before Chambliss could step in. Did the outburst mess up Mark Littell, the Royal closer who had retired five straight? Perhaps. But Chambliss was the perfect man for this moment. He had 17 homers and 96 RBI in 1976, and in the ALCS, he had set a new record, with 10 hits (in 20 at-bats), while tying Hank Aaron's 1969 mark of seven RBI.

If Littell could get past Chambliss, the bottom of the Yankees lineup was hitless. and the Royals had Brett and Mayberry due up in the 10th. But Littell couldn't even get one pitch past the Yankees first baseman. Chambliss ripped the reliever's fastball toward right-center. He stood and watched, not quite believing what he had done. But when right fielder Hal McRae went up wishing and came down despairing, Chambliss leaped into the air, exultant. The Yankees had made it to the World Series—if they could get out alive.

Before Chambliss was even halfway around the bases, fans had breached the playing field and were rampaging toward their new hero. Between second and third, Chambliss momentarily disappeared, tripped up by one fan as another tried swiping his helmet. His unruly entourage expanding exponentially, Chambliss tucked his headgear under his arm and headed toward third. Well, not to third exactly, since someone had made off with the base. Chambliss went wide around the thickening crowd and skated the edge until he got near the Yankees dugout, where he lowered his shoulder and knocked another maniac aside, escaping into the safety of the dugout and clubhouse.

Amid the celebration, Nettles asked Chambliss if he'd touched home to make the run official. There had been no way to get there and no plate left if he had, but Nettles sent him back out, where umpire Art Frantz was waiting. Wearing a jacket to disguise his superhero identity, Chambliss was escorted by two cops and picked his way through the remaining crowd to touch the area where home plate should have been.

That sufficed. Not that the Yankees would have brooked any dispute. With the humor and menace that symbolized those 1970s Bronx Bombers, Thurman Munson declared afterward that no official could have deemed Chambliss a modern Fred Merkle. "I saw about 50,000 people touch home plate—he could have been one of them," Munson said. "I want to see them take it back."

45

Dr. J Leads the Nets Back from 22 Down to Win the Final ABA Finals, May 13, 1976, Nassau Coliseum

Julius Erving, the greatest player the ABA had ever seen, topped his own high-flying standards in the first five games of the 1976 Finals, soaring for 39 points per game as his New York Nets grabbed a 3-2 lead. But the Nets played appallingly through the first two-thirds of Game 6, allowing the Denver Nuggets to waltz to an 80-58 lead. With 5:07 left in the third quarter, a Game 7 felt inevitable.

Dr. J resuscitated his team and showed he was far more than a dunking machine—with steals, blocks, rebounds, passes, and his calm leadership (plus a couple of dunks, of course), the native Long Islander led the Nets to one of the greatest basketball playoff comebacks ever. When they clinched their second title in what proved the final ABA game ever, it was a fitting finish: The short-lived league was, if nothing else, always entertaining—it never succeeded financially, but it brought flair to the game with teenage stars, three-point shots, and slam dunks that stood in stark contrast to the more staid NBA.

When the ABA began in 1967, a challenge seemed realistic, given that the NBA was less than two decades old and still not a force on national television. But despite attracting some world-class talent, the ABA struggled constantly. The Nets were forced out of Manhattan by the Knicks and initially landed in an armory in Teaneck, New Jersey. The next year they tried for Newark but failed, instead ending up at the Long Island Arena in Commack. The court and arena barely met amateur standards, much less professional ones. Their record of 17-61 matched the surroundings, but no one really noticed since the team averaged 1,100 people per game, drawing just 516 for one contest. Things gradually stabilized: The Nets moved the Island Garden in West Hempstead; made the playoffs; moved into the newer, larger Nassau Veterans Memorial Coliseum in Uniondale; and even reached the finals in 1972. Before the 1973–1974 season, the Nets grabbed Erving from the broke Virginia Squires. He won the MVP and led the team to its first championship.

During the 1975–1976 season, Erving earned his third scoring title (29.3 points) and third MVP. He also wowed everyone in the league's new All-Star Game event: the Dunk Contest. While Denver's David Thompson was dazzling, Erving clinched his win by taking off from the free throw line and not returning to earth until after he had slammed the ball through the net.

Denver finished with 60 wins and the league's best offense; the Nets had the second-best record, with 55 wins, with John Williamson and Brian Taylor as Erving's main support acts.

Now the Nets were back in the Finals, but the league's future was very much in doubt. The commissioner, ex-Knick Dave DeBusschere, held a press conference during Game 3, revealing that the Virginia Squires had just folded, leaving the ABA with just six teams. The Finals could only be seen nationally on a tiny cable outlet called Home Box Office. Given the chaos, it's easy to be dismissive of Erving's exclamation point of a performance throughout this final Final. But before calling the ABA a lesser league, it's worth noting that the Nuggets were coached by Larry Brown, featuring future NBA stars Thompson, Dan Issel, and Bobby Jones, plus Ralph Simpson and Marvin Webster.

But Erving was Afro, head and shoulders above them all—people who saw him play in the ABA would later compare him to Magic Johnson, Larry Bird, and Michael Jordan without hesitation. He scored 45 in Game 1, notably a game-winning 18-footer from the corner with one second left and Jones in his face. After Game 4, when Erving featured a backhanded dunk, two running hook-dunks, a dunk behind his head on an offensive rebound, and a one-fingered put-back on another, Jones confessed, "He destroys that adage that I've always been taught—that one man can't do it alone. To be honest, I enjoy watching him."

Jones probably didn't enjoy the end of Game 6, however. The comeback was sparked by the Nets' full-court press on defense and featured big plays by numerous Nets, but it revolved, as always, around Erving. He drove along the baseline from the left, and when his path to the basket was cut off, he went behind the glass, switched the ball from his left hand to his right, took off, reversed direction, and scooped his long right arm under the backboard and rolled the ball into the basket off the glass. (He later did something similar for Philadelphia on national television against Kareem Abdul-Jabbar and the Los Angeles Lakers in Game 4 of the 1980 Finals.) Erving finished the third quarter with 29 points, bringing the Nets to within 14.

He scored only two more in the fourth—knowing Denver was keying on him, he took the ball at the top of the key, luring the double team and then kicking the ball to teammates. John Williamson, who had just four first-half points, poured in 16 points in the fourth as the Nets outscored the Nuggets, 34–14. The biggest basket came with the Nets down 104–101, with 3:14 left—Erving missed a free throw, but backup center Jumbo Jim Eakins put the ball in, got fouled by Marvin Webster, and hit the free throw—and suddenly the game was tied.

In the waning seconds, with New York up, 110–106, the ball landed in the hands of Rich Jones, who had four steals and nine rebounds but was 0–11 shooting. He hit his first shot, a layup, to seal the win. The fans couldn't take it anymore—with several seconds left they stormed the court in celebration.

Erving's 31 points was a low for him in the series, but his line score featured 5 assists, 19 rebounds, 5 steals, and 4 blocked shots. He averaged 37.7 points and 14.2 rebounds for the series. "If this was the ABA's last game at least we went out in high style," Erving said afterward.

The league was, indeed, done. The Nets, Nuggets, San Antonio Spurs, and Indiana Pacers were allowed entry into the NBA—at a steep price: $3.2 million in cash and no access to that year's draft picks or any NBA television money for three years. The Nets still felt confident and traded Eakins, Brian Taylor, and the 1977 and 1978 first-round draft picks to the Kansas City Kings to add Tiny Archibald to their lineup.

Then the other shoe didn't so much as fall as it did kick the Nets in the face. The NBA decreed that to invade the Knicks' territory, the Nets had to pay the Knicks a crippling $4.8 million penalty. The cash-strapped Nets reportedly offered Erving to the Knicks instead (the Knicks foolishly passed), then sold the soul of the team to the Philadelphia 76ers for $3 million, ruining the franchise for five years.

Still, in May 1976, all that was merely an uncertain future, and the present was dominated by Dr. J, the unstoppable force of the ABA champion New York Nets.

46

The Upstart Islanders Stun the Comeback Rangers in the Playoffs in OT, April 11, 1975, Madison Square Garden

On April 11, 1975, at the Nassau Coliseum, New York's hockey landscape turned upside down in just 11 seconds.

The New York Islanders entered the NHL in 1972, and sank beneath the ice, winning just 12 games (with 60 losses and six ties). The following year they managed 19 wins. For their third season, the Islanders were a greatly improved team, with a lineup that would build the foundation of their 1980s dynasty: second-year player Denis Potvin (and his brother Jean), Billy Harris, Bobby Nystrom, rookie Clark Gillies, Garry Howatt, and goalies Billy Smith and Chico Resch. But even while scooting past respectability into a winning record, it was hard to imagine the Islanders as a Rangers rival, on the ice, in the media, or with the fans. The Rangers were an original NHL team and after years of disaster had been on solid ground for almost a decade: The team was in its ninth straight winning season and playoff spot; in the previous four years, the team had reached the semifinals three times and the Stanley Cup Finals once. Even as the Islanders learned to win, they could not beat the Rangers—in their first four games of the 1974–1975 season, there was one tie and three Rangers wins.

But the day after the second loss to the Rangers, Islanders general manager Bill Torrey, boosted his offense by acquiring 33-year-old veteran and two-time All-Star Jean-Paul Parise from the Minnesota North Stars. Two days later, Torrey nabbed another scoring forward from Minnesota, Jude Drouin. While Potvin and Gillies were the stars, Resch later said that acquiring Parise, who played alongside Phil Esposito on Team Canada, "brought a legitimacy."

On March 29, the Islanders finally outscored the Rangers, 6–4. In the season finale on April 6, they repeated the results with the same score, pushing the Islanders into a virtual tie with the Rangers, with 88 points apiece. (The Rangers had more wins and home ice advantage.) The new playoff system featured 12 playoff teams, and the second- and third-place teams from each division faced off in a best-of-three preliminary round.

The Islanders proved themselves worthy in enemy territory in Game 1, with Harris, Potvin, and Gillies scoring in a 3–2 win. But the Rangers annihilated them, 8–3, in the next game. It came down to one game at Madison Square Garden. The favored and more experienced Rangers attacked early and often, but Billy Smith held them at bay. With four minutes left in the opening period, Bob Bourne rushed into Rangers territory in the middle of the ice, drawing Brad Park and Ron Harris. That left Gillies open, and he took Bourne's pass and scored from 25 feet out.

In the second period, Denis Potvin scored on a power play and, four minutes later, a shorthanded goal. Desperate, Rangers coach Emile Francis yanked goalie Gilles Villemure for Eddie Giacomin. The sluggish Rangers finally re-awakened early in the third period, when Bill Fairbairn got them on the board.

Still, with seven minutes left, the Islanders held a 3–1 lead. Then the unthinkable happened: Fairbairn scored again, and just 14 seconds later Steve Vickers tied the game at 3–3. The Islanders' success in the first two periods was eradicated. But while the Islanders were rattled, Billy Smith halted the Rangers' momentum, forcing the game into overtime. The Islanders retreated to the locker room, wounded but still alive.

Coach Al Arbour knew he needed to steady his team and go on the offensive to begin overtime so he started his most experienced players on the front line: Eddie Westfall and the two former North Stars, Drouin and Parise.

Overtime is sudden death, but scoring is rare enough in hockey that said death usually takes time. Not here. Drouin beat Jean Ratelle on the face-off, sending the puck to Dave Lewis, who sent it back toward Drouin, the puck moving along the boards near the corner of the rink. Drouin seized control of the puck.

Perhaps 10 seconds had passed. Many fans were still returning to their seats from the bathroom or concessions. No one suspected that the Rangers' season had just one second left.

Giacomin slid in Drouin's direction. Parise said after the game that he was in the wrong place at the right time—he and Drouin usually had a set play in that situation. "When he gets the puck in the corner, I usually go behind the net," he said. "But this time I decided to stay in front because nobody checked me."

Drouin saw him there and sent the puck flying toward the goal crease; Parise slipped between Park and Giacomin and, just as Park hit him, knocked the puck into the net. Eleven seconds into overtime—the fastest ever in postseason history—and the Islanders were victorious. The crowd was stunned, the Islanders were jubilant. (When they left the Garden, their bus was pelted with beer bottles, and they required a police escort out of Manhattan.)

"That series really put us on the map," Nystrom later recalled.

The loss sent the Rangers spiraling—they failed to make the playoffs the next two years, then lost in the preliminary round. Ironically, their next moment of glory came in 1979, as a David, toppling Goliath, when they beat the Islanders, who seemed on the verge of Stanley Cup greatness.

This triumph was a turning point for the Isles. In the next round against Pittsburgh, they became the first team in three decades to recover from a 3–0 deficit in a seven-game series. They almost did it again in the semifinals, losing three straight, then forcing the Philadelphia Flyers, the eventual champions, to the full seven games. Eventually, this briefest of overtimes would help the Islanders fulfill their expectations by winning the Stanley Cup in 1980. And 1981. And 1982. And 1983.

47

The "Ya Gotta Believe" Mets Win in a Miracle Finish in the 13th against the Pirates, September 20, 1973, Shea Stadium

"Ya gotta believe." If ever a team earned its slogan, it was the 1973 New York Mets, a team that provided joy, hope, and inspiration with their unlikely journey from the cellar to the World Series.

The Mets almost buried themselves that season due to a lack of firepower and depth, especially when a rash of injuries took down John Milner, Jerry Grote, Cleon Jones, Buddy Harrelson, and Jon Matlack. Stopper Tug McGraw was injury-free but flat-out awful, blowing save after save.

The Mets sank from first place on April 29 to last place by July 26. On August 16, they were 12 games below .500 with just 44 left to play; however, the entire division was so mediocre that when president M. Donald Grant gave a desultory speech urging the Mets to keep plugging away, it wasn't totally ludicrous. Then McGraw, who had just taken up self-actualization, playfully mocked his boss, shouting his new personal mantra, "Ya gotta believe."

The Mets had a war cry, and soon they had an unhittable closer. In 19 appearances, McGraw pitched 41 innings, with an ERA of 0.88 and 38 strikeouts, garnering five wins and 12 saves, bounding off the mound at inning's end, banging his glove on his leg, and whooping it up. Still, progress was slow—on August 30, they were just 6½ games out of first but still in last place. By September 11, they'd reached fourth, five games under .500. Yet, they were just three games out of first.

By September 20, the Mets were 75–77, and tied for third. The day was marked by Willie Mays's emotionally draining retirement announcement. But the Mets stayed focused. Three times in that game first-place Pittsburgh took a one-run lead, but each time the Mets rallied, finally forcing extra innings on ninth-inning pinch hits by Ken Boswell and Duffy Dyer.

CHAPTER 47

In the 13th, Pittsburgh's Richie Zisk singled, and with two outs Dave Augustine smashed the ball to deep left field. The ball was way back. It was going . . . going . . . but the Shea fence was perhaps a half-inch too high, and the ball stayed in the park. Still, Zisk, running with two outs, would certainly score—except the ball ricocheted on a straight line to the one spot it had to go—right into Cleon Jones's glove. Jones whirled and fired to third baseman Wayne Garrett, who spun and relayed the ball home to rookie catcher Ron Hodges, who blocked the plate and put the tag on a stunned Zisk. It was a Mets miracle.

In the bottom of the inning, Hodges singled home the winning run, pushing the improbable Mets into second place, just a half-game behind the devastated Pirates. The next night, ace Tom Seaver pitched the Mets into first. The Mets would shock Cincinnati's Big Red Machine in the NLCS and push the powerful Oakland A's to seven games in the World Series.

There were other big wins, but none better summed up this season, affirming not only McGraw's slogan, but also another one coined that September by their sagacious manager, Yogi Berra: "It ain't over till it's over."

48

Secretariat Ends Horse Racing's Triple Crown Drought by Dominating at the Belmont Stakes, June 9, 1973, Belmont Park

There were other horses in the Belmont Stakes that June day in 1973, really there were. Why, right out of the gate a horse named My Gallant grabbed the lead, and later on, Sham briefly nosed in front. But one by one they fell away, distant and irrelevant, so far back that they seemed to exist only to magnify the magnificence of the leader, the majestic Big Red running so fast the others fell out of range of the television cameras; Secretariat's lead was so large the announcer couldn't even fathom it, clearly underestimating it as the horse streaked across the finish line and into history. For the greatest racehorse of all time, the Belmont Stakes was his masterpiece.

It had been a quarter-century since Citation had earned the Triple Crown, and horse racing had suffered since then. It was in dire need of a new superstar. Yet, even though Secretariat was the first two-year-old unanimously voted Horse of the Year, some remained skeptical that he could win it all, especially since his sire, Bold Ruler, had lacked stamina, as did Bold Ruler's other offspring. In January 1973, Secretariat's development was further hindered when owner Christopher Chenery died, leaving a massive estate tax burden; the horse's training was curtailed until he was sold to a syndicate for a record $6.08 million. That price heightened expectations and increased the pressure on trainer Lucien Laurin and jockey Ron Turcotte. At Aqueduct for the $50,000 Gotham Stakes, a one-mile race that would be the first of two big tests before the Kentucky Derby, the heavily favored Secretariat carried a whopping 126 pounds. He hit the stall's side coming out of the gate, wobbled, then won by three lengths anyway, tying a track record. Turcotte showed that his eyes were on bigger prizes—after the finish line he kept Secretariat going for an extra quarter-mile to equal the Kentucky Derby distance.

CHAPTER 48

Secretariat leaves the entire field behind with his record-setting performance at the Belmont Stakes as he wins the first Triple Crown in 35 years. *ASSOCIATED PRESS*

Now people openly talked about Secretariat as a once-in-a-lifetime horse, a Man o' War, a Seabiscuit, a Citation. But equally important, Secretariat's fame spilled beyond the track's borders. Sports fans who wouldn't have known Bold Ruler from Northern Dancer were champing at the bit, eagerly awaiting the Triple Crown races.

He had one more Aqueduct tune-up, the Wood Memorial, but he was suffering from an abscess in his mouth and finished third, staining him in the press. William Nack recalled later in *Sports Illustrated*, "In the most important race of his career, Secretariat had come up as hollow as a gourd. I couldn't help but suspect that Secretariat was another Bold Ruler, who ran into walls beyond a mile."

Secretariat's loss encouraged other owners to enter the Kentucky Derby, bringing the field to 13. Secretariat started the Derby in last place and then lingered far back as a horse named Shecky Greene led with Sham challenging him. A half-mile in, Secretariat suddenly appeared on the outside, outrunning everyone with ease, winning by 2½ lengths and setting a Derby record at 1:59 4/5.

Only five competitors bothered showing up for the Preakness Stakes. This time the champion made his last-to-first move early, with a stunning charge on the first turn that decimated the field. The official timer was inaccurate, but almost 40 years later race officials reevaluated the footage and lowered Secretariat's time to 1:53, an unmatched record.

By the time the Belmont started, Secretariat had made the covers of *Time*, *Newsweek*, and *Sports Illustrated*, becoming, as Nack observed, a "cultural phenomenon, a sort of undeclared national holiday from the tortures of Watergate and the Vietnam War." Turcotte planned to sit behind Sham and then pull away, but his horse was pulsing with energy so he just turned him loose early, picking his head up in the first turn. Sham made a gallant effort and briefly held a lead, but by the backstretch Secretariat had left everyone behind, with the camera having to pull back just to keep Sham in the frame. Turcotte said later he was essentially a passenger until 70 yards from the end, when, remembering the Preakness timing controversy, he urged his horse to finish fast to leave no doubt about a record here. Secretariat responded, coming through at 2:24, a time that has never been challenged. While announcer Chic Anderson shouted that the horse had won by 25 lengths, the final distance was actually measured at 31 lengths, another seemingly unbreakable record.

Although horse racing still recedes into the shadows of the sports pages for much of the year, the story of Secretariat made the Triple Crown races a bigger annual story, so that horses from Seattle Slew to Justify would streak briefly across the athletic firmament—even though they will never, ever catch Big Red.

49

The Knicks Finally Beat Boston in Game 7, April 29, 1973, Boston Garden, Boston

The odds, and history, were firmly stacked against the New York Knicks on April 29, 1973. They had blown two straight games, forcing a decisive seventh game in the Eastern Conference Finals. They'd have to beat the Boston Celtics, owner of the NBA's best record, at 68–14, in Boston, on the fabled parquet floor, where only Red Auerbach's men knew the dead spots. The Celtics defined NBA greatness and had never lost a seventh game, boasting 10 straight such wins.

But the Knicks had defied odds before, winning the 1970 championship after Willis Reed was severely injured. In November, this 1972–1973 team scored 19 straight points against Milwaukee to turn an 86–68 deficit into an 87–86 win. And in this series, they'd come from 16 points down to win in double overtime.

This was the Knicks' last shot at a second crown. The core of 1969–1970 remained—future Hall of Famers Willis Reed, Walt Frazier, Bill Bradley, and Dave DeBusschere—with Earl Monroe, who'd tortured them for years in Baltimore, replacing Dick Barnett and Jerry Lucas, imported from Golden State to ease Reed's burden. But the front line was old and vulnerable—Lucas and DeBusschere were 32, Reed's knees seemed twice that age—and ascendant Boston and 1971 champion Milwaukee were younger and at least as potent as New York and 1972 champion Los Angeles.

The teams took turns routing one another in Games 1 and 2. The Knicks won Game 3 on the road and had a double-overtime win at home. Boston star John Havlicek hurt his shoulder, but Boston won Game 5 on a lucky shot and Game 6, too. In Boston, Knicks reserve Phil Jackson claimed the Celtics engaged in their usual sabotage tactics, pulling the fire alarm at the Knicks' hotel the night before Game 7, then assigning them a new locker room with a low ceiling and an oversized training table.

MVP Dave Cowens made up for the injured Havlicek (who contributed only four points in 23 minutes) by scoring regularly over DeBusschere, and the Celtics led after one quarter, 22-19. Coach Red Holzman shook things up, benching Monroe, who was hobbled by an ankle injury, for defensive specialist Dean Meminger. "The Dream" forced Jo Jo White to shoot jumpers instead of driving, limiting White to just two second-quarter points.

Meminger suggested that he and Frazier press more, and Holzman also sent his forwards into Boston's backcourt, chewing up the 24-second clock and rushing the Celtics out of their planned plays. Holzman also urged Meminger to shoot more so Boston couldn't sag off him and clog the middle. Meminger contributed nine second-quarter points as the Knicks snatched a 45–40 halftime lead.

In the third, DeBusschere ran into foul trouble, so Holzman reverted to tradition and put his centers, first Lucas and then Reed, on Cowens—they held him to two points in that quarter as the Knicks put the game away, building up a 68–53 lead en route to a 94–78 win that Holzman called the most satisfying of his career. In the second and third quarters combined, the Knicks held Boston to just 35 points. Frazier played 47 minutes, with 25 points and 10 rebounds, but it was a vintage all-around team effort, with five players scoring in double figures and five hauling in at least six rebounds.

To become champions the Knicks still had to beat the 60–22 Lakers. No team had ever beaten two 60-win teams in the playoffs to become champion. The Knicks again seized the chance to show what they thought of such history.

50

The Fight: Ali–Frazier I, March 8, 1971, Madison Square Garden

It was simply called "the Fight," but there was nothing simple about it. The 1971 heavyweight championship battle between Muhammad Ali and Joe Frazier at Madison Square Garden had enough twists and turns—personal and political, in the ring and on the streets—to justify the endless articles, books, and documentaries that have explored its lingering echoes.

The Ali–Frazier story line is so battered by mythology and misperception that its legacy may always be unsatisfyingly ambiguous. It revolved around Ali's outsized personality as a symbol of antiwar activism and black pride. Yet, his political views were somewhat manipulated by the Nation of Islam, a hateful and hypocritical cult of personality. Ali's portrayal of Frazier as the establishment bad guy and an Uncle Tom was cruel and inaccurate. But strip away the backdrop and Ali–Frazier I still remains the greatest fight in New York City's history, an electrifying display of sustained suspense, brilliant athleticism, and sheer human spirit. It lived up to and even surpassed the hype, producing 15 rounds the world will never forget.

The story began in 1967, when Ali famously declared, "I got no quarrel with them Viet Cong." He was convicted for refusing induction into the armed forces and stripped of his world heavyweight title. As Mark Kram argues in his book *Ghosts of Manila*, the politically naïve Ali was played by the Nation of Islam's leaders, the morally corrupt Elijah Muhammad and his son Herbert. (Ali had even cut off Malcolm X to stay in their good graces and spouted their fantastical beliefs about a "Mothership" that would whisk away blacks to outer space.) Still, once cast in this role, Ali played it bravely, even as everything he'd single-mindedly worked for was taken away. In 1967, criticizing the war was not

Muhammad Ali was "the Greatest," but Joe Frazier was the undisputed heavyweight champion after he floored Ali in the 15th round of "the Fight." *LOC/ World Journal Tribune photo by Ira Rosenberg/Library of Congress, Prints and Photographs Division, NYWT&S Collection [LC-USZ62-115435]*

fashionable, and everyone from Joe Louis to Sugar Ray Robinson to Red Smith slammed Ali. Whites who'd disdained the brash loudmouth's rhyming boasts now called him a traitor.

Although almost contemporaries, Ali seemed to represent a different generation than Frazier. Smokin' Joe had grown up dirt-poor in a Gullah community in South Carolina and earned a living in a Philadelphia slaughterhouse before turning pro. He was heavyweight champ but often regarded as the illegitimate king. Frazier initially liked, even admired, Ali, befriending him during Ali's years in exile. Knowing he'd need to fight and beat Ali, Frazier talked on his rival's behalf to the press and even boxing officials. He reassured Ali that his day would come and even occasionally loaned him a couple hundred dollars.

But the manic showman also perplexed the soft-spoken warrior, leaving him hurt or angry. Once Frazier drove Ali from Philadelphia to New York, chatting about the millions they'd reap together. "He was a brother," Frazier recalled later. But in Manhattan, Ali commandeered the sidewalks, shouting, "I want my title! He ain't the champ, he's the chump."

Once, Ali, facing jail time and desperate to whip up pressure for a boxing license, showed up at Frazier's gym. With a rabid crowd in tow, he challenged Frazier to a fight right then and there. The police, unable to cope with the throngs, ordered the two to a nearby park. Frazier's manager, Yank Durham, wouldn't let him go, figuring he might get beat or hurt with no payday. Ali badmouthed Frazier in absentia in front of 20,000 blood-hungry voyeurs. When Ali picked a fight with Frazier in the street, Frazier went to Ali's house to issue stern words of challenge. The friendship was over.

After 1968, with Martin Luther King and Robert Kennedy dead, and the antiwar movement surging, Ali became an iconoclastic voice that blacks and the alienated counterculture rallied around. Bowing to relentless pressure, boxing authorities finally let Ali back in the ring in 1970. He made short work of Jerry Quarry, then bested Oscar Bonavena. He was rusty but ready.

The Houston Astrodome and Madison Square Garden each offered a $2.5 million purse for an Ali–Frazier fight. But Jerry Perenchio, a show biz manager with no boxing experience, swooped in with $5 million (courtesy of backer Jack Kent Cooke). To earn it back, he booked the Garden and sold the closed-circuit TV rights regionally for a fortune. Although the world was ready to tune in, Ali still played carny barker but stooped to ugly low blows.

He proclaimed himself the "People's Champion" and rhymed, "This might shock and amaze ya, but I'm gonna retire Joe Frazier," before crossing the line, calling Frazier "too ugly" and "too dumb to be champ," a vicious insult that played on white America's prejudice but also one between lighter- and darker-skinned blacks. He isolated Frazier by declaring, "Ninety-eight percent of my people are for me. They identify with my struggle. If I win, they win. I lose, they lose."

In *Jet* magazine, Ali called Frazier the "unheralded white-created champion for the primary enrichment of two white businessmen," although he was being paid by those same men and had started with the backing of wealthy whites.

Then he called Frazier and any black rooting for him an "Uncle Tom." For the straightforward Frazier, this was an outrage. He'd been forced to leave home after talking back to whites; he had migrated North and taken a low-paying, dangerous job; and he was a Baptist who read the Bible, worked diligently, and took quiet pride in his achievements. In a way, he personified black America. "I tommed for him," Frazier cried out, since he'd appealed to white power brokers to help Ali. "He betrayed my friendship."

Frazier's children were taunted at school, while death threats and bomb threats warranted constant protection. Ali so stained Frazier's image that months later, the editor of *Black Sports* sneered in print, "Is Joe Frazier a White Champion in a Black Skin?" That editor, Bryant Gumbel, later admitted that he was terribly wrong but said that it seemed Frazier "was one of them and Ali was one of us. We weren't interested in the fairness of it all."

At a prefight photo session, photographer George Kalinsky put the men in a ring to simulate action. Ali started teasing and testing Frazier, who snarled, "Let's go at it," and Frazier soon drove a real left hook into Ali's stomach, surprising and frightening Ali.

The training and pressure left Frazier fatigued and burdened with high blood pressure, but if Ali thought he could unnerve Frazier, he'd badly misread his opponent. For Frazier, Ali's "sadistic" attempt to "deblacken" him made him ready to kill or die in the ring.

Finally, March 8 arrived. The Fight.

After separate weigh-ins to avoid another incident, the police, afraid of the surging crowds, wouldn't let Ali leave the Garden, making him a prisoner of his own creation, left to restlessly prowl the building.

Seven hundred press credentials were issued and 500 more turned down. More than 300 million viewers in 35 nations tuned in, while the local crowd featured the likes of Joe Louis, Jack Dempsey, Sugar Ray Robinson, Willie Pep, James Braddock, Gene Tunney, Coretta Scott King, Jesse Jackson, Andrew Young, Ralph Abernathy, Julian Bond, Count Basie, Aretha Franklin, Bing Crosby, Miles Davis, Diana Ross, Sammy Davis Jr., Elvis Presley (reportedly), one or more ex-Beatles, Dustin Hoffman, Barbra Streisand, Bill Cosby, Hugh Hefner, Senator Ted Kennedy, Mayor John Lindsay, Joe Namath, and Walt "Clyde" Frazier, along with thousands dressed even more flamboyantly than the dandyish Knicks guard. Frank Sinatra worked as a photographer for *Life* magazine, while Burt Lancaster handled broadcasting duties.

In the ring came Ali: age 29; 6-foot-3; 215 pounds; 31-0, with 25 knockouts; dressed in red. And then Frazier: age 27; 5-foot-11; 205 pounds; 26-0, with 23 knockouts; dressed in green.

Before the opening bell, Ali danced in circles wide enough to accidentally-on-purpose bump Frazier's shoulder. Frazier merely glared into Ali's eyes. He had a game plan: let Ali protect his pretty face by leaning back, then pound, pound, pound the body and arms until Ali came down to his height, exposing his head.

At the start, Frazier rushed at Ali, who looked surprised. Ali soon settled in, looking like the young Cassius Clay, flicking his fists and dancing away or standing in and throwing long, hard blows. He set the tempo early, scoring points, winning rounds. But bobbing and weaving is a tiring business, and Frazier didn't care how much he had to take. Stamina wouldn't have mattered to the Ali of the 1960s, but he couldn't dance with his old speed and endurance. By the third, Ali's feet were flattening, his back searching for ropes to lean on. He was fighting on Frazier's terms.

Even as he waved away Frazier's best attacks, telling everyone he couldn't be hurt, the fight was shifting. Ali's flurries were ineffective, and Frazier pushed the pace, unceasingly driving lefts and rights to the body. In the fourth round, Frazier connected with a left hook to the jaw, avoided the clinch, and punished

Ali's ribs, sending pain shooting down to his hips. Frazier pinned Ali against the ropes, landing another hook to the head.

When Ali taunted, "Do you know I'm God?" Frazier growled back, "God, you're in the wrong place tonight. I'm taking names and kicking ass." He even played Ali's game, aping his wounded foe by dropping his hands to his sides and laughing derisively when Ali hit him. Frazier wobbled a bit, but Ali's ribs were hurting.

Ali had predicted a sixth-round knockout, so Frazier came out aggressively, bashing him against the ropes, while Ali resorted to pitter-patter punches. He was giving away rounds when he could not afford to—he either misjudged his opponent or had nothing more to offer and was just holding on, awaiting a second wind. In the eighth, the crowd chanted Ali's name, until Frazier changed their tune with lefts and rights to Ali's head; by round's end, his name was being cheered.

Finally, in the ninth, Ali emerged, whipping a series of rights to the head, followed by combinations that left Frazier bleeding from his left nostril. Frazier retaliated with devastating force, striking Ali with eight unanswered punches. After 10 rounds, the ref had Ali slightly ahead, while the two judges favored Frazier. A decision was up for grabs.

Round 11 changed the equation. Frazier trapped Ali in a corner, then left the ground to detonate a deadly hook. Ali's knees buckled, and he fell into the ropes. He stumbled away, arms at his sides, shoulders slumped, seemingly out on his feet. No one had ever seen Ali like this. Frazier warily watched, unsure if this was some Ali trick. Ali survived the round and the next one too, but Frazier had clinched a decision, meaning Ali needed a knockout.

Again, Ali somehow rejuvenated himself. Frazier at one point asked in his corner, "What is keeping this motherfucker up?" Ali began landing long-range shots but was stunned by the depths of Frazier's will. Ali had more energy than Frazier but not enough to finish him off.

The 15th round provided the Fight with the perfect exclamation point. Both men were tired but still punching hard. With both fighters in the middle of the ring, Frazier leaped and launched a bomb with his left. Ali pulled back but not quickly enough, taking it on the jaw. He toppled backward to the canvas, his feet in the air. Frazier was surprised when Ali rose up, but he had accomplished his mission. Ali had nothing left and had to simply endure more punishment until the bell.

Frazier won a unanimous decision and heard the sweetest words in his life when Ali came over and said, "You're the champ."

In his dressing room, Ali's jaw grew obscenely swollen. But there was little celebrating by the other side: Frazier spent weeks in the hospital, which he found embarrassing, knowing Ali would eventually brandish this against him. Rumors even circulated that Frazier had died. He hadn't, but some of his drive had; he was flattened by George Foreman and lost a 12-round nontitle rematch with Ali at the Garden. Ali, meanwhile, pulled off his momentous upset over Foreman in Zaire to again become king of the heavyweights. He gave Frazier a shot at regaining his glory, and their final go-round in Manila was another visceral display of magnificent cruelty as the two men hammered one another to the edge of death until Frazier's trainer, Eddie Futch, stopped him from coming out for the final round.

For years thereafter, the rivalry simmered and occasionally boiled—in 1988, Ali mocked Frazier for laughs in front of a celebrity crowd, and Frazier got drunk and tried attacking Ali, stopped only by the physical intervention of Foreman and another ex-champ, Larry Holmes. Frazier had to content himself with verbal blows; after Ali lit the 1996 Olympic flame, he said, "If I had the chance, I'd have pushed him in."

It took until the twenty-first century before the two men made peace with one another, but they always had to live with each other: Without beating Ali, Frazier would not have been a genuine champion, and without surviving Frazier, Ali's claims to being "the Greatest" would have rung hollow. The Fight resonated because of the sociopolitical mess that ensnarled both men and because their skill and will elevated the event itself above those outside forces.

51

Willis Reed Hobbles to the Rescue,
May 8, 1970, Madison Square Garden

The Captain to the Rescue. The heroic saga of Willis Reed and Game 7 of the 1970 NBA Finals is so well known that even New York Knicks fans who weren't born yet can visualize the wounded leader limping out of the Madison Square Garden tunnel, hear the din of the crowd building to a frenzied roar, and sense the sagging psyche of the Los Angeles Lakers.

But the mythologizing has obscured reality in ways that both understate and overstate the great center's inspiring performance. The story has been rubbed so smooth that all we hear about is Reed's remarkable physical courage and how he won the opening jump and scored the Knicks' first two field goals, sparking the stunning win over Los Angeles and their Goliath, Wilt Chamberlain.

It's all true, but it's not enough. Reed truly was the soul of that team, but he did more than just lift his teammates' spirits. Many people think he left shortly after his second basket, but he played into the second half, with a physical game that prevented Chamberlain from taking over. Still, he contributed just four points and three rebounds. This is a story of not only one man, but also a remarkable team, one unique in its cohesiveness, one so deep and talented it could win even without its biggest star. The ultimate hero was New York's most skilled all-around player, Walt "Clyde" Frazier, who once quipped, "People don't even know I was in the game." It was his swishing and dishing, as it were, his 36 points, 19 assists, and 7 rebounds, that carried the Knicks to their elusive first championship.

The Knicks were a charter member of the NBA and almost its first dynasty. They reached three consecutive NBA Finals, beginning in 1951, but were thwarted thrice, the last two times by the Lakers and the sport's most dominant player—that team was still near actual lakes in Minneapolis and the player was George Mikan. In the 1960s, the Knicks became a laughingstock—they lost on Christmas 1960, by 62 points; Elgin Baylor set an NBA scoring record against them with 71 points, which lasted until Chamberlain, then, with the Philadelphia Warriors, scored 100 against New York.

Gradually, failed-coach-turned-front-office-wizard Eddie Donovan pieced together a contender. He drafted the little-known Reed out of Grambling in 1964. The Rookie of the Year was tough (taking on the entire Lakers bench in a fight in 1966), talented (averaging more than 20 points and 14 rebounds per game in four years leading up to the championship), and team-oriented (moving to power forward when Donovan acquired fellow center Walt Bellamy).

In 1965, Donovan traded for Dick Barnett and drafted Dave Stallworth and Bill Bradley; the next year, he picked Cazzie Russell. In 1967, he snatched Phil Jackson and the reticent, conservatively dressed Frazier from tiny Southern Illinois University—Knicks scouts noted his dazzling play at the Garden in the National Invitation Tournament.

Scout Red Holzman became coach and molded a unified, balanced team: What they lacked in size and superstars they made up for with intelligence, versatility, unselfishness, and crisp ball movement. The final move came in 1968, when Donovan traded the inconsistent Bellamy and Howard Komives to Detroit. This enabled Reed to shift back to his natural position and truly take control of the team, while Komives's departure yielded playing time for Bradley; the trade brought Dave DeBusschere, a rugged power forward who could defend and rebound like few others.

In 1969, the Knicks were almost flawless, reeling off a then-record 18 straight victories and finishing 60–22. They attracted new fans to professional basketball and a media swarm as well. They bounced Earl Monroe's Baltimore Bullets and Lew Alcindor's Milwaukee Bucks to reach the Finals. There they encountered an immensely talented Lakers squad led by the indomitable Chamberlain, the incomparable Jerry West, and an old but dangerous Elgin Baylor.

The Knicks waltzed through Game 1 behind Reed's 37 points, but Chamberlain blocked Reed's shots at the start and end of Game 2, as the Lakers toughed out a 105–103 win. In L.A., New York showed its resilience after West hit a 63-footer at the buzzer by prevailing in overtime. The Lakers again evened the series with an overtime win. Then the series took a shocking and, for New York, seemingly devastating turn early in Game 5.

Eight minutes in, Reed collapsed to the floor, clutching his hip and writhing in agony. Already playing on battered knees, the league's MVP had hurt his right thigh muscle and the tensor muscles around the hip. Reed was done for the night, likely for the series. Surely Chamberlain would take over now. But led by the 6-foot-6 DeBusschere, New York shut down the towering center and came back from 16 down to win, 107–100.

But Chamberlain dominated Game 6 with 45 points and 27 rebounds in a 135–113 rout that was so emphatic it made the notion of a "decisive" seventh game seem a mere formality—unless, of course, Reed could play.

Reed had skipped Game 6, returning home for intensive treatment. "I'll play if I have to crawl," he'd vowed. He arrived early on May 8. On the court he tested his leg and found that he could drag it but couldn't pick it up without extreme pain. Holzman wanted Reed out for pregame warm-ups for moral support, but Reed stayed behind as team physician Dr. James Parkes searched for the right spots to inject the half-dozen shots of cortisone and Carbocaine that would numb Reed's leg. This inadvertent change ended up enhancing the boost Reed gave his teammates. It was past 7:15 when Parkes finally began. Because Reed's legs were so huge, the doctor needed six-inch-long spinal needles to reach the muscles; Reed was in agony during the 20-minute process.

As the Knicks and Lakers loosened up, the sold-out crowd scanned nervously for Reed. A wild roar went up when a latecomer emerged, but it was only Cazzie Russell. The game was late in starting, and Laker officials began grumbling.

Then, slowly emerging from the dark tunnel, came the personification of desire, determination, and hope. As Reed dragged his right leg onto the court, the fans, vendors, and security guards all let loose a sustained and deafening ovation that shook the Garden. The Lakers looked deflated, nakedly watching Reed as he took a few shots (doing the bare minimum to hide how crippled he was). He had to shoot flat-footed instead of jumping, but at least he was out there shooting.

Finally, the game began. Reed couldn't jump for the opening tap, but Bradley stole a pass and got the ball to Frazier, who decided to maximize the Knicks' psychological edge. He found Reed open at the top of the key and fed him the ball.

Reed drained the shot for the first basket of the game. There were still 47 minutes and 42 seconds to play, but the game and the championship were essentially over. "People always talk about last shots that win games, but I think the first shot won a game," Reed said.

The Knicks believed themselves a team of destiny, while the Lakers sensed impending doom. Reed hammered home those themes by hitting another shot for a 5–2 lead. He'd miss his three other attempts, but it didn't matter. In the first 14 minutes, Bradley, DeBusschere, and Frazier hit 15 of 21 shots.

Chamberlain said later that players on both teams had the "inescapable feeling . . . that no matter what the Lakers did, individually and collectively, the Knicks would find a way to win, and we would find a way to lose."

Realizing his limitations, Reed dedicated himself to setting screens and picks. Knowing he wouldn't last the entire game, he didn't hesitate to foul Chamberlain, keeping the sport's most dominating player from getting comfortable. Although Reed's face often contorted in pain—especially after he hurt his hip again going for a first-quarter rebound—he kept Chamberlain as far from the basket as possible, while the slick Frazier led an aggressive ball-hawking effort that flustered the Lakers and disrupted their game plan. While Reed was on the floor, the Lakers got Chamberlain the ball 17 times, but he shot just 2-9. He'd finish with only 21 points and 16 shots, going just 1-11 from the line.

The Knicks led, 69-42, at halftime. Reed got another injection during intermission, made another late entrance, and played six more minutes in the third, departing after picking up his fourth foul. He'd played 27 minutes—far more than the Knicks ever could have expected. But it was Frazier's performance—among the greatest Game 7 showings in any NBA Finals—that carried the Knicks.

At the start of the playoffs, Holzman had asked Frazier to pass more and shoot less, and Frazier had averaged just 14.9 points, six below his season average. In this game, however, New York needed his scoring, and Frazier shot 12-of-17 from the floor and 12-of-12 from the line. Yet, Frazier never betrayed Holzman's "hit the open man" credo—his 19 assists tied a playoff record and topped the entire Lakers team.

After coasting to a 113-99 win, the Knicks had their first championship and New York had its third since the Jets pulled off their own stunner in January 1969; on May 8, 1970, the defending World Series champion Mets were playing at Shea Stadium, and most of the fans were listening to the Knicks on transistor radios, chanting, "We're number one." While the Jets had been roguish underdogs and the Mets lovable-losers-turned-miracle-workers, the Knicks championship was not an upset—before Reed got hurt, the Knicks and the Lakers were considered even. But the Knicks had their own identity, representing basketball at its most cohesive and most artistic—a true team game.

After the NBA's bush league days of the 1950s and the Boston Celtics' dynasty of the 1960s, this Finals resonated in part because of featuring the nation's two most important and glamorous cities, which fueled both fan and media interest in the sport, but also because in a time of great disharmony for both New York and the country, this notion of a group of individuals, black and white, hitting the right notes, perfectly in tune with one another, was a wonderful and much-needed symbol. "We exemplified an idea," Frazier said.

The Amazin' Mets Win the World Series, October 16, 1969, Shea Stadium

"There Are No Words."

At 3:17 p.m. on October 16, 1969, an ordinary fly ball to left field by Baltimore's Dave Johnson was caught by Cleon Jones. This was one of the most thrilling plays in New York sports history. Suddenly, somehow, the New York Mets were World Series champions.

There have been thousands upon millions of words spilled about the Miracle Mets, about their ascension from lovable losers to David slingshotting Goliath, about what their World Series victory meant to the city, its mayor, baseball, and underdogs everywhere. The miracle of the early Mets was always about the love showered on them by their banner-wielding admirers, so it's fitting that the day's emotions were best captured when diehard fan Karl Ehrhardt, known as "Sign Man," whipped out his banner decreeing, "There Are No Words."

Using words to declare language insufficient is Stengel-esque eloquence, capturing both the rapturous explosion about to envelop Shea Stadium and the implausible absurdity of the notion that the Charlie Browns of sports had won it all. Or you could choose one word, uttered repeatedly by Casey Stengel himself—the original Mets manager served as a reporter and baseball ambassador during the 1969 World Series and delivered this loopy verdict: "Amazin', Amazin', Amazin', Amazin'."

At their birth, the Mets linked themselves to New York's National League past through colors (Dodgers blue and Giants orange) and players (Gil Hodges, Duke Snider). Then they lost a record 120 games. Yet, with Stengel at the helm and players like Marv Throneberry raising baseball ineptitude to a comic art form, the Mets became a unique hit with fans. The first pitch of 1963, by Roger

Craig, was way outside, allegedly prompting one smart aleck to yell, "Wait till next year!" This was a team that, as Ed Kranepool once said, "celebrated rainouts." But with the Mets losing by 13 with two outs and the bases empty in the ninth, fans began chanting, "Let's go Mets"—with enthusiasm, not cynicism. In 1964, the last-place Mets lured 1.7 million faithful to their new Shea Stadium, more than the American League champion Yankees.

But novelty eventually wears off, and the losers would stop seeming lovable. To head off that crisis, the Mets stocked talent (Tug McGraw and Ron Swoboda in 1965, Jerry Grote and Cleon Jones in 1966) and transformed themselves with three Big Bangs.

A controversial commissioner's decision about contracts and college eligibility handed the Mets Tom Seaver, who became the 1967 Rookie of the Year. Then Gil Hodges was hired as manager. The former Marine had an air of quiet authority; the former Dodger was respected and occasionally even feared by his young players. There were baby steps toward respectability. In 1968, with lefty Jerry Koosman joining Seaver, the team won 73 games, a franchise record. For 1969, Hodges's stated goal was 85 wins.

The Mets may have graduated from joke to contender without making the jump to winner, but on June 15, 12 days after reaching .500, they acquired Donn Clendenon, giving them a third legitimate big bat. The first baseman fit well into Hodges's lineup manipulations (he platooned four of eight positions) and pumped out 12 homers in 202 at-bats, complementing Tommie Agee (26 homers overall) and Jones (who hit .340).

But for true believers who don't subscribe to evolutionary theories, the Mets—still 9½ games out of first in mid-August—provided evidence that destiny or divine force was in play. This team swept a doubleheader, winning both editions, 1–0, when their pitcher drove in the sole run. Great teams make their own good luck, but the '69 Mets seemed to trip over it throughout the season. In the 13th inning, against the San Francisco Giants, Hodges employed a four-man outfield against Willie McCovey. McCovey drilled a ball to left-center, but Jones was right there to make a leaping catch, taking away a homer. Against Los Angeles, the Mets won in the ninth, when three Dodgers watched Jerry Grote's high pop fall between them. The St. Louis Cardinals' Steve Carlton set a major-league record, striking out 19 Mets, but New York won, 4–3, because Swoboda blasted two two-run homers with two strikes on him. Most famously, in September, against the Chicago Cubs, a black cat darted at Chicago's first batter, Don Kessinger, ran in front of the Cubs dugout, and hissed at manager Leo Durocher. The Mets won, 7–1.

The Mets won 38 of their last 49, and finished with 100 wins and 2.2 million fans, the most in baseball. A *Daily News* headline declared, "The Moon: Astronauts Took Nine Years, Mets Eight." The *New York Post* wrote a tribute poem parodying Milton's *Paradise Lost*. The *New York Times* adapted Shakespeare to the '69 Mets. (For Seaver: "'And put the world's whole strength into one giant arm.'—Henry IV.")

Many experts said Hank Aaron's Braves would set matters straight in the newfangled division playoffs. The Mets swept Atlanta. "We ought to send the Mets to Vietnam—they'd end the war in three days," Atlanta general manager Paul Richards said.

The Baltimore Orioles won at least 90 games in all but two full seasons from 1965 to 1983. They were just beginning a run of five postseason births in six years with 109 wins. They featured future Hall of Famers at the plate (Frank Robinson), in the field (Brooks Robinson), on the mound (Jim Palmer), and on the bench (Earl Weaver). Their top four hitters—the Robinsons, Boog Powell, and Paul Blair—outhomered the entire Mets team; the O's scored 147 more runs than New York and allowed 24 fewer runs. "They're so good that I wouldn't mind managing their bench," quipped Kansas City manager Joe Gordon.

In the year of Joe Namath, Neil Armstrong, and Woodstock, Mets fans believed anything could happen. But the old-school O's, with their no-nonsense players, expected to annihilate New York. "We're here to prove there is no Santa Claus," Brooks Robinson sneered.

This was to be the biggest mismatch since the Baltimore Colts prepared to dismiss the New York Jets in the Super Bowl earlier that year. . . .

Oops.

New York had more than mystique and good fortune. They had two unsurpassed starters—Seaver and Koosman—and a team that was smart (22 players had gone to college) and opportunistic—they'd score just 15 runs in five games, yet almost always produced on offense or defense with the game on the line.

Game 1 satisfied the conventional wisdom when Don Buford smacked a homer on Seaver's second pitch of the game, Brooks Robinson's nifty barehanded play stifled a rally, and Baltimore won, 4–1. But the Mets won the next day on three two-out singles in the ninth and in Game 3, when Agee made two spectacular catches. Seaver redeemed himself in Game 4, retiring 19 of 20 Orioles. In the ninth, Swoboda made a diving, tumbling catch; in the 10th, a throw to first on J. C. Martin's bunt ricocheted off Martin's wrist and Rod Gaspar scored from second.

Finally, everyone believed. The Mets were for real. When Game 5 began on October 16, the Mets had allowed just two runs in 32 innings. When Koosman yielded three runs in the third, the Mets remained confident, and Koosman backed it up by going the full nine and retiring 19 of the last 21 batters.

To make up the three-run deficit, the club conjured one amazing Mets moment after another. In the sixth, Dave McNally snapped a curve at the feet of Cleon Jones. Jones argued that the pitch had nicked his foot before caroming toward New York's dugout. Hodges strode up, displaying the ball with a tell-tale black shoe polish smudge. The umpires reversed their call and awarded Jones first base. The ball might have hit Jones—equipment manager Nick Torman became a mini-celebrity for his shine job—but many speculated that Hodges had someone mark up the ball on their foot in the dugout. One account says Koosman later admitted to the deed.

The Mets, who'd won throughout the year by relentlessly capitalizing on such gifts, struck immediately. Clendenon, soon to be Series MVP, blasted a pitch off the loge section in left field for his third Series homer. The gap was just one run. They tied the score in the seventh in unlikely fashion.

The Mets had acquired infielder Al Weis largely because he was too old to be called for Vietnam duty. He batted just .192 in two seasons with the Mets and had just six homers in 1,446 career at-bats. He'd never hit homers at Shea. Sure, he was batting .444 in the Series, but that was four singles, nothing more. So, no one, not even Weis, expected his shot off McNally to clear the 371-foot mark in left-center. Weis put his head down and ran hard, only realizing when he was at second base that the boisterous cheering meant the ball was gone.

In the eighth, Swoboda, a .235 hitter who hit .400 for the Series, drove home the go-ahead run, and with two outs the Mets added another on an error and some heads-up running: Boog Powell misplayed Jerry Grote's low liner but could have made a play if reliever Eddie Watt hadn't been late covering first. When Watt dropped the throw, Swoboda, hustling all the way from second, made it 5–3.

Koosman was so nervous and excited before the ninth inning he couldn't control his warm-up tosses. He walked Frank Robinson, bringing up the tying run in Powell, who'd hit 37 round-trippers that year. But Powell grounded into a force. Brooks Robinson flied to Swoboda. Two outs. Davey Johnson, who would manage the next Mets championship team, lifted a fly to left.

"Keep dropping down to me, baby," Jones said. "Keep dropping down." He caught the ball and went down on one knee. Then the Mets ran for their lives as Shea Stadium imploded in a frenzy of turf-tearing fans. It was, Swoboda said, the "most appropriate loss of institutional control I can ever recall."

In the clubhouse, Mayor John Lindsay joined them. For months during his struggling reelection campaign, his handlers had unsuccessfully tried making the elegant WASP seem like just another New Yorker. Then they shoved him into the Mets' celebration. When Tom Seaver doused him with champagne in a front-page photo op, their problems were solved; Lindsay celebrated with them again at City Hall after a ticker-tape parade, which, along with his parades for the Jets and the Apollo 11 astronauts, gave New York a "Fun City" flavor that helped mask its divisions and problems. On Election Day, the Mets picked up, if not a win, then a save.

In Manhattan, fans dancing in the street at 34th Street stopped traffic for an hour, while downtown a spontaneous outburst of 1,000 tons of impromptu confetti poured out of windows, more than during the formal Apollo 11 parade.

Long after that glorious autumn slipped away, long after the Mets entered the dark winter of the mid-1970s, 1969 retained its unique glow, with those Mets becoming the patron saints of underdog dreamers in every sport and all walks of life.

"A lot of things were separating people then—Vietnam, campus unrest, the generation gap, race riots—and at times like those, people look for a fairy tale to soothe them," Seaver once said. "We were that fairy tale."

53

Tommie Agee Saves the Day, Then Does It Again, October 14, 1969, Shea Stadium

It's rare to make a career-defining catch in a World Series game. To top it three innings later is unique. In Game 3 of the 1969 World Series, Tommie Agee's defense saved the Series for the Mets.

The Baltimore Orioles brusquely dismissed Tom Seaver and the Mets in Game 1, raising the question of whether the Mets were for real. Jerry Koosman's masterful pitching and a flurry of clutch two-out hits in Game 2 showed New York could compete. It remained to be seen, however, whether they could outplay the masterful O's in an entire series.

Game 3 was pivotal for reasons of momentum and strategy. It would be the Mets' first effort without their two aces. Rookie Gary Gentry (3.43 ERA) faced Baltimore's Jim Palmer (16–4, 2.34 ERA). Manager Gil Hodges started an array of lefty bats: Ed Kranepool at first, Ken Boswell at second, Wayne Garrett at third, and Art Shamsky in right.

Game 3 was also historic. Most municipalities wait a generation or even two for a glimpse of the Fall Classic, but New York hadn't endured a four-year drought since 1911.

The Mets spiraled through 27 center fielders in just six seasons before acquiring Agee from the White Sox in 1968. After Bob Gibson hit him in the head on the first pitch of spring training, Agee hit just .217, with five homers, that year. But he bounced back in 1969, hitting .271, with 26 homers, 97 runs scored, and 76 RBI. He'd bashed two homers in the playoffs before going hitless in the first two Series games. In the bottom of the first, Agee slammed a liner over the center-field fence. When Gentry, an .081 hitter, doubled in two runs, New York led, 3–0.

CHAPTER 53

In the fourth, the Orioles had two on with two outs when lefty pull hitter Elrod Hendricks lined a ball to deep left-center. Agee "ran for several minutes," Roger Angell wrote in the *New Yorker*. It was actually about 40 yards, but the Miracle Mets did seem to demolish such basics of physics as the space–time continuum.

Just before the wall, Agee made a dazzling backhand grab. The ball—a sure triple—almost snuck through the webbing. He had saved two runs.

The Mets made it 4–0 in the sixth when Boswell singled and scored on Jerry Grote's double. But the lead was endangered the next inning when Gentry walked three straight hitters. Hodges called on 22-year-old Nolan Ryan. Paul Blair greeted him by slashing a ball into the gap in right-center. Running in the opposite direction from his earlier catch, Agee again covered the Great Plains of Shea in a heartbeat. And when the wind made the ball dip at the last minute, he dove then skidded across the ground, stretching out to make a one-handed catch at the warning track. Agee had single-handedly saved five runs—or six, as the speedy Blair claimed he'd have had an inside-the-park homer if Agee had missed.

In the eighth, Kranepool made Hodges look smart, giving the Mets an extra cushion with a home run, 5–0. With two outs in the ninth, Ryan, like Gentry, went wild, and the Orioles loaded the bases with an infield hit and two walks. Blair was next. This time Agee was not needed—with two strikes, Ryan buckled Blair's knees with a curve to end the game.

The Mets had caught the momentum in a crucial game in the webbing of their center fielder's glove.

54

Broadway Joe Makes Good on His Guarantee, January 12, 1969, Orange Bowl, Miami

Joe Namath never posted the greatest numbers. It just doesn't matter. Joe Namath won only two postseason games. It just doesn't matter. Super Bowl III was far from Joe Namath's greatest statistical showing, and it was the unsung defense that proved crucial to football's biggest upset, the New York Jets' 16–7 win over the Baltimore Colts. It just doesn't matter.

It just doesn't matter because in football's greatest underdog story, it was Namath who was the superhero, who led and inspired the Jets, who saved the Super Bowl as a concept and legitimized the AFL–NFL merger, and it was Namath who transformed football as it headed into a new decade and a new era.

Well, not Joe Namath—Broadway Joe. This larger-than-life persona, the brash talker with the hard-eyed confidence and ferocious desire to win, that's who won Super Bowl III and created the lasting image, wagging his finger to symbolize that he and his team were indeed number one, stunning the sports world while becoming an American idol.

The Jets' turnaround began when Sonny Werblin took over and hired coach Weeb Ewbank, who had masterminded the Baltimore Colts to two NFL championships over the New York Giants. A move into Shea Stadium, which boosted attendance, and a league rights deal with NBC both provided spending money, which Werblin used to splurge on Namath.

In 1965, the NFL's St. Louis Cardinals offered the University of Alabama star $200,000 and a Lincoln Continental. The Jets, understanding the publicity bonanza a talented, personable quarterback might reap in New York, doubled the offer. This ignited more outrageous spending, which prompted the NFL to offer the AFL a merger in 1966. Although the leagues wouldn't combine until 1970, they began sharing a draft and squaring off in a championship game.

But the championship showdown merely reinforced the notion that the AFL was bush league. Vince Lombardi's Green Bay Packers annihilated the Kansas City Chiefs, 35–10, in 1967, and the Oakland Raiders, 33–14, in 1968.

In 1968, the Jets were AFL champs. They were outsiders in the big city, but since the Mets, Yankees, Knicks, Rangers, and Giants hadn't won at all or in years, this scrappy bunch attracted a new following in a city looking for sports heroes.

Still, the NFL champion Baltimore Colts seemed unstoppable, even after quarterback Johnny Unitas was injured in the preseason. Earl Morrall guided the club to a 13–1 record and a 34–0 playoff win. The Jets were a bunch of no-bodies led by a long-haired loudmouth with a white mink coat and a llama rug and zebra pillows in his apartment. (The hair issue sounds overblown today, but back then the NCAA was threatening to revoke scholarships for athletes with hair deemed too long.)

Oddsmakers put the spread between 17 and 19 points, and Jimmy the Greek specifically tacked on three extra points "for the NFL mystique and Don Shula's coaching." Of 55 writers polled, 49 picked the Colts, with *Sports Illustrated*'s Tex Maule projecting a 43–0 rout.

Pete Rozelle was so alarmed that he held a press conference in which he promised to consider rejiggering the championship—just formally named the Super Bowl—so as to allow two superior (read NFL) teams to meet for the title. "Rozelle Indicates Tomorrow's Super Bowl Contest Could Be Next to Last," the *New York Times* declared.

But Rozelle's comments attracted far less attention than Namath, who lived beneath a floating spotlight in Miami. Namath was the starkest possible contrast to crew cuts like Morrall, Unitas, and Shula. When Ewbank thanked the players' wives for their support, Namath thanked "all the broads in New York."

Namath infuriated Shula by declaring Morrall inferior to himself and all the "top young quarterbacks in the AFL." Namath represented a new era, a risk-taking, wide-open game that reflected the swinging '60s, while the NFL largely retained its 1950s mindset. Namath knew these fighting words might provoke Morrall, but he also wanted the Colts defense to focus on Don Maynard, who was hiding an injured left hamstring.

Then came "the Guarantee."

Days before the game, Namath was at the Miami Touchdown Club giving his acceptance speech as the first AFL player selected as Player of the Year. When a Colts supporter heckled him, Namath, drinking Johnnie Walker, broke from his semiprepared rambling to audible a bold declaration: "The Jets will win Sunday. I guarantee it."

Namath wasn't just mouthing off—he'd studied the Colts and been genuinely unimpressed by their traditional zones. The Jets defense was shocked by Baltimore's static offense. Most older NFL quarterbacks couldn't handle Baltimore's pressure, but Namath knew his fast feet, deep backpedal, and rapid release gave him an edge. The Jets' relative youth would hold up better in Miami's heat.

The media made only passing mention of Namath's comment, but it did get both teams' attention. Shula commented curtly, "He's given our players more incentive." Then, at the start of the broadcast, announcer Curt Gowdy relayed Namath's boast to the entire nation.

All Namath's sizzle—broads, booze, and controversies—obscured the ultimate gamer, a tough guy who played through unimaginable pain and spurred his men to greatness. A gambler who won big but frequently lost because of interceptions, he was smart and ambitious enough to subvert his personal style for this game. In Super Bowl III, he quarterbacked like a stereotypical NFL quarterback, with restraint and precision, while the Colts, reacting to Namath's declarations, played a riskier, sloppier game.

The Jets came out loose, while the Colts were on edge. "If we blow it, we destroy the whole season," Shula said.

The first quarter was a scoreless affair but not a meaningless one. The Jets made two strong statements, while the flustered Colts frittered away two huge opportunities. The game's first drive delivered what Jets offensive lineman Randy Rasmussen called the "tone-setter." Running back Matt Snell plowed headfirst into safety Rich Volk, temporarily forcing him from the game with a concussion. The Jets would not be intimidated. (When Volk was hospitalized after the game with convulsions, Namath sent flowers.)

When the Colts sped to New York's 19, it seemed like NFL superiority flexing its muscles, but they wanted that first touchdown badly—so badly they played tight and blew it. Willie Richardson dropped one pass, Morrall overthrew another, and then linebacker Al Atkinson hurled Morrall down. A missed field goal kept the game scoreless.

Namath, who audibled frequently in the first half, knew the Colts secondary never helped on deep plays, so he sent Maynard flying down the right side. Bad leg and all, Maynard blew past everyone. A step slower than usual, he couldn't reach the 55-yard bomb, but this play and a similar one the next quarter altered the Colts' defense. When the Colts rotated toward the strong side and frequently doubled the injured Maynard—who caught no passes all day—it opened up the weak side.

Still, when the Jets fumbled deep in their own territory, it seemed the sort of gaffe that doomed previous AFL teams. But Morrall, wanting to shut up

Namath, played like an overeager rookie. He fired hard into traffic on third down, and Atkinson deflected the pass into the hands of diving cornerback Randy Beverly.

Soon thereafter, Namath patiently captained a 12-play, 80-yard touchdown drive. Morrall continued to gamble and lose. A pass from New York's 16 was intercepted at the two by former Colt Johnny Sample, and just before the half Morrall's pass over the middle was picked off by safety Jim Hudson.

Shula decided to give Morrall just one more chance. But Baltimore fumbled on the first play, and after New York chewed up the clock and kicked a field goal, Shula allowed his starter one more series. Morrall lost two yards on three plays. When the Jets added another field goal for a 13-0 advantage, it meant Morrall's replacement, the great Unitas, would not have time to mix in a ground game and would be easier to defend.

Unitas seemed weak early on, and the third quarter ended with the Jets having yielded 10 yards on seven plays.

After Namath's two passes to George Sauer totaling 50 yards in the fourth, he let Snell and Bill Mathis pound the line. A field goal pushed the lead to 16-0, with 13:26 left. Baltimore was crumbling now—Beverly intercepted Unitas in the end zone, and the Colts' Tom Matte lost his cool and attacked Sample, who ducked his charge and flipped him away.

Jets fans did start squirming after kicker Jim Turner missed a field goal and Unitas, facing a 4th and 10 at his own 20, dug into that old bag of magic, completing a 17-yard pass that sparked a touchdown drive.

Down 16-7, with 3:19 left, Baltimore recovered their onside kick in Jets territory, and Unitas moved 25 yards to New York's 19. But on 4th and 5, Larry Grantham deflected Unitas's pass. It was over.

Snell gained 121 yards, and Sauer caught eight passes for 133 yards. Beverly made two crucial interceptions. Namath's numbers—17-for-28 for 206 yards, no fourth-quarter passes—seemed dinky by his standards, but as he ran off, wagging his index finger high, there was no question about the MVP. Namath's teammates gave him the game ball, but Namath said he'd donate it to the AFL as a symbol of the league's vindication. Afterward, when Jets management planned to give the players watches, Namath berated them, forcing them to come up with diamond-encrusted rings, like those received by Lombardi's Packers.

Many Jets failed to grasp their conquest's historical magnitude—eradicating the demon Raiders had been more emotional—and they even left their Super Bowl trophy behind the front desk in the hotel (an unfortunate indicator, along with the watch incident, of cheap, sloppy mismanagement to come).

But the impact was tremendous. In a country reeling from the horrors of 1968, everyone zeroed in on this feel-good story. Even such lesser stars as defensive lineman Gerry Philbin got endorsement deals.

For New York, the Jets also kicked off an astonishing run: The Mets would win their first World Series that fall, and the Knicks captured their first NBA championship the following spring.

Namath was an iconoclastic icon, the heroic antihero on whom the NFL, and television could piggyback for as long as his knees could bear it. Emboldened AFL owners went into realignment meetings with the NFL and successfully insisted on staying together. (Baltimore was one of three teams forced to shift into the new AFC.) Thanks to Namath, the game opened up—quarterbacks like Dan Fouts took to the air, and such receivers as Lynn Swann and John Stallworth became Super Bowl legends.

This new, more exciting, and colorful game was ready for prime time. *Monday Night Football* rode in on the wake of Super Bowl III. And the championship became a major event, growing from 20 million viewers in 1969, to 102 million by 1978. By living up to its new name in 1969, the Super Bowl took a giant leap toward the national holiday stature it has since attained. And it was all because Joe Namath was truly super.

55

The Jets Avenge Their "Heidi" Loss and Win the AFL Title, December 27, 1968, Shea Stadium

The New York Jets' improvement in the Joe Namath era went from incremental to exponential until, with one fourth-quarter bomb, it accelerated to explosive.

The brash young quarterback from Alabama had been Rookie of the Year in 1965, before leading the Jets to their first .500 season in 1966, their first winning season in 1967, and, finally, an 11–3 record and first place in the East in 1968.

The team was Namath's, but it was more than just him: George Sauer finished second in the AFL with 68 catches, while Don Maynard finished second in yards among receivers, averaging 22.7 yards per catch; Matt Snell and Emerson Boozer were fourth in rushing among backfield tandems; Jim Turner was the most prolific scorer among kickers and Curly Johnson had the second-highest yard-per-punt average; and Johnny Sample and Jim Hudson were among the leaders in interceptions.

Together they were almost at the promised land, one step away from the Super Bowl; however, their opponents in the AFL championship would be the 12–2 Oakland Raiders, the defending AFL champs, whose extra notch in the win column was the infamous "Heidi Game." NBC had cut away from an apparent Jets 32–29 victory with 50 seconds left, to show the movie *Heidi*, only to have Oakland storm back to a mind-boggling 43–32 triumph. Namath's Jets had lost six of seven in his career to the swaggering, sinister Raiders. Twice Oakland intercepted him five times in a game, once they'd nearly killed him by shoving his face in the mud until he choked on it, once they fractured his cheekbone. Oakland loved cheap or late shots, and their target was always the same: Namath. Cut out the heart and kill the team.

The 1968 Raiders were more than nasty and intimidating, they owned the second-best defense and the best offense. But the Jets, fourth in defense and second in offense, had the ultimate intangible—Namath in his prime and ready to lead.

With temperatures near freezing and winds gusting as fast as 50 miles an hour, the field was a wreck, churned up but with no give. Namath was unfazed. He started with a four-play, 56-yard scoring drive, capped by a 14-yard touchdown pass to Maynard. Later, with the Jets up, 10-0, Oakland's Fred Biletnikoff burned Sample to catch a 29-yard touchdown pass, prompting coach Weeb Ewbank to yank his cornerback.

Namath's bruised coccyx and sore right thumb got banged up, and his left ring finger was dislocated. He got a shot to numb the latter and had it taped to the ring finger. Then Ben Davidson sacked Namath and drove a knee into the quarterback's head, giving him a concussion. He also endured a body slam on the half's penultimate play. At halftime, the Jets led, 13-10, but Namath was so disoriented he didn't know where he was.

In the third, Oakland's Daryle Lamonica completed passes of 37 and 40 yards, giving the Raiders first and goal from the six. But Hudson made three straight tackles, and Oakland settled for a game-tying field goal. A revived Namath helmed a 14-play drive to regain the lead. The Super Bowl felt within reach until Sample, who had returned, was again beat by Biletnikoff, this time for 57 yards to open the fourth quarter. The Jets held Oakland to a field goal.

Then it happened, one of those plays that turns a game, specifically, one of those plays that always seems to spin these Jets–Raiders wars in Oakland's favor. In his own territory, Namath looked downfield to Maynard, but cornerback George Atkinson snatched the pass on the run. The Raiders scored on the next play: 23-20, Oakland. The Raiders had done it again. They always did—they were just better or tougher—or something—than the Jets.

But on first down, Namath began his redemption. He saw Atkinson and fellow cornerback Willie Brown playing prevent defense, at least seven yards back to avoid getting beat deep. Namath fired a quick, short pass to Sauer. Having laid the trap, he cautioned his team to stay ready for an audible. At the line, he saw his opening: Both corners moved up to stop Namath from pecking away and throwing underneath. Namath audibled, keeping both running backs blocking for protection and sending three receivers deep. Namath faded almost 10 yards and shifted toward the left hash mark, buying time. He lofted the ball far and wide, across to the right sideline, where Maynard sprinted past Atkinson. Maynard looked over his left shoulder, to where the pass should be, but the wind carried it past, over his right. Maynard swirled around and made the catch before being shoved out of bounds at the Oakland six.

Namath next drew inspiration from the oddest of places. According to Mark Kriegel's biography, the quarterback recalled a dumpy guy named Petey the Cabdriver. This guy drank regularly at Namath's bar, Bachelors III, so he told the quarterback in person that the Jets were too risk-averse near the goal, always running, never passing. Namath called a play-action pass. Perfect protection gave him time to find Maynard, the fourth option, free in the end zone. Sidearm, Namath zipped the ball past three defenders to his receiver. In three plays, Namath had moved the team back into the lead.

He had struck so quickly, however, that Oakland had time left for two drives. The first stalled on the Jets 26. But on the next one, Lamonica hit Biletnikoff for 24, and Warren Wells for 37 more. A penalty moved the ball to the Jets 12. Was the *Heidi* theme beginning to play?

Lamonica called a short pass out in the flat to Charley Smith, a play the Raiders had worked on all week and saved for just this sort of opportunity. But Lamonica felt pressure, and his pass floated awry. The Jets' Ralph Baker realized that Smith was behind Lamonica, meaning the play was considered a lateral. He scooped up the loose ball, and while his 70-yard romp was nullified—the ball was dead upon recovery—the Jets had possession, and the game.

They beat Oakland with the dramatic and unpredictable play the Raiders typically pulled off and were champions of the AFL. What had seemed unthinkable was now not enough. Even though the NFL's Baltimore Colts and the media wrote them off for the Super Bowl, the Jets knew how good they really were. Namath, in fact, was ready to guarantee victory.

56

Arthur Ashe Wins the First U.S. Open, September 9, 1968, West Side Tennis Club

In 1968, tumult and turmoil were inescapable: the King and Kennedy assassinations, the Tet Offensive, the Soviet invasion of Czechoslovakia; it was a year of riots in cities and black fists raised at the Olympics. In New York, there was a student takeover at Columbia, a public school strike, and a radical transformation of the local tennis tournament—tennis finally opened its doors to professionals, and in the first U.S. Open, in a sport as white as its dress code, a black man won the U.S. crown for the first—and only—time.

Tennis began as a diversion for the British upper class, and even when it reached the United States, class lines remained sharply etched—it was an amateur sport played by those who could afford to. Although the middle class began following the sport after Bill Tilden rose to stardom in 1920, public courts remained scarce, participation was minimal, and the biggest tournaments were held at private tennis clubs. (No Jews, blacks, or other outsiders allowed, thank you very much.)

The game suffered from a split personality that arose after Tilden helped develop the professional game. The International Lawn Tennis Association ensured that the most prestigious tournaments remained strictly and haughtily amateur. To keep the best players around to entertain society crowds, "amateur" tournaments lured them with expenses and under-the-table money, giving rise to the phrase "shamateurism." Although some players made a decent living and remained subservient to the system, most, from Don Budge to Jack Kramer to Ken Rosewall to Rod Laver, won their titles then turned pro, traveling from city to city with another top player, playing the same foe nightly, toiling like carny performers.

CHAPTER 56

Finally, in 1968, revolt arrived. Top pros like Rosewall and Laver were form-ing new circuits and grabbing the best amateurs, so the British Lawn Tennis Association and United States Lawn Tennis Association helped force change from within, transforming Wimbledon and the U.S. championship into "open" tournaments. At Forest Hills, the pros (all Australian) were seeded highest: Rod Laver, Tony Roche, Ken Rosewall, and John Newcombe. Arthur Ashe was seeded fifth.

Ashe grew up in segregated Richmond, Virginia. At his first hometown-sanctioned tournament he was turned away because he was black. Determined, not deterred, Ashe became the first African American to play in the Maryland boys' championships. The skinny boy with the power game earned a tennis scholarship to UCLA, winning both an individual and a team NCAA champion-ship in 1965.

In 1963, Ashe also became the first African American to represent the United States in Davis Cup play. Radical blacks subsequently chastised Ashe for playing for "white America," but he preferred working within the system. Similarly, in 1968, he told black Olympians that he would not publicly support a boycott—their participation and public display of strength had a far more last-ing impact.

By 1968, Ashe, 25, had been drafted into the U.S. Army. He could play in tournaments if he served on a national team but had to remain an amateur to be eligible for Davis Cup play. According to army policy, playing the Open was considered Davis Cup preparation.

The pros at the Open were unaccustomed to playing outdoors and on grass, and unfamiliar with the new players after years on their insular and largely indoor tour. Laver lost to Cliff Drysdale, another pro, in round 16, and Ashe disposed of Drysdale. He had an easy semis foe in Clark Graebner, while speedy Dutchman Tom Okker upset Rosewall. (The pros acclimated by the following year, particularly Laver, who won the Grand Slam in 1969.) Rain and scheduling conflicts pushed the first Open final back to Monday, so just 7,100 fans witnessed Ashe's powerful serve and aggressive volleying, which offset his numerous errors and Okker's court coverage. Ashe pounded 26 aces, including 15 in the 64-minute, 14–12 first set. But Ashe also surprised Okker with a deft touch on his lobs whenever Okker took the offensive. After Okker edged him in the second set, 7–5, the two men traded 6–3 sets, bringing the final to a fifth set.

Down 0–1, Okker rushed the net at 30–30, only to watch a perfect lob float overhead. After Ashe hit a forehand winner for the break, he needed only to hold serve the rest of the way, and he did just that. He blasted one last ace in the last game at 5–3, which he captured at love.

Okker took home $14,000 as runner-up, but Ashe's strict amateur status meant he got nothing more than his free hotel room and $28 daily stipend. The champion, who brought his father out of the stands and embraced him during an emotional trophy presentation, didn't mind. He had made history. "There would be only one first U.S. Open," Ashe said later.

He was the first American men's tennis champion since 1955, which provided cachet and a platform for leadership in and out of tennis. "If Ashe doesn't win, he doesn't become 'Arthur Ashe,'" said tennis writer Joel Drucker.

When Ashe turned pro, he helped force tournaments to dole out prize money properly; he became a founding father of the Association of Tennis Players and, in 1973, was a leader of a Wimbledon boycott that gained more rights and money for players. He also cofounded a program to teach tennis to economically disadvantaged youth. Ashe devoted considerable time and capital, calling attention to South Africa's apartheid, and after his playing days he became involved with the United Negro College Fund and created the Safe Passage Foundation, which oversaw an inner-city tennis program and another program that worked to boost the graduation rates of minority athletes. After a heart attack, he became national campaign chairman of the American Heart Association, and, in 1992, when he publicly acknowledged he had AIDS, he launched a foundation to help raise money and remove the stigma that haunted the disease.

That 1968 tournament also had an instantaneous and monumental impact on the U.S. Open and tennis overall. Advance sales for the 1969 Open tripled, and the sport's upscale audience drew more television coverage and dollars, which fueled viewership and participation. The number of people playing tennis tripled between 1970 and 1974, when Chris Evert and Jimmy Connors, representing a truly "Open" generation, generated a new wave of excitement, virtually reinventing the sport.

That growth would push the sport from the private Forest Hills club to the very public National Tennis Center. And when the sport outgrew Louis Armstrong Stadium shortly after Ashe's tragic death in 1993, the United States Tennis Association built a new stadium alongside it. It was named for a man who was not the greatest tennis player of all time but who achieved greatness as a human being, symbolized the potential in everyone, and did it all in large part because of what he had achieved at the very first U.S. Open final: Arthur Ashe.

This Time Ralph Terry Finds Success in the Ninth Inning of a Game 7, October 16, 1962, Candlestick Park, San Francisco

It was the quintessential sports moment, a finale so fraught with tension that it almost felt scripted: Game 7 of the World Series, the bottom of the ninth inning, the score 1–0, and the home team sending the top of the order to the plate. Every imaginable factor would come into play in the final three outs—the weather, managerial and coaching decisions, the right fielder's overlooked defensive skill, the imprecise positioning of the second baseman, a quest for redemption by an all-time World Series goat, and the menacing presence of three future Hall of Famers at the plate. The inning has been broken down and analyzed endlessly, but add it all up and the final showdown of the 1962 World Series between the New York Yankees and the San Francisco Giants reveals nothing less than the magnificent and endless intrigue of baseball.

This World Series should have been a slugfest. The defending champion Yankees featured Mickey Mantle and Roger Maris, who combined for 63 homers, while three other players hit at least 20 dingers. While the Yankees led the American League in runs scored, the Giants led everyone, thanks to Willie Mays, Orlando Cepeda, Felipe Alou, and Willie McCovey. But the 101-win Giants had to mount a last-minute charge to tie the Los Angeles Dodgers, forcing a replay of the 1951 playoff—the Giants even overcame a 4–2 ninth-inning deficit in the deciding game (the score when Bobby Thomson hit his famous home run).

Whitey Ford beat the exhausted Giants, 6–2, in Game 1, then Giants 24-game winner Jack Sanford evened things up with a three-hitter against the Yankees' 23-game winner, Ralph Terry. The teams split the next two games. Game 5 pitted Sanford and Terry against one another again; the score was 2–2 in the eighth before New York captured the win, 5–3. The teams returned to San Francisco, where a deluge of rainstorms postponed the action for three days before Billy Pierce's three-hitter forced a seventh game. The extra days off meant Game 7 would again match Sanford and Terry.

There had been only two other best-of-seven Series in which two pitchers faced one another three times—Detroit's Hal Newhouser versus Chicago's Hank Borowy in 1945, and Milwaukee's Warren Spahn versus New York's Whitey Ford in 1958—but neither showdown produced consistent duels. (Subsequent confrontations, for example, the Yankees' Mel Stottlemyre versus the Cardinals' Bob Gibson in 1964, the Dodgers' Sandy Koufax against the Twins' Jim Kaat in 1965, and the Mets' Jon Matlack against the A's Ken Holzman in 1973, also produced uneven results.)

But Sanford and Terry exceeded expectations. Sanford yielded seven hits and four walks but pitched out of almost every jam: The Yankees got their lone run in the fifth on a bases-loaded double play.

That lone run loomed awfully large. Terry was perfect through 5⅔ innings before allowing a harmless single to Sanford. In the Giants' seventh, Mays was robbed of an extra-base hit by Tom Tresh; McCovey followed with a triple that would otherwise have tied the game. With the tying run 90 feet away, Terry fanned Cepeda. The Yankees chased Sanford in the eighth, but reliever Billy O'Dell came on with the bases full and no outs, and performed a Houdini-esque escape of his own.

Terry took his two-hitter into the bottom of the ninth. The Yankees needed three more outs to earn back-to-back titles for the fourth time.

Baseball had not had a 1–0 clincher since the Giants beat the Yankees in 1921, and this one was soon in jeopardy. Catcher Elston Howard muffed Matty Alou's pop foul near the Giants dugout. (Terry later claimed that one of the Giants, possibly manager Alvin Dark, bumped Howard.) Given new life, Alou dragged a bunt for a hit. Trouble had begun.

Matty's brother Felipe had hit 25 homers and bunted just twice all year, but Dark turned conservative at the wrong time and called for a sacrifice. After one failed attempt, Dark changed his mind, but Alou whiffed. Terry fanned Chuck Hiller, too, but to finish the Giants he'd have to defeat perhaps the best ballplayer since Babe Ruth. Willie Mays led the league with 49 homers in 1962, and he wanted one more. Terry, unfortunately, knew about Game 7 ninth-inning home runs—two years earlier, he'd surrendered a shocker to the Pittsburgh Pirates' Bill Mazeroski.

Trying to avoid the goat tag again, Terry pitched Mays away. Mays roped the ball into right. Had it not been for the excessive rain, the ball would have skittered into the corner, allowing Alou to score from first. But the wet field slowed everything down, and Maris, always underrated as a fielder, hustled over, cut off the ball, and made a perfect relay to second baseman Bobby Richardson. The play has long been a debate topic in San Francisco: Most Giants agreed with third-base coach Whitey Lockman's decision to slam the brakes on the speedy Alou because it's bad baseball to make the final out at the plate with two of your best hitters coming up. But Mays disagreed, saying Richardson's throw home was a bit off-line and might have been worse had he felt the pressure of a runner steaming home; Mays always maintained he would have run through Lockman's stop sign (and run over Yankees catcher Elston Howard, if need be).

With Alou on third and Mays on second, Yankees manager Ralph Houk visited Terry to talk tactics. Up next was the lefty McCovey, who had homered off Terry in Game 2 and just tripled off him. The following batter was Orlando Cepeda, a more feared hitter then. But, like Terry, Cepeda was a righty, and his only Series had come off the lefty Ford. The choice seemed obvious. Yet, Houk inexplicably deferred to Terry's decision to go after McCovey, albeit carefully.

Terry's idea of careful, however, conjured Mazeroski memories: He left the first pitch right out over the plate. McCovey, not expecting to see a strike, was so surprised he overreacted and hit a long, hard foul. The next pitch was a ball. On the 1–1 pitch, Terry tried coming inside on McCovey, but the slugger stepped back and took a vicious swing. He crushed the ball, smoking a liner toward the outfield in a spot that, in normal circumstances, would have resulted in a two-run hit. McCovey was such a dead pull hitter that most National League teams shifted their second baseman in the hole against him and often pulled their shortstop on the right side of the bag. But Yankees second baseman Bobby Richardson wasn't as familiar with McCovey's tendencies and failed to play him as far toward right as he should have. Out of position, Richardson inadvertently was perfectly positioned.

It was a moment McCovey would long relive in his dreams. Richardson took one step, read the topspin, and put his mitt out. For a fraction of a second as McCovey's bat met the ball, the Giants and their fans had begun leaping out of their seats—they were World Series champions. But before the jubilation could travel from their brains to their vocal cords, the ball smacked into Richardson's glove, choking off the cheers.

This would be the last Yankees championship for 15 years, and thanks to this memorable ninth inning, Terry, the goat of the 1960 Series, was the Most Valuable Player of the 1962 Series.

58

Roger Maris Beats the Babe, October 1, 1961, Yankee Stadium

Sometimes I think it wasn't worth the aggravation. Maybe I wouldn't do it over again if I had the chance.

—Roger Maris, on hitting 61 home runs in 1961

Put a big fat asterisk next to the 61st home run of the season Roger Maris hit on October 1, 1961. Not the one with a negative connotation that then-commissioner Ford Frick had in mind, but more of a star, a positive symbol indicating that this is the true home run record, that Maris is the only person to hit more home runs than Babe Ruth without the aid of andro, creatine, cream, clear, and the other substances swallowed, injected, and rubbed on during the modern muscle era.

To top it all, Maris faced more stress and pressure than Ruth in 1927, Mark McGwire and Sammy Sosa in 1998, or Barry Bonds in 2001. When Ruth hit 60 homers, he sought only to break his own six-year-old mark of 59, which topped his 54 from 1920, which shattered the high-water mark of 29 he'd attained in 1919. In other words, Ruth existed in his own universe. Had he finished 1927, with 57 or 59 four-baggers, he would have remained baseball's most important, most popular, and most successful star. McGwire and Sosa faced a media brigade unlike anything Ruth or even Maris ever saw, but most of the interviews were friendly, even fawning. It would be years before McGwire and Sosa, and others, would shame themselves in front of Congress and the nation. In 1998, McGwire and Sosa were credited with saving baseball, not accused of betraying it. And they were chasing Maris, not Ruth, so there was no sense of a hero being demeaned. If Bonds didn't get such a lovefest, it was due to his lifetime of surliness; besides, he didn't seem to care. And while his 2001 performance was a marvel, the record was only three years old, and long-ball totals were so inflated that the chase did not resonate the same way.

Maris, by contrast, was chasing Ruth's ghost while racing alongside superstar teammate Mickey Mantle and being harassed by the commissioner, the press, and fans, who all felt this precious record should not fall into the hands of a mere mortal—and a bland one at that. Only Hank Aaron would have it worse, being subjected to vicious racial hatred when he broke Ruth's career home run record. By season's end, Maris's hair was falling out in clumps, and he was surviving on coffee and Camels, unable to think straight, trapped inside the swirling media vortex.

Maris had grown up in Fargo, North Dakota, and was heading to the University of Oklahoma on a football scholarship when the Cleveland Indians offered him $15,000. In the minors, he learned to pull for power. By 1957, he was in the majors, streaky and injury-prone with Cleveland and then Kansas City. The Yankees—who treated the cash-poor Kansas City A's like their farm team, making 15 trades for 59 players from 1955 to 1960—snatched up Maris. His hitting style would be perfect for the "House That Ruth Built," with its short right-field porch.

In 1960, Maris hit 25 homers by June 30; he finished with 39 and won the MVP Award, helping the Yankees reclaim the American League crown.

But the Yankees were stunned by Bill Mazeroski's home run in Game 7 of the 1960 World Series—the once-invincible Bronx Bombers had now won just two crowns in the previous seven seasons. In 1961, they'd have something to prove. The Yankees' 240 long balls, almost half of them hit by the "M&M boys," set a record that stood until the steroid era. Maris and Mantle blasted the Yankees to 109 wins—the third most at the time for any World Series champion. Manager Ralph Houk flipped Maris and Mantle in 1961, batting Maris third, where he'd see better pitches, and Mantle, a superior all-around hitter, fourth. When Maris hit his first homer in the 10th game, Mantle already had seven. After 27 games, it was 10–3, Mantle. Then Maris bashed 12 long balls in 16 games and 23 homers in 36 contests. He'd also hit five homers in five games twice in July and seven in six games. But as he attracted attention, he endured more droughts.

In June, Maris was asked if he might break the record. The reluctant star already had a rep for being surly; he hated such speculation and was surprised it was already starting. "How the fuck should I know?" he responded.

By July 2, Maris had 30 homers—eight ahead of Ruth's pace—and Mantle 29. Mantle had been a shy hick when he first came to New York, and despite his popularity, high expectations had caused perpetual disappointment in some fans and writers, his biggest flaw being that he wasn't Joe DiMaggio. But with Maris threatening Ruth's record, Yankees followers coalesced around Mantle, the 10-year veteran, as the pure Yankee, their true love, and the deserving one. Mantle gamely struggled to stay in the homer race, even when his body broke down at season's end, attaining new stature in the eyes of the writers and fans at the expense of Maris, his good friend and roomie.

Then Frick, a former ghostwriter for and buddy of Babe Ruth—and a classic "back when men were real men" guy—issued a decree. "Any player who may hit more than 60 home runs during his club's first 154 games would be recognized as having established a new record," Frick wrote, referring to the fact that the American League had just added two teams and expanded its schedule from 154 to 162 games. "However, if the player does not hit more than 60 homers until after . . . there would have to be a distinctive mark in the record books."

Although Maris replied, "A season's a season," most baseball writers, in a *Sporting News* poll, backed the commissioner, and so did many players: Stan Musial, Warren Spahn, the Yankees' Whitey Ford, and the Mick himself supported the asterisk. "If I should break it in the 155th game, I wouldn't want the record," Mantle declared on a day he and Maris each had a home run erased when an incomplete game was rained out.

Maris's bat then went largely quiet. It wasn't just Frick. You can't spell "pressure" without "press," and the television, radio, and newspaper sportswriters piled on. Television's growth forced newspapers to go beyond game reports and seek quotes, color, analysis, and, of course, controversy. This was better and more truthful journalism than the gee-whiz mythmaking of Grantland Rice and his 1920s comrades, but it could be malevolent, birthing the permanent tabloidization of the media.

Just as Mantle hadn't been DiMaggio, now reporters held Maris accountable for not being his aw-shucks, life-of-the-party teammate. Maris didn't help his cause with such comments as, "I'll be glad when the season is over."

Some writers chastised Maris for his low batting average or inability to hit lefties; others pointed out that expansion had so diluted pitching talent that every American League record should be considered suspect. They didn't mention the advent of night baseball, West Coast travel, relief pitchers, and the influx of talent accompanying integration, which made life harder for Maris than it had been for Ruth.

On August 2, both sluggers had 40 homers. More reporters attached themselves to the race. Maris's inability to play along cost him, with local headlines like, "Maris Sulks in Trainer's Room" and "Maris Fails," shading public perception until even New York fans booed him.

After 125 games, Maris's 50 homers stood ahead of Ruth's 154-game pace. Then Mantle got an infection, and an abscess followed—he'd finish with 54 homers, languishing in a hospital, leaving Maris more exposed both in the lineup and in the race against Ruth (and Frick). Stuck at 58, he ran into a rainy doubleheader in games 152 and 153, and was blanked.

Before the fateful 154th, he told Houk, "I can't stand it anymore." Then he hit his 59th—beating Hank Greenberg and Jimmie Foxx—while the wind held up another blast. The Yankees clinched the pennant, but while his teammates celebrated, Maris got the third degree from the media about what would happen if he "belatedly" passed Ruth.

The *Milwaukee Journal* decreed that the record should only be broken "by someone of greater baseball stature." It further stated, "[Maris] is not more than a good big-league ballplayer. There just isn't anything heroic about the man."

October 1 arrived, the season's final day. Maris was stuck on 60. That was Ruth's number. To come so far but end there hurt. Maris wanted the record. In the first, Boston Red Sox pitcher Tracy Stallard got Maris to pop to left. In the fourth, Stallard missed, high and away, then missed low and inside. The fans started booing him. The 2-0 sat fat, and Maris whipped his 35-inch, 33-ounce lumber through the strike zone, his weight shifting into the ball. He watched it soar through space, not returning to earth until it was 365 feet away, six rows deep in right field.

This was the Yankees' 240th home run. It was Maris's 132nd run scored, tying him (with Mantle) for the league lead, and his 142nd RBI, giving him that crown. And since the Yankees' 109th triumph would finish with no other scoring, it marked the only time Maris won a 1-0 game with a home run.

Only one number mattered. 61.

Briefly, the number flashed through Maris's mind—the first time he thought specifically of a number as he hit one—then he circled the bases in a "complete fog." One fan ran out and shook his hand near third base, and his teammates refused to let the modest Maris disappear into the dugout until he had waved his cap to the crowd, which cheered so long the game was delayed even after Maris sat down. "It was," he admitted, "the greatest thrill of my life."

A local teen named Sal Durante caught the ball and was brought down to meet Maris and pose for pictures. In the sixth and the eighth, Maris, taking home run cuts, whiffed and popped up. Still, he had 61. Yet, the media mob didn't let up, grilling him afterward with such queries as, "As you were running around the bases, were you thinking about Mickey Mantle?"

Frick never backed down, but the numbers legitimize Maris: He hit 61 home runs in 698 plate appearances; Ruth hit 60 home runs in 691. The last eight games did not make the difference. No one claimed Maris was Ruth's equal—Ruth's 1927 average was almost 100 points higher than Maris's in 1961, and he belted almost twice as many doubles and twice the triples, drew 44 more walks, scored 26 more runs, and drove in 22 more runs. The big man even stole six more bases. But Maris's home run mark was fairly earned. (One trivia note: A week later, Whitey Ford set a new World Series record, pitching 32 consecutive scoreless innings, breaking a mark set by a long-ago Boston Red Sox hurler: Babe Ruth.)

The following year, Maris was taken to task for mustering "just" 33 homers and 100 RBI. He didn't find peace until being traded to St. Louis in 1967, but he found appreciation a decade later when new Yankees owner George Steinbrenner cajoled him into returning for Old-Timers Day, where Maris was loudly cheered.

By the time he died of cancer in 1985, the reevaluation had begun in earnest. When McGwire and Sosa began their assault in 1998, Maris's mark had lasted longer than Ruth's, earning him the stature he finally deserved. His mark was eradicated, of course, but the subsequent steroid controversy has only enhanced the aura around Maris's all-natural 61. The record books no longer call him the single-season home run king, but in the ultimate irony, the press and the fans are on his side. Maybe if Maris could know that, he'd decide it was worth the aggravation after all.

59

Pat Summerall Kicks a Field Goal in the Snow, December 14, 1958, Yankee Stadium

In the best of circumstances, Pat Summerall probably could not have made a field goal from near midfield. These were not the best of circumstances: The thermometer read 25 degrees; large, wet snowflakes tumbled from the sky; the wind howled; the field was a mess—and it was the fourth quarter with the New York Giants' season on the line.

"I could barely see the goalpost," Summerall recalled later.

Owner Wellington Mara peered down from the press box, barely making out Summerall in the descending gloom. "He can't kick it that far," Mara speculated aloud. "What are we doing?"

Offensive coach Vince Lombardi was furious. Sure, Charlie Conerly had failed to complete a pass on first, second, and third downs, but Lombardi would rather try once more than accept the inevitability of a failed kick. Normally, head coach Jim Lee Howell deferred on strategy. Not this time.

The Giants were not losing—the score against Cleveland was 10–10—but the Browns were one game ahead in the standings on the season's final day, so a tie would give Cleveland the Eastern Division title, sending them to the NFL Championship Game and leaving New York out in the cold.

Paul Brown's Cleveland squads were accustomed to winning big games. The Browns won all four titles in the upstart AAFC; when the league folded into the NFL, the Browns edged the Giants in a 1950 tiebreaking playoff game to go to the championship, then returned to the championship game in six of the next seven years. The only year the Browns stumbled was 1956, when the Giants won it all, but Brown drafted running back Jim Brown and, in 1957, topped New York once more.

The 1958 season seemed like more of the same. The Giants struggled to a 2–2 start, and the Browns began undefeated. But Big Blue won in Cleveland and entered this final game 8–3, while the Browns were 9–2.

On the Browns' first play from scrimmage, quarterback Milt Plum faked a pitchout, then handed off to Jim Brown, who'd set a new NFL record that year with 1,527 rushing yards. Brown burst through the middle and raced 65 yards virtually untouched for a touchdown.

In the swirling snow, Cleveland's Lou "The Toe" Groza missed two field goals from less than 40 yards, while Summerall missed a 45-yarder, but both men made one, giving the Browns a 10–3 halftime lead. In the third quarter, Cleveland's drive stalled at the Giants 12, and Paul Brown opted for trickery, faking the field goal and trying to run it in. The Giants shut down the play, and many Browns were so furious they lost focus.

In the fourth, the Giants finally mounted two solid drives. On the first, Bob Schnelker's seven-yard touchdown catch tied the game. With less than five minutes left, they reached the 33-yard line and sent Summerall into try a field goal that would give New York the lead.

The Giants had traded for Summerall that season despite his 45 percent average with Chicago; after all, he could also play tight end and defense, and even return kicks. He started terribly, missing seven of his first 10 attempts, along with two extra points. He'd settled down, hitting seven of his next 11 field goal attempts, but the week before this game he'd injured his leg and had been unable to practice. He told defensive coach Tom Landry he could not kick off but maybe could hit extra points or a short field goal. Now 33 yards proved too long, and Summerall missed. But the Giants defense stopped Cleveland with time for one last drive. On second down near midfield, Conerly fired a short pass to Frank Gifford, who appeared to catch it and take a few steps before being hit by a Cleveland linebacker, causing him to drop the ball. Cleveland's Walt Michaels scooped it up, racing the length of the field toward a game-clinching touchdown—or not. Head linesman Charley Berry ruled the pass incomplete. Paul Brown argued vociferously, but there was no instant replay and no way to change Berry's mind. (Michaels later said Brown made sure Berry never officiated another Cleveland game.)

The Giants' situation remained bleak, but they still had the ball and, with a little more than two minutes left, one final chance. But that third-down play fizzled when Alex Webster, free near the goal line, lost the pass coming out of the snow and dropped it. Despite the vehement argument of Lombardi, Howell again turned to Summerall.

CHAPTER 59

When Summerall was born, his right foot faced completely backward; when he was six months old, the doctor broke the bones and turned the foot around. He'll walk, the doctor said, but don't expect him to run or play on it. In 1956, when Summerall was with Chicago, he kicked three field goals to beat Cleveland, 9–7. Afterward, Paul Brown sneered, "Enjoy it. It'll never happen again." Here was a chance to prove Brown as wrong as the doctor.

Due to snow covering the field, no one knows exactly how long the kick was—the record books marked it at 49 yards, but estimates by players and reporters ranged from 45 to 55. No matter what, it was a daunting prospect. When Summerall arrived in the huddle, Conerly was shocked, barking, "What the fuck are you doing here?" So much for a vote of confidence.

As Summerall got set, Browns defensive back Kenny Konz screamed and shouted to distract him. The snap was perfect, and Summerall let fly.

He knew instinctively he had the distance, but as the ball weaved toward the side, he wasn't sure it would remain on line. The ball disappeared into the snowy night, and when Summerall heard the cheering and the celebrating, he knew he'd made it. The Giants led, 13–10.

An ecstatic Summerall floated back to the sideline, where Lombardi greeted him, not in joy, but in disbelief that he had been wrong too, saying, "You know, you son of a bitch, you can't kick it that far."

But he could, and he did.

The kick's impact lasted long after the ball cleared the goalpost. It gave Summerall a celebrity's shine, earning him his first radio job after the season. And it discouraged the Browns, who were lackluster in the next week's tiebreaking game, which New York won, 10–0. In the NFL Championship Game against Johnny Unitas and Baltimore, the Giants would lose one of the closest and most important championship games ever, but they'd be elevated to immortals in the process.

60

The Yankees Resurrect Themselves with a 10th-Inning Win, October 8, 1958, County Stadium, Milwaukee

The magic was gone. When Milwaukee's Warren Spahn blanked the New York Yankees in Game 4 of the 1958 World Series, an era seemed over. Formerly omnipotent, the Bronx Bombers had failed to reach the World Series in 1954, lost to (gasp!) Brooklyn in 1955, and, after squeaking by the Dodgers in 1956, fallen to Milwaukee in 1957—in a Game 7 at Yankee Stadium no less.

In 1958, New York staggered to a 29–32 finish, so when they dropped three of the first four in the Series, the end seemed nigh. Only once, in 1925, had a team rebounded from a 3–1 deficit. After Game 2, Lew Burdette, who accumulated his fourth Series win against the Yankees in two years (and hit a three-run homer), sneered that the Yankees "would have trouble in our league," an echo of Spahn's harsh dismissal from 1957.

Such boasting contained a kernel of truth—the National League had integrated far more rapidly than the American League and had more strong teams; the league had won three of the four previous Series and would win five of the following seven. The Braves, who had moved to their new city from stodgy old Boston just six years earlier, represented the future. The segregationist, tradition-bound Yankees, who won just 92 games that year (fewest of the franchise's World Series champions until 2000) by beating up such perennially underfinanced weaklings as the Athletics, looked like a relic. (Indeed, the same could be said of New York in general, which, in 1958, lost its two National League franchises to westward relocation.)

The Yankees, however, weren't through yet. Goliath would get up off the floor and smite David but hard, winning three straight to capture the Series. If so many other great Yankees triumphs did not already dominate these lists, all three victories might merit a place on them. But beating Spahn in extra innings in Game 6 stands out.

The turnaround began in Game 5, when Bob Turley pitched a complete-game shutout. With the Yankees clinging to a 1–0 lead in the sixth, Elston Howard made a diving catch on a sinking liner and turned it into a double play. Pumped up, the Yankees churned out six runs in their turn as Burdette finally wore down.

Still, the Yankees needed to take Game 6 to force yet another winner-take-all showdown. The years 1955 to 1958 mark baseball's only stretch of four straight seven-game Series, and while the two Dodgers–Yankees battles are more renowned, the Braves–Yankees matchup proved every bit their equal for electrifying baseball.

For Game 6, Milwaukee manager Fred Haney got greedy and started his ace, Spahn, on two days' rest (on top of 10 innings in Game 1) instead of Bob Rush on three days' rest. Spahn wanted the assignment. Early in his career, a different Braves manager, Casey Stengel, had questioned his courage when he refused to throw at Pee Wee Reese, and he wanted to avenge himself. (He'd pitched poorly in the 1957 Series.)

Spahn gave up a first-inning homer to Hank Bauer, but Milwaukee tied it in the first and knocked out starter Whitey Ford in the second with three singles and a walk for a 2–1 lead. The Yankees escaped only when Howard made another big defensive play, throwing Andy Pafko out at home.

The Yankees scratched out a run in the sixth on Yogi Berra's sacrifice fly to tie the game, and Stengel called on closer Ryne Duren. Duren fanned seven in four innings, allowing just two baserunners. But Spahn was equally magnificent, and the game went to the 10th inning.

Haney left Spahn in for his 29th inning in a week. It would be the Braves' downfall. Spahn gave up a leadoff homer to Gil McDougald, then two-out singles to Howard and Berra. Moose Skowron greeted reliever Don McMahon by singling home an insurance run, and the Yankees led, 4–2.

But Duren, who'd averaged less than two innings per appearance all year, was also out of gas. With one out, he walked Johnny Logan, bringing up the Braves' big bats. Representing the tying run would be Eddie Mathews (averaging 38 homers annually in six seasons), Hank Aaron (averaging 32 in his first four full years), and Joe Adcock (who hit 19 in just 320 at-bats that year).

Duren found that proverbial something extra on his fastball to pick up his eighth and final strikeout on Mathews (with Logan taking second in the process). And he kept Aaron and Adcock in the yard—but he couldn't get them out. Aaron singled home Logan, making it 4–3. Then Adcock singled Aaron to third, putting the tying run 90 feet away and the winning run on first.

Stengel called on the one person besides Duren he'd seen dominate the Braves: Bob Turley.

Pinch-hitter Frank Torre (then known for his .309 average, not for being Joe's older brother) lifted the ball toward right field, but it never got there: Second baseman McDougald snared it for the final out. In the year of the movie *Damn Yankees*, those damn Yankees had forced a seventh game. The Yankees won that one, too, beating Burdette again as Turley once again saved the day with 6 1/3 innings of one-run relief.

When it was over, the loquacious Stengel, for whom this would be the final Series crown, had the following last words: "Well, I guess we showed them we could play in the National League after all."

61

Carmen Basilio and Sugar Ray Robinson Go to War, September 23, 1957, Yankee Stadium

Sugar Ray Robinson was a flashy fighter, flamboyant showman, and Harlem entrepreneur, admired by sportswriters and adored by the public. Carmen Basilio loathed him.

"When he died, I said, 'I don't give a shit,'" Basilio once said. "There's no sense in putting on any act."

Robinson's supporters saw a stylish slugger, a technical and tactical master, and a symbol of hope for both aspiring blacks and a new generation of athletes—his fierce sense of ownership in negotiating his fights paved the way for the likes of baseball's Curt Flood. Basilio, a former onion farmer and proud ex-Marine, saw a haughty son of a bitch and a show-off who liked gouging opponents in business dealings as much as in the ring. When Basilio vacated his welterweight title in 1957, to challenge Robinson for the middleweight crown, the champ—still fighting at age 36, only because the IRS had him on the ropes—demanded that Basilio accept a mere 10 percent of the purse, half the customary amount for a challenger. When Basilio balked, Robinson backed down, but the bad feelings lingered.

So, when Basilio climbed into the ring in Yankee Stadium, he was going after the title and going after Robinson.

The 30-year-old Basilio, with youth on his side, was the slight betting favorite, but he was giving away five inches and almost seven pounds. Only one twentieth-century welterweight champion had dethroned a middleweight belt-holder before—that was Robinson, who slaughtered Jake LaMotta in 1951.

Robinson was the initial predator, sticking and feinting, and using his reach to keep a safe distance, while landing jab after jab after jab. Basilio lacked Robinson's defensive skills and cut easily: Robinson drew blood from Basilio's nose and left eye. But while Robinson sometimes disdained everything about boxing except the fat checks, the aggressive Basilio relished the confrontations and kept charging inside to pound Robinson's body.

"When people buy a fight ticket, they're paying to see blood and knockdowns," he said. "Every time I go into the ring, I expect to be busted up; it's as much a part of the business as the boxing gloves."

When Robinson slowed, Basilio got punches off quicker and with more snap. He lacked Robinson's knockout power, but he could hit. In the famous 11th round—considered one of the most enthralling boxing rounds ever—Robinson briefly rallied with hard rights to the body before Basilio countered with three blazing rights to the jaw that sent Robinson sailing into the ropes. Some reports estimated that Basilio landed 34 straight punches before the bell. But Robinson persevered, coming back in the 12th and pummeling Basilio with several combos that left the challenger wobbly.

Basilio also demonstrated determination and resilience rarely seen even in the upper echelons of sport. He held on even after Robinson sliced his face with another eruption of jabs in Round 13. Basilio was launching wild punches, but one right to the jaw rattled Robinson, shifting the momentum yet again. Robinson, having gone through his second, third, and fourth winds, had nothing left in reserve. In the last two rounds, he landed some good punches, but Basilio set the pace and inflicted more damage.

The referee scored the fight to Robinson, 9–6, but the two judges voted for Basilio, 9–5–1 and 8–6–1. A ringside poll of the press gave 19 votes to Basilio and eight to Robinson, with seven draws.

The new middleweight champion had taken such a beating that he locked himself in the dressing room out of embarrassment. Robinson was also a wreck, although he downplayed how badly he had been hurt, prompting Basilio to sneer, "Robinson wouldn't tell the truth to God." Worse still, the IRS decked him with a tax bill for $514,000 to snatch his earnings.

In an odd way, the loss helped secure Robinson's legacy. He was such a savvy a fighter and so headstrong that virtually no one could beat him twice—he avenged losses to LaMotta, Randy Turpin, and Gene Fullmer in rematches. By losing the fight and the belt to Basilio, Robinson set himself up for the unthinkable. The following year, in his last great fight, Robinson switched to more right-hand leads and uppercuts, and after he and Basilio bashed one another for another 15 savage rounds, Robinson came out on top in the split decision, regaining the middleweight title for an unprecedented fifth time.

CHAPTER 61

Basilio may not have liked Robinson after those fights, but he certainly respected him. "He had guts, and he was a terrific fighter," Basilio said. "You'd be crazy to deny that."

After what Basilio endured in the ring with Robinson, it's hard to imagine anyone better qualified to speak on the subject.

62

The Giants Crush the Bears in the NFL Championship Game, December 30, 1956, Yankee Stadium

In November 1956, the New York Giants led the Chicago Bears, 17–3, after three quarters. Feeling confident, offensive coach Vince Lombardi ordered his men to play conservatively and kill the clock. Fifteen minutes is a lot of time to chew up against an elite team, and when Chicago snared a 17–17 tie Lombardi was furious with himself. Never again would he keep such a tight rein on his offense for such a long period of time.

The next month the Giants and Bears met for the NFL championship. The story is one of lessons learned—the lessons of that November tie and the Giants' 1934 championship win against Chicago. It was also a story of lessons taught—lessons about the power of this burgeoning sport to attract the attention and dollars of a nation.

The 9–2–1 Bears were slight favorites—their league-leading offense scored 100 more points than the 8–3–1 Giants. But these Giants were a balanced, smart team—the offense overseen by Lombardi, the defense by Tom Landry. The lineup featured five eventual Hall of Famers (Sam Huff, Andy Robustelli, Roosevelt Brown, Frank Gifford, and Em Tunnell), plus a half-dozen NFL head coaches-to-be and coordinators-in-waiting.

Everything had gelled, from the preseason trade for Robustelli to anchor the defense to the move from the decrepit Polo Grounds to first-class Yankee Stadium. Attendance jumped to 45,000 from 25,000, and Giants games suddenly became the place to be in New York.

The team hadn't played for a championship in a decade. Yet, the players were loose and confident. Dick Modzelewski, Huff, and others played poker the night before, and in the locker room before the game they clowned around.

CHAPTER 62

After a night of sleet, the temperature hovered in the low teens, while winds rattled at 30 miles per hour.

But Giants owner Wellington Mara remembered the 1934 "Sneaker Game" and was prepared. He asked Robustelli, who owned a sporting goods store in Connecticut, for 48 pairs of thick, rubber-soled sneakers. The sneakers arrived right before game time. The first play set the tone: Gene Filipski charged the opening kickoff back 53 yards, while the Bears, who were trying shortened cleats, shimmied around, uncertain of their footing. Then Don Heinrich connected on a third-down, 21-yard pass to Frank Gifford, and Mel Triplett churned out 17 yards, lugging several Bears into the end zone. Blink and you missed it: The Giants led, 7–0. The Bears were stunned.

Less than two minutes later, Chicago back Rick Casares coughed up the ball near Chicago's 15, and Robustelli scooped it up. After Ben Agajanian lofted a field goal, Jimmy Patton picked off a pass and ran 26 yards to Chicago's 37, setting up another field goal. Blink and you missed it: The Giants led, 13–0. The Bears were essentially beaten.

Recalling Lombardi's dictum, there was no letup. The halftime score was 34–7. The Bears were buried alive. The Bears finally switched to flat-soled sneakers, but it was too late. The Giants were too much to handle no matter what the footwear. The Giants tacked on another touchdown in the third and another in the fourth; it's notable that they scored both from the air—the first on a nine-yarder from Charlie Conerly to Kyle Rote, the second an 11-yarder from Conerly to Gifford—when they easily could have stuck to running plays. At 47–7, the Giants were finished scoring. The Bears were just finished.

The game was not front-page news in New York—football hadn't yet earned such prestige—but it helped blaze the trail. Everything was coming together: Attendance was rising; CBS and NBC (which had earlier rejected football) had begun televising games in 1956, and NBC carried the championship.

In the aftermath, the nation's top communicators, both in newsrooms and on Madison Avenue, took a new look and saw the NFL as an action-packed drama with charismatic stars, a game America might be ready to tackle. Players like Charlie Conerly and Gifford suddenly had an air of glamour, landing endorsements and radio and television gigs. This, in turn, paved the way for the excitement surrounding the 1958 title game between the Giants and the Baltimore Colts. Later known as the "Greatest Game Ever Played," it catapulted the NFL toward where it is today: a supremely lucrative sport with its deciding game not only front-page news, but also a national holiday.

"We won in Madison Avenue's backyard," Kyle Rote said later. "These ad-men were young guys—bright and sharp—but they'd never had an NFL cham-pion in their own backyard. This propelled football far beyond what it would have been had a Green Bay won the title or a Cleveland."

63

Don Larsen Pitches a Perfect
Game in the World Series,
October 8, 1956, Yankee Stadium

Imagine this scenario: The defending World Series champions, having played in three of the previous four Series, win the first two games of the Fall Classic. Their rival evens the Series but spends two of its best pitchers. The champs know the fifth game is key to earning back-to-back titles and a shot at the coveted "dynasty" label. So, the champs start their Game 1 winner, a veteran with one of the best winning percentages of all time. Their foes are left with a middling muddle of mediocrity—a hard-partying righty who was rocked by the champs in not only the previous World Series, but also Game 2 of this one.

That was the setup before Don Larsen took the mound at Yankee Stadium on October 8, 1956.

From this side of history, most Yankees World Series crowns have an aura of inevitability, and it's often the truth—think 1927, 1950, or 1998. But, in 1955, the Bums from Brooklyn had reversed their curse to beat the Bombers. With the Yankees' aura stripped away, the World Series would finally be battled on equal footing, and Game 5 tilted the Dodgers' way, with Sal Maglie starting against Larsen.

Larsen's perfect game—while certainly a bolt of lightning in a lackluster career—was a singular achievement that also came at a crucial moment in baseball history.

Had Larsen fallen on his face in Game 5, as he had stunk in Game 2's 13–8 loss, the Dodgers would have wielded a tremendous advantage, going home to Ebbets Field for Game 6 with the pitching matchup in their favor. And had the Dodgers won the 1956 World Series, we'd look back at this rivalry differently. The Yankees reign would have seemed less imposing. A domino effect is even imaginable: Would Casey Stengel have survived after the Yankees lost to Milwaukee in 1957? Would a new manager have won in 1958? Larsen's win also fortified the Dodgers' place in history: They were not a dynasty, but rather the ultimate victims of a Yankees machine that cranked out big plays and big games from the unlikeliest of sources. That elevated Brooklyn's 1955 triumph to the holy grail stature it has retained for 50 years and ironically gave the club a more sharply defined identity after it left Brooklyn.

Don Larsen and Yogi Berra celebrate after Larsen does the unthinkable, achieving World Series perfection. *Library of Congress, Prints and Photographs Division [LC-USZ62-103254]*

History is, of course, often written in broad strokes. The Dodgers symbolized falling short, when they'd dominated the National League for a decade. And Larsen was better prepared for his historic success than one might think. He'd won nine games in the minors and nine in the majors in 1955. Heading into 1956, manager Casey Stengel said that Larsen could be a "big man in this business—any time he puts his mind to it." Admittedly, his mind often wasn't there—Gooney Bird, as he was called, crashed his car into a telephone pole at 5:00 a.m. during spring training, and he was maddeningly inconsistent on the mound, often getting bumped to the bullpen. Still, he had electric stuff. In September, he'd abandoned his full windup for an abbreviated version that steadied his control, conserved his energy, and disrupted the hitter's timing. He'd reeled off four straight wins.

But in Game 2, he walked four and didn't last through the second inning. With no travel days in a "Subway Series," the teams churned through more pitchers, and so Larsen got his shot at redemption.

Early on, it seemed equally likely that Maglie, who had thrown a no-hitter weeks earlier, would make history—as both he and Larsen reeled off nine straight outs.

In the first inning, Pee Wee Reese worked the count to 3–2, before striking out looking. That was Larsen's only three-ball count of the day, a vital indicator that his struggle with command was under control. In the second, Larsen got lucky: Jackie Robinson smacked a liner that third baseman Andy Carey couldn't handle, but shortstop Gil McDougald alertly grabbed the ricochet and nailed the aging Robinson by a half-step. In the fourth inning, Larsen survived another scare when Duke Snider ripped a seeming home run that bent foul by inches.

Staked to a 1–0 lead on a Mickey Mantle home run, Larsen gave up two long balls in the fifth but survived both: Mantle made a backhanded grab of Gil Hodges's 400-foot blast in deep left-center, then Sandy Amoros's shot hooked just foul. Suddenly there was that nervous energy that flows through the stands and dugouts when a no-hitter is a serious possibility. After five innings, the two pitchers had retired 30 men, while yielding just one hit. The Yankees eked out another run in the sixth, but an even bigger rally was cut short when Hodges fielded Mantle's grounder, stepped on first, and then threw home to trap Hank Bauer in a rundown.

By the seventh, Larsen was a bundle of nerves—his hands shook in the dugout as he tried lighting his cigarette. In past World Series, three Yankees (Herb Pennock, Monte Pearson, and Red Ruffing), along with the Cardinals' Burleigh Grimes, had lost no-hitters in the eighth. In the dugout, Larsen said to Mantle,

"Wouldn't it be funny if I pitched a no-hitter?" Afraid of baseball's no-hitter jinx, Mantle moved away.

The fans at Yankee Stadium were reaching new decibel levels. Dodgers manager Walter Alston asked Robinson to ruffle Larsen. After a first-pitch strike, Robinson went to talk to Hodges on deck. The fans, knowing Robinson was looking to disrupt the pitcher's rhythm, jeered, but Larsen easily retired Robinson.

Larsen faltered briefly, offering Hodges a flat nothing of a fastball, but when Hodges zinged it, Carey snagged it just off the ground for the out. Amoros popped to center. Larsen was three outs from perfection.

Larsen led off the bottom of the eighth and received a thunderous ovation. He received another one on his way back to the dugout after striking out.

There were almost 70,000 regular-season major-league games from the American League's birth in 1901 to 1956, but just three perfect games, and none in 34 years. No one else had ever thrown a no-hitter, much less a perfect game, in the Series. Only the Yankees' Floyd Bevens, now watching at home in Oregon, had reached the ninth—in 1947, he'd walked 10, then lost the no-hitter, the shutout, and the game with two outs.

The crowd was so loud Larsen couldn't hear his teammates' encouragement. He just concentrated on reaching the mound, since his legs had turned to rubber. "My fingers didn't feel like they were on my hand," he later recalled.

Carl Furillo fouled off two pitches, took a ball, and then fouled off two more. It was excruciating. Finally, he lifted a slider to right. Roy Campanella, perhaps anxious, chased a 1–1 slider off the plate and grounded to second.

Larsen had thrown 92 pitches, 66 for strikes. He had one batter left, a pinch-hitter for Maglie, veteran lefty Dale Mitchell. Larsen felt a calm wash over him. He walked around behind the mound, waiting.

Catcher Yogi Berra just wanted the basics, figuring Mitchell would be especially flustered because he had never batted against Larsen's no-wind-up motion, which made pitches seem to arrive extra quick. Larsen's fastball missed, low and outside, just the fourth time all afternoon he'd fallen behind a hitter.

Another hard one caught the outside corner. No one could hear umpire Babe Pinelli over the screaming fans. Larsen's slider was low, but Mitchell chased it. Strike two. One more to go. Back to the fastball. Mitchell barely got the bat out to foul it off.

Larsen needed a break. He took off his cap. He picked up the rosin bag. He was ready. Berra called for another heater, low and away. Babe Pinelli had been umpiring for 22 years and was retiring after the season. This was his final game, his final inning behind home plate. He was so tense he could barely breathe.

The pitch came in. It was close. Mitchell started his swing, then checked it. Pinelli's arm went up. Strike three. The game was over. Larsen had achieved the unthinkable. Berra leaped into his arms, and the Yankees began celebrating. Perfection accomplished. And the World Series had tilted back to the Yankees.

The Dodgers managed to win Game 6, but their offense never recovered, scraping together just one run in the 10th inning. When the Yankees exploded for nine runs in Game 7, Brooklyn posted nothing but zeroes. Larsen was World Series MVP.

Larsen never regained that day's magic, and he flubbed his starts in Game 7 of the next two World Series. But October 8, 1956, was more than unique—it was influential. Before Larsen, few people differentiated between no-hitters and perfect games. Even Larsen never thought about a "perfect game." This game made people appreciate the distinction between a no-hitter and retiring 27 straight batters, something that happened only 17 times in the next six decades (more than half in the expansion-riddled, muscle-bound, free-swinging years since 1990).

The game also represented a capstone: The years 1947 through 1956 were the greatest years in New York City baseball. The Yankees, Dodgers, and Giants won all but one World Series and made history in every way imaginable. This Series would mark the last hurrah for that magical era. Larsen provided a finishing touch that was—in a word—perfect.

64

"Next Year" Finally Arrives for Brooklyn, October 4, 1955, Yankee Stadium

It was a routine roller to Pee Wee Reese, the easiest and most wonderful task in the world. Time stood still in the bottom of the ninth as an entire borough prepared to explode with delirious joy.

Reese, the 37-year-old shortstop and captain of the Brooklyn Dodgers, had been a rookie in 1941. That year the Dodgers and their fans celebrated reaching their first World Series in more than two decades, even excusing Mickey Owen's dropped third-strike fiasco in the ninth inning of the crucial fourth game with the hopeful cry of, "Wait till next year."

"Next year" was 1942: The team won 104 games but blew a nine-and-a-half-game lead against St. Louis in under a month.

"Next year" was 1946: closer still, losing to St. Louis in baseball's first tie-breaker playoff.

"Next year" was 1947: Jackie Robinson inspired a magical season, but the Yankees stopped them in the seventh game of the World Series.

"Next year" was 1949: the Yankees—again.

"Next year" was 1950: The Phillies broke their hearts on the season's final day.

"Next year" was 1951: In case you hadn't heard, the Giants won the pennant.

"Next year" was 1952: *Herald-Tribune* reporter Roger Kahn wrote, "Every year is next year for the Yankees."

"Next year" was 1953: those Damn Yankees.

"Next year" was 1954: watching the Giants—the only rivals Brooklyn hated more than the Yankees—win it all.

Now it was Game 7 of the 1955 World Series, and there couldn't have been more on the line. There are perennial losers, like the pre-2016 Chicago Cubs or the pre-2004 Boston Red Sox, who probably think they understand that level of suffering, but they're wrong. No other team, especially one with the same core of players, has ever come so close so many times in one generation—10 times in 14 years, eight in the last nine—and this bittersweet success was especially excruciating because most of the pain was inflicted by the teams of New York, a distressing reminder of Brooklyn's second-tier status since losing its independence at the turn of the century.

So, in the ninth inning, having navigated through perilous territory, clinging to a 2–0 lead, Pee Wee Reese gathered up the grounder and threw across the diamond to Gil Hodges. And finally it was done. On October 4, 1955, "next year" finally arrived.

In the beginning, it hadn't seemed like "next year." The start of 1955 saw the folding of the *Brooklyn Eagle*, the only daily paper devoted to a borough. The youthful Milwaukee Braves, not the aging Dodgers, were the National League favorite. In spring training, sophomore Brooklyn manager Walter Alston clashed with veterans like Robinson, Roy Campanella, and Don Newcombe. Opening Day was postponed for bad weather, and the game, played on an unscheduled day, drew only 5,000 fans.

But when the distractions fell away, the Dodgers won their first 10 games and 22 of 24. They clinched the pennant on September 8, the earliest date in league history. Still, the Yankees. The Dodgers dropped the first two Series games, and no team had ever come back from such a deficit. It seemed time to dejectedly look ahead, once more.

Back at Ebbets Field for Game 3, a desperate Alston turned to 23-year-old Johnny Podres. After an injury-plagued second half he'd almost been left off the World Series roster. Podres responded with an 8–3 win. Duke Snider hit three homers in Games 4 and 5, as the Dodgers pounded out 13 runs. But in Yankee Stadium for Game 6, another inexperienced lefty, Karl Spooner, was raked for five first-inning runs. Whitey Ford's easy 5–1 win swung momentum back to the Bronx Bombers.

For Game 7, Alston again turned to Podres. With Robinson suffering an Achilles tendon injury, Alston put Don Hoak at third and added Don Zimmer at second base, moving Junior Gilliam to left and Sandy Amoros to the bench.

Podres scattered eight hits, but Tommy Byrne, who had stopped the Dodgers in Game 2, along with relievers Bob Grim and Bob Turley, allowed only five. It was a game in which every out, every base loomed large. This year the little things broke for Brooklyn. With two out and two on in the third, Gil

McDougald's slow roller seemed a sure infield hit, but as Phil Rizzuto slid into third, the batted ball hit him and he was automatically out, quashing the rally.

In the fourth, by contrast, Campanella doubled with one out, and when Carl Furillo grounded to short, Campanella read how slowly the ball was hit and surprised everyone by advancing to third, even though the play was in front of him. Byrne pitched to slugger Gil Hodges instead of walking him for the weak-hitting Hoak. With two outs and two strikes, Hodges fisted an inside curve to left for a single, bringing home Campanella—who would not have scored from second.

Brooklyn made a defensive gaffe in the Yankee fourth—Snider and Gilliam let Yogi Berra's pop fall between them for a fluke leadoff double—but Podres was unfazed and retired three straight hitters. In the sixth, the Yankees again made a fundamental mistake. After Reese singled, Snider surprised everyone with a bunt. Byrne grabbed the ball and flipped toward first baseman Moose Skowron. But Skowron was off the bag; he swiped his glove at Snider, who knocked the ball loose. After a sacrifice and an intentional walk, Grim came on, but Hodges's fly out was deep enough to score Reese for a 2–0 edge.

To replace Zimmer and strengthen the defense, Alston moved Gilliam back to his natural spot at second, returning Amoros to left. That maneuver saved the Series.

Billy Martin walked, and McDougald bunted for a hit. With the lefty pull hitter Berra up, the Dodgers defense shifted toward right. Podres drove Berra off the plate on the first pitch, then pitched him away on the second. But it wasn't away enough from Berra, a notorious bad-ball hitter, who stung a slicing liner toward the left-field corner. As Amoros ran and ran and ran, there was enough time to imagine headlines proclaiming Berra the hero and the Yankees the champions. Then Amoros ran out of room. In the corner, he stopped short, stuck out his glove, and caught the ball. Using his left hand to brace himself on the fence, he whirled and made a perfect throw to Reese, who relayed to Hodges at first. McDougald was past second and easily doubled off.

It's impossible to make an objective comparison of Amoros's catch with other classic World Series catches—but even if Al Gionfriddo made a more difficult play in 1947, its impact was muted when the Dodgers lost the Series, and even if Willie Mays's 1954 catch was more spectacular, it was in Game 1, not Game 7, and his throw, however astonishing, did not yield a double play. Amoros's heroics matter more, not because he made a better catch, but because this was Brooklyn at the precipice, and Brooklyn had never before made the leap into the promised land. Had Amoros not gotten there in time, the Dodgers might well have gone once more into the abyss. Had Gilliam, a righty, still been in left, he'd have had to reach across his body to backhand the ball and probably would not have made the catch—and "next year" might never have arrived.

There was still a runner in scoring position, but Podres retired Hank Bauer. In the seventh, with two out and one on, he retired Mickey Mantle; in the eighth, Podres again faced Berra with two on but induced a harmless pop to right, then fanned Bauer.

In the ninth, Podres easily retired Skowron and Bob Cerv. It was up to Elston Howard. After relying heavily on his changeup in Game 3, Podres had thrown more fastballs in Game 7, especially as the late-afternoon shadows grew longer. Against Howard, he fired four straight heaters, running the count to 2–2. Once more he tried blowing the ball by Howard, but the Yankee fouled it off. Campanella called for yet another fastball, but Podres, afraid Howard had timed it, shook off his batterymate for the first time. He returned to his changeup, and Howard, off balance, hit that final grounder toward Reese.

Reese, the only player ever to have lost five World Series to the same opponent, scooped up the ball and fired. In his excitement, he threw off target, low and wide. But this was not another Mickey Owen moment. Hodges reined in the throw, Podres leaped into the air, and up in the broadcast booth Vin Scully announced, "Ladies and gentlemen, the Brooklyn Dodgers are the champions of the world."

Then Scully was silent. Everyone else, however, let loose—the players, the fans, the entire citizenry of Brooklyn. During the next quarter-hour, the telephone company reported the highest call volume since V-J Day; the system was so overloaded that most callers couldn't get a dial tone.

The day was an endless celebration of honking horns, impromptu block parties, and a borough-wide swelling of exhilaration and relief. On Court Street, someone put a jukebox outside for dancing in the street, along with a keg of free beer; on Smith Street, a candy-store owner handed out free cigars; on Utica Avenue, a deli set up a hot dog stand outside and gave franks away.

That night, 2,000 fans partied in the street outside the Bossert Hotel while the Dodgers and their families whooped it up inside. It was a moment to be savored. Those who experienced it can recall the emotions vividly, because as tremendous as this triumph seemed, it grew more so in retrospect. If not for 1955, there might never have been a "this year," a shining moment to recall. The Boys of Summer were entering the autumn of their careers, especially Robinson and Reese, the spark and soul of the team. And although few realized it at the time, the team itself was not long for Brooklyn.

The year 1956 would be Robinson's final season and Reese's last as an everyday player; in the Series the team would again succumb again to the Yankees. In

1957, the Braves finally surpassed the Dodgers. The final blow came when the Dodgers confirmed what everyone had been dreading: The team was leaving home for sunny Southern California. There would be no "next year."

Brooklynites were left with no one to root for but plenty of memories to cherish. And no game spoke louder about their underdog outlook and their perpetual "wait-till-next-year" optimism than Game 7 of the 1955 World Series, when Gil Hodges, Johnny Podres, and Sandy Amoros grabbed the future and held on, finally corralling it back into the present.

65

Willie Mays Makes "The Catch," September 29, 1954, Polo Grounds

"A kiss is just a kiss," went Bogie's song in *Casablanca*.

A cigar is just a cigar, Sigmund Freud famously insisted.

But a catch is not just a catch. Not when it's "The Catch."

The Catch is the greatest defensive play in baseball history, even though Willie Mays and other experts insist it wasn't the best Mays ever made, and even though "The Throw" that followed is really the heart of the play.

Mays's memorable over-the-shoulder haul of Vic Wertz's long, long, long fly in Game 1 of the 1954 World Series at the Polo Grounds justifies its accolades because it was more than just a catch. It was a confluence of factors: Mays's growing stature; technology; circumstance; The Throw; and the aftermath, from a pipsqueak pinch-hit home run to a World Series sweep to a sudden tilt toward the National League that lasted more than a decade.

First, Mays himself.

Earlier, such black stars as Jackie Robinson, Don Newcombe, and Larry Doby had been older, more established Negro League players. Mays was the first young black player nurtured through the minors by a major-league club. His astonishing skills, smarts, and great joy seduced anyone who saw him play. Unlike Robinson, Mays didn't have to be a pioneer, so he could be an idol, a superstar, making his cap fly off on purpose to give fans an extra thrill. Fans came to spring training workouts to watch him play pepper. As major leaguer Ted Kluszewski once said, "I'm not sure what the hell charisma is, but I get the feeling it's Willie Mays."

As a rookie in 1951, he helped propel the Giants to the National League pennant. When he left for the U.S. Army in 1952, they were in first; without him, they finished second, then fifth in 1953. A mythology built up around him. *New York Herald-Tribune* writer Roger Kahn was assigned to the Giants in 1954, and had never seen Mays play but heard so much in spring training that he satirized the breathless descriptions, writing, "Willie Mays is 10 feet nine inches tall. He can jump 15 feet straight up. Willie's arms extend roughly from 157th Street to 159th Street. . . . Willie can throw sidearm from the Polo Grounds to Pittsburgh. . . . The best evidence indicates he is a step faster than electricity."

Then Kahn watched Mays play and realized the hyperbole had been an understatement. "This is not going to be a plausible story, but then no one ever accused Willie Mays of being a plausible ball player. This story is only the implausible truth."

That, of course, proved a perfect summation of Mays's entire 1954 season. Mays hit 36 homers in the first 99 games, threatening Babe Ruth's 60. But manager Leo Durocher asked him to hit for average to help the team—Mays hit just five more homers but raised his average to .345, winning the batting title on the season's final day, carrying his team (inferior in many regards to Brooklyn and Milwaukee) to the pennant.

Everyone had now heard about Mays, but they too needed to see him to believe him. Thanks to television, everyone could. Bobby Thomson's "Shot Heard Round the World" brought coast-to-coast sports to television in 1951, but just three years later the total number of televisions had more than doubled to 32 million. Television really did bind the nation together in a new way that's hard to fathom in today's multichannel, multiplatform, streaming universe. When Wertz hit the ball, it wasn't just the ticketholders watching, an entire nation turned its eyes to Mays. He gave them an up-close look at genius in action and provided instant proof that live television captured the immediacy and intensity of sports. (Ironically, Mays's Catch owes much of its impact to the famous series of four still photos that froze this fleeting moment forever.)

Then there's circumstance: A great catch in a World Series accrues more weight than one during a pennant race, which matters more than one in late April. Mays made dozens of seemingly impossible plays throughout the year, with stories taking on a John Henry–esque folktale flavor.

In the minors, Mays caught a ball in left-center while climbing the wall—he then somersaulted and threw on target to second. As a rookie, Mays caught a fly to right-center with a runner on third; to avoid throwing across his body on the dead run he improvised a new move, coming down hard on his left foot, spinning counterclockwise away from the infield and around, letting fly a bullet to the plate. In Pittsburgh, Mays raced to deep right-center, but the ball hooked less and sank faster than expected, so he reached back and barehanded it on the dead run. Once, with two outs in the ninth, Mays charged full-speed from center for a popup. At the last second, he avoided a terrible collision by dancing around backpedaling second baseman Chuck Hiller. Hiller and the umpire both thought Hiller made the catch, but his glove was empty, and Mays, who had disappeared into the clubhouse, had the ball tucked inside his.

Mays himself cited different favorites in different interviews: In the minors, he reached over the center-field fence, caught the ball barehanded, landed, and fired a strike on the fly to home plate 405 feet away; at Ebbets Field in 1952, he made a diving catch at the fence, knocking himself unconscious but holding on to the ball; and at the 1955 All-Star Game, he robbed Ted Williams with a leaping catch in right-center.

But this was the World Series, and it turned the tide against a heavily favored Cleveland team that had won 111 games. In the bottom line of history, that counted more.

Wertz opened Game 1 by tripling in two runs in the first off Sal Maglie, making predictions of an Indians rout seem prescient. The Giants tied it in the third, and it remained 2–2 until the eighth inning, when Larry Doby walked and Al Rosen got an infield hit. Durocher brought in southpaw Don Liddle to face the lefty Wertz.

Liddle threw one pitch. Wertz crushed it. The ball hurtled through space, hard, fast, and not terribly high to center, the harsher trajectory slicing off its hang time. Mays always played a shallow center field, but with a ground-ball pitcher and the go-ahead run on second hoping to score on a single, he'd crept extra close. Mays raced head down toward the spot where he and only he knew the ball would land. That spot was about 460 feet from home plate. When the ball fell to earth, Mays was there to intercept it. Joe DiMaggio and Hank Leiber each made longer catches during the 1936 World Series but on much higher flies—Mays would have made those plays, but no one but Mays could have made this one.

If the Catch was the picture-perfect demonstration of Mays's speed and grace, the Throw was a dynamic display of his brains and brawn.

Mays, knowing his own speed and uncanny judgment, never doubted he'd outrun Wertz's smash, but, as he told Roger Kahn, "That wasn't the problem."

Doby could easily score tagging from second on a ball that deep, while letting Rosen advance would also make it easier for the Indians to win the game and set the tone. That's what Mays was calculating as he ran toward the ball.

Mays knew his dead run posed a major problem. "Suppose I stop and turn and throw. I will get nothing on the ball, no momentum," he told Kahn. "To keep my momentum, to get it working for me, I have to turn very hard and short, and throw the ball from exactly the point I caught it. The momentum goes into my turn and up through my legs and into my throw."

Mays slowed almost imperceptibly before catching the ball. He stopped, whirled, and hurled the ball to second baseman Davey Williams without looking. His hat flew off, and his momentum carried him downward, so he landed on his stomach. His teammates expected him to make the catch. (Rosen, thinking he was going to score on a triple, had already rounded second and had to scramble back to first.) But no one was prepared for this throw. Even if another center fielder somehow had the speed and mental dexterity Mays did, no one else had the calculation, coordination, and strength to pull it off. Doby tagged up but could advance no further than third. The rally crashed in Mays's glove and died with his throw. Liddle was lifted for Marv Grissom, who escaped the jam when the wind kept Jim Hegan's long fly in the park. The entire Series turned around on Mays's play.

In the 10th, Wertz walloped one into the gap in left-center. Mays called this play more difficult and crucial. Yet, it's usually overlooked. This ball should have slithered through to the wall, either a leadoff triple or an inside-the-park homer. Mays, playing Wertz to pull, scooped the low bounce barehanded on the run and fired to third base, halting Wertz at second. The Indians were not only stopped, but also disheartened. After using pinch-hitters during that failed rally, the Indians inserted backup catcher Mickey Grasso. Mays, ever alert, noticed he didn't throw to second in warm-ups. Covering up a sore arm? Mays drew a one-out walk, then lit out for second. Grasso's throw bounced well before the base. Mays's steal provoked the Indians into walking Hank Thompson, giving Durocher the opportunity to send up pinch-hitter extraordinaire Dusty Rhodes.

On a hanging curve from Bob Lemon, the lefty Rhodes lifted a soft pop toward the right side. Indians second baseman Bobby Avila started going back for it. But the wind or the fates or something carried it to the short porch 257 feet away in right. Hit some 200 feet less than Wertz's eighth-inning out, Rhodes's shot was a game-winning three-run homer.

In the clubhouse, Durocher walked toward Mays, his hand outstretched. One-pitch Liddle intercepted him; accepted the congratulations mockingly; and quipped, "I got my guy." (The following year, when Don's son Craig needed a glove for Little League, Mays tossed him his leather from 1954, saying. "Take care of this." Craig later loaned the Rawlings glove that had made The Catch to the Baseball Hall of Fame.)

In the next three games Wertz produced eight hits, but the Giants scored in 11 different innings and Mays was involved in eight of those, while Rhodes drove in seven in just six at-bats. The Indians were not as great as their 111–43 record—they beat up weak teams and were just 11–11 against the stronger Yankees and Chicago White Sox. Having coasted through the final weeks, Cleveland was unprepared for a stiff challenge and collapsed after Mays's Game 1 performance. The Giants swept the Series, the first time an American League team had been swept since 1922. The loss was devastating—the Indians were awful for 40 years and still have not won the World Series since then.

This World Series and Mays's performance demonstrated just how much the game had changed since integration. With his dramatic flair, superior talent, aggressive style, and keen understanding of the game, Mays headed a new class of black and Latino superstars developed by the more welcoming National League. The American League had won 15 of previous 19 World Series, but the National League, led by Mays, Hank Aaron, Roberto Clemente, Bob Gibson, and Lou Brock, would reel off eight titles in 12 years. (Other than the Yankees, Cleveland—the first American League team to integrate—was the only American League team to reach the Series between 1947 and 1958.) Only when Frank Robinson went from Cincinnati to Baltimore in 1966 would things even out.

Mays's persona and performance, and his defining Game 1 catch, paved the way for this second wave of integration, encouraging owners and fans alike to open their eyes and hearts to these players. When Indians manager Al Lopez said, "Willie Mays made that great catch and we were never the same," he was talking about his club in that World Series, but he could have been talking about us all.

The Yankees Win a Fifth Straight World Series on Billy Martin's Series-Record 12th Hit, October 5, 1953, Yankee Stadium

Five World Series titles in a row. Babe Ruth never won more than two in a row; Joe DiMaggio's best run was "only" four straight titles and five in six years. George Steinbrenner's teams never won more than three straight. Look back through the prism of the Yankees Century, created by Ruth and reimagined by Steinbrenner, and you have to marvel at October 5, 1953, when the Yankees were crowned champion for the fifth straight year.

The earlier dynasties had been built around superstars and stability. From 1926 to 1928, Ruth, Lou Gehrig, Tony Lazzeri, and Bob Meusel routinely ranked among the league leaders, and the Yankees fielded the same regulars at every position but catcher. The 1936–1939 squad had six hitters together—featuring Gehrig, DiMaggio, and Bill Dickey—until 1939, when Gehrig fell ill. The 1949–1953 Yankees were different. Yes, their staff was anchored by Allie Reynolds, Vic Raschi, and Eddie Lopat, but they rarely had the league's best pitching or the best offense. This team was supposedly so monotonous and metronomic in its ruthless efficiency that cheering them on was likened to rooting for U.S. Steel. Yet, they were unbeatable mostly because manager Casey Stengel slyly fit pieces together, creating a team greater than the sum of its parts. His modern approach shaped and foreshadowed the changes in the way champions were built.

Yogi Berra was at catcher and Phil Rizzuto at shortstop throughout, but everything else was mix-and-match Stengel style. First base might have Tommy Henrich or Johnny Mize or Joe Collins. At second, Snuffy Stirnweiss gave way to Jerry Coleman, who was replaced by Billy Martin. Bobby Brown, Billy Johnson, and Gil McDougald held down third base. (McDougald later moved to shortstop.) The crowded outfield corners included Cliff Mapes, Johnny

Lindell, Hank Bauer, Gene Woodling, and Irv Noren; in center, an aging DiMaggio gave way to a still maturing Mickey Mantle. Berra was really the only consistent threat. In hunting down their record fifth championship in 1953, the Yankees won more frequently and impressively than ever before. Raschi, Reynolds, and Lopat had help from veteran Johnny Sain and youngster Whitey Ford. Mantle set the tone in the fourth game when he hit his famous 565-foot home run in Washington. New York won 99 games, the most during this stretch. For the first time since 1947, the Yankees led the league in scoring, and for the second time they allowed the fewest runs.

Baseball's 50th World Series featured a rematch against Brooklyn, their fifth meeting in 13 years. This Dodgers team was confident. They had been through the crucible—losing the Series in 1949, the pennant on the last day in 1950, the devastating playoff in 1951, and the Series in Game 7 in 1952—but their core was intact, and they'd won 105 games thanks to their most overpowering offense ever. They'd hit 208 homers (to the Yankees' 139) and scored 955 runs (to the Yankees' 801). Gil Hodges, Roy Campanella, and Duke Snider were among the league's most dangerous power hitters. Carl Furillo won the batting crown, and Brooklyn even led the league in stolen bases.

But in the Series, the bantam would rule the roost. Fittingly for Stengel's squad, it would be a less famous name, a second baseman in just his second full season, the only time he'd ever bat 500 times: Billy Martin. Weighing in at 155 pounds, Stengel's protege was turbulence personified, constantly getting into scraps with foes. Yankees general manager George Weiss tried trading him, but Stengel dissuaded him. In 1953, Martin enjoyed what would be his best year offensively, with 24 doubles, 6 triples, 15 homers, and 75 RBI.

Martin's bases-loaded triple in the first inning kick-started Game 1. With the Yankees clinging to a 6–5 lead in the eighth, Martin slapped Brooklyn down by singling for his third hit of the day, then stealing second to spark a three-run rally. In Game 2, Brooklyn led, 2–1, until the seventh, when Martin smacked a home run. (Mantle's blast later won it.) Brooklyn won the next two games, despite three more hits from Martin. In Game 5, Martin added a single and a homer as the Yankees coasted, 11–7.

In Game 6, the Yankees drew first blood for the fifth time as Carl Erskine was knocked around for three runs in two innings. Whitey Ford struck out seven and scattered six hits through seven innings, allowing only a run in the sixth, when Jackie Robinson doubled, stole third while Ford held the ball, then scored on a groundout.

In the bottom of the eighth, Rizzuto was thrown out at the plate trying to score on a grounder. Then in the ninth, Furillo smashed a two-out, two-run home run, knotting the game at 3–3 and giving the Dodgers momentum.

Throughout the Series, Yankee pitchers issued just 14 walks, and the defense tied a record with just one error. The Dodgers provided 24 free passes and made seven defensive blunders. In the bottom of the ninth, Clem Labine committed baseball's original sin and walked leadoff hitter Hank Bauer. With one out, Mantle hit a weak dribbler no one could get.

The winning run was on second base, and the one hitter the Dodgers didn't want to see was coming up: Billy Martin.

Martin had already doubled, and one more hit would be his record-setting 12th, but more crucially, it would likely produce a record-tying eighth RBI and end the season. Labine had to pitch carefully, but he couldn't walk Martin with just one out. He had to stop him. Except he couldn't. On a 1–1 count, Martin smacked the ball back up the middle. Bauer scored easily. The Yankees, World Series champions in 1949, 1950, 1951, and 1952, were champions in 1953.

Martin's 12-hit record would later be tied for a six-game Series and broken in a seven-game Series. But this game gave the 1953 Yankees a record no other baseball team is likely ever to match, much less surpass. They are the champion of champions.

Billy Martin's Lunging Catch of Jackie Robinson's Popup Saves Game 7 of the World Series, October 7, 1952, Ebbets Field

Call it fate; call it fortune; or call it the baseball gods. Whatever your term, these forces always beamed munificently on the Yankees. Well, perhaps it would be more accurate to say the Yankees signed them to a lucrative, long-term contract no other team could afford.

But in Game 7 of the 1952 World Series against the Brooklyn Dodgers, those otherworldly powers suddenly rebelled and took an active role against the Bombers, using Ebbets Field's low sun and high wind to put the Yankees' dynastic aspirations in peril. Then Billy Martin stepped in. Martin never liked leaving a ballgame in the hands of anyone else—rival players, meddling owners, muddling teammates, or fate. This feisty fireball wanted, even needed, to mix 'em up, to thrust himself into the action. And the Yankees second baseman saved his team with one of the most sensational infield plays in World Series history.

The Cleveland Indians, with three sluggers and three 20-game winners, had seemed on paper like the best team in the American League in 1952. But the Yankees replaced Joe DiMaggio with a kid named Mickey Mantle in center field, and manager Casey Stengel again proved he was unparalleled in getting the most out of his players. When Jerry Coleman was drafted by the U.S. Army, Stengel moved Gil McDougald from third to second base. When Bobby Brown was conscripted, Stengel stuck Martin, one of his pet projects, at second and shifted McDougald back to third. The Yankees won the pennant by two games.

The Dodgers rode their overwhelming offense to a 60–22 start before their shallow pitching almost blew a 10-game lead to the New York Giants. With his weak rotation exposed, Brooklyn manager Charlie Dressen made his lord of the bullpen, Joe Black, a starter for the Series.

Black, the Rookie of the Year, boasted, "There's nothing in that lineup to be scared of," and he backed it up in three strong starts. But with the Yankees trailing 2–1 in games, Stengel outmaneuvered Dressen. During the regular season, Yankees first baseman Joe Collins hit 18 homers; his Brooklyn counterpart, Gil Hodges, had 32 homers. Both men were hitless through three games. Dressen lacked the bench depth and nerve to bench his first baseman (Hodges finished the Series 0-for-21), but Stengel called on Johnny Mize, a Hall of Fame slugger who was almost 40 and had managed just four homers in 137 at-bats. In Game 4, Mize homered again to help the Yankees even the Series. Mize hit a three-run blast in Game 5, but Brooklyn won and went to Ebbets Field needing just one win in two games. Throughout the year, the Dodgers had had a feast-or-famine offense: Hodges would hit four homers and they'd win 19–3, but they'd lose a game when they failed to get a runner home from third with less than two outs. The Series turned on two balls that never left the infield.

In Game 6, with the game tied and a runner on first, Brooklyn rookie Billy Loes dropped the ball while on the mound for a balk. A comebacker ricocheted off Loes's leg, and the runner scored. After the Yankees won, Loes was widely mocked for saying he lost the grounder in the sun, but given how low the sun was in the sky, he might have been unable to see the ball after his pitch. Still, that sort of thing only happened to Dem Bums, never the Bombers.

Meanwhile, Stengel had bypassed his bullpen and got a save out of ace Allie Reynolds, his scheduled Game 7 starter. So, he turned to Eddie Lopat, a lefty, against a righty-heavy lineup that feasted on lefties in tiny Ebbets Field. But Stengel coaxed three shutout innings out of Lopat. Staked to a 1–0 lead on Mize's RBI single, Lopat faltered in the fourth, but when Brooklyn loaded the bases, Stengel once again called on the 37-year-old Reynolds—who'd started Game 1 and Game 4, then relieved in Game 6 on one day's rest—to give whatever he had left. Hodges mustered his lone Series RBI by flying out, but Reynolds whiffed George Shuba and got Carl Furillo on a grounder.

Game 7 was tied at 2–2 after five, but Black was tiring, which would be expected from a rookie reliever starting for the third time in six days. Dressen had no one in the bullpen to bail him out, however, so he sent Black back for the sixth. Mantle launched a home run over the top of the scoreboard. After Mize singled again, Preacher Roe came on and foiled that rally but yielded another run in the seventh. The Yankees led, 4–2.

Reynolds told Stengel his arm was shot, so Stengel, while replacing Mize with Collins for defensive purposes, brought Vic Raschi in for the seventh.

CHAPTER 67

Raschi pitched well only when rested, and he'd gone almost eight innings the previous day on top of a complete game four days prior. With shadows cutting across the infield, the tension mounted, and the Brooklyn faithful grew louder and louder as Raschi went 3–2 on every batter—Furillo walked, and with one out Billy Cox singled and Pee Wee Reese walked, loading the bases. Stengel wanted a lefty against the red-hot Snider, who had tied Babe Ruth and Lou Gehrig with four homers in a Series and set a new record with 24 total bases. He called on Bob Kuzava, even though he hadn't pitched at all in the Series and had control problems. Kuzava fell behind, 3–2, but got Snider to pop up on a tailing fastball. Two outs.

With right-handed Jackie Robinson up, Stengel came out of the dugout to make another pitching change. Then he abruptly turned back, as if he'd just had a hunch—after all, Kuzava loved busting righties inside with that same fastball (the equivalent of today's cutter), and Stengel had brought him in with the bases loaded in the ninth inning of Game 6 in 1951, where he'd gotten three straight righties out.

Robinson stayed alive with a 2–2 count by fouling off several pitches—one was a long, hard foul into the left-field stands that brought Stengel back out for a peek. When Robinson pulled the next pitch for a hard, foul grounder, Yogi Berra went halfway to the mound to remind Kuzava not to leave the ball out over the plate.

The next pitch was in on Robinson's hands, and he lifted a meek infield pop that should have quashed the Dodgers threat. On the left side of the infield, Gil McDougald and Phil Rizzuto took a few steps in, then realized the wind would keep the ball on the other side of the diamond. Kuzava stood on the mound. It was clearly the first baseman's ball. Collins, looking directly into the low sun cutting across the grandstand roof, could not see a thing. As Dodgers circled the bases with great haste, the baseball gods seemed to have finally thrown in their lot with the underdogs.

If the ball fell safely, the game would be tied, but the momentum would belong to Brooklyn. Then Martin noticed just how clueless Collins looked.

Like Stengel and his mentor, John McGraw, Martin saw everything on a ball field. In Game 4, Martin had saved a crucial run by spotting Dressen clutching his left shoulder; recognizing the suicide squeeze sign from when Dressen coached for Martin's minor-league team in Oakland, Martin called out to Reynolds; the Yankees nailed the runner at the plate.

With Collins frozen, Martin started moving, but the capricious wind blew the sphere back toward home plate, closer to Kuzava and Berra. As the ball hurtled toward earth, Martin shifted gears and raced full speed across the infield, his hat flying off, and lunged on the dead run, grabbing the ball perhaps two feet from a total fiasco.

Noisy Ebbets Field fell silent. There were two more innings, but the Dodgers were dead. Even fate and fortune couldn't beat the New York Yankees. As Charles Einstein wrote in his syndicated story, they could have skipped the entire Fall Classic—memorable though it was—if they'd read the record books carefully, "down in the small print where it says the Dodgers don't win World Series and the Yankees do."

68

Sugar Ray Robinson Melts against Joey Maxim, June 25, 1952, Yankee Stadium

The bell rang for the 14th round. The favorite of the press and public, the man clearly leading on points, sat on his stool, unmoving. Sugar Ray Robinson may have been the greatest fighter ever, and he may have been a better boxer than his opponent, but he had finally confronted a force even more unstoppable than himself: Mother Nature.

A third weight-class title—the light heavyweight championship—had seemed so tantalizingly close. But Robinson could not grasp it, not now, not ever, as oppressive heat and humidity conspired with the dark side of that informal "pound for pound" title to sap him of his strength and fierce will.

Born Walker Smith, Robinson moved to Harlem from Detroit and earned pocket change dancing outside of theaters. His fancy footwork also gave him a future in boxing. To participate in an American Amateur Union fight for which he was too young, the 15-year-old was given another fighter's card: Ray Robinson. Later a sportswriter wrote that his style was sweet as sugar. Sugar Ray was born.

As a welterweight, Robinson was indestructible, losing only once in more than 120 pro fights. In 1951, he captured the middleweight title, butchering rival Jake LaMotta. He was a masterful strategist who possessed an unheard-of skill set—he punched with the best but was fast and graceful on defense; he had style and elegance, yet could explode with fury.

The flamboyant and confident Robinson, with his flashy pink Cadillac and stretch of Harlem businesses, was also a symbol of postwar prosperity and opportunity for blacks, someone on whom they could hang their hopes and aspirations. He inspired Muhammad Ali, but his presence was most powerful in New

York's black community, which often saw Robinson up close. Robinson had some of his greatest triumphs in Chicago and some of his most brutal defeats in New York, but this was home turf, and his fights here, for better or worse, had an extra glow.

Robinson's struggle against Joey Maxim to become only the second three-division champion in the twentieth century (after Henry Armstrong) had been postponed because of rain. The new date proved a scorcher: At fight time, 10:00 p.m., it was still 90 degrees. The stadium lights and densely packed crowd made it 104 degrees inside the ring.

Robinson's reach advantage as a welterweight and middleweight evaporated against this bigger man, and he weighed just 157 pounds to Maxim's 173. Blows that would damage a lighter man inflicted far less hurt against Maxim, who could take a punch and often fought heavyweights. Maxim fought a stolid, cautious fight, staying in the center of the ring, conserving energy, and forcing Robinson to come after him.

The crowd was disappointed, with people stamping their feet to urge more action. Maxim's tactic seemed a recipe for defeat, but on this night it proved shrewd, as Robinson spent 13 rounds stalking his own self-destruction.

Robinson led easily on points, but Maxim absorbed everything he threw—jabs, body blows in the clinch, and even a crunching shot to the jaw in the seventh. Imagine the tortoise and the hare in a ring instead of a race. In this epic war of attrition, the hare should slow down and pace himself, but *New York Times* columnist Arthur Daley noted that Robinson perhaps "became too enamored by his own magnificence."

By the ninth, Robinson felt groggy. Maxim hit him clean on the jaw, and Robinson would have no memory of anything that came after. The first participant to melt away, however, was the third man in the ring, referee Ruby Goldstein, who was so exhausted after the 10th round he became the first ref ever to leave a championship bout. Replacement Ray Miller was handed a scorecard with notations blurred with sweat. Coming in fresh, Miller pushed the pace, quickly breaking up the increasingly frequent clinches, which harmed the tiring challenger. (Robinson complained later that the fight should have ended when Goldstein left.)

In the 11th, Robinson mustered everything he could into a looping right that landed squarely on Maxim's jaw—it was the same shot that had floored middleweight Randy Turpin nine months earlier—but the heavier Maxim staggered without going down. Robinson meandered around the ring, unable to summon the energy to capitalize on the opening. Shuffling to his corner at the bell, Robinson looked far weaker than Maxim.

CHAPTER 68

Winning individual rounds was irrelevant now—if Robinson remained on his feet, he'd win the fight. In the 12th, Maxim snapped the smaller man's head back twice with lefts, and Robinson needed smelling salts to return for round 13. He was virtually out on his feet, and his infrequent punches were slow and sloppy, with his arms hanging limp by his sides in between each draining effort.

Maxim seemed relatively fresh, throwing crisp punches. Even glancing blows wobbled Robinson, and a combination sent him reeling. Desperate, Robinson countered with a huge right, which became the lowest moment in his glorious career. His flailing blow missed Maxim completely; Robinson lost his balance, falling hard on his face. Sugar Ray Robinson had knocked himself down.

The trip to the canvas was humiliating—Maxim stepped casually over him and walked away—but also excruciatingly painful. Robinson pulled himself up but offered little resistance as Maxim battered him along the ropes. When the bell saved him, he was unable to make it back to his corner, staggering senseless and bent over before his handlers rushed to fetch him. They went at Robinson with ice packs and smelling salts. When the bell rang to commence round 14, Robinson, leading handily on all three cards, was unable to rise and could barely shake his head to indicate he was through.

Back in his dressing room, Robinson, who had melted off 16 pounds in the previous hour, was delirious. His wife Edna Mae and the doctor decided that the vain Robinson would be happier at home than in a hospital. His blood was so hot that his body was covered with fever blisters. He couldn't keep food or liquid down for two days and remained irrational most of that time, although he came to his senses long enough to ask pridefully, "He didn't knock me out, did he?"

Robinson did not recover fully for six months and then announced his retirement. During the next two years, he made his living as a cabaret performer, tap dancing without worrying about getting hit. But his appeal diminished, and after getting slugged by business and IRS woes, Robinson was forced to return to the ring. He reclaimed his middleweight title in 1955, and held it on and off until the age of 39. But Robinson, whose genius for strategy and determination enabled him to defeat in a rematch anyone who managed to defeat him—Jake LaMotta, Randy Turpin, Gene Fullmer, Carmen Basilio—never sought to avenge his loss to Maxim, nor did he again venture into the ring as a light heavyweight. That was a once-in-a-lifetime fight.

69

The Giants Win the Pennant,
October 3, 1951, Polo Grounds

"The Giants win the pennant . . ."

Bobby Thomson's playoff-ending home run for the New York Giants against the Brooklyn Dodgers has probably insinuated itself into your life, even if you were born decades after the event, maybe even if you don't follow baseball. This seminal sports moment became part of our collective unconscious—for the first time that newfangled box in the living room united the nation for a magical, spontaneous moment.

No one outside Wrigley Field had seen Babe Ruth's called homer, few people owned televisions when Ted Williams reached .400 on the last day of 1941, and only local viewers could see the Yankees overcome the Red Sox on the final day of 1949. This was different. President Harry Truman had made the first coast-to-coast telecast of any kind in September, and this game marked the first sports event broadcast nationwide. Although television was still in its infancy, so many people in so many states saw Thomson's home run, meaning so many had a more intimate, visceral stake in the creation of this generational memory. This was when sports and television first became intertwined, when popular culture strengthened its hold on the American psyche.

"The Giants win the pennant . . ."

Maybe your tie remains clear and direct. You, your father, or your grandfather are from New York, or were a Giants or Dodgers fan, so the moment remains a potent stew of folklore, American history, and personal passion: Where were you when John Kennedy was killed, when Neil Armstrong took one giant step—when Bobby Thomson did the impossible?

Maybe in college you read Yale historian J. R. H. Hexter's 1968 scholarly essay "The Rhetoric of History," which elevated the Giants' stretch run and triumph over Brooklyn to a lofty analytical plane. Maybe you saw the clip and heard the shouting on the *M*A*S*H* episode when Charles Winchester took a knife to the newsreel replaying the famous scene. Maybe you watched one of the numerous documentaries that continued cropping up well into the twenty-first century.

"The Giants win the pennant . . ."

Maybe you purchased Don DeLillo's opus *Underworld* in 1997, just to read his elegiac prologue, "Pafko at the Wall," or mailed a letter using the 1999 postage stamp commemorating the homer. Maybe you followed the front-page news in 2001, and subsequent media brouhaha about the Giants' 1951 sign-stealing, or bought your child or grandchild the 2005 picture book entitled *The Shot Heard Round the World*.

"The Giants win the pennant . . ."

October 3, 1951. The Polo Grounds. The ninth inning. Find your thesaurus, for this was the most blood-tingling, hair-raising, mind-boggling, breathtaking, heart-stopping single moment in New York team sports history. New York's major-league teams played about 40,000 games in the twentieth century, and the Knicks, Rangers, Jets, football Giants, and such college teams as CCNY, Fordham, and St. John's played thousands more. This game, this inning stands above them all.

When Red Smith wrote, "The art of fiction is dead. Reality has strangled invention. Only the utterly impossible, the inexpressibly fantastic, can ever be plausible again," he aptly summed up not only the ninth-inning action, but also the season-long narrative.

On May 25, the fifth-place Giants promoted Willie Mays from Triple A. The rookie started just 1-for-25, but his infectious charm loosened up the club, while his fielding firmed up a mediocre defense. Putting Mays in center allowed manager Leo Durocher to move Thomson from center to third and lock Monte Irvin in left; both had been struggling but carried the offense after that.

The team climbed to second place, even as Brooklyn buried the rest of the league. Still, anything the Giants did, the Dodgers did better. After snatching an August 8 doubleheader, Brooklyn manager and former Durocher protégé Charlie Dressen boldly decreed, "The Giants is dead." The Dodgers won again the next day and celebrated as if they'd reached the mountaintop. Jackie Robinson yelled, "Eat your heart out, Leo," and he, Pee Wee Reese, Carl Furillo, and others pounded bats on the wall separating the two teams' clubhouses, loudly singing, "Roll out the barrels, we got the Giants on the run."

The Giants and Dodgers had rarely been good the same year. Yet, their rivalry was bitter. It dated to 1889, when the Giants beat Brooklyn (then the Bridegrooms of the American Association) in the "World's Series" despite Brooklyn's manipulation of the rules and umpires. It remained so vivid that when Durocher, the longtime Brooklyn skipper, jumped to the Giants in 1948, it was considered heresy by fans of both teams.

A loss to Philadelphia dropped the Giants 13 games back (and just one ahead of the Phillies). But then they tore off 16 straight wins, including a three-game sweep of Brooklyn, and they finished the season 37-7.

The Giants had begun pilfering pitch calls in the Polo Grounds on July 19, but didn't get hot until three weeks later. Sure, they went 20-3 at home, but their offense actually declined; they went 17-4 on the road, while scoring more runs, so it seems the tactic hurt rather than helped them. Ultimately, it was stellar pitching that made the difference—along with the Dodgers' choke job.

Brooklyn discovered that after the peak, what's left is the descent. The Dodgers had nothing but time for their long slide down. Eventual MVP catcher Roy Campanella got repeatedly banged up. As the standings tightened, so did the team. Dressen acted panicky, particularly with his pitchers. When he started Ralph Branca on two days' rest, the pitcher's tricep acted up, and he struggled the rest of the way. Dressen's September dispute with red-hot rookie Clem Labine turned into a season-sabotaging grudge—furious when Labine ignored instructions to pitch from the full windup with the bases loaded (to gain more velocity), Dressen ignored Labine thereafter, burning up his exhausted and diminished starting rotation and his bullpen, too. Labine might have won one game or at least eaten enough innings to let Don Newcombe and Preacher Roe rest. "His vindictiveness cost him the pennant," Labine said later of Dressen.

The Giants and Dodgers were tied on the season's final day. The Giants beat Boston; the Dodgers rallied from 6-1, down in Philadelphia, and in extra innings Robinson made a game-saving catch and blasted a home run. It was time for a best-of-three playoff, a format invented in 1946, for Brooklyn and St. Louis.

Game 1, at Ebbets Field, turned on a single pitch, thrown by Ralph Branca, and smacked into the stands by Bobby Thomson for his 31st homer. Branca had already yielded eight homers to the Giants, including two by Thomson, that year. The Giants went home to the Polo Grounds with two chances to win one game.

Out of options, Dressen finally relented and gave the ball to Labine, who pitched a six-hitter in a 10-0 shutout. In the third with the bases loaded, Labine struck out Thomson on a 3–2 curve that was low and outside. "That guy wasn't going to get the chance to hit one in the seats," Dressen said.

October 3, 1951.

It was a last-minute weekday game on a cold, gray day—lights would be needed by the third inning—and with televisions showing it everywhere in New York, 22,000 seats went empty. In attendance were General Douglas MacArthur, Toots Shor, Jackie Gleason, Frank Sinatra, J. Edgar Hoover, and many of the American League champion Yankees.

Sal Maglie, who had beaten the Dodgers five times, against Newcombe, had rescued Brooklyn in the season's final weekend. At one point, Maglie retired 13 of 14, but Newcombe pushed his scoreless inning streak past 20. In the seventh, Monte Irvin doubled; when Whitey Lockman bunted, Brooklyn's backup catcher, Rube Walker, threw unsuccessfully to third. (Would the sidelined Campanella have made that choice? Would he have succeeded?) Lockman screamed for time. Durocher's men played sneaky baseball, so they recognized it elsewhere: Lockman had spotted Billy Cox trying to pull the hidden-ball trick on Irvin.

Thomson's sacrifice fly to center tied the game, 1–1. But in the eighth, the Dodgers scored one run on a wild pitch, and two balls sent toward third became run-scoring hits. Neither were errors, but Thomson handled neither and suddenly looked like the goat. The Dodgers led, 4–1, and were six outs from rendering the Giants' monumental effort meaningless.

On the bench, a weary Newcombe told Reese, Robinson, and Dressen he was done. Reese encouraged him to keep going, while Robinson said, according to various reports, "God-dammit, get in there and pitch," and also, "You keep pitching out there until your fucking arm falls off." Newcombe breezed through the eighth. But Dressen then left him in for the ninth, when the Giants had their best hitters coming up.

Alvin Dark hit a two-strike pitch off the end of his bat for a cheap hit. Inexplicably, Dressen had Gil Hodges hold Dark on first, and Don Mueller, a master of bat control, poked a ball through the hole. First and third. Dressen went to the mound but made no change. After the breather, Newcombe got Irvin to foul out.

In the press box, Brooklyn announced, "The Dodgers will hold a victory party tonight at the Hotel Bossert, beginning at 6:00 p.m."

With the right-field wall 254 feet away, Newcombe pitched away to the lefty Lockman. Lockman went with the pitch, knocking it to left for a double: 4–2. Then everything stopped. Mueller was on the ground at third, torn tendons in his ankle. He was carried off on a stretcher (Clint Hartung replaced him), giving Dressen a free trip to the mound. Always a know-it-all—he'd tell his team, "Just stay close, I'll think of something"—Dressen had been reduced to an indecisive wreck. He asked his pitcher and infielders what they thought. Reese, the captain, told him to make a change.

In the last phone call, Coach Clyde Sukeforth had told Dressen that Branca had finally loosened up and was throwing hard, while Carl Erskine had just bounced a curveball. Of course, Thomson was a fastball hitter and owned Branca, while Erskine wanted his curve diving downward. And Labine, a curveball-sinker-ball specialist who had mastered the Giants, sat nearby, ignored yet again.

Dressen signaled for Branca, who charged in confidently. Normally the manager would discuss the situation, but this time he nervously flipped Branca the ball from five feet away, said, "Get 'em out," and scurried to the dugout. One thing Dressen didn't do was tell Branca to walk or pitch around Thomson, which would have meant putting the winning run on base. Yet, behind Thomson were slumping rookie Willie Mays and the bottom of the order.

It was the Glasgow-born, Staten Island-raised Thomson against Branca, the youngest of 17 kids from Mount Vernon. Everyone and everything else receded, creating the head-to-head confrontation that makes baseball unique among team sports.

Branca's first pitch was a nice, fat fastball. Thomson took it for a strike and chided himself for letting it pass. Thomson's hits had been to left or center, so Branca hoped to imitate Labine and get him on a curve away. First, however, he'd set up Thomson with a fastball up and in. In hindsight, Branca admitted that if he wanted to get Thomson on a curve, he should have thrown the curve.

The fastball zoomed high and tight but not up or in enough. Thomson whipped the bat around. The wood connected with the ball. A hard, spinning line drive. The fence was only 315 feet away in left but 16 feet high. Andy Pafko was at the wall. The ball might not have gone out at Ebbets Field, just as Thomson's Game 1 homer in Brooklyn might not have gone out at the Polo Grounds. But that's baseball, that's life. At this time, in this place, the ball made it. Pandemonium erupted as Thomson floated around the bases, and the Giants and their fans poured onto the field.

"Thomson settled a five-month argument in just seconds," Grantland Rice noted.

Branca trudged off the field and sagged, inconsolable on the clubhouse steps, moaning, "Let me alone, let me alone. Why me?" He was the last man to leave. In Brooklyn, number 13—Branca's unlucky uniform number—hung in effigy. (Brooklyn switched Branca to number 12 in 1952; he promptly suffered a freak injury and never fully recovered. He did, however, eventually form a lasting friendship and built a lucrative autograph signing business with Thomson.)

Meanwhile, Thomson appeared on Perry Como's television show, took a taxi to the Battery, rode the Staten Island ferry, hopped another cab to the firehouse where his brother worked, and then went to dinner with his family. The World Series, which the Yankees won (for the third straight year), seemed almost anticlimactic.

It wasn't just television that gave this historic home run extra cachet—it was also the old-fashioned radio. On television, announcer Ernie Harwell simply said, "It's gone," and let the images speak, but on radio Giants announcer Russ Hodges let his own deliriously giddy excitement convey the emotions of the moment.

Radio stations did not tape broadcasts then, and this classic call would have faded, draining the moment of much of its staying power, if not for the "Miracle of Larry Goldberg" (and his mother Sylvia). Goldberg, a Giants fan in Brooklyn, showed his mother how to use his reel-to-reel tape recorder, then left for work, asking Sylvia to tape the ninth inning on WMCA, 570 AM. Goldberg sent the tape to Hodges. The Giants' sponsor, Chesterfield, gave him $100 and box seats for 1952, then put Hodges's call out on a promotional record that still sends chills through its listeners more than 60 years later:

Branca throws. There's a long drive. It's gonna be. I believe.

The Giants win the pennant! The Giants win the pennant! The Giants win the pennant! The Giants win the pennant! Bobby Thomson hits it into the lower deck of the left-field stands. The Giants win the pennant! And they're going crazy. They're going crazy. Wheyyyywhoooooo!!!!

70

CCNY Wins Its Second National Championship . . . of the Month, March 28, 1950, Madison Square Garden

B efore the fall came the last days of innocence. For college basketball—especially in New York—1950 was a transcendent moment when the city was the center of the basketball world; college players were hardworking, upstanding young men; and CCNY's basketball team rocked the rafters of Madison Square Garden and bathed its hometown in sports glory.

For now, at least, erase everything that followed: the 1951 revelations that CCNY's stars were deeply enmeshed in a widespread point-shaving scandal that stunned the United States and haunted the city hoops scene for generations. Instead, live in the blissful ignorance that prevailed during that dizzying 18-day run in March 1950. CCNY's Beavers won both the National Invitational Tournament (NIT) and the NCAA Tournament in an era when the NFL and particularly the new NBA were still so small-fry that the Knicks played at the 69th Street Armory or shared Madison Square Garden bills. College football's season was long over and largely irrelevant in New York schools, and baseball—the city's true love—was still in spring training. All eyes were on Madison Square Garden, college basketball's mecca since the first successful doubleheader staged there in 1934.

CCNY had never reached the finals of the prestigious NIT, nor the smaller, less-heralded NCAA Tournament. As 1949–1950 began, Coach Nat Holman's charges, mostly sophomores, seemed a year away from contention. The team looked immature and wildly unpredictable, besting top-ranked St. John's, then falling to unheralded Niagara. With five losses before season's end, CCNY was almost shut out of the postseason before beating Manhattan College and NYU, snatching the final NIT slot. As the 27th-ranked team, with no All-America stars, CCNY seemed destined for an early exit. These erratic kids would never survive the defending NIT champs from San Francisco, third-ranked Kentucky, sixth-ranked Duquesne, and Bradley, the nation's numero uno. And only a strong showing in the NIT would earn them a NCAA slot.

CCNY's roster was mostly blacks and Jews who faced quotas at most private universities. They commuted from throughout the city: The center was sophomore Ed Roman, from Taft High School in the Bronx; the forwards were Irwin Dambrot, the only senior and only married starter, who'd also gone to Taft, and Ed Warner, an orphan from Harlem, from De Witt Clinton High in the Bronx; the guards were Floyd Layne, also an outstanding lefty pitcher, from Benjamin Franklin High in Manhattan, and playmaker Al Roth, from Erasmus High in Brooklyn, who'd turned down numerous scholarships because his immigrant family wanted him close to home. Key players off the bench were sixth man Norm Mager, a senior, from Lafayette High in Brooklyn, and Roth's Erasmus teammate Herb Cohen.

Some disliked the cold, imperious Nat Holman, but they bought into his coaching style. One of early basketball's greatest players, Holman put an emphasis on team play that reverberated a generation later when his protege, Red Holzman, taught the same fundamentals to the New York Knicks. The Beavers were undersized but quick. They excelled at rotating on defense, helping out and clogging the middle. At season's end, Holman occasionally shifted Warner into the low post, freeing Roman to shoot from outside.

The team gelled at the right time, challenging tournament foes with an aggressiveness on both ends that reflected childhoods spent playing rough-and-tumble half-court games on the warped rims of city playgrounds. (Of course, they also stopped taking gamblers' bribes in the postseason.)

CCNY's other edge was the hometown crowd, which virtually shook the Garden's walls and rattled opponents with the strange but unforgettable chant, "Allagaroo-garoo-garah, allagaroo-garoo-garah; ee-yah, ee-yah; sis-boom-bah." ("Allagaroo" was most likely a corruption of the French phrase "allez guerre," meaning "on to war.")

CCNY demolished San Francisco by 19 points. Kentucky's legendary coach, Adolph Rupp, was a hard-core segregationist and provided the New Yorkers with unintended inspiration when some of his players, who had never faced blacks in an official game, refused to shake hands with CCNY's starters. Holman shrewdly gave his backup center, 6-foot-7 African American Leroy Watkins, the opening jump against Kentucky's seven-footer, Bill Spivey, to rattle the Wildcats. Watkins controlled the ball, and CCNY raced out to a 13–1 start. They won, 89–50; the Kentucky legislature proposed flying the state flag at half-mast.

CCNY's 10-point trouncing of sixth-ranked Duquesne put them in the NIT finals and earned them a spot in the NCAA Tournament. Facing the quintessential Middle America team—Bradley from Peoria—CCNY was motivated to prove that city kids were best at the city game. The Beavers looked frazzled early, trailing the Braves, 29–18, but they clawed within three by intermission. In the second half, the lead changed hands seven times. Bradley led, 56–55, but Warner—soon to be the first black tournament MVP—poured in several crucial buckets, sparking a 14–5 run. CCNY won, 69–61.

The Beavers were NIT champs and the new darlings of New York. Classes were canceled, and 6,000 students attended a celebration. The team was honored at City Hall, too. These players were embraced because they were part of the city fabric—they'd starred at your high school or grown up down the block from your cousin. The day after the finals, Ed Roman was playing pickup games at Claremont Park. Floyd Layne said CCNY was to New York what the Dodgers were to Brooklyn, a strange approximation but accurate in its sense of intimacy. And these were real students—you had to be to go to the "poor man's Harvard." During the tournaments, while the visiting teams concentrated on basketball, CCNY students attended class.

The quest was on for a second championship. No one had ever won both, and CCNY got a quick lesson in why: They were tired and now faced three more matchups with elite teams. The Beavers trailed second-ranked Ohio State by 52–49, before escaping with a 56–55 win. There were 14 lead changes against North Carolina State before CCNY won, 78–73.

All that remained was a rematch against Bradley. The Braves had played man-to-man defense in the NIT, but Coach Forrest Anderson, knowing his team was also fatigued, started in a zone. Ed Roman spread them out, however, by shifting from the pivot to the outside and pouring in 12 points in the first 12 minutes as the Beavers raced to a 39–32 halftime lead. Bradley returned to man-to-man defense but ran into foul trouble while CCNY built a double-digit lead. Then Roman fouled out, and the weary Beavers grew sloppy. Bradley's full-court press whittled the lead to 66–61, with two minutes left.

In the days before shot clocks, five points seemed fairly safe. But Bradley's whirlwind of a guard, Gene "Squeaky" Melchiorre, swiped a pass and scored, 66–63. CCNY built the cushion to 69–63, with just 57 seconds left. But after a Braves free throw, Melchiorre grabbed a loose ball and scored, then intercepted a pass and converted again. In 17 seconds, almost the entire lead vanished: 69–68, CCNY.

With 30 seconds remaining, Melchiorre again nabbed a pass and burst full tilt for the basket. Dambrot raced back and used the angle to cut off Melchiorre. The Brave pulled up for a short jumper instead, and—well, if you lived in Peoria, you thought Squeaky was fouled and the Braves were cheated out of their shot at victory. But in the Garden, Dambrot cleanly blocked the shot. He grabbed the ball and fired to Mager, downcourt by himself. Mager laid it in, and it was all over. CCNY 71, Bradley 68.

The Beavers were the first squad to wear two crowns and the first NCAA champ with black starters. And they'd done it as a team—Dambrot scored 15 points, Mager and Warner 14, Roman 12, and Layne 11. If the city was excited by the first win, it was delirious after the second. In his superb rumination on that championship season and the scandal that followed, *The Game They Played*, Stanley Cohen wrote that this team seduced the city, even people who didn't follow basketball, because they were true New Yorkers, underdogs who made good through determination and hard work. "The national champions were kids like us—Jews and blacks mostly, sons of immigrants and grandsons of slaves—and they had taught us, demonstrated, that we could share equal footing with the best that America could offer." Newspapers throughout the nation touted this unique feat, and Holman earned an appearance on *The Ed Sullivan Show*. Heady times indeed.

A year later, of course, it all crashed down. Worst of all was the revelation that the 1949–1950 narrative was false: At least two regular-season losses were games in which the team shaved too closely. Seven key team members were implicated. The team and school were accused of doctoring transcripts to ensure eligibility. The school never played at the Garden again, and the NCAA soon moved its games from this den of iniquity. Had CCNY stood alone, forgiveness might prove elusive, making it difficult to separate the great from the terrible. But the scandal permeated college hoops—even Bradley and Kentucky were caught up and pulled down. "I don't condone what they did or give it a pass, but I don't think you can take away from the fact that in spite of what they did during the regular season, they were able to accomplish something unique," Cohen said a half-century later.

The much-repeated American myth is that life in the 1950s was simpler, more wholesome. That is patently false. Yet, while it's healthy to demythologize our heroes and see their human flaws, sometimes we also need to celebrate their achievements. Let's freeze this moment then: a time when the smiles, the laughter, the chants and cheers, the proclamations and celebrations really were pure and wonderful.

71

Columbia Ends Army's Winning Streak, October 25, 1947, Baker Field

Seconds before the first half ended at Baker Field on October 25, 1947, Army kicker Jack Mackmull missed an extra point, low and to the left.

No big deal. What was one measly point to the Black Knights? West Point had racked up 93 points in four games in 1947, without yielding a single point to their opponents. In fact, Army had not lost in 32 straight games, dating to 1943. The 2–2 Lions were coming off bad losses to Yale and Penn.

Coach Lou Little and his men wanted this game for reasons beyond their won–loss record. For the Lions, pride was at stake. The previous year, Army humiliated them, 48–14, which was particularly galling for the militaristic Little, an infantry captain in World War I, and the 29 Ivy Leaguers who had just served as enlisted men in World War II under West Point–trained officers. After the 1946 blowout, tackle Hank O'Shaughnessy ran into a lieutenant colonel who had verbally run down O'Shaughnessy and his team. O'Shaughnessy wore a knee brace because of a shrapnel wound, after having landed at Normandy, fought at the Battle of the Bulge, and earned a Bronze Star, Silver Star, and Purple Heart. He wanted revenge.

"They thought they were going to run over us," Columbia left guard Joe Karas recalled later. "They were very mouthy, making wise cracks on the line."

At first Army backed up its trash talking, driving for a touchdown on its first try, then adding another to start the second quarter. Cadets shook white handkerchiefs at Columbia's fans, telling them to surrender. Then Columbia broke West Point's scoreless streak when quarterback Gene Rossides and receiver Bill Swiacki teamed up for completions of 14 and 32 yards on a 69-yard scoring drive.

CHAPTER 71

Army invaders scored again on Rip Rowan's 84-yard gallop, which preceded Mackmull's failed kick. With a comfortable 20–7 lead, the content Cadets cruised into the locker room. The Lions, however, were not dispirited—they'd been stopped on the goal line and knew they'd come close to putting a scare in Army.

Little had ripped his players the previous week for lying down against Penn, but at halftime against Army, when Little saw his players shouting and revving one another up, he quietly stepped aside; for the first time ever, he neither gave a speech nor drew a single play on the blackboard.

In the third quarter, the teams shoved back and forth, but the Lions were wearing down the Cadets and controlling the game's tone. When the final 15 minutes began, Rossides connected twice to Bill Olson to advance into Army territory. Then Rossides went deep to Swiacki; with defender John Shelley seemingly attached to him in the end zone, Swiacki lunged for Rossides's low pass, stretching out and scooping up the ball just before it hit the ground. (Coach Earl Blaik and Shelley forever insisted that Swiacki trapped it.) The Lions were within six.

Army marched to the Columbia 28, but the Lions' defense held and Army botched its fourth-down snap, giving Columbia decent field position. Again, Rossides moved the Lions, and again he called Swiacki's number at crunch time. Scrambling toward one sideline, Rossides floated the ball diagonally back across, leading Swiacki, who dove and came up with the pass at the Army three.

Everyone was stunned. Two plays later, the Lions scored. The extra point was deflected by a Cadet, but the ball still cleared the upright. That gave the Lions the extra point—literally. They led, 21–20.

There was still 6:38 to go, but the Lions were now the predator and the Cadets the prey. Army was "beaten emotionally," recalled Columbia's Ventan Yablonski afterward.

After a final interception, the Lions celebrated as their fans stormed the field, tearing down the goalposts in celebration. The sole policeman joined the festivities.

On the subway platform afterward, Columbia students waved white hankies at their former tormenters, some of whom were reduced to tears. O'Shaughnessy saw the same lieutenant colonel he'd encountered in 1946. Triumphant, O'Shaughnessy asked, "How do you like Columbia now?"

72

Cookie Lavagetto Ruins Floyd Bevens's World Series No-Hitter, October 3, 1947, Ebbets Field

The year 1947 was historic for baseball: Jackie Robinson smashed the color barrier, and the World Series was televised for the first time. It was also the year New York reasserted its place as capital of the sports world, surpassing even its 1920s heyday. For the next decade, the Yankees, Dodgers, and Giants would dominate baseball, in television's spotlight; boxing would flourish at Yankee Stadium and Madison Square Garden; the football Giants would come into their own as champions and Madison Avenue's darlings; the Knicks would emerge as an annual contender in the fledgling NBA; and CCNY would reach the apex of college basketball before being felled by scandal. But the most memorable moment of the biggest event—the World Series—featured two also-rans whose careers would end that October.

In Game 4, Floyd "Bill" Bevens started for the Yankees. The 6-foot-3, 215-pound pitcher had emerged from seven years' toil in the Yankees farm system to pitch impressively from 1944 to 1946, going 33–23, and finishing among the ERA leaders his third year. But arm problems in 1947 led to a dismal 7–13 season.

Brooklyn's Cookie Lavagetto had been a solid but unremarkable infielder before the war, spending five years in Brooklyn's starting lineup. But at age 35, he was a bit player, earning only 69 at-bats in 1947.

The brief moment when Bevens and Lavagetto's lives intersected was so dramatic that it guaranteed both men lasting fame, even as it marked their baseball demise. The Yankees led the Series, 2–1, so Brooklyn needed the win. Yet, the Dodgers' pitching was so thin that manager Burt Shotton started rookie Harry Taylor; even though Taylor was nursing a torn elbow tendon, Shotton hoped that, against the underwhelming Bevens, he might be passable. Taylor lasted 11 pitches, getting yanked after walking Joe DiMaggio with the bases loaded. Hal Gregg pitched well in relief, but the Yankees added a second run in the fourth.

Bevens, meanwhile, was unhittable, despite several close calls: Snuffy Stirnweiss robbed Pee Wee Reese of a single on a grounder up the middle in the first, and Johnny Lindell made a diving outfield catch in the third. But Bevens created his own trouble. He walked four in the first three innings, inspiring Shotton to order his players to work the count. In the fifth, Bevens walked two more, and one, Spider Jorgensen, scored on a groundout, making it 2–1, New York.

Still, Bevens plowed on. With each out, the Ebbets Field fans grew louder and more frantic with both hope and dismay—the television engineer shut off the crowd microphone because the shouting was drowning out Red Barber's broadcast. The Chicago Cubs' Ed Reulbach had made it to the seventh inning of a World Series game with a no-hitter in 1906, and two Yankees had recently lasted until the eighth, Monte Pearson in 1939 and Red Ruffing in 1942. But no one ever completed the task.

In the eighth, Brooklyn's Gene Hermanski launched a long fly toward the wall in right, where Tommy Henrich leaped and made the catch. For just the second time, Bevens retired the Dodgers in order.

Three outs from history. In the ninth, the Yankees threatened to break open the game, but Henrich bounced into a bases-loaded double play.

Bevens took the hill for the bottom of the ninth. Bruce Edwards smashed the ball to left, but Lindell grabbed it near the fence. Two more outs. Bevens was tired now and if not for the no-hitter might well have been lifted, but he stayed on, even after tying a World Series record by issuing his ninth walk, to Carl Furillo. Jorgenson fouled out. Twenty-six down, one more to go. But then came a close call, a questionable strategic maneuver, a managerial hunch, so many small decisions accumulating so rapidly that it could make skeptics believe in fate and destiny.

Shotton belatedly sent the speedy Al Gionfriddo to run for Furillo. Then he looked down the bench for a pinch-hitter for the pitcher. Pete Reiser had been suffering dizzy spells from a horrific crash into an outfield wall that summer, and in Game 3 he broke his ankle stealing a base. The doctor ordered him to sit out, but Reiser had built his legend violating such orders. Shotton growled, "Aren't you going to volunteer to hit?" Reiser knew the question was a demand. He could barely hobble to the plate, but the Yankees didn't know how bad his injury was and saw only a dangerous lefty.

With the count 2–1 on Reiser, Bevens threw twice to first. Gionfriddo took off on the next pitch. He stumbled, but the throw was high, and while shortstop

Phil Rizzuto was convinced he'd nailed Gionfriddo, umpire Bill McGowan called the runner safe.

The tying run was in scoring position. Yankees manager Bucky Harris ordered Bevens to walk Reiser intentionally even though it would put the winning run on base. He would be second-guessed for eternity. But Harris was no fool. With the count 3–1 and the World Series walk record looming, Bevens might have grooved a strike to Reiser, a more potent hitter than anyone the Dodgers had left. There was no clear answer.

Reiser limped to first, where Eddie Miksis replaced him. Shotton suddenly called back the next hitter, Eddie Stanky, in favor of Harry "Cookie" Lavagetto. Lavagetto, whose wife had given birth to their first child earlier that day, was as shocked as Stanky.

Bevens fired a fastball. Lavagetto swung hard but missed. After 136 pitches, the no-hitter was still alive.

Bevens threw another fastball, up and away. Lavagetto went with it, driving the ball hard to the right, where Henrich faced an impossible dilemma: go for a near-impossible catch to preserve the no-hitter or play conservatively and field the ball off the wall to stop the winning run from scoring.

Henrich went for the catch but missed by several feet. The ball clanged off the wall just above an ad for the new Danny Kaye movie, *The Secret Life of Walter Mitty*. Henrich couldn't recover, and the ball rebounded away.

Bevens was banished from the record books—the no-hitter was gone.

Gionfriddo scored easily—the lead was gone, too.

Miksis raced home ahead of Henrich's off-balance throw—the game was gone as well.

Bevens was no longer the little-guy-turned-unlikely-hero. Instead, Lavagetto was at the center of Bedlam on Bedford.

Broadcaster Red Barber was so startled that he exclaimed over the air, "I'll be a suck-egg mule."

For the Dodgers and Lavagetto, the jubilation proved short-lived. In Game 5, with the Dodgers again trailing 2–1, with two outs in the ninth, Lavagetto again pinch-hit with the tying run on second. Knowing everyone expected him to repeat his success, he became overanxious and whiffed. After pinch-hitting a game-tying sacrifice fly in Game 6, he failed again in Game 7, a game in which Bevens largely redeemed himself, giving up just one run-scoring double in almost three innings of clutch relief, which helped the Yankees win both the game and the World Series.

The Bevens–Lavagetto game ultimately provided an ideal bookend with Don Larsen's 1956 perfect game—one marked the first year of the great rivalry between the Yankees, Dodgers, and Giants, while the other ended that era. The games are apt symbols as well. Larsen's game was neat and tidy, perfection leading to yet another championship for the U.S. Steel of baseball. This win, like the one in Game 6—highlighted by Gionfriddo's astonishing catch of Joe DiMaggio's long blast—fit the Dodgers: It was dramatic and unpredictable, ending with a burst of elation that set up the heartbreak that followed. But if you're going to lose in the end anyway, well, what a way to go.

Jackie Robinson Shatters the Color Barrier, April 15, 1947, Ebbets Field

The ninth-inning home run. The two-minute touchdown drive. The buzzer-beater jump shot. In life, such exhilarating successes are exceedingly rare; for many people, most days follow a relatively predictable routine—comfortable perhaps but sometimes disquietingly mundane. The heart of our insatiable passion for sport is that vicarious ride on an emotional roller coaster, never knowing what will come next: the adrenaline rush of a stunning victory or the heart-stopping blow of a devastating defeat.

In that sense, the most magical, memorable, monumental day in New York City's sports history was a nonevent: a man walked out to play first base. Yet, when Jackie Robinson took the field for the Brooklyn Dodgers on April 15, 1947, his one small step was a giant leap, shattering the long-standing color barrier in a moment so inherently dramatic it transcended sports. It was a turning point in history, a moment crucial to the civil rights movement and one of the most important days of the twentieth century.

There was an inevitability to the breaking of the color line, but there was no guarantee it would happen here, even if the city's relative liberalism and central place in baseball history made it fitting. And there was no certainty it would be done right—the right team, the right player. Had Dodgers boss Branch Rickey picked the wrong man, someone lacking Robinson's baseball skills and inner strength, integration might have been derailed for years, and opponents of integrated schools, buses, and lunch counters would have had ammunition to delay the entire movement. When Robinson proved that he and the black and Latino men who followed truly deserved to share the playing field with whites, he laid the groundwork for everything that followed—from Harry Truman's integra-

Jackie Robinson shakes up baseball and the United States in his first game with the Brooklyn Dodgers. *Library of Congress, Prints and Photographs Division [LC-USZ62-122139]*

tion of the U.S. Army to Rosa Parks's refusal to go to the back of the bus, to the March on Washington and Martin Luther King's "I Have a Dream" speech.

Robinson did not take his role lightly and view himself as merely an athlete, although he was one of the century's finest. He was the first UCLA athlete to letter in four sports—a fast-breaking point guard, an unparalleled broken-field running back, and a champion long-jumper, along with baseball, his weakest sport.

He was prone to a quick and fierce temper, especially when he believed whites were insulting or exploiting him. In the army, he successfully faced down court-martial charges after refusing to move to the back of a bus, and in the Negro Leagues he led his team, the Kansas City Monarchs, to prod gas stations, restaurants, and hotels to open their doors to blacks. But Rickey persuaded the combative competitor to transform himself.

"Mr. Rickey, do you want a player who is afraid to fight back?" Robinson famously asked at their first meeting when Rickey tested Robinson by baiting him with horrible insults.

"No," Rickey said. "I want a player with guts enough not to fight back."

Brooklyn signed Robinson on October 23, 1945. He became the first black in the minor leagues in 1946, making a sensational debut with the Dodgers' Montreal farm club, leading them to a win against the Jersey City Giants with a three-run homer, three singles, and two stolen bases; twice he teased opposing pitchers into sending him home on balks. His .349 average that year set a team record.

Obstructionist owners, skeptical sportswriters, and balking ballplayers still stood in his way. That offseason, owners met with Commissioner Happy Chandler—who had replaced unrepentant segregationist Judge Landis—and voted 15–1 against integration. But Chandler bravely gave Rickey the go-ahead in private, knowing the owners were too image-conscious to protest publicly. In spring training, a rebellion broke out among Southerners on the Dodgers. Popular right fielder Dixie Walker organized a petition against promoting Robinson. Rickey and Dodgers manager Leo Durocher stood firm. After learning of the insurrection, Durocher woke the players in the middle of the night to set them straight.

"Well, boys, you know what you can do with that petition. You can wipe your ass with it," Durocher reportedly said. "I'm interested in one thing. Winning. . . . This fellow is a real great ballplayer. . . . He's going to put money in your pockets and money in mine."

Rickey then brought the full force of his personality down, lecturing each player individually and smashing plans for organized action. (When Kirby Higbe still seemed discomfited, Rickey traded him.) Just before Rickey officially announced Robinson's promotion there was a stunning distraction. Chandler suspended Durocher for the entire season, citing his association with gamblers and other unsavory behavior. (Durocher's public accusations that former Dodgers boss Larry MacPhail, now running the Yankees, had himself consorted with gamblers may have sparked the suspension.) The resulting media frenzy provided some cover, diverting attention from Robinson's call-up.

On the day of Robinson's debut, the *Daily News* sports headline was not about integration, but the search for a new manager, while the *Baltimore Sun* editorialized, "This year sees a Negro, Jack Robinson, having his first chance in the big leagues, but the really big change, of course, is the absence of [Durocher], the most colorful personality in recent baseball history." (Coach Clyde Sukeforth served as interim manager for the first few games until Burt Shotton took over.)

Tuesday, April 15, 1947, dawned wet and cold. More than half of the Ebbets Field crowd was black, many proudly wearing "I'm for Jackie" buttons. Robinson was nervous but ready. Fifteen photographers hovered around the new first baseman, snapping pictures beforehand. "I'll be number 42," he'd joked to his wife Rachel that morning. "Just in case you have trouble picking me out."

All eyes were on number 42 when he stepped in the batter's box against the Boston Braves' Johnny Sain in the bottom of the first. Robinson made solid contact and tore down the line. He just beat the throw—or so he thought—but umpire Al Barlick called him out. Robinson whirled, ready to argue, before reining in his emotions and returning to the dugout. After popping out his second time up, Robinson hit into a double play in the fifth. Then, in the seventh, with Brooklyn trailing, 3–2, Robinson demonstrated those intangibles that would make him the Dodgers' catalyst for the next decade. With a runner on first, Robinson laid down a perfect bunt. His speed forced Earl Torgenson to hurry his throw, and the ball glanced off Robinson's shoulder, ricocheting into the outfield. Suddenly there were Dodgers on second and third. Pete Reiser slammed a double, and Robinson sprinted home to give the Dodgers a lead they wouldn't relinquish.

Robinson later wrote of his Opening Day performance, "If they expected any miracles out of Robinson, they were sadly disappointed," but no miracles were needed on that first day of a new nation.

Robinson's most famous quote—later his epitaph—was, "A life is not important except in the impact it has on other lives." He'd affected people from his first days in the organization. In 1946, his minor-league manager, Clay Hopper, had initially asked Branch Rickey, "Do you really think a nigger is a human being?" Yet, by year's end, Hopper was telling Robinson, "You're a great ball-player and a fine gentleman. It has been wonderful having you on the team."

In the majors, Robinson's impact spread far and wide. Black papers covered his first game like a new Emancipation Proclamation: The *Afro-American* devoted seven stories, seven photographs, an editorial, and a cartoon to it. While Robinson's debut gave blacks hope that a better, fairer day was coming, the change he inspired in whites was equally significant. On Opening Day, when Robinson left the clubhouse an hour after the game, he was surrounded by 250 fans hoping to see, speak to, or touch him. Most were white.

"By applauding Robinson, a man did not feel that he was taking a stand on school integration, or on open housing," Roger Kahn later wrote in *The Boys of Summer*. "But for an instant he had accepted Robinson simply as a hometown ballplayer. To disregard color, even for an instant, is to step away from the old prejudices, the old hatred. That is not a path on which many double back."

Robinson became baseball's biggest draw since Babe Ruth. The Dodgers set a road attendance record of 1.8 million, propelling the National League to its highest attendance figure ever. After just a few weeks, he became, at least during meals and card games, just another Dodger to most of his teammates. As Durocher had predicted, Robinson was worth money, leading Brooklyn to the World Series.

Even the influential white press transformed itself. On Opening Day, they'd been skeptical about his chances and integration in general. Many writers seemingly believed blacks might not be smart or skilled enough for baseball or that their readers felt that way—the *Washington Post* devoted one paragraph to Robinson, the *Pittsburgh Post-Gazette* two, and the *Baltimore Sun* three. As a result, many whites did not initially appreciate how momentous that game was. But Robinson's star radiated brightly, and writers gave him ink and respect. That fall, *Time* put him on its cover. The *Sporting News*, long a segregationist magazine, named him its first Rookie of the Year. That year marked the first televised World Series, and as television's reach grew, more and more people could see blacks and whites playing side by side, hugging one another after victories, consoling one another in defeat.

Fifty years after Robinson's first game, baseball commissioner Bud Selig—who saw Robinson play at Wrigley Field in 1947—honored the Dodgers legend by retiring his number from all of baseball and declaring April 15 an annual Jackie Robinson Day. Robinson's legacy was not built simply on this one day, of course. He won the MVP in 1949, propelled the Dodgers to the World Series six times in his 10-year career, and infused the entire sport with a spark and an aggressiveness that was common to the Negro Leagues but had too often been absent from the plodding white version. True integration came slowly, but the National League owners adapted first, and as its new wave of stars—Willie Mays, Roberto Clemente, Hank Aaron, Frank Robinson—built upon Robinson's style, it became the game's dominant league.

Those accomplishments ultimately trace back to a hitless afternoon at the ballpark, an Opening Day that was truly an opening, the birth of a new era. "Whenever I hear my wife read fairy tales to my little boy, I'll listen," Robinson wrote about that first game in a column for the *Pittsburgh Courier*. "I know now that dreams do come true."

74

Army and Notre Dame Shut One Another Out in the "Battle of the Century," November 9, 1946, Yankee Stadium

A rmy didn't win. Army didn't even score. Notre Dame didn't win. Notre Dame didn't score, either. But on November 9, 1946, in front of 74,000 screaming fans, a 0–0 tie added up to much more than nothing. This grudge match, the culmination of a storied rivalry, was one of the most breathlessly hyped sports events of its generation but still exceeded expectations for pure drama.

The relationship between these foes had undergone a seismic shift. Their annual contests had begun in 1913, with Knute Rockne catching passes in Notre Dame's 35–13 upset of undefeated Army. After Rockne became coach, his team racked up the wins against Army, but the showdowns, fought in New York City, helped elevate college football to its central place in the American sports landscape.

Eventually, Notre Dame's dominance diminished anticipation for the game—Army didn't even score off the Irish from 1938 to 1943. World War II changed everything. College rosters were depleted as star players and coaches entered the service, but West Point was a rare exception. The Cadets assembled one of the most fearsome teams ever, headed by "Mr. Inside" and "Mr. Outside," Doc Blanchard and Glenn Davis, respectively.

In 1944, Army humiliated a severely weakened Notre Dame squad, intercepting eight passes and running up a 59–0 score. The next year, Army served a 48–0 walloping. By their annual Yankee Stadium showdown in 1946, the West Pointers had racked up 25 straight games without a loss. But Notre Dame had returned to form, winning its first five games by a combined score of 177–18, climbing to number two in the rankings.

The press churned out proclamations about the "Battle of the Century." The quarterbacks, Arnold Tucker (Army) and Johnny Lujack (Notre Dame), were competing for All-America honors. Army coach Earl Blaik was a lieutenant colonel but stayed on the sidelines during the war, while Frank Leahy missed two years at Notre Dame to serve in the U.S. Navy. Leahy and Blaik actively disliked one another.

Notre Dame closed practices to reporters and even parents. The team was so fearful of Army spies they'd run only basic plays when planes flew overhead. Students created SPATNC (Society for the Prevention of Army's Third National Championship) and sent off pestering postcards to Blaik.

Reportedly, 1 million ticket requests were turned away, and Notre Dame alone had to return $500,000 to people who had sent in money for ducats snapped up the moment they became available. Tickets costing $3.30 were scalped for $200.

There were 20 photo news syndicates, 5 newsreel companies, 4 radio and television teams, and 95 print reporters in the press box. The packed stadium favored the Irish, thanks to New York's huge Catholic population and their decades of success. On the field were four past or future Heisman Trophy winners—Blanchard, Davis, Lujack, and Notre Dame's Leon Hart—and more than a dozen All-Americans, an assemblage never again equaled. Given the offensive firepower on both sides, many expected a nonstop assault on the end zones.

Not quite.

The quarterbacks each produced only 52 yards passing, and Army's Davis and Blanchard mustered only 80 yards on 35 carries. Notre Dame gained 30 more yards overall but was plagued by turnovers and penetrated Army territory just twice.

The lack of scoring was partly due to leg injuries nagging Lujack and Blanchard, both coaches' conservative approach, and the era's macho mindset in which easy field goals were disdained as unmanly. Leahy's unwillingness to trust his second unit raised questions; even after Lujack got kicked in the head, Leahy ignored backup quarterback George Ratterman, although some thought Ratterman a superior passer.

Both teams had done endless advance scouting, eliminating surprises that often create big yardage gains. And both rugged defenses were superb, turning in big plays and stiffening up when the other team threatened.

Early on, Army recovered a Notre Dame fumble on the Irish 24, but Blaik played it safe, hurling Blanchard up the middle on second, third, and even fourth down. Notre Dame repelled him each time.

The biggest defensive plays were made by the two offensive stars—in this era of the two-way player, Lujack and Tucker showed they could perform at either end. In the second quarter, Notre Dame's Jerry Cowhig took a lateral near midfield and exploded past the Army line, down to the 30, the 20, the 12, before

Tucker chased him down, saving a touchdown. Three plays later, the Irish eschewed "settling" for the field goal and failed on 4th and 1 from the three.

Shortly before halftime, Lujack returned the favor when Tucker slithered for 30 yards to the Notre Dame 30, before Lujack finally grabbed him. The half ended before Army could score.

In the third, Tucker intercepted a deep pass by Lujack at the Army 10 and burst up the sideline for 32 yards. Army's misdirection made it look like Davis was getting the ball on first down, but instead Blanchard tore through a stunned Notre Dame line. Suddenly, Mr. Inside was outside, momentarily free of the stifling Irish defense. He got past Notre Dame's secondary, heading for glory. There was no one left but Lujack, who cut off the angle, foiled Blanchard's last fake, and smashed the runner to the ground at the Notre Dame 36. It was the game's defining play. Army reached the Notre Dame 12, but a halfback-option pass was intercepted by future Irish coach Terry Brennan. In the fourth, Army was stronger. Yet, Notre Dame continued its narrow escapes, stopping Army just inches from a first down on the Notre Dame 33, intercepting the ball on their own 10, and recovering one of their own fumbles on their five.

Near game's end, Army was again sweeping through Notre Dame territory when a sack and fumble halted their march. With 48 seconds left, Army's last chance died when Blanchard caught a pass at Notre Dame's 20 but his feet landed out of bounds.

Both teams trudged off after their terrible tangle still unbeaten. Players felt a curious blend of elation and despair. Army outplayed Notre Dame, with more drives and more real chances to score. Yet, Blaik was despondent for failing to capitalize on opportunities, while Leahy was happy to have averted disaster. Notre Dame was deemed the psychological victor for stopping the top-ranked team, avenging the wartime routs, and ensuring that Army could not score off a Leahy-coached team.

When both teams finished the season undefeated, Army, which barely edged Navy, was perceived as less convincing than the Fighting Irish, who beat their opponents by a combined 271–24. Notre Dame was crowned champion.

The game, alas, was a farewell performance. At year's end, the schools released a statement saying the rivalry, especially on the Gotham stage, had spun out of control, growing too big and unwholesome for collegiate sports. (The confrontation relocated to Indiana the following year, then ended.) Their rivalry had been big business since 1923, and there was speculation that Blaik simply couldn't abide losing to Leahy and Notre Dame anymore. But if it had to end, there was no better way to go out, with a scoreless game that scores high on the list of classics.

75

Tony Zale Drops Rocky Graziano, September 27, 1946, Yankee Stadium

Here's the 33-year-old middleweight champ, a hard, precise hitter but a shy, mild-mannered family man from America's steel mill towns. He is reduced to underdog because of four years of rust that accumulated on his body and his crown while he served in World War II.

Here's the betting favorite, the 24-year-old hometown boy, a scattershot windmill of a slugger. Up from the streets of New York, the challenger is a rambunctious character with a penchant for fighting dirty and getting in trouble outside the ring—while the champ was protecting the United States, this former juvenile delinquent was punching a captain, going AWOL, and getting sent to Leavenworth, before being dishonorably discharged by the military.

Anthony Zaleski was born in Gary, Indiana, and worked in the mills. By the time he volunteered for the U.S. Navy in 1942, he was Tony Zale, the "Man of Steel" and middleweight champ. His punches to the body inspired fear and awe. Thomas Rocco Barbella was born on the Lower East Side and spent his youth prowling those streets or getting packed off to reform school. He was kicked out of the U.S. Army for running away to box, which he did using a friend's name, Rocky Graziano. He was still known more for his prison record than his boxing record. Where Zale once said, "If my mother had ever caught me stealing, she'd have broken my neck," this "Dead End Kid" joked he'd steal "anything beginning with an 'a': a car, a piece of jewelry, a purse."

Zale, after knocking out everyone in a half-dozen warm-up bouts, wanted Graziano for his first defense because Graziano's roguish charm meant more tickets sold. Graziano made sure Zale paid the price for the bigger payday.

The New York crowd rooted for Graziano, who would need to attack early— Zale was the better boxer but a slow starter and had just recovered from pneumonia. Yet, Zale stunned Graziano with a left hook to the jaw early in the first, flooring him for a four count. Graziano recovered and then some, pounding Zale's head, bouncing him off the ropes. In the second round, Graziano seemed on the verge of victory, ruthlessly beating Zale, splitting his lip, and, with four big rights to the head, sending him down. Zale was saved by the bell.

The violence was, in the manner unique to boxing, simultaneously excruciating and exhilarating. And it only increased: Zale revived in his corner, only to take another beating in round 3. In the next round, despite injuring his right hand, he recovered to pummel Graziano's body. In the fifth, Zale attacked the body again, but Graziano stayed in and rifled shots into Zale's head. Zale was so disoriented he headed for the wrong corner afterward, fueling calls for referee Rudy Goldstein to stop the fight.

But Graziano was in uncharted waters: He built his record knocking out ambitious welterweights who couldn't handle a heavier foe. By contrast, Zale was a genuine middleweight and a true champion.

In round 6, Graziano turned desperate or perhaps just more uninhibited. Going for the kill left him vulnerable, and Zale—knowing his body blows have an accumulative effect—waded in, blasting Graziano with a right just under his heart. Finally, he launched a left hook to the jaw that sent Graziano crashing to the canvas. Graziano, who'd gone the distance in every previous fight, could not recover in time. The fight was over. The defeated man pulled himself up just after the 10 count and raged that he wanted more. He had to be led away by handlers. Those few seconds might have cost him a victory—Zale was so battered he could barely stay on his feet.

The rivalry joined boxing's pantheon, as Graziano knocked out Zale in Chicago the next year to claim the middleweight title, only to have Zale exact revenge in 1948, in Newark, by shredding Graziano in three rounds. The fights lasted just 15 rounds total but put the men in hyphenated company alongside Dempsey–Tunney, Pep–Saddler, Ali–Frazier, Hagler–Hearns, and Robinson–LaMotta. It was not the modest Man of Steel but the gregarious Graziano who captured the public's imagination and became a media star, but even then Graziano's fame was always linked to Zale and his powerful knockout punches.

76

Joe DiMaggio Hits in His 45th Straight Game, a New Record, July 2, 1941, Yankee Stadium

The number 56 is among the most celebrated in sports. Yet, this most hallowed statistic is an accidental icon. When Joe DiMaggio's hitting streak reached its 56th game, no one knew it had reached its furthest point; the number is bittersweet, symbolizing the end of the line. Back when the "Yankee Clipper" had America singing his song, the numbers that mattered most were 42 and 45: the marks that broke George Sisler's modern record of 41 and Willie Keeler's all-time skein of 44 straight games.

The day DiMaggio broke Sisler's record was more dramatic because his bat was stolen between games of a doubleheader, and he went hitless in the first three at-bats of the record-breaker with a new bat. The day he broke Keeler's record, July 2, at Yankee Stadium, was more important, particularly with the gift of hindsight: In 1978, Pete Rose equaled Keeler's 44-game streak, so had DiMaggio not surpassed 44, he wouldn't solely own the modern record.

Initially, DiMaggio was merely shaking off a slump, not making history. The previous year was his first without reaching the World Series. In 1941, things initially looked bleaker: On May 15, the fourth-place Yankees fell to 14–15, 6½ games out of first after a 13–1 loss. DiMaggio managed one single, a good day considering he'd batted .194 in the previous 20 games. Headlines belittling the weak Yankees offense laid much of the blame on DiMaggio.

There were plenty of distractions: DiMaggio's wife Dorothy was pregnant; his manager, Joe McCarthy, was shuttling newcomers in and out of the lineup; Lou Gehrig was dying; and big-leaguers were getting draft numbers as the country slowly, inexorably headed toward war.

That loss was day one of the "streak." DiMaggio's hitting steadily improved, although what was more noticeable early on was that the Yankees started win-

Joe DiMaggio's 56-game hitting streak may be baseball's unbreakable record. *Library of Congress, Prints and Photographs Division [LC-USZ62-76272]*

ning, as catcher Bill Dickey hit .391 in his own 21-game hitting streak. Interest in DiMaggio's streak was negligible until Memorial Day in Boston, where Red Sox star Ted Williams had started his own streak on May 15. (It ended at 23 games.)

Since DiMaggio had hit in 61 straight games in the minors, New York writers thought he had a legitimate shot at the club record of 29.

DiMaggio tied the Yankees record in a game against Cleveland and reached 30 thanks to a generously scored bad-hop single off Luke Appling's shoulder. Attention spread to the national press and from the sports pages to the front pages. The focus was on Sisler's 1922 record. But the *World-Telegram* started hyping Keeler's 1897 streak as the ultimate goal. Records set before 1900 are generally dismissed as ancient history, with good reason. In 1897, a crucial rule favoring slap hitters decreed that foul balls did not count as strikes. But once Keeler's ancient accomplishment was dug up, the record became a challenge DiMaggio had to meet.

When DiMaggio set the righty record with 34 straight games, radio stations were daily interrupting regular programming to announce DiMaggio had gotten his hit. (The Yankees were not on radio because no sponsor shelled out the $75,000 rights fee, although WINS provided 15-minute highlight recreations each evening.)

The Yankees moved into first place after the 37th game. The streak almost ended the next day. Against St. Louis submariner Eldon Auker, DiMaggio was 0-for-3 in the eighth. With the Yankees winning, this was their final turn, so DiMaggio, due up fourth, needed help. With one out, Red Rolfe walked. Tommy Henrich, terrified that he'd hit into a double play and kill the streak, returned to the dugout and asked McCarthy if he could bunt. McCarthy approved, and afterward DiMaggio smacked a double.

June 29 was DiMaggio's chance to both tie and pass Sisler in a doubleheader in Washington. The Yankees needed an extra train car for all the writers traveling with the team. In the opener, DiMaggio rammed a sixth-inning double, but between games a fan swiped DiMaggio's bat from the rack. DiMaggio was unnerved, because of superstition and because that bat had been just right—a 32-inch, 36-ounce bat with a half-ounce personally sandpapered off at the handle. Using an unfamiliar new bat, DiMaggio went hitless in his first three trips to the plate.

Henrich, who had earlier borrowed some of DiMaggio's lumber, thrust one of those sticks at DiMaggio in the seventh, and DiMaggio singled to pass Sisler. (The fan who stole the bat went home to Newark and boasted about it; DiMaggio's mob-connected friends found him and got the stick back for the streak's last stretch.)

All that remained was Keeler. DiMaggio tied the record in the second game of a doubleheader. One more hit and he would stand alone. The next day, July 2, was a scorcher, almost 95 degrees. Boston's 41-year-old Lefty Grove—scheduled to go for his 300th win—bowed out at the last minute; the Red Sox started Dick Newsome.

DiMaggio got a good read on Newsome with his first at-bat, crushing the ball deep to right-center, where Stan Spence made a fine running catch. In the third, DiMaggio jumped on another pitch, but this long drive hooked foul. He grounded out to third.

On a 2–0 fastball in the fifth, DiMaggio looked overeager. He chased a high fastball and popped up, but the ball drifted into the stands. Newsome tried another high fastball. DiMaggio turned on it. Whipping his quick, compact swing from his wide stance, he lashed a hard liner over Ted Williams's head and over the fence for a home run. He had hit in 45 consecutive games.

Teammate Lefty Gomez quipped that DiMaggio had broken the record of Keeler, a singles hitter, in perfect style. "Joe hit one today where they ain't," he said.

His teammates, who had long held back, afraid of pressuring or jinxing the great man, rushed out to greet him. Afterward, DiMaggio acknowledged that 45 had been the magic number. Breaking his pose as Mr. Unflappable, he also admitted that the pressure was getting to him and that he'd been swinging at bad pitches to avoid being walked. Relaxed, he hit safely in the first inning of each of his next five games. In the streak's final 11 games, he hit .545, going 24-for-44, leaving fans slack-jawed in awe. It took two great stops at third base by Cleveland's Ken Keltner to end the streak at 56. DiMaggio then hit safely in his next 16 games.

During the run, DiMaggio tallied a .408 average, 15 homers, 55 RBIs, 56 runs scored, and just 7 strikeouts. (By the time he was finished, his average was .375.) The Yankees won 41 and lost just 15 during the streak, taking over the league. Ted Williams would lead the league that year with his remarkable .406 average and 37 home runs, but while DiMaggio finished just third and fourth, respectively, in those categories, he was the league's MVP, as the Yankees won the pennant and their fifth World Series title in the six years since DiMaggio first donned pinstripes.

DiMaggio graduated from baseball star to American idol. On July 2, he'd needed a police escort to get past the fans, and each day added luster to his legend. Les Brown and his band recorded a new song that streaked up the charts. The lyrics to the chorus, "Jolting Joe DiMaggio, Joe . . . Joe . . . DiMaggio . . . we want you on our side," took on extra significance after the United States entered World War II that winter. More than 60 years after the fact, only Rose has broken the 40-game barrier, leaving DiMaggio's streak intact as baseball's most remarkable mark.

77

Joe Louis Comes Back to KO Billy Conn, June 18, 1941, Polo Grounds

Billy Conn was close, so close, to beating the indomitable Joe Louis and pulling off the most astonishing upset in boxing, perhaps in all of sports.

"I'd tasted some of Joe's best blows, and I was still standing," Conn said later about sipping at the goblet of greatness. "I wasn't surprised, but now I was sure. I felt I could win if I went to work."

Confidence is a wonderful thing, but in the wrong place and at the wrong time it spells doom. Being trapped in a square ring with Louis, one of the strongest punchers of all time, desperate for a knockout, definitely counts as such a situation.

Louis had steamrolled everyone in sight, so his team stirred up new interest by stepping up the pace of his conquests to unparalleled levels. The "Bum of the Month Club" campaign, taking on all comers, one per month, drew new crowds. Conn, the Pittsburgh Kid, was number seven on the list. He was no bum, but he was no heavyweight either—25 pounds lighter than Louis, the light heavyweight champ was given little chance. Still, he boasted that his quickness would be Louis's undoing: "I'm going to knock him out, win his title, and hold it for 20 years."

That cockiness packed the house and carried Conn further than anyone expected. He spent the early rounds in fleet retreat, but after stinging Louis in round 3 with a combo and left hook, Conn began attacking. But he came inside too much, and Louis pummeled him back. Conn needed smelling salts before round 6, and Louis followed up with a shot to the body that buckled Conn and blows to the face that opened cuts by his nose and right eye. The fight seemed done, to be quickly forgotten.

But in the seventh, Louis hurt his right wrist, muffling his chief weapon. The pain wouldn't subside until the 10th, and by then Conn had stopped fleeing and started blocking Louis's punches, enabling him to counterattack. At the end of the ninth, Conn, who was mouthing off, badly hurt the champ with a right to the body.

Even as Louis's wrist improved, he could do little more than trade blows and tie up Conn, hoping to slow him down. In round 12, Louis opened a cut over Conn's other eye, but the challenger smashed the champ back onto his heels with a left hook to the jaw. The champ had to clinch to stay erect. Conn's success planted a seed in his mind, a bad seed.

Conn was ahead in scoring, and if he won just one more round, he could run, if not hide, all the way to the championship. Louis was completely exhausted, but he had spotted a flaw—Conn left himself open when unfurling his long hook—and decided to risk it all to exploit that weakness.

In round 13, Louis absorbed a left hook to the face for the opportunity to detonate his rights. His first two landed too high, however, barely harming Conn but giving him false confidence. His flood of unanswered punches made him gamble for the KO. As he reached back for the big blow, he dropped his left—and Louis stepped into the opening, zapping a chopping right to the head. This one was right on target, stopping Conn cold.

Louis seized control, and his volley of heavy artillery sent Conn down for good just six minutes and two seconds from victory. Hubris stopped Conn just short of the heavyweight throne, although this salt-of-the-earth fighter probably would have scoffed at such a fancy Greek word. He was too proud of his own heritage for that. "I lost my head. You can't trade punches with that man," he said afterward. And with a rueful grin, he took a jab at himself: "What's the use of being Irish if you can't do something stupid once in a while?"

78

Lou Gehrig Proclaims Himself the "Luckiest Man," July 4, 1939, Yankee Stadium

Words like grace, courage, and heroism often find their way into sports-writing, but the finest and truest display of those traits on a ball field came in a simple speech from a dying man. With just a few words in front of the Yankee Stadium crowd on July 4, 1939, Lou Gehrig provided a poignant and powerful reminder not to take life and its joys for granted. The speech has stood the test of time as a piece of great American oratory, a testimony to Gehrig's dignity and humanity, and that potential in everyone.

Ironically, those brief moments ensured that Gehrig, a remarkable power hitter with an unmatchable work ethic, would be remembered mostly for how he handled himself when he was deprived of that which had made him famous.

Gehrig had lived the fairy-tale version of the American Dream. The child of immigrants had achieved unimagined success, a two-time MVP who became the game's highest-paid athlete. Yet, Gehrig never got the accolades he deserved. He was a quiet, colorless guy obscured by Babe Ruth, the game's loudest, most colorful, and greatest player. After the Babe's departure, Gehrig watched, un-complaining, as the press anointed another soft-spoken, colorless immigrant, Joe DiMaggio, as the second coming of Ruth, conflating his elegant playing style with a personality.

Gehrig's numbers were—well, no one ever called anything Gehrig-esque, but they were the closest thing to Ruthian outside of the Babe himself. In 10 of 12 years from 1926 to 1937, Gehrig placed in the top three in home runs, RBI, runs scored, and total bases. He was also in the top three in batting average seven times. Gehrig's remarkable consistency gradually allowed people to take him for granted—especially because what he did during each game was eventually overshadowed by the fact that he never missed one. Gehrig's consecutive-game streak started generating press in 1930, when Joe Sewell, owner of the longest active run, missed one game. It began earning headlines in 1932, the year before he broke Everett Scott's record of 1,307 games, and it defined him until 1939, when he was felled by amyotrophic lateral sclerosis (ALS).

Gehrig endured sporadic criticism by playing through a broken thumb, a broken toe, back spasms, lumbago, and other injuries, occasionally to the detriment of the club. Yet, his relentless devotion and pride in being a Yankee was at his core and crucial to his greatness. Gehrig diligently transformed himself from an atrocious fielder into a solid, even strong, one and approached every game like a thrilled rookie—down eight runs in the ninth inning, he'd run hard to first on a weak grounder.

In 1938, Gehrig struggled, falling below .300 for the first time since 1925. Calls grew louder for a day off to get his strength back. His wife Eleanor asked him to stop the streak at 1,999; Gehrig played in his 2,000th game. Manager Joe McCarthy said it was Gehrig's decision, but he did drop Gehrig in the batting order. Gehrig compensated for his loss of strength by ordering lighter bats and guessing more on pitches. Clearly exhausted, he twice pulled himself out after one inning that September, which brought a fresh round of criticism, with some fans calling the hardest-working man in sports a phony.

That winter, Gehrig began falling and dropping things with increasing frequency. By spring training, something was obviously wrong. His muscles had withered, his body ached, and his balance was wobbly. Easy grounders rolled through his legs, and once he missed 19 straight pitches in batting practice. Gehrig started the exhibition season 3-for-35, as writers called him washed up, speculated on the cause of his demise, and wondered when he would bench himself.

When the season started, the fans, who had occasionally booed him in 1938, realized this was no normal slump and began cheering Gehrig for his effort with all their might, even after strikeouts. On April 30, in the ninth inning of his 2,130th consecutive game, Gehrig fielded a routine grounder and flipped to the pitcher for the out. When his teammates congratulated him for a basic play, Gehrig realized he had been reduced to a pitiable creature.

On May 2, 1939, in Detroit, Gehrig took himself out of the lineup. McCarthy gave Gehrig the honor of delivering the lineup card to the umpire. As he headed back to the dugout afterward, the public address announcer said, "How about a hand for Lou Gehrig, who played 2,130 games in a row before he benched himself today." Gehrig tipped his hat to the roaring fans, went down the steps, and wept.

CHAPTER 78

He would never play again. On June 13, Gehrig checked into the Mayo Clinic in Minnesota, where specialists diagnosed his illness. He was 36. The modest Gehrig downplayed the disease, implying that he might someday be crippled without letting on that ALS's progress is often rapid and eventually fatal. It seems only Eleanor Gehrig, Yankees executive Ed Barrow, and a few others learned the truth. Still, in Philadelphia on June 29, Athletics owner-manager Connie Mack requested that Gehrig come onto the field, and the fans gave him an eight-minute ovation. Gehrig didn't like such attention, so his teammates chipped in for a trophy they could present in the clubhouse. The writers, however, promoted the idea of a Lou Gehrig Appreciation Day, and Barrow agreed, scheduling the event between games of a doubleheader.

On July 4, 1939, a dozen members of the 1927 Yankees crowded into the clubhouse—Bob Meusel, Waite Hoyt, Mark Koenig, Joe Dugan, Herb Pennock, Bob Shawkey, and Tony Lazzeri, to name a few. Everett Scott and Wally Pipp, who Gehrig had replaced at first base in 1925, were also on hand. Gehrig was so nervous and so moved by the presence of his ex-mates that he hid in McCarthy's office. Before the game, the 1927 stars raised their old championship pennant in center field. The Yankees dropped the opener, but no one cared.

As a brass band played, the Yankees and Washington Senators lined up on either side of the mound, and the 1927 squad gathered near home plate, notably Babe Ruth, who had not spoken with Gehrig since a petty feud that dated to 1934. Barrow and Gehrig walked out together. Mayor Fiorello La Guardia, U.S. postmaster general James Farley, McCarthy, and Ruth spoke glowingly of him. The Yankees retired number 4, the first time that had ever been done. While being showered with gifts, Gehrig kept his head down, silently wiping tears away as the inscription from his teammates' trophy was read aloud.

Finally, it was Gehrig's turn. The fans chanted, "We want Lou! We want Lou!" Gehrig shook his head at emcee Sid Mercer. No. It was too much for him. Afterward, Gehrig told reporters that it was the only time in his life he was ever frightened on a baseball field, saying, "I'd have rather struck out in the ninth with the score tied, two down, and the bases loaded than walk out there before all those grand people."

Mercer apologized to the crowd, explaining that Gehrig was "too moved to speak," and the crew prepared to dismantle the microphones. But he had always been one to follow his manager's orders, and when McCarthy asked that he give it a shot, Gehrig stepped forward. The stadium fell utterly, deafeningly silent.

Fans, for the past two weeks you have been reading about the bad break I got. Yet, today I consider myself the luckiest man on the face of this earth. I have been in ballparks for 17 years and have never received anything but kindness and encouragement from you fans. Look at these grand men. Which of you wouldn't consider it the highlight of his career just to associate with them for even one day? Sure, I'm lucky. . . . When the New York Giants, a team you would give your right arm to beat, and vice versa, sends you a gift—that's something. When everybody down to the groundskeepers and those boys in white coats remember you with trophies—that's something. When you have a wonderful mother-in-law who takes sides with you in squabbles with her own daughter—that's something. When you have a father and a mother who work all their lives so you can have an education and build your body—it's a blessing. When you have a wife who has been a tower of strength and shown more courage than you dreamed existed—that's the finest I know. So I close in saying that I may have had a tough break, but I have an awful lot to live for. Thank you.

The band played a German folk song, and Ruth threw his arms around his former slugging partner; everyone wept or cheered.

Since few knew the truth about Gehrig's prognosis, the event felt more like a valedictory celebration than a living memorial. Still, his speech had a powerful, indelible impact on everyone who witnessed it. In the *Herald-Tribune*, Richards Vidmer noted a deep understanding that Gehrig was more than a mere jock, that he "stood for something finer than merely a great baseball player—that he stood for everything that makes sports important in the American scene."

When Gehrig died two years later, subsequent viewings of the film clip of his speech and the somewhat altered climax of the popular biopic *Pride of the Yankees* added a layer of heartbreaking poignancy.

By avoiding self-pity and focusing on our better nature, Gehrig transcended sports, providing an eternal reminder of what really matters. For that, Gehrig—a stouthearted, hardworking, and honest man, a caring son, and a loving husband who faced the worst life had to offer with determination and optimism—truly was a hero.

79

The Giants Hold Off the Packers for the NFL Championship, December 11, 1938, Polo Grounds

In the brutal 1938 championship game between New York and Green Bay, the fearsome Packers amassed 378 yards to the Giants' 212 and had twice as many first downs in the second half, and they also pulled off a 40-yard touchdown pass, a 66-yard breakaway on a screen, and a 34-yard run. Yet, the defending champions could not fend off the Giants, who displayed a vigilant opportunism, swooping in at crucial junctures to alter the game's dynamic.

It was a pitched battle, with intermittent fisticuffs and numerous injuries. The Giants' Johnny Dell Isola left on a stretcher with a spinal injury, Ward Cuff departed with his sternum possibly fractured but returned, and Leland Shaffer stayed in with a broken bone in his leg. Even the biggest names weren't exempt: NFL MVP and Giants leader Mel Hein was temporarily knocked out with a concussion, while Green Bay's unstoppable wideout Don Huston missed much of the second half with an injured knee.

The Giants yielded yardage willingly in a game plan designed by Hein, who knew the gravest danger was not grinding drives, but lightning strikes; he'd ordered his unit to grudgingly give inch after inch to prevent explosive outbursts. The Giants couldn't completely contain Green Bay, but the defense produced their own stunners. On Green Bay's second possession, future Giants coach Jim Lee Howell blocked a punt, giving New York the ball on the Packers seven and setting up a field goal. The Giants blocked a punt on the next possession, too, and Howell recovered the loose ball on Green Bay's 28. Four plays later, Tuffy Leemans, the league's second-leading rusher, scored a touchdown for a 9–0 Giants lead. Later, Green Bay closed within 9–7, but Hein recovered a fumble near midfield, and Giants quarterback Ed Danowski hurled a 20-yard touchdown pass. Again, Green Bay struck back, when Wayland Becker caught a short pass but broke free for 66 yards to set up a touchdown. At the half, New York was clinging to a 16–14 lead.

In the third quarter, the Packers seized the lead, 17–16. Thus, for the first time all day the Giants offense needed to mount a sustained drive. They did. Or rather, Hank Soar did. Soar, later the first-base umpire in Don Larsen's perfect game, carried the team by carrying the ball five times and catching one pass to move the ball 39 yards to the Packers 23. Then Ed Danowski lofted a ball downfield. Two Packers defenders were there, but Soar hauled it in at the six. With Clark Hinkle trying to drag him down, Soar shoved his way into the end zone.

New York had to protect that 23–17 lead for one more quarter. Green Bay mounted two last marches, but both times the Giants defense cut them down, with an interception inside New York's 30 and a fumble recovery. The Giants' victory made them, not Green Bay, the first NFL team to win two championship games. With their fourth appearance since the title game had started six years' earlier, the Giants could unofficially but proudly claim the crown as the NFL's first modern dynasty.

80

Joe Louis Annihilates Max Schmeling,
June 22, 1938, Yankee Stadium

Two friends strolled along the Harlem River on a June evening. "How you feel, Joe?" Freddie Wilson asked. This was no idle question. His buddy was Joe Louis, set to fight a rematch against Max Schmeling at nearby Yankee Stadium that very night. At stake were personal pride and a heavyweight crown, as well as the hopes and dreams of a race and a nation.

"I'm scared," Louis replied. Timidity was not what one expected from the heavyweight champion.

"Scared?"

"Yeah, I'm scared I might kill Schmeling tonight."

Louis's barrage of blows didn't kill Schmeling, but he did demolish the challenger with an abruptness and ferocity rarely seen in heavyweight title fights. And in leveling Schmeling at just 2:04 of the first round, Louis delivered a short jab to Germany's Nazi nationalism and a more telling blow to the deeply bred racism in the United States, thus earning his place in the pantheon of American heroes.

Joe Louis Barrow was born in 1914, the grandson of slaves and the seventh child of an Alabama sharecropper. His father died when Joe was four; his mother Lillie remarried and, in 1926, took the children north to Detroit. Louis built his muscles carrying blocks of ice at work and spent the money his mother gave him for violin lessons on a locker at a gym where he took up boxing. He was an immediate success, making it to the Golden Gloves finals in 1933 and winning the national AAU light heavyweight championship soon thereafter. Louis turned pro in 1934, his career steered by an array of blacks determined to forge a new black heavyweight champion. They carefully crafted his persona as the antithesis of Jack Johnson, whose flamboyance, gloating, and public dalliances with white women stirred up racism and even violence. They taught Louis to aim for knockouts so judges wouldn't get the chance to favor white foes and avoid drinking, smoking, boasting, being photographed with white

Front page from the *Cleveland Call Post*, featuring Joe Louis's victory over Max Schmeling. *Schomburg Center for Research in Black Culture, Photographs and Prints Division, the New York Public Library*

women, or being "too black." They taught him to be flawless, and he almost was—he not only floored his opponents, but also became a role model for many, notably Jackie Robinson. (Louis was not perfect—he had numerous affairs with both black and white women, from Lena Horne to Lana Turner—but he was discreet.)

Louis's team later hired Mike Jacobs, a savvy New Yorker looking to break Madison Square Garden's tightfisted control of the city's fight game, and he got William Randolph Hearst's newspapers on his side, building Louis's celebrity. When Louis made his New York debut in 1935, against Italian Primo Carnera, right when Benito Mussolini was preparing to invade Ethiopia, the press touted this matchup as U.S. democracy versus Italian fascism. Louis KO'd Carnera in six rounds to become as big a star in black America as Satchel Paige.

In his first 18 months as a pro, Louis scored 23 knockouts in 27 straight wins, earning $371,645, when the average yearly salary was $1,250. He seemed destined for the heavyweight crown, with one fight before a title shot: Europe's first German champion, Max Schmeling, who had conquered the United States in 1930, by beating Jack Sharkey. Schmeling's title was both tainted and short-lived: He won when Sharkey was disqualified for low blows and, after one defense, lost the rematch to Sharkey on a controversial decision.

Schmeling, who wore opponents down while he searched out their weaknesses, trained hard and diligently studied footage of Louis, nine years his junior. "I saw something," he cryptically told the press before their June 1936 fight. What he had seen was Louis briefly dropping his defenses between lefts. If he could take the pounding, Schmeling knew he'd find an opening for his big right.

He found it in the fourth, dealing Louis his first-ever knockdown. Louis, expecting another quick knockout, had devoted himself to golf, eating, his wife, and other women instead of training. Schmeling ground down Louis before punching him out in the 12th. White America did not feel it had much at stake, but blacks were distraught—there were even reports of suicide and depression attributed to Louis's loss.

"I walked down Seventh Avenue and saw grown men weeping like children and women sitting on the curbs with their heads in their hands," Langston Hughes said afterward. More than a fighter, Louis symbolized hope for blacks. But he had been reduced, Lena Horne said later, to "just another Negro getting beaten by a white man."

The Nazis were ecstatic. Having ordered the press to minimize the fight in case Schmeling lost to a black man, they now flew him back home on their new airship, the *Hindenburg* (talk about bad omens), feting him at a dinner with

Adolf Hitler and propaganda minister Joseph Goebbels, and releasing the fight as a feature film (*Schmeling's Victory: A German Victory*).

Schmeling was next in line for a shot at champion James Braddock. Schmeling desperately wanted his title back, but he also loved his celebrity at home. He had once circulated in Berlin with playwrights, actors, and other artists, many of whom were Jewish. Now he allowed Hitler to use him for propaganda purposes. He never joined the Nazi Party, although that may have been because Hitler thought him more useful outside of it.

Mike Jacobs capitalized on growing political pressure and boycott threats by playing up fears that Schmeling, as a Nazi tool, would win, take the title to Europe, and refuse to defend it. Louis landed the rights to fight Braddock and beat him in eight rounds. But his victory felt hollow. "I've got to beat Schmeling before I'm the real world champion," he said.

In June 1938, Louis got his shot. By then Hitler had flexed his muscles, annexing Austria and threatening Czechoslovakia. The Nazis touted Schmeling (whose manager, Joe Jacobs, was Jewish) as a representative of Aryan superiority, and he earned the enmity of the American public by going along, singing the Nazi anthem and doing the Sieg Heil at fights held in Germany while shilling for Hitler. He also lied to the American press, pretending there was no persecution of Jews, and promised that Hitler had no grand designs.

Now there was genuine concern among whites about what it would mean if "our guy," the American, lost to "one of them." Protesters outside Schmeling's hotel in Manhattan harassed the German, and the press portrayed Louis as the protector of American values. It's hard to fathom how sudden and shocking a transformation this was in public perception—Louis, who the white press had routinely called things like a "wild animal," was transformed from a near-savage to democracy personified, a beacon equal to the Statue of Liberty. President Franklin Roosevelt dined with the champ at the White House, publicly squeezing his biceps and pronouncing, "Joe, we need muscles like yours to beat Germany."

For Louis, this fight was mainly personal—he wanted to avenge his sole loss and was riled by reports that Schmeling said he wasn't smart enough to change his style. Yankee Stadium was packed, and 70 million people, more than half the population, tuned in on radio. Movies and dances throughout the nation were interrupted for the broadcast. The fight played throughout the Western world in English, German, Portuguese, and Spanish. That night, everything was on the line. As Dave Kindred put it in the *Sporting News* decades later, "Lose, he's just another guy. Win, he's Joe Louis forever."

The hostility toward Schmeling was palpable. He entered the ring protected by 25 cops but was still bombarded by apples, cigarette butts, and banana peels. Louis, who had run out of steam in their first fight, had no plans to pace himself. Schmeling was not expecting such aggression, and Louis snapped off two sharp left hooks to the face and a right to the chin before the German set himself. Schmeling managed only two ineffectual punches the entire fight. Louis pursued him immediately, drilling him in the head and body, slamming him to the ropes. Louis threw every punch in his arsenal, and they all connected.

Louis sent Schmeling to the canvas twice. Then Schmeling, trapped against the ropes, turned to escape yet another right but took the blow near his kidney, fracturing a vertebra. His high-pitched howl tore through the crowd. Soon thereafter, Schmeling's handlers threw in the white towel. That was against the rules in New York, so referee Art Donovan paid it no heed. He could not, however, ignore the beating Louis was delivering. After just 124 seconds, Donovan stopped the fight.

The entire nation, black and white, celebrated with a giddy mixture of joy and relief. But it was a particularly wondrous night for black America. The police commissioner closed off 30 blocks in Harlem for revelers, and 100,000 people poured into the streets and bars. "There was never a Harlem like the Harlem of last night. Take a dozen Christmases, a score of New Year's Eves, a bushel of July 4ths and maybe—yes maybe—you get a faint glimpse of the idea," the *Daily News* wrote.

In Germany the reaction was quite different. The Nazis cut off radio transmission once they realized what was happening. Schmeling was portrayed as the victim of illegal hits, with film doctored with footage from 1936 added to make it seem as though Schmeling had put up a fight. Louis's victory may have embarrassed and infuriated Hitler, but it did little to slow him down. The us-versus-them mentality encouraged by the triumph did, however, eventually help Roosevelt when making the case for entering the war.

More lasting was the effect on the home front. Louis's triumph over Schmeling was the biggest event in black America at the time, especially because black writers had just begun getting boxing credentials. In the days before major civil rights victories, it was white Americans rooting hard for a black man that started the process of breaking down racial barriers. Louis won even more white loyalty during World War II when he joined the U.S. Army and donated more than $100,000 in proceeds to the army and naval relief funds. (He also helped get blacks—notably Jackie Robinson—into officer training school.) Jesse Owens had anticipated some of these accomplishments in the 1936 Olympics, but that performance happened overseas, was not a mano-a-mano matchup, and was in track, which lacked boxing's clout. The heavyweight champion was the Man. And the Man, for black and white Americans, was now Joe Louis.

81

Lazzeri, DiMaggio, and the Yankees Make a Statement against the Giants and Start a New Yankees Dynasty, October 2, 1936, Yankee Stadium

The Babe Ruth era was over. The Yankees, who had played in seven World Series during his tenure, finished second for three straight years starting in 1933; they'd reached just one World Series in the last seven.

Manager Joe McCarthy was dismissively called "Second Place Joe" and it seemed, despite the steady greatness of Lou Gehrig, that their days as the powerhouse were done.

Sure, they had some skinny new Italian kid from San Francisco who had shredded the Pacific Coast League, but the 21-year-old, named Joe DiMaggio, missed April because he burned his foot on a machine after being too shy to ask why it felt so hot.

Then the rookie debuted in May and gave the Yankees the jolt they needed. DiMaggio had three hits in his first game, then batted .323, with 206 hits, 29 homers, and 125 RBI in 138 games. He graced the cover of *Time* magazine. Teaming with Gehrig and Bill Dickey, he helped the Yankees win the pennant by 19 games. But the proving ground would be the World Series, and not just any World Series but a Subway Series, the first since 1923.

The Giants had won the World Series in 1933, and had 12 league titles to the Yankees' eight. Both had won four championships, so 1936 was the battle for supremacy. Giants ace Carl Hubbell shut out the Yankees to open the series. Game 2 would be crucial—no team had won a best-of-seven after losing the first two games. The Yankees did more than make a statement—they issued a manifesto, declaring that while Ruth was exceptional, his era would not be an exception. A new dynasty—one that some historians deem the most impressive of all Yankee reigns—was taking hold, built on a blend of slugging, pitching, and defense. Game 2 linked the glory of the old and new, highlighting Tony Lazzeri, a holdover from the Murderers' Row lineup of the 1920s, and DiMaggio, who finished with a personal touch that made it clear these were his Yankees.

With two on in the first, DiMaggio surprised everyone by dropping a bunt for a single, filling the sacks for Gehrig, who drove home a run with a fly to right. In the third inning, the Yankees led, 5–1, and had loaded the bases again when Lazzeri came up. Nearing the end of his career, Lazzeri, a fellow Italian American from San Francisco, had (with shortstop Frankie Crosetti) been a valuable mentor to the young DiMaggio. Now, Lazzeri smashed the second ever World Series grand slam to blow the game open.

The Giants managed three in the fourth, perhaps because the Yankees' famously flaky Lefty Gomez was growing bored—he stopped pitching to watch a plane fly overhead. But the Yankees padded their lead with one in the sixth and two in the seventh. In the ninth, the Yankees added enough flourishes to make this a game for the record and history books.

Jake Powell singled, stole second, and went to third on a fly-out. Yes, with an eight-run lead in the ninth, the Bombers played small ball. Gomez singled him home, then Crosetti, Red Rolfe, and DiMaggio singled in succession. One out later, Dickey cracked a homer to make it 18–4. That gave Dickey five RBI, tying a single-game Series record—set by Lazzeri earlier that afternoon. Every Yankee had at least one hit and one run. They broke or tied 12 records. No other team has scored 18 in a Series game before or since. It remains the most lopsided rout in Series history and a clear sign of what the Yankees had in store for their opponents.

One more sign soon emerged. Before the ninth inning, there was an announcement asking everyone to remain seated after the game until President Franklin Roosevelt departed in a car driven through the center-field gate. DiMaggio corralled two easy flies. Then, with a runner on second, Hank Leiber blasted the ball some 475 feet from home plate—a home run in many other ballparks but in Yankee Stadium's Death Valley merely an excuse for DiMaggio to display his long, graceful strides and knack for making even the most difficult plays look easy. He caught the ball on the dead run and took two steps up the stairs in center field toward the clubhouse. Suddenly, he remembered the president.

The immigrant's son from Fisherman's Wharf stopped short and stood at attention, waiting. He later told writers that as the president's car rolled by, Roosevelt gave him a wink and a wave, and the "V" sign for victory.

In the years to come, DiMaggio would ensure that Yankees pinstripes continued to symbolize victory just as surely as did Roosevelt's V sign; the club would capture 16 of the next 18 World Series games, while capturing four straight titles.

"I've always heard that one player could make the difference between a losing team and winner, and I never believed it," Giants manager Bill Terry said about DiMaggio after that 1936 Series. "Now I know it's true."

Ned Irish Launches College Basketball with the First Doubleheader, December 29, 1934, Madison Square Garden

When Ned Irish was a young sportswriter, he went to cover a college basketball game at Manhattan College in 1933. The game was sold out and the doors shut. Irish crawled through a small athletic department window, ripping his suit pants. He then had an epiphany that changed basketball and the city: If basketball's appeal had outgrown this tiny gym, maybe it could fill a much larger arena. And so, on December 29, 1934, Ned Irish brought hoops to the Garden.

That's how the legend goes.

In reality, in 1931, Irish and other sportswriters staged a tripleheader basketball benefit for Mayor Jimmy Walker's Unemployment Relief Fund at the Garden. Despite the Depression, the event sold out. It packed the house in 1932, and 1933, too. Irish, a 29-year-old Brooklyn native, was not only a sportswriter for the *New York World-Telegram*, but also publicity man for the football Giants, and he sensed the sport's potential. So, on December 29, 1934, Ned Irish officially brought hoops to the Garden.

This twin bill was the start of something new, something big, something very New York—it was the beginning of college basketball's elevation to major sports status and the turning point for the Garden, which thereafter became a mecca for college basketball and sports in general.

The Garden had faced troubled times since its main force, Tex Rickard, died in 1929, just months before the Depression hit. Million-dollar profits shrank to $130,000 in 1931, and by 1933 the Garden was losing money. (Hockey was the main sports attraction, along with boxing between the Jack Dempsey and Joe Louis eras.) Although it may be too strong to say this doubleheader saved the Garden, it did propel the arena toward the future by delivering Irish as a basketball director—he would build college hoops and help launch the National Invitation Tournament (NIT), the Basketball Association of America (which evolved into the NBA), and the New York Knicks, for whom he served as president until 1974.

Showing savvy and foresight, Irish worked out a sweet deal, getting the rights to host six doubleheaders without laying out a penny. "The Garden was dark a lot of nights," he once explained. "The only guarantee the Garden wanted was that its percentage of the gate would average the cost of renting the building."

Irish understood not only business, but also basketball. According to Dennis D'Agostino, author of *Garden Glory*, a book about the Knicks, many teams still played on courts drawn in chalk on hard surfaces and in "cages" (the netting that surrounded the court, keeping the ball constantly in play). For this doubleheader, Irish brought in a real wood basketball floor and installed glass backboards so that patrons sitting behind them could see the action. He also fed this information to his press-box colleagues, who effusively previewed the event. "Metropolitan college basketball will step out of its cramped gymnasiums and gloomy armories tonight into the bright lights and spaciousness of Madison Square Garden," trumpeted the *New York Herald-Tribune*.

By today's standards, the games were boring—with no shot clock and jump balls after every basket, the final tallies were so low they resembled football scores. But on this long-ago winter's night, the games between St. John's and Westminster College, and NYU and Notre Dame, thrilled the appreciative crowd of 16,188, while thousands more were turned away.

The story of these games was not the specifics of Westminster's 37–33 win or NYU's 25–18 triumph in the headliner. In the first game, St. John's led, 16–12, early in the second half but couldn't finish off the "big" Westminster squad with 6-foot-4 giants. In the second game, NYU used a 10–0 second-half run to extend its two-year winning streak to 20 games.

Irish added more dates to his schedule, and thanks to his relentless promotion, the eight doubleheaders drew almost 100,000 people. In addition to putting college basketball and the Garden on the map at the same time in the same place, the Garden doubleheaders improved the game itself by encouraging standardized rules and officiating.

Soon more top teams wanted in as the New York press made schools famous, players celebrities, and hoops a major spectator sport. By 1938, basketball was so big that the Garden debuted the NIT. The NCAA later joined the NIT there. The sport took off, giving birth to new professional leagues that would develop into the NBA. By the time the point-shaving scandal chased many of college's biggest games away in 1951, the Knicks were ready to step in as a new basketball attraction. And when the Big East Tournament was born in the 1980s, its roots traced back to Irish's inspiration. On some level, all college basketball, down to March Madness' nationally televised Final Four, owes a debt to a couple of low-scoring games on a cold December night in New York and the man who brought them to life.

83

The Giants Win the NFL Championship in the Sneaker Game, December 9, 1934, Polo Grounds

Abe Cohen was five feet tall and 140 pounds. He toiled as a tailor. Cohen was also the MVP of the New York Giants upset of the undefeated Chicago Bears in the 1934 title game—if MVP stands for Most Valuable Procurer.

Cohen did not play a down for the Giants, but he did run the best route of the day—to the Manhattan College supply room.

This game was another crucial step forward in pro football's development. In 1925, Red Grange pumped life and money into the floundering young league. In 1930, the Giants' defeat of Knute Rockne's Notre Dame All-Stars in a charity exhibition demonstrated the pro game's superiority to skeptics. The NFL held its first championship game in 1933, which the Bears won in a down-to-the-last-play thriller. Now the powerful New York press could see a big game and perhaps deem it as exciting, and as worthy of their attention as the Rose Bowl or the annual Army–Navy or Army–Notre Dame games. A blowout by heavily favored Chicago—who outscored their foes 286–86 in their 13–0 regular season—might have dampened their enthusiasm, but they got a hard-fought game that turned on a behind-the-scenes twist, one the writers could use to mythologize the day, making this the first NFL game for the ages: the "Sneaker Game."

That morning, a cold spell took a turn for the worse. The weather barely broke double digits when team president Jack Mara inspected the Polo Grounds field—it was a solid block of ice with the tarpaulin frozen to it. Mara called coach Steve Owen, who warned his players at breakfast. "Why don't we wear sneakers?" asked captain Ray Flaherty, who had done just that at Gonzaga University with great success.

Great idea, but where do you find sneakers on a Sunday morning? Owen, Flaherty, and tackle Bill Morgan hit the phones, but every sporting goods store was closed. Owen called running back Ken Strong at home in Queens since Strong worked an offseason job with a sporting goods firm, but Strong didn't have a key to that building.

Dejected, Owen phones and his men headed to the Polo Grounds. In the locker room was little Abe Cohen, who loved football so much he tailored Manhattan College's uniforms and volunteered on game days to help the Giants trainers. He also had a key to Manhattan College's supply room. Owen called Cohen's play, sending the little man off in search of a taxi to the school. At least that's the story told after the game—decades later, Wellington Mara speculates that Cohen may have broken in to get the sneakers.

Getting to Manhattan College at 242nd Street takes time even when the streets aren't slick with ice, so Cohen was gone a while. The Giants got an early field goal, but the Bears' bigger, stronger line shoved the Giants around, and Chicago held a 10–3 halftime lead.

Into the Giants locker room strode Abe Cohen, mission accomplished. He scrounged up nine pair of sneakers. Both teams had worn their cleats down to nubs, but not all the Giants players embraced the idea. Then they saw Ken Strong moving well in sneakers and were convinced.

When Chicago's coach, George Halas, learned of the switch, he urged his men to step on their feet. But you can't step on what you can't catch up to. The Giants were able to make sharp cuts that left the Bears slipping and sliding. "We had to mince about," Bears star Bronko Nagurski recalled.

Despite an injured leg, Strong tore off on a 15-yard punt return that set up one touchdown, a 42-yard touchdown run, and another touchdown on a reverse—an unthinkable call if the team had played in cleats. Lewis Burton of the *New York Journal-American* wrote in celebration, "To the heroes of antiquity, to the Greeks who raced across the Marathon plain, and to Paul Revere, add now the name of Abe Cohen."

At the All-Star Game, Carl Hubbell Strikes Out Ruth, Gehrig, Foxx, Simmons, and Cronin in a Row, July 10, 1934, Polo Grounds

When the stands are packed, the pressure is on, and as the first two guys get on base, you may think you're in trouble. But when you look at the next few hitters and see that the easiest out, the weak link, is Babe freakin' Ruth, you *know* you're in trouble. That's where Carl Hubbell found himself on July 10, 1934, at the Polo Grounds, for the second annual All-Star Game.

Expectations for the screwballer were particularly high. The game was being played in Hubbell's home park. Prior to the game he'd been honored with the MVP Award for 1933 for pitching the New York Giants to a World Series crown.

Hubbell didn't invent the screwball, although he threw it so often that his arm actually turned inward. The pitch, which a southpaw like him could make break away from righties, was a variation of the "fadeaway" that made his Giants predecessor, Christy Mathewson, a legend. "Hub" mastered it and hurled a record 46.3 straight scoreless innings in 1933; he'd won 24 straight throughout two years, a new record.

But he yielded a leadoff single to Charlie Gehringer and walked Heinie Manush. Now came the heart of the order:

Babe Ruth: Sure, the aging Bambino would finish his last season as a Yankee with just 22 homers and a .288 average, but no one equaled his flair for drama—he'd already crushed the first All-Star Game home run the previous year.

Lou Gehrig: The Iron Horse was headed for the Triple Crown, with 49 homers, 165 RBI, and a .363 batting average, while striking out just 31 times.

Jimmie Foxx: The Philadelphia muscleman was the only one of the bunch who'd finish 1934 among the strikeout leaders, ending with 75, but his 44 homers, 130 RBI, and .334 average made him almost as dangerous as Gehrig.

CHAPTER 84

Al Simmons: Foxx's teammate, like Gehrig and Foxx, would finish with more than 100 runs and 100 RBI, while his .344 average would be fourth in the league.

Joe Cronin: Washington's future Hall of Famer was far less intimidating, but he too would drive in more than 100 runs in 1934. And he fanned just 28 times that season.

Going over the lineup before the game, Hubbell had come to a realization: "We couldn't discuss weaknesses . . . they didn't have any." The goal was to keep the curve and fastball out of the strike zone and throw only the screwball for strikes. That hadn't worked against Gehringer and Manush.

Hubbell was never a strikeout pitcher. To get out of this jam he wanted a grounder from Ruth, who'd be easy to double up. Looking for a pitch he could launch, Ruth took ball one, then was frozen by three consecutive low screwballs. Strike one, strike two, strike three.

Gehrig too was confounded by the scrooge—he took a big rip at the last one but wasn't particularly close. (The two runners pulled off a double steal on that pitch.)

With Foxx up, Hubbell went for the K. Nothing but screwballs sent Foxx down swinging, too.

Hubbell had fanned Ruth, Gehrig, and Foxx on 12 pitches. And after the National League took a 1–0 lead, he whiffed Simmons and Cronin, both going down swinging, victimized by screwballs they couldn't quite fathom.

Then, perhaps because weak-hitting pitcher Lefty Gomez, with his .104 lifetime batting average, was on deck, Hubbell let up briefly. Bill Dickey managed a single. Whiffing Gomez was a cinch. (Gomez jokingly complained, because if Dickey had struck out, the streak would have reached seven and Gomez would have been forever lumped in with baseball's greatest sluggers.)

Hubbell hurled another scoreless inning and left with a 4–0 lead. The American League stormed back with a six-run fifth to win, 9–7, with Foxx, Simmons, and Cronin combining for 7 hits, 5 runs, and 4 RBI. It barely registered. All anyone talked about was Hubbell slaying one dragon after another.

Major-league officials had put the game in New York to give the new event stature and media exposure. A boring game could have killed the entire experiment. But Hubbell's feat elevated the All-Star Game, and for the next 60 years it truly was the centerpiece of the baseball season.

85

Columbia Pulls Off a Stunning Rose Bowl Upset, January 1, 1934, Rose Bowl, Pasadena

S ome numbers lie. Others don't.

Check these stats from the 1934 Rose Bowl between Columbia and heavily favored Stanford.

First downs: Stanford 16, Columbia 6.

Total yardage: Stanford 272, Columbia 114.

Scoring threats: Stanford 6, Columbia 3.

The only number that counts, however, is the final score:

Columbia 7, Stanford 0.

Back then the Rose Bowl was the sole New Year's Day event, and the best West Coast team picked its opponent. Stanford's first choice was undefeated Princeton, but the Tigers, who had trounced Columbia's Lions, 20–0, refused the invite because of an agreement with Yale that restricted postseason games.

Other choices included Army, Nebraska, Duke, Pitt, Michigan, and Minnesota, but Stanford asked Columbia to the big dance. Some writers grumbled that Stanford was looking for an easy time—Lou Little's Columbia squad had some excellent players, but it was far from great and lacked depth. Columbia would be outweighed by about 17 pounds per man, and cocaptain and leading lineman Joe Ferrara was declared ineligible after failing physics and French midterms.

The Lions arrived in sunny Southern California to find the worst deluge of rain Los Angeles had ever experienced—18 inches fell during the three days preceding the game. Mudslides, flooding, and the resulting car crashes claimed dozens of lives.

CHAPTER 85

At the stadium, the players' benches floated along the sidelines, and the field was submerged. The game was almost canceled, but 25 fire engines and two electric pumps slurped water from the field for hours. The weather and Stanford being the heavy favorite meant only 35,000 bothered to show up, the smallest Rose Bowl crowd ever, although once Columbia proved its mettle, another 5,000 arrived at halftime.

The surface remained treacherous, and rain continued during the game. A mudfest might favor Stanford's heavier, sturdier backs—Bobby Grayson's 152 yards was more than the entire Columbia team—yet the muck inhibited Stanford's superior offense, as they completed only two of 12 passes and fumbled the slippery ball away five times. In the end, they always fell shy of the goal line.

Columbia reached the end zone only once—on a stunning two-play drive in the second quarter—but that would prove enough. Starting at Stanford's 45, quarterback Cliff Montgomery made his sole completion (in just two tries), hitting Red Matal, who splashed to the 17.

Throughout the week the Lions had practiced trick plays to spring on their bigger, stronger opponents, hoping Ivy League brains could triumph over brawn. Now Montgomery decided to try one. Knowing Stanford expected a rushing play through the line, he called KF-79. K stood for kicker (the quarterback was often called the kicker then), who handed the ball to F (the fullback). The offensive line overloaded the right side, and the K, Montgomery, slammed in as if carrying the ball, while the F, 23-year-old sophomore Al Barabas, glided the opposite way through the left side's seven and nine slots.

The execution worked to perfection. Montgomery had set up the play by faking handoffs to Barabas and halfback Ed Brominski early in the game. Now Montgomery "faked" a handoff to Barabas but actually stuck the ball to the runner's left hip. Pretending he still had the ball, Montgomery plunged into the right side. The entire defense fell for it, attacking the line, while Barabas sauntered by untouched—no one from Stanford even saw him until he was at the 10. Just as he coasted into the end zone the sun burst out from behind the clouds.

No one expected that to be the last word in scoring. With Little relying on only 17 players the entire game, the Lions tired. Time after time, Stanford pushed downfield. Yet, each time Columbia dug in. Once Stanford had first down on Columbia's three, but the Lions allowed only two yards in four plays, forcing a fumble on the final effort. When Stanford had a second down on the eight, the Lions—armed with a rare wave of fresh substitutes—tossed the Cardinals back two yards on two plays. Desperate, Stanford took to the air, but Columbia intercepted Grayson's pass. Columbia kept Stanford's slate blank, walking off with a shocking 7–0 victory.

In New York, the Lions were hailed as conquering heroes. Newly sworn-in mayor Fiorello La Guardia, who had promised not to waste time on such trivial nonsense as official greetings, was at Pennsylvania Station to welcome the team home; the city celebrated with a parade from 34th Street uptown to the Columbia campus.

Even the Lions themselves remained forever amazed at what they accomplished. At a reunion 15 years later, Little showed filmed footage of the game. When the second half was about to begin, Barabas said, "Lou, don't show the second half. They might beat us."

86

Babe Ruth "Calls" His World Series Home Run, October 1, 1932, Wrigley Field, Chicago

Ladies and gentlemen of the jury, we will now hear closing arguments in the never-ending case of the "called" home run versus "it's just a myth."

Well, no, actually, we won't. Babe Ruth's mammoth blast into the Wrigley Field bleachers on October 1, 1932, deserves its place as the World Series' most celebrated long ball, one of the final highlights for the man who essentially was baseball. Although it's impossible to definitively close the debate on whether Ruth actually pointed to center field, indicating where his hit would land, the point is moot, since Ruth certainly "called" his home run by taunting Chicago Cubs pitcher Charlie Root and the entire Cubs bench in a wondrous and unique flourish of showmanship that left little doubt about what his plans were.

By 1932, Ruth was old—at 37, he was aging in a hurry, often leaving games during the late innings. By 1932, Ruth was fat—he'd once been big but muscular; now the extra padding slowed him down. By 1932, Ruth had been dethroned as home run king—he swatted 41, but the 58 four-baggers of Philadelphia's Jimmie Foxx had made it the first time since 1918 that Ruth had at least 500 plate appearances but lost the crown.

Nonetheless, in 1932, Babe Ruth was still Babe Ruth, and his output—Foxx's superiority notwithstanding—was still prodigious. And Joe McCarthy's Yankees were back on top, with one of their strongest teams ever. The Philadelphia A's had reigned for three years as the Yankees' pitching faltered and their secondary players struggled. In 1932, Ruth and Lou Gehrig led an offense that scored 1,002 runs, and New York led the league in ERA en route to winning 107 games.

Still, all anyone remembers is Ruth's home run in Game 3 of the World Series against Chicago, the team that had fired McCarthy in 1930.

Ruth and his teammates found extra incentive when the Cubs voted only a half World Series share for midseason pickup Mark Koenig, despite his .353 average—that stinginess rankled because Koenig had been the Yankees' shortstop in the 1920s. New York easily won the first two games at Yankee Stadium amid fierce bench jockeying from both sides. The Cubs directed much of their vitriol at the Yankees' biggest target, Ruth.

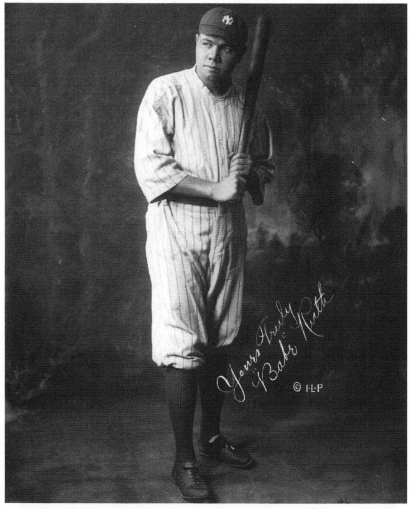

Babe Ruth, baseball's biggest star, always had a flair for the dramatic, and his called home run in the 1932 World Series instantly became part of baseball lore. *Courtesy of the Library of Congress [LC-DIG-ppmsca-39089]*

CHAPTER 86

But New York was a love-in compared to Game 3, where the Cubs injected their insults with an extra dose of venom, particularly regarding Ruth's racial background. (The quickest way to get under Ruth's skin was to question the color of it—specious rumors had long floated about black ancestry.) The Chicago fans at intimate Wrigley joined in—Ruth and his wife Claire had been spat on by a woman at their hotel upon their arrival, and during outfield practice fans hurled lemons at Ruth every time a ball was hit toward him. Ruth picked them up and tossed them back. Then he and Gehrig awed the crowd with their display of might during batting practice.

When the jeering resumed in the first inning, Ruth provided a most impressive rejoinder, smashing a three-run homer into the right-field bleachers. The *New York Herald-Tribune* reported that Ruth pointed to the right-field bleachers just before walloping the ball, although this "call" has been largely forgotten.

In the third, Ruth's shot to right-center was caught at the fence, but Gehrig hit the next one over. Then the Cubs struck back, tying it at 4–4 in the fourth after Ruth misplayed an attempted shoestring catch. As Cubs fans heckled him, Ruth jauntily doffed his cap. But it suddenly seemed this Series might develop into a competitive matchup.

Then came the fateful fifth, which essentially decided the Series and gave Ruth his greatest story line. He stepped in and took strike one from Root. Every fan and every Cub seemed to feel compelled to share their thoughts on Ruth's failings. Remaining jocular, Ruth turned to the Chicago dugout and raised one finger, saying, in effect, "That's just one strike, I've got two more."

Root missed inside and then outside, running the count to 2–1. Then Root pegged strike two, encouraging another outpouring of catcalls—Chicago's Guy Bush actually came a few steps out of the dugout to make sure Ruth could hear his contributions. Ruth remained unperturbed. He shooed the Cubs back into their dugout and held up two fingers.

What happened next is the stuff of myth.

Ruth certainly pointed his bat before the next pitch. Perhaps he did point toward center, although it seems unlikely, since he was a pull hitter and the wind was gusting toward right. Perhaps he pointed his bat at Root—Gehrig said there was one final heated exchange between pitcher and hitter, which Ruth finished with, "I'm going to knock the next pitch right down your goddamned throat." Perhaps he pointed at his enemies in the Cubs' dugout, as stated by some recent analysis of two contemporary home movies.

Imagine standing in front of a hostile crowd, holding up two fingers, pointing your bat, and saying, as Chicago catcher Gabby Hartnett reported, "It only takes one to hit it." Anything short of a rocket off the fence would be a failure, and a strikeout would have doomed Ruth to public humiliation for at least the remainder of the Series. But Ruth was rewriting Mighty Casey and changing the ending.

Root delivered an off-speed pitch low and outside, a difficult pitch to lift out, but Ruth got the bat down and whacked the ball up, up, and away. It soared more than 430 feet to center, the longest home run ever hit in Wrigley. Ruth had shut up his antagonists, but he himself was cackling and shouting at the fans and the Cubs as he rounded the bases, clasping his hands over his head like the champion he was.

Only Joe Williams in the *New York World-Telegram* specified that "Ruth pointed to center," but others made it abundantly clear that this was a "called" home run. Gehrig complained to Fred Lieb that night, asking, "What do you think of the nerve of that big monkey, calling his shot and getting away with it?" In the *New York Times*, John Drebinger wrote, "In no mistaken motions Ruth notified the crowd that the nature of his retaliation would be a wallop right out the confines of the park."

Yes, other journalists looking to fill inches, sell papers, and glorify themselves ginned up accounts with revisionist histories that unnecessarily embellished the moment. But Ruth had made his intentions clear. And the home run was not only climactic, but also timely, giving the Yankees a 5–4 lead. On the very next pitch, Gehrig smacked another home run—also his second of the day—to make it 6–4. The Yankees won, 7–5, and swept the humbled Cubs. Gehrig's 9 hits, 3 homers, and 8 RBI, as well as his 529 average, constituted the best World Series performance by anyone since 1928—when Gehrig was equally great.

But as always, even when Gehrig was the star, Ruth was the story. And in this case, the story was one of baseball's best, a case where you could print the legend but know it was indeed fact.

87

Notre Dame Wins One for the Gipper, November 10, 1928, Yankee Stadium

Johnny O'Brien spent the entire game on the sidelines. With dusk settling late in the fourth quarter, he was wrapped in a blanket to ward off November's chill. This sophomore on the struggling Notre Dame team didn't expect to see action in the big game against Army at Yankee Stadium.

With two minutes remaining, his team started driving, hoping for a startling upset against the undefeated Cadets. At Army's 16, everything crumbled: The snap from center went awry, and the ball bounded through the backfield. Star running back Jack Chevigny recovered it but was injured, knocked out of the game, leaving the team facing 3rd and 26 on Army's 32.

This was a different game than football today: Substitutions in mid-drive were rare—usually made only for an injury—and subs could not speak to teammates on the first play, preventing coaches from sending in plays. Coach Knute Rockne sent Bill Dew in for the wounded Chevigny, but he also slipped in O'Brien for John Colrick. O'Brien, who would letter in track, was willowy, fast, and well rested. He ran deep, slipping past Army's tiring All-American, Chris Cagle. Johnny Niemic faded to the 43 to buy time, then looped a soft pass to O'Brien, crossing the middle. O'Brien bobbled the throw, then entered the end zone, giving the underdogs a 12–6 lead.

Notre Dame's fans, players, and coach were electrified. Rockne wrapped the kid—forever to be known as "One Play O'Brien"—in a hug, supposedly the only time Rockne ever embraced a player on the sidelines. And yet this dramatic sequence and the rest of the action would eventually be overlooked, as the 1928 Army–Notre Dame matchup became the greatest football game no one really remembers.

The sole image people conjure of the game is a sepia-toned reminiscence of Rockne's touching "Win One for the Gipper" speech. The saga of the speech—which won the big game, launched a movie, and catapulted an actor into the presidency—is pure Hollywood hokum, a story that evolved away from the truth, while leaping from tabloid newspaper to national magazine to silver screen and into the nation's lifeblood. But the biggest problem is that the shadows of this tall tale obscured a genuinely thrilling showdown.

By 1928, the Army–Notre Dame rivalry had 15 years of tradition and was the preeminent regular-season game. It had graduated from West Point to Ebbets Field, to the Polo Grounds, and finally to the grandeur of Yankee Stadium. This game was in such demand that the teams gave away rights for both NBC and CBS to broadcast it on radio; traffic and subway overcrowding left the stands half-empty at game time, but the stands eventually filled, and 5,000 diehards peered in from rooftops, fire escapes, and elevated train platforms.

Notre Dame, after dominating for years, had been routed, 27–0, in 1925, and 18–0 in 1927. Laid low by injuries and inexperience, Rockne's team came in with a 4–2 season record. Talk was simmering that it might be time for Rockne to move on. Another Army trouncing would compound matters, and even Rockne sounded down, calling his players "Minute Men," quipping, "They'll be in the game one minute, and the other team will score."

That afternoon, however, Rockne's boys resembled the original Minutemen, gamely sticking it to the more powerful British Regulars. The teams battled to a scoreless standstill in the first half, with favored West Point even unable to reach midfield.

After the break, however, Cagle ran for 19 yards, then passed for 39 to set up the game's first touchdown. Notre Dame's pounding ground game soon tied the score. The taut back-and-forth of the third quarter set the stage for the unforgettable final minutes. Notre Dame, buoyed by new confidence, marched to Army's 37. Although Frank Carideo missed a 55-yard field goal, Notre Dame had Army reeling. On their next possession, Notre Dame started on their own 47, and Carideo, Chevigny, Frank Collins, and Niemic blasted their way down to Army's 16. That was when a bad snap and Chevigny's injury paved the way for O'Brien's touchdown catch.

Any chicken-counters underestimated Cagle's determination and skills. He returned the kickoff 55 yards, and one play later he broke free again, almost running to the 10-yard line. But having been involved in virtually every offensive and defensive play, Cagle was near collapse and had to be helped off the field, according to many reports.

CHAPTER 87

Cagle's replacement, Dick Hutchinson, seemed equal to the task, firing a third-down pass through traffic to Charlie Allen on the four. He then called a keeper and came within inches of the end zone. Army set for one final play, but suddenly the ref blew the whistle, ending the game and preserving Notre Dame's 12–6 upset. Some claimed Army had earned another first down—and thus another play according to the rules—but their protests were in vain.

But don't credit the win to the Gipper.

George Gipp played for the team in 1919 and 1920, a talented player but hardly an inspiration. He was aloof and selfish, a drinker and a gambler, who was always in trouble and on the verge of being expelled. When he died of pneumonia and strep throat in 1920 (some rumors hint at venereal disease), his image was closer to that of today's soiled, surly athlete than the wholesome gentleman deified in the popular imagination by the whitewash in *Knute Rockne, All-American*.

Rockne was indeed an impressive, multifaceted man. He worked through college as a janitor and then a chemistry research assistant; aside from playing football, he played flute in the orchestra, starred in student plays, and graduated magna cum laude. As a coach, he was a gifted teacher, an acute talent assessor, and a brilliant tactician. He designed equipment and uniforms that were wind-resistant and less bulky but provided more protection. His teams produced five unbeaten seasons and a 105–12–5 record.

Yet, Rockne grew into an icon because he was also an impresario, a masterful performer who deftly manipulated school officials, players, and the media. He transformed Notre Dame into a national team by traveling the country, challenging the toughest competition. And boy, could he talk. He was shrewd enough to dole out his motivational speeches sparingly and was talented enough to move reporters and other bystanders to tears. But to score points with his listeners, Rockne was quick to stiff-arm the truth—he once tried inspiring his team to win against Georgia Tech by telling a fib about his own perfectly healthy son Billy being hospitalized. In his book on coaching, Rockne wrote, "The history or traditions of the school are a great thing to recite to your team. . . . Exaggerate these as much as you can."

He did just that with Gipp, who was never called "the Gipper" by anyone, especially himself. In 1928, some columnists had written fondly of Gipp while glossing over Gipp's tumultuous life. Perhaps this inspired Rockne, who knew his young squad was impressionable. From there, everything gets murky. Some say Rockne, who probably was never alone with Gipp for a deathbed scene, passed on Gipp's request before the game, when boxer Jack Dempsey also offered encouragement. Others, with the belief that Rockne wouldn't compete with a heavyweight champ, place the speech at halftime. Still others say he didn't talk about Gipp at all. Years later, sportswriter Grantland Rice attempted to insinuate himself into the scene—he testified to the speech's veracity by claiming that the night before, Rockne told him and another man he might ask the team to "pull one out for Gipp." But Murray Sperber's *Shake Down the Thunder* reveals that Rice was in Atlanta and the third man, Hunk Anderson, was in St. Louis.

The story first appeared two days after the game in a *Daily News* article with the headline, "Gipp's Ghost Beats Army." Written by Notre Dame alum Francis Wallace, it sounds like a pregame speech in which Rockne said straightforwardly, "On his deathbed George Gipp told me that someday, when the time came, he wanted me to ask a Notre Dame team to beat the Army for him."

The tabloid's tale was forgotten until 1930, when Rockne "recounted" it in *Collier's*. The ghostwritten version sounded unnatural, with Rockne uttering such awkward phrases as, "His eyes brightened in a frame of pallor," and declaring that Chevigny shouted, "That's one for the Gipper," after scoring the winning touchdown.

That article embellished the speech into a tearjerker: "Some time, Rock, when the team's up against it; when things are wrong and the breaks are beating the boys—tell them to go in there with all they've got and win just one for the Gipper. I don't know where I'll be then, Rock. But I'll know about it, and I'll be happy." But it also placed the speech at halftime, which made little sense since the boys weren't up against it or suffering bad breaks—they were surprisingly holding their own against a better team.

After Rockne died, this version resurfaced in his posthumous autobiography and, in 1941, in the movie, starring Pat O'Brien as Rockne and Ronald Reagan as Gipp. In the rewriting and retelling, the story's sentiment resonated. It might not have mattered during the Roaring Twenties, but this triumph over adversity was a perfect tale for a nation subsumed in the Great Depression, a nation on the verge of war, and, in 1980, a politician speaking of a bright, new future during hard times. Reagan, who further distorted and dramatized the story to suit his purposes, shared both Rockne's ability to inspire and his loose grasp of truth and reality.

Had Army scored on that last play, the Gipper might never have surfaced, since no one recounts inspirational speeches after losses. Perhaps Reagan would not have become president. (Sperber says many Reagan Democrats were Catholics responding to his "Win one for the Gipper" approach.) But maybe it's time to bench the Gipper anyway. Sure, dispelling the myth strips away the connection to Hollywood and the White House, diminishing the game's importance, but whatever Gipp did or didn't do and whatever Rockne did or didn't say, the truth is that Notre Dame's play in the second half was inspiring enough, and both Army and the Fighting Irish gave New York a football game to remember.

88

The Babe Hits 60,
September 30, 1927, Yankee Stadium

The 1927 New York Yankees were one of baseball's greatest teams. The team won 110 games, losing just 44, the second-best winning percentage for any World Series champion. (Two teams won more games in the 154-game era but lost the World Series, while the 114-win Yankees of 1998 had a lower winning percentage. Only the 1909 Pittsburgh Pirates, who won 110 but lost only 42, fared better.)

This deep roster outscored opponents by a record 376 runs, with the best ERA in the league and that celebrated Murderers' Row lineup: Tony Lazzeri had 102 RBI and was just fourth on the team; Bob Meusel hit .337, which was also just fourth; and Lou Gehrig outpaced everyone with a .373 average and 175 RBI.

But these stars still orbited around one man: Babe Ruth. Fittingly—although no one could have known it at the time—the Yankees' winning percentage was .714, which would, of course, be Ruth's final home run total. Of those 714, 60 came in this singular season.

By September 6, Ruth had 44 home runs but was deadlocked with Gehrig, who had hit the most homers ever by someone not named Ruth. With the pennant race long decided, this dynamic duo generated most of the ink devoted to baseball. The excitement was so great that more radio stations began broadcasting baseball games, prompting more people to buy this new entertainment device. Still, with just 24 games left, an assault on Ruth's 1921 record of 59 homers seemed absurd.

Then the "Sultan of Swat" reclaimed his royal throne by swinging his hefty Louisville Slugger as if it were Excalibur yanked from a stone. He clouted five homers in three games, then added another three in three games beginning on September 11. This gave him 52 long balls with 15 games left. That ended the tussle with Gehrig and began a new home run race with his only true competition: himself.

Ruth, who put a notch in his bat to commemorate each new blast, was openly musing about 60. The press also championed the charge to baseball's Camelot. From the wide-open West to the city's skyscrapers to such folk heroes as Paul Bunyan and John Henry, the United States had long been infatuated with the grand and the gargantuan. So, Ruth and his appetites and feats seemed quintessentially American.

The 1920s were the golden age of hero worship, as the American press and public mythologized great talents like Ruth, Bill Tilden, Jack Dempsey, and Red Grange, which had begun to fade, and Ruth was frustrated by the perception that he had peaked in 1921, and that at 32, he was heading downhill. In the spring of 1927, America crowned a new celebrity king when Charles Lindbergh flew across the ocean in the *Spirit of St. Louis*; then Gehrig challenged Ruth's supremacy on the Yankees and throughout baseball. Gehrig's emergence spurred Ruth on. On June 30, both men hit their 25th homers. For Ruth, who had won seven home run titles in nine years (failing only when he'd missed at least 40 games), this was a challenge. By mid-August, Gehrig—in just his third season—led, 38–35, and had become a favorite subject for the mighty scribes of the day, who called him "Slambino" to Ruth's "Bambino" and the "Prince of Punch."

While those titles implicitly deferred to Ruth as "King," some columnists began predicting Gehrig would wear the crown by season's end. Ruth freely credited Gehrig's fearsome presence behind him in the cleanup slot with forcing teams to pitch to him more often, although he still walked 138 times. But by September 22, when Ruth blasted his 56th round-tripper—carrying the bat around the bases to stop people from stealing it—few were still paying attention to the young first baseman, even as he broke Ruth's RBI record of 170.

Ruth skidded into a brief dry spell, and with just four games remaining the record was slipping away. Then he swatted a grand slam for number 57 (no other *team* would top 56), and on September 29, Ruth regained his stroke, crushing a solo home run and another grand slam for 58 and 59, plus a triple and a fly out to the fence.

That left two games for one blast. The Washington Senators' lefty Tom Zachary, the opposing starter on September 30, said later he did not want to give Ruth a single good pitch. He walked Ruth on four pitches in the first. Ruth managed to poke singles his next two times up, which was wholly unsatisfactory. Letting Ruth reach first, however, was dangerous too: Ruth had scored after each single, creating a 2–2 tie. In the eighth inning, shortstop Mark Koenig tripled with one out, and Zachary knew walking Ruth with Gehrig and Bob Meusel waiting would not solve anything.

He came after Ruth with a fastball for strike one. After a high ball, Zachary broke off a curve at Ruth's knees to back him off the plate. "I don't say it was the best curve anybody ever threw, but it was as good as any I ever threw," he'd later recall.

Ruth waded right into the pitch, reaching down and jerking it deep to right, well inside the foul pole.

"Put it in the book in letters of gold," the *New York Times* decreed. "It will be a long time before anyone betters that home run mark and a still longer time before any aging athlete makes such a gallant and glorious charge over the comeback trail."

The fans tossed special "Homer 60" hats in the air and shredded paper to create instant confetti. Even sportswriters were on their feet applauding. When Ruth returned to the field for the ninth, the fans waved handkerchiefs in celebration, and Ruth in turn saluted them. The Yankees won, 4–2, and when Ruth trotted in after catching the final out, fans jumped down from the bleachers to congratulate him. In the clubhouse afterward, Ruth was jubilant and almost defiant in his pride, boasting, "Sixty, count 'em, 60! Let's see some other son of a bitch match that!"

The Yankees swept Pittsburgh in the World Series and won four straight again in the 1928 World Series, but this one game stood apart from the rest. In the 34 years until the 162-game schedule came along and Roger Maris finally matched and passed Ruth, 60 was baseball's preeminent magical number. Hack Wilson, Jimmie Foxx, Hank Greenberg, Ralph Kiner, and Willie Mays all fell short. It was perhaps more potent a symbol than Cy Young's 511, Joe DiMaggio's 56, Ted Williams's .406, and Ruth's 714. Ruth's 60 became shorthand for baseball's love affair with the home run and the Yankees' dominance. But most of all, 60 symbolized Ruth's greatness. Ruth had proved once and for all that this was his team—and that he was baseball.

Harry Greb Bests Mickey Walker,
July 2, 1925, Polo Grounds

Harry Greb was two weight classes and 30 pounds lighter than Jack Dempsey. Yet, he embarrassed the great heavyweight so badly during a 1920 sparring session that Dempsey's manager never again let Greb publicly spar with him, much less fight him. Greb, the middleweight champ, was the only man to defeat Gene Tunney, briefly capturing the light heavyweight title. And he did it all while blind in one eye.

He was one of the best—and dirtiest—fighters of his generation. But so was Mickey Walker, the "Toy Bulldog." He spent three and a half years as welterweight champ and another four as middleweight champion. Their 1925 Polo Grounds bout capped off a festival of fisticuffs with 15 rounds of astonishing ferocity.

Some boxing historians argue that Greb's 1922 win over Tunney—a vicious 15-rounder in which Tunney reportedly lost two pints of blood—has historical heft and should be Greb's entry to this list. But while Tunney's singular loss is statistically notable in retrospect, Greb was not a champion then and Tunney was not yet a figure of national renown, so it was just another fight at the Garden.

By contrast, this was a hotly anticipated spectacle, a charity fund-raiser that reaped almost $100,000 for local hospitals and attracted a heavyweight crowd that included a who's who of New York politicians, plus a coterie of movie and theater stars, and baseball legends.

At 32, Greb, the middleweight champ, was seven years older than Walker. Despite being unusually disciplined during training, Greb strained to shed 18 pounds to meet weight specifications. Greb could handle a shot to the jaw or even a thumb in the eye like few others—in 1921, a foe's digit detached his retina, blinding him in that eye, but he kept it secret so he could keep fighting. (Live by the thumb, go blind by the thumb—this illegal gouging was one of Greb's favorite moves.) He was remarkably quick on his feet, but mostly the "Human Windmill" was known for fast, relentless punching. "It was like fighting an octopus," Tunney said.

"I thought somebody had opened up the ceiling and dumped a carload of boxing gloves on me," opponent Pat Walsh recalled.

Greb defended his crown as the underdog thanks to a devious ploy. Just before the showdown, Greb, who often bet his entire purse on himself, took two showgirls to Lindy's, a gamblers' hangout, and staggered around "drunk." It was an act, and a successful one: By fight night, the odds were stacked against Greb.

Walker, the welterweight champ, shared Greb's aggressive, anything-goes style but punched even harder. He too preferred whiskey and women to roadwork, and seemed best suited to barroom brawls. Yet, he was a skilled golfer and painter whose works later hung in respected galleries.

In the ring, the two men fought savagely. Even the clinches bristled with mauling and wrestling. Once, Greb worked his way behind Walker and then punched; twice the ref was knocked to the floor trying to separate them. (Greb is said to have done it on purpose.)

Greb adopted a rope-a-dope variation, hoping to tire out Walker. But fighting in close he absorbed endless blows to the stomach, ribs, and heart. The newspapers' accounts are rife with repetition—"Walker hooked another left to the body. . . . Walker hooked a terrific left to the body. . . ."—conveying the terrible beating Greb endured. By the fifth round, fans were calling for the ref to stop the fight, but Greb's savvy was paying dividends: Walker would have been far more dangerous throwing long punches, and his inside game was neutralized by Greb's weight advantage and constant clinching. So, although Walker was way ahead on the scorecards, the damage was minimized and he was growing weary.

In the fifth round, Greb backed Walker into the ropes with a barrage of blows until Walker smashed Greb's face with his best punch. Greb simply spit out a few teeth and continued fighting. In the sixth round, momentum shifted. What made this fight remarkable was that the momentum seemed to change in every round.

Greb lacked a knockout blow, and Walker possessed a tenacious spirit, so the two men just kept exchanging punches, sneaking inside to smash kidneys, grab arms, and use thumbs to unseemly advantage. Greb was more expert at such tricks. Walker's lip got bloodied and split, his nose bloodied and battered, his right eye cut and puffed. But he kept coming. Walker snatched the ninth round, but Greb won the 10th, using his windmill delivery to slash Walker's face and body. In round 11, Walker escaped Greb's clutches with a left that sent Greb reeling, clinching desperately until the bell.

By the 13th round, any decision would go to Greb, so only a knockout could save the challenger. Overeager, Walker left himself open in round 14, but Greb moved in so quickly he inadvertently trapped Walker against the ropes, leaving the sagging body nowhere to fall. Walker, essentially out on his feet, somehow still managed one last flurry before the bell. In round 15, both men fired shot after shot, even as the final bell rang. Greb had suffered tremendously, but he hobbled out the winner.

The fight lingered long after the last punch—a little embellishing here, a sordid detail added there, until it sounded like something out of the Roman Coliseum. Stories abound about Greb twirling Walker around to make him dizzy, Greb biting his foe, and Walker becoming so disoriented he started crying. Rumors surfaced that Walker asked Greb to carry him the last few rounds so the fight would go the distance. The cherry atop the swirling sundae of myth is the woolly tale about Walker and Greb encountering one another at a Manhattan bar that night and coming to blows on the street, although many historians dismiss the tale as outright malarkey.

Both boxers' fortunes would soon change dramatically. Losing sight in his good eye and weakened by again shedding the necessary weight, Greb lost to Tiger Flowers, then lost a rematch on a decision everyone from the referee to Tunney to the New York Athletic Commission thought unjust. Greb bitterly said Flowers would lose his next title defense. But it would not come against Greb. Injured in a car crash and unable to breathe properly, he underwent surgery for his nose but died on the operating table. Two months later, Flowers did indeed lose the middleweight crown, dethroned by Mickey Walker.

90

The Four Horsemen of
Notre Dame Triumph over Army,
October 18, 1924, Yankee Stadium

One fateful fall afternoon, George Strickler stepped into the fray and wiped clean the slate of sports journalism, unleashing rivers of purple prose that flowed on black ink across this great nation, lifting a university, a genre of journalism, and an entire sport.

That's an approximation of how Grantland Rice, the *New York Herald-Tribune*'s master of breathless extravagance, might have started this recounting of the 1924 Notre Dame–Army game at the Polo Grounds. It's both more poetic and less descriptive than the simpler but more accurate modern style that has forsaken him.

The myth is that Rice alone remade the sports landscape with his account of the game, which famously began, "Outlined against a blue-gray October sky, the Four Horsemen rode again."

But it was Strickler, a lowly Notre Dame student press assistant, who helped produce one of the biggest scores in sports history without playing a single down. With a stray pop culture reference, a goofy photo op, and a large assist from the legendarily hyperbolic Rice, he begat the iconic "Four Horsemen of Notre Dame." In one great rush, this accident of history forever enhanced the school's backfield and its overall stature, all of college football, and even sportswriting as a field.

Notre Dame and Army made headlines beginning with their first game at West Point in 1913. The football's circumference had been reduced to make passing easier, and Notre Dame, featuring an end named Knute Rockne, became the first to feature a real aerial attack. They stunned Army, 35–13, that year. Rockne became coach in 1918, and transformed Notre Dame into foot-

The Four Horseman of Notre Dame symbolize American mythmaking at its finest. *Library of Congress, Prints and Photographs Division [LC-USZ62-26735]*

ball's powerhouse; his team grew so popular that free admission games at West Point gave way to the big game in the big city. In 1923, the rivals debuted at Ebbets Field and turned 15,000 people away.

College football was coming of age. Thanks to the unlikely combo of Strickler and Rice, October 18, 1924, at the Polo Grounds, would be its coming-out party. New York was only an hour south of West Point. Yet, thousands of "Subway Alumni" made it feel like a Notre Dame home game. The stars were the backfield of Harry Stuhldreher, Jim Crowley, Don Miller, and Elmer Layden. In the second quarter, Crowley slithered for 15 yards on a reverse. Layden ate up six more through left tackle. Miller pushed through for almost another 10, Stuhldreher connected with Crowley for 12 yards, and Crowley rushed for five more. Miller rampaged around the right side for 20 yards. Crowley drove within yards of the goal line, and Layden. Up just 6–0 at halftime, Notre Dame had dominated the second quarter, racking up eight first downs, yielding none.

During halftime the game headed for the history books. Strickler commented to several sportswriters that Notre Dame's backfield reminded him of a Rudolph Valentino movie, *The Four Horsemen of the Apocalypse*, which he and the players had recently watched. Just making conversation, that's all. Except that Rice, the fabulist par excellence whose presence lent the game an air of importance, translated the observation into American sports mythology.

In the third quarter, Layden intercepted a pass. Crowley ditched two would-be tacklers, stiff-armed another, and raced 21 yards for a touchdown. Notre Dame almost scored twice more, stopped once by an Army interception and once by Army's tough four-down stand on their own nine.

The 13–7 win was hardly overwhelming. The *World* credited Notre Dame for having a "soundly coached team," but it seemed like just another W in a long string of them—this team had only lost twice in two years and was en route to a 10–0 season.

But Rice was someone who once said, "When a sportswriter stops making heroes out of athletes, it's time to get out of the business." Inspired by Strickler's halftime snippet, he showed why he would be in the business for decades to come:

> Outlined against a blue-gray October sky, the Four Horsemen rode again. In dramatic lore they are known as Famine, Pestilence, Destruction, and Death. These are only aliases. Their real names are Stuhldreher, Miller, Crowley, and Layden. They formed the crest of the South Bend cyclone before which another fighting Army football team was swept over the precipice.
>
> A cyclone can't be snared. It may be surrounded, but somewhere it breaks through to keep on going. When the cyclone starts from South Bend, where the candle lights still gleam through the Indiana sycamores, those in the way must take to storm cellars at top speed.

Unfortunately, as journalist Red Smith would later point out, to see players outlined against the sky you'd need to lay on the field. Moreover, for all their skills, this foursome, topping out at 162 pounds, was hardly physically imposing; Army was not swept away (they kept it closer than any other 1924 foe).

Also, how and why does one "surround" a cyclone?

The article ran on the *Herald-Tribune*'s front page and was syndicated in 100 newspapers, but the story still easily could have died the death of so many daily reports. Rice largely ditched the Horsemen concept after the first paragraph, playing up his cyclone imagery while throwing around references to tigers, antelopes, tanks, and motorcycles. (He'd still be recycling his "South Bend cyclone" phrase in 1929.) He moved on afterward, not bothering to preview Notre Dame's next game.

The savvy Strickler, however, called his dad back in South Bend and had him rent four horses from a corral. Strickler posed the four athletes on the steeds, clutching footballs (looking a bit uncomfortable). He sent the photo to wire services and newspapers throughout the country, and they rode the ploy for all it was worth. Soon every columnist referred to the newfound celebrities as the "Four Horsemen," and Rice, the 1920s Roaring Hypester, was touting further them as a way of praising his own acumen.

Notre Dame would play better games and have better backfields, but this confluence of events made these men and this game symbols of the golden age. It was an era when sportswriters polished history to a gleam, creating larger-than-life legends. In this postwar boom, the Jazz Age public was ready to think big. Sport was moving front and center—this was the first game broadcast on the radio, airing on two New York stations and their affiliates. By the following year, newspaper coverage was double that of 1915. Although this interest stemmed from genuine public demand, sportswriters like Rice certainly stirred the pot. From 1921 to 1930, attendance at college football games doubled and receipts tripled, while universities devoted financial resources to the sport, building huge new stadiums. A skeptical minority complained about the business of sports usurping academics and sportsmanship, but cheering fans drowned out those voices.

As countless publications echoed Strickler's photo echoing Rice's article echoing the original game itself, the reality faded—the four players, Notre Dame, college football, and the sportswriter and his "gee whiz" approach to sportswriting got surrounded by the cyclone of glory.

Jack Dempsey Outslugs Luis Firpo, September 14, 1923, Polo Grounds

Boxing is the "sweet science," a complex sport with layers of nuance involving footwork, psychology, and strategy. Sure, sounds good, but what fight fans really want is a slugfest. For a feast of flying fists, nothing topped the fast and furious Jack Dempsey–Luis Firpo punch-a-thon at the Polo Grounds. It lasted less than two rounds and was marred by rule violations and poor refereeing. Yet, it's hailed as among the most thrilling fights of all time.

The ninth of 11 children, Jack Dempsey worked an array of jobs while living in "hobo jungles" out West. He began boxing in saloons and mining towns. His ducking and sidestepping techniques were influential, but the ferocity of his attacks made him a legend. In 1919, he won five straight first-round knockouts, then captured the heavyweight title by flattening champ Jess Willard. The "Manassa Mauler" firmly established himself as boxing's biggest draw with the sport's first million-dollar gate, for which he punched Georges Carpentier senseless in the fourth.

The only other top-flight contender was Harry Willis, who was black, and promoter Tex Rickard wouldn't let Dempsey fight him because Rickard was afraid of another potential black champion in this racist nation so soon after the turbulent reign of Jack Johnson. So, questions remained about whether Dempsey was a true great, whether he'd respond if hit hard. With few worthy foes, Dempsey barely fought in 1922 and into 1923, until Rickard decided if he couldn't get quality, he'd get a good draw. He settled on Argentinean Luis Angel Firpo, "the Wild Bull of the Pampas."

The 6-foot-3, 216-pound Firpo was big, tough, and phenomenally strong but so raw he was barely a boxer. He'd worked as a laborer, butcher, and drug-

Jack Dempsey's brawl against Luis Firpo lasted less than two rounds, but it is one of boxing's most memorable bouts. *Library of Congress, Prints and Photographs Division [LC-USZ62-94046]*

store clerk before boxing for exercise and then for money. He was less wild bull than reticent miser—he wore cheap clothes and refused to pay for trainers, managers, or sparring partners. He trained simply by fighting more bouts. (After becoming wealthy thanks to this fight, he turned quite generous and once gave Dempsey a gift of $20,000.) Firpo shrewdly secured foreign film rights to bouts leading up to and including the Dempsey fight. He initially demanded payment from the press for interviews or photos. The night before the fight, he supposedly sat in his hotel room calculating how much he'd owe in taxes.

That same night, fans camped out at the Polo Grounds for bleacher seats. More than 80,000 packed the ballpark on fight night, and tens of thousands more were turned away. When a van arrived containing 3,800 tickets for last-minute sales, it was attacked by fans who were forcibly removed by cops. The best seats were filled with society names like Astor, Belmont, Morgan, Gould, Vanderbilt, Rothschild, and Whitney, and former champs Jim Corbett and Jess

Willard. The New York Yankees and visiting Chicago White Sox were there, along with Giants manager John McGraw; Babe Ruth attracted all the buzz as he walked in.

The fight was almost called off at weigh-in when the doctor thought Firpo's left elbow was dislocated and fractured. Firpo smashed his fist hard onto a table, gritting his teeth and forcing a smile through the agony. The New York Medical Commission chairman deemed the limb dislocated but not broken and jerked it sharply back into place. Firpo sweated profusely but didn't utter a sound. His swollen arm was bandaged until the fight.

At 10:02 p.m., the ring exploded with a purposeful violence no one could have imagined. The action was so frenetic that every newspaper account differs about what actually happened. Dempsey rushed Firpo instantly, but for one brief moment Firpo showed surprising agility and technique, sidestepping the champ's first blow and delivering a quick left that sent Dempsey to one knee and the fans to their feet. They would not sit down again. (A bench toppled over, taking down Babe Ruth; he angrily came up swinging at the nearest target, who happened to be middleweight Mickey Walker.)

Dempsey was more surprised than hurt and was up without a count. He roared in, but the two men got tangled and clinched. When the ref shouted, "Break," Firpo naively let his hands drop; Dempsey floored the challenger with a body blow. Firpo popped back up, for the moment. During a vicious tango in the clinches, Dempsey's left to the top of the head sent Firpo to the canvas again.

This moment altered this fight and boxing history. Dempsey did not retreat to a neutral corner, and referee Johnny Gallagher failed to make him. Firpo rose, and Dempsey slammed him back down with a body blow. Again, Gallagher was lax, so Dempsey stalked Firpo like prey, knocking him down, lurking nearby, and pouncing as soon as Firpo pulled himself up. After the fourth knockdown, Firpo didn't get up until Gallagher hit nine. And Dempsey was right there with a big right that knocked the challenger down—again.

Somehow Firpo hoisted himself up and dropped Dempsey to all fours briefly with an overhead right. While trading blows, Dempsey landed a right cross that again toppled Firpo, who tried getting up and covering up simultaneously. Dempsey left no room and thrashed him once more. After this record seventh knockdown in one round, Dempsey nonchalantly stepped over his fallen foe and lounged in the corner with his arms against the ropes, surveying the havoc he had wreaked. Amazingly, however, the bell still had not rung.

Firpo not only hauled himself up, but also escaped the corner and caught Dempsey off guard, backing the champ into the ropes. He fired a volley of rights, then stung Dempsey with a left uppercut, followed by a crashing right overhead. The blow seemingly stayed connected to Dempsey's head as he went down and out, through the ropes, completely out of the ring. (Some say the ropes weren't strung tightly enough.)

George Bellows's classic painting, which hangs in the Whitney Museum, commemorates this notorious moment. Dempsey was lucky to escape—if he'd stayed upright, another blow would have knocked him out. He tumbled into the press row, jamming his hip on a wooden board and banging his neck and head on the reporters' typewriters. It was almost impossible for Dempsey to resurrect himself before a 10 count. But the referee reacted slowly, and the writers shoved Dempsey up and back into the ring. They later claimed they were not unfairly abetting the American, merely removing an obstacle to their writing. They also declared that Dempsey—despite being dazed and semiconscious—snarled in a rage, "Get me back in there. I'll fix him."

Gallagher should have disqualified Dempsey, but he remained a passive bystander. Dempsey—who wouldn't remember leaving or climbing back in the ring—was groggy, swaying with his chin unprotected. Yet, Firpo was so surprised to discover the fight was still on and so weakened himself, he couldn't land the final big blow. The brief letup allowed Dempsey to tie up Firpo until the round ended.

Dempsey prompted some boos when he threw a few extra weak punches after the bell, but he was unaware of the bell, unaware of the chaos around him, unaware of pretty much everything. In his corner, Dempsey's manager, Jack Kearns, asked where the smelling salts were; he couldn't hear trainer Jerry Ludvadis shouting back that the salts were in Kearns's own pocket. Kearns instead dumped a bucket of cold water over Dempsey's head. When Ludvadis reached for Kearns to pull the salts out, Kearns, not understanding the trainer's actions, punched Ludvadis. Kearns finally found the salts, and they helped Dempsey snap to—kind of: He innocently asked what round it was and was surprised to find out he'd made it through only one.

In the second round, Firpo reared back for another right. But Dempsey had that move read and stepped in with a left. They seemed to wrestle a bit, but soon Firpo was back on the canvas. This time he arose with blood gushing from his face. Firpo missed a wild right, then desperately tried clinching, but the champ tore free and fired a left uppercut to Firpo's jaw and a right to his face. The mighty Argentinean toppled. This time for good. Firpo rolled over onto his stomach but couldn't pull himself up. At 58 seconds of round 2, the count reached 10.

The fight raised a hue and cry from preachers and editorials denouncing the primitive blood lust it incited. While the press gushed about the drama,

Dempsey, who rushed over to help Firpo up afterward, was ripped for unethi-
cal, even treacherous behavior. Rules would be strengthened to force boxers to
return to the neutral corners during a knockdown; in 1927, Dempsey would
lose the famous "Long Count" fight to Gene Tunney because the ref refused
to count until Dempsey moved, giving Tunney at least an extra four or five
seconds. Dempsey lost that fight but gained new stature for his dignity in defeat.

By bravely withstanding such an assault, Firpo became a hero, and his tour
of Latin America and South America with his film reaped a fortune, creating
demand for Firpo's Fedoras, Firpo's Fantasy Perfume, and other products.
Streets and soccer teams were named for him throughout Latin America and
South America. He retired soon thereafter, a millionaire.

In the United States, boxing flourished as never before. The golden age
would last 50 years—paralleling the heyday of its working-class fan base.
Dempsey admitted that Firpo rightfully should have won when he flew out of
the ring, but his stature was enhanced by the victory, as he almost became equal
to Babe Ruth as an American hero of folktale proportions.

92

Babe Ruth Christens the "House That Ruth Built" with a Home Run, April 18, 1923, Yankee Stadium

The hero had fallen and fallen hard. But with one dramatic swing, Babe Ruth knew he could set things right again. "I'd give a year of my life if I can hit a home run in the first game in this new park," the Sultan of Swat said just before inaugurating Yankee Stadium.

Ruth's exploits often seem lifted straight out of American folklore, and Yankee Stadium's debut is both a pivotal chapter in the saga of this larger-than-life figure and a turning point in modern America. Ruth and the Yankees were creating a new world, birthing an affluent society's obsession with sports and celebrity. The Stadium, like the city's skyscrapers that would soon follow, was unlike anything the United States had seen, a New York blend of arrogance and accomplishment. That first game helped create the narrative arcs of both baseball—the Yankees' dominance, the love of the long ball, the hunger for stadium building—and New York, as it defined itself with major real estate deals and stunning architectural monuments.

Ruth had transformed baseball and transfixed the nation with his home run bashing. He was the living, breathing postwar symbol of the American Century, of New York's grandeur and the fast-flying Jazz Age. The Stadium was to be a physical representation of Ruth's power, New York's supremacy, and baseball's magnificent future. That was the idea when the Yankees hatched their plans in 1921. By the time the Stadium opened in 1923, Ruth seemed washed up, a tragic symbol of American hubris, which meant the Stadium could become baseball's *Titanic*. Thus, when Ruth smashed a home run in that first game, it was no ordinary four-bagger. It reversed the tide and set the Yankees and baseball history back on course.

The team started in Hilltop Park in Washington Heights in 1903, just as John McGraw began a Giants dynasty that defined baseball. The small-ball, nitty-gritty Giants finished first or second 19 times in 23 years and led baseball in attendance 10 times. In 1913, the Yankees signed a 10-year lease as the Giants' Polo Grounds tenants. They seemed harmless so the Giants happily collected rent money while playing on the road. Then Ruth arrived, and everything changed.

In 1920, Ruth hit 54 home runs and set a record with an .847 slugging percentage. McGraw disdained this home run fad, but one number particularly galled him: The Yankees' attendance more than doubled, drawing almost 1.3 million—400,000 more than the Giants. The Giants wanted the upstarts out, and not just because of McGraw's growing jealousy of Ruth. With Sunday blue laws repealed in 1919, the Giants wanted every Sunday gate for themselves. McGraw boasted that the Yankees would never find enough open space in Manhattan, declaring, "They'll have to move to the Bronx or Long Island. The fans will forget about them, and they'll be through."

The Yankees looked in Long Island City and over the railroad tracks on Manhattan's West Side before settling on the South Bronx. The Yankees were not the first to build a modern ballpark, following Detroit's Navin Field, Boston's Fenway Park, and Chicago's Wrigley Field. But "The Yankee Stadium," as it was called, was different—no other ballpark had ever been so grandiose as to call itself a stadium.

Before television and merchandising, team revenue stemmed largely from gate receipts, so the Yankees wanted space for the anticipated masses, especially as Ruth topped himself in 1921, with 59 homers and 171 RBI, leading the Yankees to their first World Series (which they lost to the Giants). The Yankees would gain a tremendous advantage in revenue that would pay for the best scouts, front-office executives, and athletes. In other words, it was not just Ruth but the combination of Ruth and the new coliseum that laid the groundwork for baseball's dominant franchise.

Every detail was breathlessly announced: the 15-foot copper facade, the 950,000 board feet of Pacific Coast fir shipped via the Panama Canal, the 2,200 tons of structural steel, the 1 million brass screws bolted into the seats, the 16,000 square feet of sod.

Some suggested calling this majestic stage Ruth Field. In most ballparks, right field was the "sun field," but since Ruth played right, left fielders would have to wage that battle. Center and left-center were impossibly deep ("Death Valley" was 490 feet), but right field was a mere 295 feet, eminently reachable for a left-handed pull hitter. (Ruth, however, said, "I cried when I left the Polo Grounds," only 256 feet down the line.)

But as the Stadium was rising, Ruth was self-destructing. He drew a six-week suspension in 1922, from Commissioner Kenesaw Mountain Landis, for a rule-breaking postseason barnstorming tour. He spent much of his time off at the racetrack, then slumped when he returned. When he was ejected for throwing dirt in an umpire's face, he was booed by Yankees fans and charged into the stands after one particularly vociferous heckler. He was only suspended for one game but earned several days off that year for arguing with the umps, and he got into a fistfight with teammate Wally Pipp. The Yankees won the pennant despite Ruth managing only 406 at-bats and finishing just third in home runs, with 35. In the World Series, Ruth chased an onslaught of off-speed pitches out of the strike zone, going just 2-for-17, with no homers, as the Giants took the crown yet again.

The press called Ruth an "exploded phenomenon" and a "tragic figure" who had "flashed like a comet." The *Sporting News* declared, "The baseball public is on to his real worth as a batsman." Knowing Ruth needed motivation, his agent, Christy Walsh, organized an offseason banquet, where New York's press and power brokers called on the Babe to reform. State senator Jimmy Walker, in a melodramatic touch, struck Ruth's soft spot, saying Ruth had "let down the kids of America." He added, "You carouse and abuse your great body, and it is exactly as though Santa Claus himself suddenly were to take off his beard to reveal the features of a villain. The kids have seen their idol shattered and their dream broken."

A repentant Ruth began sobbing, almost uncontrollably. As Walker comforted him, Ruth apologized and promised to both behave and play better in the future. He largely abstained from partying that winter and arrived at spring training in formidable shape. Yet, things quickly derailed when a 19-year-old girl sued Ruth for $50,000 in a paternity suit. She later admitted it was a hoax, but Ruth seemed distracted, striking out often during exhibition games, even against minor-league pitchers. As the team headed north, it seemed quite possible that Ruth would wash out, the club would collapse, fans would stop coming, and Yankee Stadium would be sneeringly called "Ruppert's Folly."

On Opening Day, general manager Ed Barrow announced the attendance at 74,217, shattering the sport's old record (47,000 at a 1916 World Series game). This was probably untrue since the Stadium held 62,000 seats, but the crowd was undeniably gargantuan, even Ruthian.

The Yankees' American League pennant was run up the flagpole, and Ruth was presented with an oversized bat in a glass case. John Philip Sousa led the

Seventh Regiment Band in a parade and "The Star-Spangled Banner." Finally, home plate umpire Tommy Connolly shouted, "Play ball."

Fittingly, the foe was Boston, from whom the Yankees had purchased Ruth. He went out easily in the first but came up in the third with two men on. Howard Ehmke worked the count to 2–2, and threw an off-speed pitch that Ruth anticipated, crushing a line drive eight rows back in the bleachers.

As the grinning Ruth reached home, he lifted his cap and waved to the crowd. His home run would be the difference in the Yankees' 4–1 triumph. It would also essentially seal the outcome of the season and even, arguably, the century.

The next day, Fred Lieb of the *Evening Telegram* dubbed the ballpark the "House That Ruth Built." Ruth kept rolling, belting 41 homers. In the 1923 Fall Classic, the Yankees finally had their own home, their own crowd. Ruth batted .368, with three homers, to defeat the Giants. It was the first Series carried nationwide on radio in its entirety; Ruth's appeal had hastened the market for this new technology.

Ruth remade the Yankees into baseball's preeminent franchise, leading them to four more pennants and three more World Series titles, while establishing Yankee Stadium as sport's most hallowed ground. Although Ruth's home run that spring day was just one of his 714 regular-season round-trippers, it retained a magical aura. In 1998, the home run ball was auctioned off for a then-record $126,500, and, in 2004, his bat was auctioned off for $1.27 million, the second-highest-priced baseball item ever. In 2005, a children's book was published called *Babe Ruth Saves Baseball*, building to that home run as the climactic moment.

In 1948, dying from throat cancer, Ruth came to Yankee Stadium one final time, putting on his uniform to celebrate the 25th anniversary of the ballpark. Barely able to speak, he slowly approached the microphone and told the fans, "Ladies and gentlemen, I just want to say one thing. I am proud I hit the first home run here against Boston in 1923."

The Giants Win, 1–0, to Capture the First Modern "Subway" Series, October 13, 1921, Polo Grounds

John McGraw versus Babe Ruth, round 1.

The 1921 World Series was the New York Yankees' first Fall Classic and the first between two New York teams. It boiled down to a simple, epochal clash: "Little Napoleon" versus the "Sultan of Swat," old-time small ball versus the new swing-from-the-heels game.

In 1921, Babe Ruth was baseball. He astonished the nation in 1920, by smashing 54 home runs. No American League team managed more than 50. But that season was rife with distractions—the deadly beaning of Cleveland's Ray Chapman, the unspooling of the Black Sox Scandal, and the appointment of Judge Kenesaw Mountain Landis as commissioner.

In 1921, all eyes were on the Sultan of Swat as he lofted 59 home runs and improved in doubles, triples, runs scored, and RBI, while hitting .378. He even stole 17 bases. Ruth transformed the Yankees, perennial also-rans, into American League champions; packed the ballpark; and forever altered the game. All the glory rained upon the big brute irked McGraw. As a player, he'd helped spark the Baltimore Orioles to three straight National League flags; as a manager, he'd led his team to seven National League pennants and seven second-place finishes since 1904. He was the undisputed master of inside baseball, playing smart, aggressively, and often dirty to piece together enough offense to back strong pitching.

Now it was the once-lowly Yankees, or one damned Yankee, in particular, grabbing the attention. Worse, Ruth had done it playing long ball, which Mc-Graw disdained. (The stereotypes were a bit simplistic. The Giants led the National League in scoring, and George Kelly's 23 homers led the league. The

Yankees, meanwhile, led the American League in earned run average, thanks to Carl Mays and Waite Hoyt, both of whom outshone any Giant hurler.)

Now Ruth and McGraw would face off—and since the Yankees were Polo Grounds tenants, the Giants would have to act as the visiting team in half the games in their home ballpark. This was technically not a "Subway Series," since it took place in one park, but it was a crucial marker. Although 1905 marked New York's ascension in the baseball world and 1947 to 1956 was the city's baseball heyday, 1921 was the year New York became the sport's capital: It began a stretch of 44 World Series that featured 45 New York clubs, including 13 Series that resided entirely in Gotham. (Brooklyn had reached the Series in 1920, but that was less a new beginning than a fluke.)

Ruth's looming presence led most to believe the Yankees would stomp out McGraw's mighty mites. Yankees pitching dominated the first two games, both 3–0 wins. No team had ever lost the first two games then won the Series, but an experimental best-of-nine format gave the Giants more time.

The Yankees broke open a scoreless Game 3, sparked by Ruth's two-run single, but McGraw's men retaliated, then pounded out an eight-run seventh in a 13–5 rout.

Ruth was forced to leave the game. In Game 2, he had cut his elbow sliding in the rocky dirt; now he'd irritated the wound in another slide. The infection that set in essentially cost the Yankees the Series. Ruth surprised everyone by playing Game 4, despite his heavily bandaged arm, and he thrilled everyone with a ninth-inning round-tripper. But the Yankees lost. (Rumors circulated that Mays threw this game: Defying Miller Huggins's orders, he threw a lackluster curve at a crucial moment and fell while fielding a bunt. This pattern repeated itself in Game 7.)

In Game 5, Ruth again stole the show in a way that must have driven McGraw mad. Playing with a tube draining pus from his arm, baseball's home run king shocked the Giants by bunting for a hit; then he scored what would be the winning run. But Ruth also struck out feebly three times and was too hurt to go on. The Yankees' morale sagged, and they were stymied in Games 6 and 7.

Looking to close out the Series in Game 8, McGraw turned to Art Nehf, his diminutive 20-game winner, while the Yankees started Hoyt, who'd beaten Nehf in two tight games.

In the first, with two out but two on via walks, the Giants' George Kelly hit a grounder that rolled through the legs of reliable Roger Peckinpaugh, allowing Dave Bancroft to scamper home.

No other Giants reached third after that, but the Yankees left two on in the first and the bases loaded in the fourth.

In the bottom of the ninth, with the World Series on the line, Huggins was desperate. He pulled Wally Pipp and sent Ruth, the real-life Mighty Casey, to the bat. But there was no long ball and no joy in Yankeedom that day as the debilitated slugger grounded to first.

Then Nehf, pitching on two days' rest, walked Aaron Ward, bringing up another threat, Frank Baker, who had earned the moniker "Home Run" when he devastated the Giants with two crucial blasts in the 1911 Series. Baker slammed a sharp grounder toward right field that looked as if it would put the tying run 90 feet from home with just one out. Instead, the Giants turned in what is likely the best defensive play to end a World Series.

Second baseman Johnny Rawlings made a diving grab. From the ground, he threw Baker out at first. Meanwhile, Ward foolishly assumed the ball got through and confidently rounded second. Kelly alertly fired a bullet to third, where Frankie Frisch welcomed Ward's hard slide with an uppercut of a tag to the jaw. The Yankees were through.

It was McGraw's first championship since 1905, and it brought him a handsome raise the following year. The only person who made more money in baseball: Ruth. In a 1922 Series rematch, McGraw's staff, following orders to feed the beast nothing but curves in the dirt, humiliated Ruth, holding him to a .118 average. The Giants swept. But McGraw's time was ending. Fans, players, and owners dug the long ball; in 1923, the Yankees would have their own stadium, and on their third try, Ruth became the first man to hit three homers in a Series. The Yankees century had begun.

Back in 1921, Nehf's Series-winning gem didn't seem unusual—there'd already been six complete-game shutouts in World Series clinchers—but with the offensive explosion that followed, there'd be just two in the next 33 years. There would not be another 1–0 clincher until 1962, when the Yankees beat the Giants. So, for the lover of the pitcher's duel and the small-ball aficionado, the end of this first all-New York series provided bittersweet poignancy. It was McGraw's triumphant return to the top but the beginning of the end of his civilization.

94

Bill Tilden Becomes Tennis's First Superstar with a Revenge Win against Bill Johnston, September 6, 1920, West Side Tennis Club

You know it when you see it, and you can't help but get excited: Your opponent is taller and stronger, and has a booming serve and a big forehand, but as you warm up you realize . . . he has no backhand. This guy's a chump. He can't beat you.

In 1919, Bill Tilden was that chump.

Tilden had lost the finals of the U.S. National Championship (forerunner to the U.S. Open) in straight sets in 1918, to R. Lindley Murray. Back in the finals at Forest Hills the next year, Tilden's lackluster slice backhand was endlessly exploited by Bill Johnston, who also ran Tilden off in straight sets.

Tilden, 26, realized his shot at greatness was slipping away. That winter, a wealthy patron gave him access to one of the Northeast's few indoor courts, in Providence, Rhode Island. Day after day he retrained himself, shaking free of his slice, learning a new grip to fire flat backhands back across the net. In 1920, he was ready to conquer.

His timing was perfect. Although the sport was still the domain of elitist private clubs, the national tennis championship had recently moved from tony Newport to Forest Hills in Queens, helping get the attention of both the press and the public. And as the Roaring Twenties dawned and a prosperous United States was going mad for sports, sportswriters gushed and fawned over new gods for a new era. New York was the center of it all. In April 1920, Babe Ruth began hitting home runs for the New York Yankees. In June, Man o' War won the Belmont Stakes in record time. That summer, Tilden unleashed his hard-earned creation and became the first American to win at Wimbledon. (Johnston had been favored but was upset early.) And, finally, at Forest Hills, Tilden

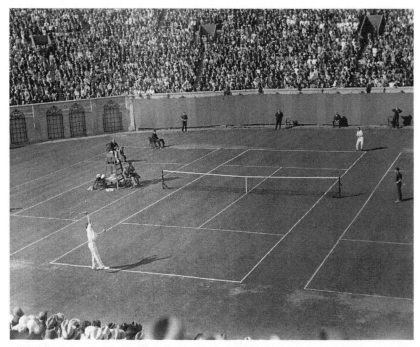

Bill Tilden remade his backhand and outlasted Bill Johnston to win at Forest Hills and become the first tennis superstar. *Library of Congress, Prints and Photographs Division [LC-USZ62-69320]*

avenged himself against his old rival, capturing the U.S. championship and becoming the first tennis superstar.

Most of the 10,000 onlookers crammed into the undersized grandstand for the finals that cloudy Monday believed that Tilden's England win was a fluke and were confident Johnston would retain his U.S. crown. Johnston, who was shorter than 5-foot-8 and would ultimately become "Little Bill" to the 6-foot-1 "Big Bill" Tilden, had a big forehand and attacked the net three times as often as Tilden. But now Tilden had strokes from both wings to complement an unstoppable serve that yielded 20 aces. (Johnston had none.)

Tilden overpowered Johnston, 6–1, in the first set but let down and was broken twice in losing the second set. Then an unexpected drama interrupted the match. A U.S. Navy airplane carrying a photographer was circling Forest Hills when the engine cut out and the plane plunged to earth, just missing the stands. Tilden felt the ground shake. Much of the crowd rushed off to the tragedy; the umpire, to prevent a stampede, urged the men to play on. Johnston's crisp volleying produced another service break at 3–3. He got within a point of 5–3, when Tilden drilled a hard-running forehand off the net cord and subsequently broke back. At 5–5, Tilden fired three aces, then broke his rival for the set with a blistering crosscourt passing shot. In the fourth, Tilden fell behind, then roared back for a 5–4 lead. On match point, he netted a volley and Johnston saved his serve with two passing shots. It started raining hard, and just as Tilden served, people began flooding the exits. Tilden saw the umpire raise his hand for time and stopped playing. But the tournament referee overruled the umpire and deemed Johnston's return worthy of a point.

At 30–30, the rain finally forced a halt, and when play resumed, Tilden had lost his rhythm, double-faulting three times. But the men were so evenly matched that the game still required 20 points before Johnston prevailed on a deep forehand Tilden couldn't handle. Johnston held for a 7–5 win, forcing a fifth set.

Johnston was exhausted, so Tilden switched tactics, laying back, forcing Johnston to play the aggressor to shorten the points. While his serve had carried him through four sets, Tilden's crisp passing shots won him the match; down a break, he reeled off four games for a 6–1, 1–6, 7–5, 5–7, 6–3 triumph.

When critics carped that he'd won merely because of a bigger serve, he promised to beat Johnston the next year just with ground strokes. He won without a single ace. The match was breathlessly pronounced the greatest in the sport's history, and the press gave it prominent play: It landed on the front page of both the *Herald* and the *Tribune*, which hadn't even put the previous year's final on the front of its sports section. Tilden was a star, and when he helped the United States win the Davis Cup—then the most prestigious triumph in tennis— he became a national hero. He would not lose a major tournament match again until 1926, beating Johnston in the finals in Queens five more times.

Along the way, Tilden created the modern foundation for spins, shot selection, strategy, and court psychology through his on-court performance and writings. He was also a consummate showman, believing, "The player owes the gallery as much as an actor owes an audience." He'd seem to tank early in matches to create dramatic finishes or purposely blow points, games, or even sets to offset a bad call in his favor; when calls went against him, he'd look to the heavens and ask, "Is there no justice?" or bully the offending linesman with an imperious glare. He was so intimidating, Frank Deford reports in *Big Bill Tilden*, that the United States Lawn Tennis Association briefly weighed a "no-glare rule," but he pressured officials into backing down.

Despite his blue-blood background and patrician air, Tilden's arrogance, showboating, and constant challenging of the established order made him an outsider. He pushed for everything from hard courts to open tennis, where pros and amateurs could compete, and flagrantly broke absurd amateur rules by accepting money for instructional films and writing tennis articles. He was the original Jimmy Connors. And like Connors, Tilden's hard-hitting, hard-charging, break-your-opponent style earned jeers but also helped tennis take a crucial step toward shedding its prissy image. After his 1920 win, interest surged so high that the West Side club quickly replaced its temporary grand-stand with a 14,000-seat stadium (which lasted until Connors's popularity forced the move to still larger quarters).

After winning Forest Hills one final time in 1929, and Wimbledon in 1930, at age 37, Tilden turned pro, creating the Tilden Tennis Tour, which attracted top amateurs, giving the pro game credibility and laying the groundwork for the Open era.

"It was not just that he could not be beaten, it was nearly as if he had invented the sport he conquered," Deford wrote in *Big Bill Tilden.* "Babe Ruth, Jack Dempsey, Red Grange . . . stood at the head of more popular games, but Tilden simply was tennis in the public mind."

The chump was the ultimate champ.

95

Man o' War Comes Back to Beat John P. Grier at the Dwyer Stakes, July 10, 1920, Aqueduct Race Course

Man o' War was not undefeated, but he seemed invincible. Sure, he'd lost once to a horse named Upset, but no one expected the great horse to lose again, especially not with his reputation on the line. So, in the homestretch at Aqueduct, when John P. Grier pushed his nose out in front, a huge cry swept up from the stands. Was the Dwyer Stakes to be the end of the great horse's legend, or could Man o' War reverse the momentum?

When that great age of sports heroes dawned in the 1920s, Man o' War broke out first, ahead of Babe Ruth, Jack Dempsey, and Red Grange. As a two-year-old in 1919, he won his debut by six lengths and captured nine of his 10 races. In that lone upset, there were three false starts—Man o' War was not even facing front when the race finally began. In 1920, "Big Red," was so dominant in the Preakness that only two horses challenged him in his next race, and only one showed at the Belmont Stakes, where he set a speed record. (He hadn't run the Kentucky Derby, which was just beginning to gain prestige, because owner Sam Riddle didn't like "western" races and believed three-year-old horses shouldn't run long races early in the year.)

John P. Grier was considered one of only two quality horses left to beat. (Riddle infamously ducked any race with Exterminator, the other viable threat.) At the Dwyer Stakes, John P. Grier was the only horse game enough to take on the champion, turning this into a match race. Man o' War was so heavily favored he carried 18 extra pounds as a handicap.

John P. Grier's jockey, Eddie Ambrose, tried desperately to get out first, but Clarence Kummer pushed Man o' War, too, and they shot out evenly. The horses were virtually inseparable through the first turn and remained together at the mile mark, beating the record time Man o' War had set at Belmont.

Horses had stayed with Man o' War early but always faded. Not John P. Grier, who battled down the stretch, then poked ahead. He was winning. The surprised crowd let loose its yell. Racing announcer Clem McCarthy burst out, "Grier's nose in front. He's got h—"

But McCarthy never got to finish the word "him." Kummer, who rarely whipped his great horse, did so, and within three strides his horse was a half-length ahead. Normality was restored.

Or was it? Grier drew even again, until Kummer resorted to the whip twice more, and Man o' War flew ever faster in the last 50 yards, a half-length in front, then a full length, then finally two lengths, finishing in 1:4975, a new world record.

Afterward, everyone marveled at John P. Grier's fortitude, although Kummer dismissed the hubbub: "The moment I went after him in earnest the race was over."

Man o' War continued ending races at will, romping through six more victories before Riddle, incensed by the dangerously heavy weights his horse was burdened with, retired him. He sired several top racers, notably Triple Crown winner War Admiral, and he was grandsire to Seabiscuit; his gene line even carried down to American Pharaoh, the 2015 Triple Crown winner.

Today most of Man o' War's wins are remembered only as a blur in which the champion far outclassed his competition. But thanks to John P. Grier's great effort and Man o' War's resounding response, people at Aqueduct still point to the Man o' War Pole, where the great horse made his unforgettable stand on the dead run.

96

Marathon Mania Reaches Its Peak, April 3, 1909, Polo Grounds

Look at them awaiting the starting gun. The quaintly named "Marathon Derby" attracted a motley collection from throughout the world, a roster that reads like something conjured by T. Coraghessan Boyle and the Marx Brothers: an Italian candy maker who gained fame by collapsing in front of the Queen of England; an Irish American shilling for his employer, Bloomingdale's; an Onondaga Indian from Canada stained by doping controversy who raced so frequently he was running himself into the ground; an Englishman whose records at shorter distances did not translate to marathon success; an Irishman from Yonkers whose world record was disregarded when the distance proved considerably off; and a waiter from France about whom no one knew anything—yet.

But this wasn't satire, and it wasn't slapstick. This was the climax of the first modern marathon era. "This was the greatest professional athletic event ever held in America," the *New York Herald* wrote in 1909. "If the Man from Mars had only been there wouldn't he have had a tale to tell of the 'crazy Americans' and the 'Marathon Derby.'"

The era began with the first Olympics in 1896, followed the next year by the first American marathon (from Connecticut to New York City) and the Boston Marathon. But the fuse for the explosion of events leading to the Marathon Derby was the 1908 Olympics.

The International Olympic Committee had standardized the race's length at 26 miles, but England's Queen Alexandra demanded that runners, departing from Windsor Castle, finish in front of her. To reach the Olympic Stadium royal box the new standard was revised to 26 miles and 385 yards.

When the front-runner, Italian Pietri Dorando, entered the stadium, he was so disoriented—from the searing heat or, some alleged, from gobbling strychnine as a performance enhancer—that he headed the wrong way. Then he collapsed. Officials helped him to his feet, and the English crowd, knowing Irish American Johnny Hayes was closing in, urged him on. Dorando collapsed three more times but each time was carried forward by sympathetic Brits. Dorando reached the finish line first, but American protests earned Hayes the gold. Hayes worked for Bloomingdale's, and some speculated he was paid just to train because of the publicity he reaped. Meanwhile, the Queen gave Dorando his own gold trophy as consolation, and he emerged as a hero in Europe.

Hayes agreed to race Dorando at Madison Square Garden. New York sports fans were primed for a grudge match between an Irish American and an Italian, who immigrants from both countries could rally around.

Dorando grabbed an early lead and turned back each Hayes charge, winning by 60 yards, as Italian supporters, overwhelming police and officials, rushed the track. Marathon madness had begun: In the next four months, the New York area hosted nine major marathons, featuring another Dorando–Hayes rematch and match races between Dorando and Onondaga Indian Tom Longboat, and between Longboat and Englishman Alfred Shrubbs.

Finally, promoters hit on the $10,000 Marathon Derby. On April 3, 1909, in front of 30,000 fans at the Polo Grounds, they would crown the greatest marathoner once and for all. Hayes's gold medal had been followed by a string of defeats. Dorando's international acclaim didn't offset his Olympic loss. Matt Maloney hoped to prove his disputed record, run from Rye to New York, was real. Shrubbs, the great middle-distance runner, needed to go the distance for once. Longboat, who faltered in the Olympics after strychnine accusations, had since bested Dorando and Shrubbs, emerging as the betting favorite. The afterthought was Henri St. Yves, a chubby, diminutive 20-year-old Parisian who worked in a London restaurant. He had won a marathon in Edinburgh but went off here at 10-to-1 odds.

People crammed Times Square to watch the updates posted in the Times Building windows.

Dorando raced out front, but St. Yves, barely five feet tall, stayed at his shoulder, passed him at the one-mile mark, and was soon two-thirds of a mile ahead. In contrast to the long, graceful strides of the others, the Frenchman's short, choppy gait looked awkward. Yet, on the soggy track its concision proved helpful. Many questioned his judgment in setting such a furious pace, especially at mile 11, when Shrubbs overtook him.

CHAPTER 96

St. Yves remained dogged, and Shrubbs wilted at mile 19. St. Yves regained his lead and maintained his brisk pace the last seven miles. Shrubbs dropped out, and Longboat, enduring foot pain caused by his heavy schedule, quit, too. Dorando finished second, four laps behind. Hayes, closing in a rush, waited too long and was unable to even catch Dorando. Maloney finished a distant fourth.

St. Yves finished in a record 2:40:50. His performance was so remarkable that the nationalism faded away, with the crowd cheering him during the playing of the French national anthem.

St. Yves won once more against nine men the next month. Although the boom faded, the marathon was established as a significant sport, and Henri St. Yves earned his place as its first undisputed champion.

97

Matty Shuts Out the A's, Again, October 14, 1905, Polo Grounds

Your first time is always something to be cherished, particularly when the circumstances are spectacularly memorable. New York's professional teams have won more than 50 championships in baseball, basketball, football, and hockey in the past 12 decades, but it will always be difficult to match the way the New York Giants brought home that very first title.

The World Series was born in 1903, between the National League and the fledgling American League. In 1904, the National League champion Giants won 106 games but refused to play the Boston Pilgrims. By 1905, agreements had been hammered out guaranteeing an autumnal confrontation. The Giants topped the National League and then proved themselves the best in baseball in the World Series, thanks to their fiery manager and one brilliant pitcher:

With each zero, the young man's stature grew. When he was done, with 27 frames of remarkable nothingness, 25-year-old Christy Mathewson was an instant icon, America's real-life Frank Merriwell.

In Mathewson, baseball found a new hero for a new age. When this tall, blond, clean-cut college man laid those golden goose eggs over three shutouts in the 1905 World Series, he ascended to baseball's throne and helped transform the New York Giants into baseball's flagship franchise.

From the start, Mathewson displayed impressive wares with his fastball, big overhand curve, and baffling fadeaway (we know it as a screwball). Mathewson, at 6-foot-2, was big for that era and, as a former Bucknell University student, a rarity in a nation where most men didn't graduate from high school. He was impeccably virtuous and quite perfectly acceptable to the WASPy press and American mainstream. He stood in stark contrast to baseball's other stars, for example, the German Honus Wagner, the malignant Ty Cobb, and, of course, John McGraw, who took over as the Giants' manager in 1902, and helped make Mathewson a star.

As a Baltimore Orioles player and manager, McGraw had been a pugnacious infielder and prime perpetrator of "inside baseball," the shrewd, sneaky small-ball style he undertook with an aggressiveness that bordered on criminal. Umpire Arlie Latham famously said McGraw "eats gunpowder every morning and washes it down with warm blood." The American League's founder, Ban Johnson, sought a wholesome public image, so McGraw was most unwelcome. He landed in New York, and despite the stark differences with Mathewson in temperament and playing style, they got along fabulously off the field, renting, with their wives, an Upper West Side apartment together.

In 1905, Mathewson won 30 games for the third straight year in a year when no other National League pitcher won more than 23. He struck out 206, while no one else topped 175. His ERA was 1.28; only one other National League pitcher was under 2.00.

Mathewson seized control of the Series immediately, retiring the first six Philadelphia batters on just 10 pitches. Relying heavily on his curve, he iced the A's, allowing just one runner to reach third. That runner, Ossee Schreckengost, was thrown out at home. This would constitute Philadelphia's best effort. New York's hurler also started the winning rally in the fifth with a single. The Giants won, 3–0.

Philadelphia's Chief Bender returned the favor in New York for Game 2, beating Joe McGinnity, 3–0. Mathewson retaliated in Game 3, heading a 9–0 rout, with nine strikeouts. Then McGinnity avenged his earlier loss, with yet another shutout, 1–0. Shutouts were relatively common at the turn of the century—the five other pre-1910 Series yielded nine. Thus, two such games were to be expected, and even three would not have been extraordinary. But with four straight shutouts, fans were abuzz.

When Mathewson took the Polo Grounds mound for Game 5, he was facing the A's for the third time in five days; to pitch another complete-game shutout, by any era's standards, would be a unique accomplishment. An overflow crowd stacked up behind the ropes in the outfield. Mathewson was the last man to appear, earning a raucous ovation. He sauntered over to McGinnity and doffed his friend's cap; McGinnity, as if in some vaudeville skit, lifted the lid off Mathewson's dome. This was a loose, relaxed team. Again, offense was scarce on both ends.

Mathewson and Bender each permitted just five hits. But Mathewson walked just one man in three starts, while Bender issued three free passes in this game alone. The Giants scored in the fifth on two walks, a bunt and a sacrifice fly. Vintage McGraw. In the eighth, Mathewson walked, advanced to third on a double, and scored a grounder.

That second run was superfluous, of course. Here's what qualified as a Philadelphia threat: In the sixth, they got two baserunners on in one inning—but not at the same time thanks to a pickoff by catcher Roger Bresnahan. No one else reached base, and of the final 10 batters, only one got a ball out of the infield.

In the ninth, Mathewson induced two weak grounders to the mound and one to short, and fans swarmed the field as the World Series champions celebrated their triumph. Soon thereafter, Bresnahan and Mathewson reappeared with a banner proclaiming, "The Giants, World's Champions, 1905."

New York's prior great sporting events—horse races, heavyweight fights, and six-day bicycle races—conferred glory solely on the participants. Only a team sport enabled rooters to feel a powerful kinship with the athletes that burnished an entire municipality's reputation. There were only two such sports worth mentioning back then, college football and, particularly, baseball. The big college football games had featured out-of-town Ivy League schools, and their swells had done most of the cheering. This was different. This was New York's moment. The 1905 World Series established the primacy of the biggest U.S. city as America's sports capital, with McGraw as its master and Mathewson—endorsing Coca-Cola ("He's proof of its wholesomeness"), sweaters, pipe tobacco, and other products—as its hero.

The Giants would be baseball's dominant team for a generation—in 21 years, they won the National League pennant 10 times, finishing second another seven. (In 1957, when the Giants departed for San Francisco, they were second to the Yankees in league pennants won.)

At the end of that third World Series shutout, Mathewson had pitched 27 innings in five days, striking out 18 and allowing just 14 hits, 1 walk, and 1 hit batsman, and prompting the *Times* to breathlessly declare him the "pitching marvel of the century" just five years into the 1900s. Ninety-five years later, it turned out they were right.

98

Charles Miller Rides (and Rides) into the Record Books, December 10, 1898, Madison Square Garden

On December 10, 1898, Charles Miller got married at Madison Square Garden, during the middle of a bicycle race, which had been going on for six days, which he was winning.

This was the last of the original six-day bike races, an endeavor that, in its outrageous demands on the human mind and body, puts today's extreme sports to shame. Bicycles had become a fad, and bike racing had become a full-fledged mania, with everything from short sprints to the "Century," a 100-mile ride. The six-day event was a combination of endurance test, torture, and freak show.

Riders navigated smoke-filled indoor ovals thousands of times for hundreds of miles each day, usually eating meals from pots while biking and enduring crashes, aching muscles, exhaustion, delirium, and often fistfights with managers who pushed them past their breaking point. Prominent racers got rooms to rest in during breaks, but lesser lights were shunted off into tiny tents. (Meanwhile, competing bands and pickpockets worked the crowds, which occasionally disintegrated into hooliganism.)

The League of American Wheelmen, cycling's governing body, loathed these events and fined everyone who participated in the 1898 race. It would be the last of its kind in New York, because a new state law would prohibit cyclists from riding more than 12 hours a day.

The solo six-day's swan song was a memorable affair. Thirty-one cyclists from as far away as Australia and Sweden set out; seven dropped out the first day, and by day 3, two riders were ordered out by medical staff. Canadian Burns Pierce was setting records, but defending champ Miller and feisty George Waller hung close, with Miller grabbing the lead when Pierce took breaks.

Pierce faded on day 4 (he'd finish third), while Miller and Waller stayed within shouting distance of one another after 1,400 miles. Day 5 decided matters. Waller led by four miles that morning when both men started sprinting; they crashed into one another, and although neither man was hurt, Waller soon came undone, veering off the track. At 8:30 a.m., while half-asleep, he slammed into a railing. He was sidelined for almost three hours while Miller maintained his steady pace, building a 30-mile lead. By Saturday, Miller had clinched the victory. All that remained was breaking the record of 1,983 miles he'd set the previous year—and marrying his fiancée, Genevieve Hanson.

Promoters promised an extra $200 if they wed in front of the crowds, and Hanson, whose mother made a last-minute trip from Chicago to give her away, agreed. Miller left the track at 3:00 p.m. At 4:40, a band played "The Wedding March" for the cheering, standing-room only crowd.

Miller emerged decked out in an outrageous racing suit, pants with one white leg and one pink, and a shirt with the colors reversed and an embroidered eagle on the back. A silk American flag was wrapped around his waist. After marrying and kissing the bride, Miller biked around for a few minutes, lapping up the applause. After a brief break, he returned and, in one last push, completed his new record, finishing with 2,007 miles in 142 hours. He'd been off the track a mere 15 hours, sleeping only 9½. After a victory lap with the other eleven survivors, Miller and his bride had their wedding dinner at the Waldorf Astoria.

The next year, a new six-day race, with two-man teams and a point system based on laps, sprang up to replace the solo one. It remained popular through the Depression, and the style became known internationally as the "Madison," after its Madison Square Garden birthplace. But those riders never knew the bliss Miller achieved on his wedding day, when he set a record that could never be broken.

The Brooklyn Atlantics Hand the Cincinnati Red Stockings Their First Defeat, June 14, 1870, Capitoline Grounds

When the visitors in the red socks snatched a two-run lead in extra innings, all seemed lost for the hometown team. Yet, clutch hitting, a wild pitch, and an untimely error helped the local boys prevail. The visitors seem haunted in the aftermath of this stunning turnaround.

This narrative sounds wonderfully familiar to those New Yorkers who rejoiced in 1986, "Mookie" and "Buckner" bubbling from their lips like a magical incantation. But this is, in fact, the long-forgotten saga of the Brooklyn Atlantics versus the Cincinnati Red Stockings, a tale of civic celebration given lasting importance as a symbol of baseball at the intersection of sport and business.

In the 1860s, Brooklyn was the center of baseball. Native sons included James Creighton, who invented the fastball and was probably the first paid professional (albeit under the table); Dicky Pearce, credited as the first to define the shortstop position and inventor of the bunt; and Candy Cummings, inventor of the curve. Although variations on "base ball" existed elsewhere, it was this "New York game" that had caught on, spread by soldiers during the Civil War.

When it spread to Cincinnati, local power brokers hired former New York Knickerbocker Harry Wright to bring glory to the Queen City. Wright was a skilled ballplayer and a savvy entrepreneur. He assembled baseball's first fully professional team, the Red Stockings, by importing from New York such players as his brother George (one of the game's greatest talents) and Asa Brainard (a pitcher whose name supposedly begat the pitching term "ace"). The only Cincinnati native was first baseman Charlie Gould, whose reliable fielding earned him the moniker "Bushel Basket."

This pro team began playing in 1869, and proved unbeatable: Their 1869–1870 winning streak has been tallied at numbers ranging from 84 to 130 games, although Wright discounted exhibitions and put the official streak at 56 games. In June 1869, these Wright brothers brought their high-flying club east and beat three establishment powerhouses, the New York Mutuals, the Atlantics, and the Brooklyn Eckfords, giving Cincinnati the credibility it needed to propel its amazing road trip—the team traveled 11,877 miles by train and boat, journeying as far as California. The Red Stockings brought baseball to hundreds of thousands of people, making the game into a national pastime.

By June 1870, when Cincinnati returned to New York, they were thought invincible. On June 13, they proved it, stomping the Mutuals, 16–3. Next came the rematch against the Atlantics at the Capitoline Grounds in Bedford-Stuyvesant. (It ran from Halsey Street to Putnam Avenue between Marcy and Nostrand avenues.)

The Red Stockings' roster was filled with former New Yorkers, but the Atlantics were playing for hometown pride, to show who was best at the New York game. With thousands shelling out 50 cents to stand the entire time and plenty more watching from holes in fences or the rooftops of nearby buildings, this game was played amid a heady excitement equal to any World Series game.

Cincinnati jumped out front, 3–0, but Brooklyn clawed back with two in the fourth and two in the sixth. In the seventh, George Wright drove home two for a 5–4 lead, but the Atlantics tied it in the next inning, when the Red Stockings catcher dropped a throw.

The game remained 5–5 after nine innings. In those days, ties often were simply called a draw. The Atlantics, thrilled to have held their own, headed off to celebrate, but Wright didn't want this stain on the Red Stockings' record, so he went to the stands and appealed to *Brooklyn Daily Eagle* journalist Henry Chadwick, the godfather of baseball rules. Chadwick decreed that extra innings were in order—setting a precedent that would make this custom more the norm than the exception—and the Atlantics had to return from the clubhouse.

When Brooklyn put two on in the 10th, George Wright purposely let a harmless pop fall to trap the runners and turn one of his patented double plays. (This maneuver prompted the infield fly rule.)

In the 11th, Cincinnati scored twice to seize a seemingly insurmountable 7–5 lead, just as Boston's 5–3 lead would seem too much in extra innings in Game 6 of the 1986 World Series.

But Brainard allowed a single, then—channeling the Red Sox's Bob Stanley—uncorked a wild pitch. Then a fly ball landed for a triple. Legend has it that a Brooklyn fan jumped on McVey's back, but McVey dismissed it, saying he shrugged off the interference attempt. (A policeman apparently subdued the intruder with his club.) Now it was 7–6, with a runner on third.

One out later, the right-handed-hitting Bob "Death to Flying Things" Ferguson, came up—and turned around to bat lefty. Ferguson simply wanted to keep the ball away from George Wright at shortstop, but he rattled Brainard and made history as the first switch-hitter. He pulled a single to right, and Brooklyn fans were as wild with excitement as Met fans would be when Kevin Mitchell tied the game in 1986. The tenuous link between these two historic but seemingly unique events was about to grow stronger.

Contemporary accounts of the final plays are murky and somewhat contradictory, but Brooklyn's George "the Charmer" Zettlein hit what the *New York World* called a "hummer" toward first base and sure-handed Charlie Gould. Sources say the ball was either too hard for Gould to reach or too hot for him to handle. It seems Gould knocked the ball down and, with no chance of getting to first in time, hurried a throw to second; that throw got past Charlie Sweasy, allowing Ferguson to dash all the way around, a la Ray Knight, with the winning run. Other sources, however, say Ferguson stopped at second and danced home on the next play, when Sweasy muffed either a grounder or a toss from George Wright.

Either way, there was joy that day in Brooklyn.

This game birthed a new era by demonstrating baseball's commercial possibilities. The National Association debuted the following year, an evolutionary step toward the National League in 1876. Teams became businesses, paying players to draw fans so that higher admission could be charged and so on, until the day finally arrived when television contracts would be negotiated in the hundreds of millions of dollars.

Meanwhile, the strange links to 1986 didn't end. After this defeat, Cincinnati's fans abandoned the team. With attendance plunging, investors backed off, and the Red Stockings disbanded. Harry Wright took his best players and moved to a city he thought would support pro baseball more avidly: Boston. When the National League formed in 1876, Boston was a founding member; later it would change its nickname to the Beaneaters, then the Braves. Decades later, when the upstart American League's Boston Pilgrims wanted a new name, they reached back to the city's proud link to professional baseball's early days and named the team after the Red Stockings, choosing the more modern "Red Sox"—inadvertently bonding the past to the future.

Finally, in 1917, Charlie Gould, a lifelong Ohioan, died at age 69—a pivotal number in Mets history—while visiting his son in New York. Not just anywhere in New York, but in Queens. Not just anywhere in Queens, but in Flushing—the future home of Shea Stadium. So, even if his gaffe (if indeed, he made one) was less damaging than Sweasy's, it is easy to imagine that his ghost lingered until the moment he stopped Bill Buckner's glove from getting all the way down, bringing joy back to the locals while haunting the spirits of red-socked players and their fans.

New York Gets Its First Glimpse of a Sports-Mad Future, May 27, 1823, Union Course

Long before MLB, the NFL, and the NBA ruled the world of sports, and long before there even was baseball, football, and basketball, much less a world of sports, there was a horse race. Not just any horse race, mind you, but a match race, one so intense, so relentlessly hyped, and so closely followed that it may well have marked the birth of our sports-mad society. When American Eclipse barreled down the track against Sir Henry at the Union Course in 1823, it seemed that everyone, not only in the city, but also throughout the young nation, went along for the ride.

American Eclipse, descended from the great English horse Eclipse, was an unbeaten nine-year-old champion born in Queens and owned by New Yorker Cornelius Van Ranst. Sir Henry was an unknown from North Carolina, while his owner, William Ransom Johnson, the "Napoleon of the Turf," was a Virginian.

This match race had more than money at stake. After the War of 1812, people had soured on the idea of importing English horses, so this showdown between two American-born steeds offered breeders of native horses a chance to prove their worth and affirm our national identity. More significantly, this was the latest in a slew of races that attracted attention by pitting North against South, sharpening a deeply felt identity split heightened by the Missouri Compromise.

This grew beyond any previous North–South showdown due to Johnson's formidable reputation and the shocking amount of gambling that quickly piled up. Backers for Van Ranst (and his partner, John Cox Stevens) and Johnson put up more than $20,000 as stakes, and then the men bet on top of that. Bankers grew nervous as folks bet all their cash holdings—one Southerner put up five years' worth of tobacco crop. It was estimated that $150,000 to $200,000 was in play.

One publication proclaimed this the biggest national event since Thomas Jefferson and Aaron Burr's battle for the presidency was decided by the House of Representatives. (Burr, along with presidential candidate Andrew Jackson and Vice President Daniel Tompkins, attended the race.) The excitement was so great that the *Statesman* headlined one story "The Races," because "who will this week look at a newspaper paragraph which is not headed 'The Races'?"

The spectacular affair transformed the Union Course in the town of Jamaica (now the Richmond Hill–Woodhaven area) into the country's most prominent racecourse. The race supposedly attracted 50,000 spectators. That is probably an exaggeration, but it was the largest sporting event to date. The New York Stock Exchange closed. Every local hotel was full, as one-third of the crowd had journeyed from the South.

To confound his foe, Johnson brought five horses north and did not publicly announce Sir Henry as his horse until a half-hour before post time. Then overflow from the stands poured onto the track, delaying the race's start. Victory required winning two of three races, each lasting four miles, exponentially longer than today's Triple Crown races. American Eclipse carried 126 pounds, almost 20 pounds more than his young rival, but his owners ensured he was well rested, while Johnson was racing his horses hard to find the perfect foe. So, the Northerners were stunned when Sir Henry aggressively took control, passing Eclipse early and turning back Eclipse's late charge, winning by a half-length and setting a new record of seven minutes, 37 seconds. With Henry's speed mark, the United States asserted its independence from England. (The Union Course's newfangled dirt track, as opposed to the traditional turf, also took hold as racing's future.) Messengers rushed to Manhattan with the news, and several investment houses closed for the day, fearing panic by Eclipse's heavy bettors.

In *The Great Match Race*, John Eisenberg blamed the loss on a tactical error by Van Ranst; to everyone's surprise, the owner had ditched legendary jockey Samuel Purdy at the last minute, replacing him with the younger, more agile Billy Craft. Craft was far less experienced, and Van Ranst blamed him for the loss. Eisenberg wrote that he was indecisive and used the whip too much, possibly cutting the great stallion's testicle. Upon learning that Purdy was in the stands that day, Van Ranst sent Stevens to grovel, but even after Purdy agreed to ride the next race, Henry remained the 3-to-1 favorite. He sprinted out, hoping to wear down the older horse, but after trailing for almost three miles, Purdy stunned the crowd when he pushed Eclipse inside and past Henry, beating him by 30 feet, in seven minutes, 49 seconds, the second-fastest winning time on record.

This time Johnson switched jockeys, dumping a rider named John Walden for veteran trainer Arthur Taylor. But it was no use. American Eclipse demonstrated a champion's stamina, leading the third race almost the entire way, even battling through a herd of fans who had spilled onto the track. He staved off one desperate rally by Henry in the third mile and won by three lengths, in eight minutes, 24 seconds.

Subsequent North–South match races further fed regional tensions, but the distinctions between horses began blurring in the 1830s, when Johnson became part-owner of American Eclipse and brought him to stud down South, while Sir Henry was bought by Stevens's brother and moved North. Thoroughbred racing endured up-and-down periods, but sports would not relinquish its hold on the public's imagination. After this race, newspapers supported the idea of spectator sports as good for society and touted races as a way of attracting tourist dollars to their city, paving the way for not only the Triple Crown races, but also the modern events, from the Super Bowl to the X Games, that define the business of the sports world.

Selected Bibliography

A bibliography is going to be somewhat limited for a book like this. Much of my research came from newspapers and magazines (local and national), especially contemporary sources for each event, and where I could I also watched as much footage as possible. I also relied heavily on statistical websites, especially Baseball-reference.com and its brethren. For the first edition of this book I also interviewed almost 20 experts on sports, from tennis to boxing to baseball; many of their insights still inform this material. There were, however, some exceptional books, newspapers, and magazines that helped along the way. The following is a selective list.

Cohen, Stanley. *The Game They Played*. New York: Farrar, Straus and Giroux, 1977.

D'Agostino, Dennis. *Garden Glory: An Oral History of the New York Knicks*. Chicago: Triumph, 2003.

Daily News

Deford, Frank. *Big Bill Tilden: The Triumphs and the Tragedy*. New York: Open Road Media, 2011.

Drucker, Joel. *Jimmy Connors Saved My Life: A Personal Biography*. Wilmington, DE: Sport Media Publishing, 2004.

Eig, Jonathan. *Luckiest Man: The Life and Death of Lou Gehrig*. New York: Simon and Schuster, 2005.

Einstein, Charles. *Willie's Time: A Memoir*. New York: Lippincott, 1979.

Eisenberg, John. *The Great Match Race: When North Met South in America's First Sports Spectacle*. Boston: Houghton Mifflin Harcourt, 2006.

ESPN

Kahn, Roger. *The Boys of Summer*. New York: Harper and Row, 1972.

Kram, Mark. *Ghosts of Manila: The Fateful Blood Feud between Muhammad Ali and Joe Frazier*. New York: Harper, 2001.

Kriegel, Mark. *Namath: A Biography*. New York: Penguin, 2005.

New York Post

New York Times

Newsday

Sperber, Murray. *Shake Down the Thunder: The Creation of Notre Dame Football*. Bloomington: Indiana University Press, 2002.

Sporting News

Sports Illustrated

Tygiel, Jules. *Baseball's Great Experiment: Jackie Robinson and his Legacy*. New York: Oxford University Press, 1983.

Index

About the Author

Stuart Miller is coauthor of *The Other Islands of New York City* and author of *Good Wood: The Story of the Baseball Bat* and *Where Have All Our Giants Gone?* He has written about sports for 30 years, and his work has appeared in the *New York Times*, the *Sports Business Journal*, the *Wall Street Journal*, *ESPN*, *Sports Illustrated*, *Sporting News*, and numerous other publications. He lives in Brooklyn with his wife and two sons.